Nunneries and the Anglo-Saxon Royal Houses

Women, Power and Politics
Series Editors: June Hannam and Pauline Stafford

Books in this series explore women's exercise of power in Britain and Europe from the ancient world onwards. In the expanding area of women's history this is an increasingly important theme, and one which provides a place for women's history and its insights within the traditional concerns of mainstream history. In view of the wide date range, 'power' is broadly conceived, involving, for instance, the religious and familial as well as the political.

Published titles in this series:

Nunneries and the Anglo-Saxon Royal Houses

BARBARA YORKE

continuum
LONDON • NEW YORK

Continuum

The Tower Building, 11 York Road, London, SE1 7NX

370 Lexington Avenue, New York, NY 10017-6503

First published 2003

British Library Cataloguing-in-Publication Data
A catalogue record for this book is available from the British Library.

ISBN 0-8264-6040-2

Typeset by Kenneth Burnley, Wirral, Cheshire
Printed and bound in Great Britain by Bookcraft (Bath) Ltd, Midsomer Norton, Bath

Contents

Acknowledgements

This book was written with the aid of a year's sabbatical funded by King Alfred's College, Winchester, and the Arts and Humanities Research Board through their Research Leave Scheme. I am very grateful to both institutions for their support. Aspects of the book have been aired at conferences or seminars at the Universities of Birmingham, Leeds, Manchester, Oxford, Uppsala and York, and at the Institute of Historical Research in London. I would like to express my gratitude for these opportunities and to all colleagues who provided me with advice and discussion on these and other occasions. I would like to thank my research students Jonathan Pitt and Ryan Lavelle for many stimulating discussions and for allowing me to cite their research, and to Rhoda Bucknell for access to her research on the Wherwell cartulary (BL Egerton 2104a). I am also very grateful to the following, who provided me with access to material in advance of publication or who clarified particular points for me: Paul Barnwell, Steve Bassett, Katrinette Bodarwé, Nicholas Brooks, Julia Crick, Sarah Foot, Lutz von Padberg, Jo Story, Alan Thacker, Leslie Webster and Patrick Wormald. I have major debts of gratitude to Pauline Stafford and John Blair, who have both encouraged me in this project and nobly read a draft of the whole manuscript, providing me with much useful feedback and advice, though they bear no responsibility, of course, for its remaining faults. John Blair also generously made available the text of his forthcoming book *The Church in Anglo-Saxon Society*, and I hope the numerous citations of it in the footnotes show how much I have gained from reading it, and from his many other stimulating publications. It is only here though that I can acknowledge the help I have also received from our many discussions on topics of mutual interest. Finally, I must thank my husband Robert for his continuing moral support and his willingness to visit the sites of so many early medieval nunneries in this country and elsewhere in Europe.

Abbreviations

AA SS	*Acta Sanctorum*
Æthelweard	*The Chronicles of Æthelweard*, ed. A. Campbell (London, 1962)
Anon., *VC*	'*Vitae Sancti Cuthberti Anonymæ*', in B. Colgrave (ed.), *Two Lives of Saint Cuthbert* (Cambridge, 1940)
A-SC	*The Anglo-Saxon Chronicle*, ed. D. Whitelock, with D. C. Douglas and S. I. Tucker (London, 1961)
A-SE	*Anglo-Saxon England*
Asser	*Asser's Life of King Alfred*, ed. W. H. Stevenson (Oxford, 1904)
B	*Cartularium Saxonicum*, ed. W. de G. Birch, 3 vols (London, 1885–99)
BAR	British Archaeological Reports (British Series)
Bede, *VC*	'*Bedae Vitae Sancti Cuthberti*', in B. Colgrave (ed.), *Two Lives of Saint Cuthbert* (Cambridge, 1940)
BL	British Library
CBA	Council for British Archaeology
Councils and Synods	D. Whitelock, M. Brett and C. N. L. Brooke, *Councils and Synods with Other Documents Relating to the English Church*, 2 vols (Oxford, 1981)
DB	Domesday Book
Dümmler	'Alcuini Epistolae', in *MGH Epistolae* IV, Vol. 2, ed. E. Dümmler (Berlin, 1895)
EHD	*English Historical Documents, I, c. 500–1042*, ed. D. Whitelock (2nd edn, 1979)
EHR	*English Historical Review*
Gesta Pontificum	William of Malmesbury, *De Gestis Pontificum Anglorum Libri Quinque*, ed. N. Hamilton, Rolls Series (London, 1870)
Gesta Regum	William of Malmesbury, *Gesta Regum Anglorum*, Vol. I, ed. R. A. B. Mynors, R. M. Thomson and M. Winterbottom (Oxford, 1998)

HE	*Bede's Ecclesiastical History of the English People*, ed. B. Colgrave and R. A. B. Mynors (Oxford, 1969)
HS	*Councils and Ecclesiastical Documents Relating to Great Britain and Ireland. III, The English Church 595–1066*, ed. A. W. Haddan and W. Stubbs (Oxford, 1871, repr. 1964)
MGH	*Monumenta Germaniae Historica*
Passio Edwardi	*Edward King and Martyr*, ed. C. Fell, Leeds Texts and Monographs, New Series, 3 (Leeds, 1971)
Plummer	C. Plummer (ed.), *Venerabilis Baedae Opera Historica*, 2 vols (Oxford, 1896)
S	P. Sawyer, *Anglo-Saxon Charters: An Annotated List and Bibliography* (London, 1968)
Tangl	M. Tangl (ed.), *S. Bonifatii et Lulli Epistolae, MGH Epistolae Selecta I* (Berlin, 1916)
Theodore, *Penitential*	*Die Canones Theodoris Cantuariensis und ihre Überliefer-ungsformen*, ed. P. W. Finsterwalder (Weimar, 1929), 285–334; translated in J. T. McNeill and H. A. Gamer (eds), *Medieval Handbooks of Penance* (Columbia, NY, 1979)
TRHS	*Transactions of the Royal Historical Society*
V. Eadburgae	*The Royal Saints of Anglo-Saxon England: A Study of West Saxon and East Anglian Cults*, ed. S. Ridyard (Cambridge, 1988), Appendix 1, 255–308
V. Edithae	[I (*Vita*) II (*Translatio*)] 'La légende de Ste Edith en prose et vers par le moine Goscelin', ed. A. Wilmart, *Analecta Bollandiana*, 56 (1938), 5–101, 265–307
V. Guthlaci	*Felix's Life of Saint Guthlac*, ed. B. Colgrave (Cambridge, 1956)
V. Leobae	*Vitae Leobae Abbatissae Biscofesheimensis auctore Rudolfo Fuldensi*, ed. G. Waitz, *MGH Scriptores*, XV (Hanover, 1887), 118–31
V. Oswaldi	Byrhtferth, *Vita Sancti Oswaldi*, in J. Raine (ed.), *The Historians of the Church of York and Its Archbishops*, 3 vols, Rolls Series, 71 (London, 1879–94), Vol. I, 399–475
V. Wilfridi	*The Life of Bishop Wilfrid by Eddius Stephanus*, ed. B. Colgrave (Cambridge, 1927)
V. Wulfhildae	'La vie de Saint Wulfilda par Goscelin de Cantorbery', ed. M. Esposito, *Analecta Bollandiana*, 32 (1913), 10–26
VCH	*Victoria County History*
Worcester	*The Chronicle of John of Worcester, Volume II, The Annals from 450 to 1066*, ed. R. R. Darlington and P. McGurk (Oxford, 1995)

Introduction

The study of Anglo-Saxon female religious

Following the Dissolution of the Monasteries and the Reformation, there was little interest from English historians in the history of Anglo-Saxon religious women, apart from brief notices by local or Roman Catholic historians.[1] In anti-Catholic propaganda and Gothick Romance, nuns were either hysterical or corrupt characters. But by the end of the nineteenth century, a much greater sympathy for the positive aspects of medieval monasticism, coupled with moves towards the greater emancipation of women, led to a renewed interest in the history of female religious communities. Lina Eckenstein, in her pioneering survey of female monasticism in the medieval west, published in 1896, made clear her hope that study of these communities would help support advances in the position of contemporary women:

> We turn to a study of the past, confident that a clearer insight into the social standards and habits prevalent in past ages will aid us in a better estimation of the relative importance of those factors of change we find around us today . . . The right to self-development and social responsibility which the woman of today so persistently asks for, is in many ways analogous to the right which the convent secured to womankind a thousand years ago. The woman of today, who realizes that the home circle as at present constituted affords insufficient scope for her energies, had a precursor, in the nun who sought a field of activity in the convent.[2]

In the twentieth century Anglo-Saxon nunneries became part of the evidence for the 'rough equality' of men and women,[3] during what was characterized as a 'Golden Age' of relative independence for women.[4] Although more recent investigations have tended to modify these somewhat rosy views of the status of Anglo-Saxon women,[5] the opportunities available to Anglo-Saxon religious women, particularly in the period of conversion and missionary endeavour, can still attract admiration, if not envy, today. Sister Catherine Wybourne makes these observations on the life of Leoba, an Anglo-Saxon nun who in the eighth century commanded a nunnery in a recently converted area of Germany:

Every Benedictine will recognize the challenge of her sanctity, attained through the ordinary means of monastic life – prayer, reading, work, and obedience – rather than because of the extraordinary events of the Anglo-Saxon mission. Far from diminishing her humanity, being a nun integrated and developed the many gifts of mind, heart and spirit with which Leoba was endowed. But there is another challenge which the Church as a whole is slow to admit. In Leoba's day, monastic life for women was not so very different from monastic life for men. The sheer number of women saints in the Anglo-Saxon calendars is evidence that women were regarded as responsible beings, capable of determining and maintaining the structures that would enable them to be faithful to their call. How ironic it is that Leoba and her companions would not be able to do in our day what they did in theirs without forfeiting the name of Benedictine *nuns*.[6]

From an early stage in the study of Anglo-Saxon female monasticism it was felt that there was a significant difference between monastic provision before and after the period of viking attacks in the ninth century. The pre-viking houses for women were identified as 'double houses', that is, joint communities of men and women, which in Anglo-Saxon England were generally commanded by an abbess.[7] Many, though by no means all of these, were founded and controlled by members of the several royal houses of seventh- and eighth-century Anglo-Saxon England. An early preoccupation in their study was to establish the origins of these foundations, and how they might relate to other examples of joint monastic provision for men and women. Mary Bateson, in a masterly survey, rightly pointed to the importance of links between the earliest Anglo-Saxon double houses and those founded by followers of St Columbanus in Neustrian Francia.[8] She disagreed with earlier conclusions that Columbanus had reproduced a system of monasticism with which he was already familiar in Ireland,[9] and stressed rather that the northern Frankish houses should be seen as a local response to the stimulus provided by Columbanus' teaching. It is an argument with which recent studies are broadly in agreement, though they would put more stress on the importance of links between Neustria and Anglo-Saxon England for spreading this form of monasticism than Bateson did.[10] Several studies have sought to compare the Anglo-Saxon double houses with comparable early Christian and medieval examples.[11] Although at one level such studies show 'that double monasteries arose in many countries and at many times as the natural sequel to an outburst of religious enthusiasm',[12] they also show how different in organization and status the female element of such communities could be, and that a range of ecclesiastical and secular features peculiar to the time of foundation needs to be taken into account when assessing them.[13] Treating the so-called 'double houses' as a distinctive element in early Anglo-Saxon religious provision has obscured both the fact that there are many similarities between all the major 'minster' churches of the seventh and eighth centuries, whether commanded by men or women,[14] and that, as in other periods and countries, not all religious women were housed in large monastic communities with substantial endowments headed by an abbess. Some foundations for women will have been much more ephemeral, perhaps no more than arrangements made for a particular generation of a family, while other religious women will have been attached to what were predominantly male communities.[15] Others might not be based in communities at all, but live on their own as hermits,[16] or even remain in the family home.[17] Widows might take a vow of chastity in order to be able to retain their independence and the control of lands received from their husbands, and, in exchange, at least part of that land would on their deaths go to the church which had provided them with protection.[18]

In the historiography of female monasticism, it has been usual to stress a complete break between the double houses of the early Anglo-Saxon period and the single-sex female houses of the later period. Very few, if any, double monasteries continued as convents of women into the tenth century and beyond.[19] The lack of continuity within the Anglo-Saxon period was traditionally attributed to those ever-popular scapegoats the vikings, though contemporary references to attacks on nunneries are few in number. Recent studies have discredited the idea of pagan aggression as a catch-all explanation for changes to ecclesiastical life in the ninth and tenth centuries,[20] and shown how the older view was the product of the selective and rhetorical presentation of recent history by King Alfred and during the monastic reform period of the later tenth century,[21] though the case for viking revisionism may now have gone too far.[22] Alternative influences towards change have been seen as coming from the religious reforms of the Carolingian Empire in the ninth century which placed a priority on the greater regulation of the lives of both male and female religious. Anglo-Saxon religious women have therefore been seen as sharing with their Frankish sisters a decline in their ability to take an active role in church affairs, since strict claustration was imposed upon them from the ninth century.[23]

Since the major nunneries of the later Saxon period continued as monastic houses until the Dissolution (though some minor houses disappeared before the Norman Conquest or soon after), it has been the practice in many studies to examine the history of the later Saxon female houses from their origins to a period in the later middle ages, and to assume that they may be seen throughout this time, or at least from the period of tenth-century monastic reform, as regular Benedictine convents.[24] However, there is a danger that such studies may assume a greater continuity of practice than was in fact the case and miss distinctive features of the later Anglo-Saxon arrangements. The major nunneries were closely associated with the Anglo-Saxon royal house, but, as a number of recent studies have stressed, they were only one strand in the provision for religious women in later Anglo-Saxon England.[25] As in the pre-viking period, religious women, either singly or in small groups, were also to be found associated with male foundations, both monasteries and secular minsters,[26] while others, especially widows, would live more informally in small congregations or in their own households after taking religious vows.[27]

Late Saxon legislation in the aftermath of the tenth-century reform movement distinguished between *mynecan* (cloistered nuns) and *nunnan* (vowesses), and many of the individual *religiosae feminae* who appear as the recipients of charters and in other records of the period would have fallen into the latter category.[28] There may have been increasing attempts as a result of the tenth-century reform movement to formalize arrangements for women wishing to live religious lives outside the major convents, and perhaps to discourage an association with male minsters. The proportions of predominantly noble women who entered the religious life were not necessarily that different between the earlier and later Anglo-Saxon periods, but the number of formal female communities was far fewer in the tenth and eleventh centuries – eight nunneries as opposed to somewhere in excess of forty double houses[29] – and so these alternative forms of provision were much more significant, especially, it would appear, for noble widows who wished to avoid remarriage. The arrangements for vowesses were a way in which kin could provide for female members wishing to take religious vows without having to permanently alienate land to a religious community and so they were inherently ephemeral.[30]

Recent trends have therefore been to recognize the variety of arrangements that existed for women wishing to follow a religious life in the early middle ages. It is now appreciated that it is quite inappropriate to expect all Anglo-Saxon congregations of female religious to have conformed to the standards of Benedictine monasticism. Until the period of tenth-century monastic reform, when all monastic communities were apparently expected to adhere to an agreed rule, the *Regularis Concordia* that prescribed and defined a reformed Benedictine discipline,[31] there was no accepted monastic rule that all religious communities followed or, indeed, against which they should be judged. No earlier rule written for, or even owned by, an Anglo-Saxon female community is known, so their manner of life has to be inferred from references in other sources such as the *Lives* of saints. In the conversion period, monastic founders established their own Rules by which their communities were to live, with the result that there was considerable variation in arrangements, some of which Bede, who had been brought up in houses strongly influenced by Benedictine principles, did not consider conformed to monastic ideals at all.[32] Even the *Institutio Sanctimonialium* of Amalarius of Metz, prescribed for female communities during the Carolingian Renaissance, seems to have departed from strict adherence to the Benedictine Rule since, although religious women were to be strictly cloistered and to eat and sleep communally, they were also permitted to have their own possessions, servants and houses.[33] It is unlikely that convent life was any stricter in later Anglo-Saxon England even after the reform period. Life in the major female nunneries of later Anglo-Saxon England seems to have had much in common with contemporary communities in France and Saxony; these are often referred to in modern literature as houses of canonesses as they followed a less rigorous regime than that enjoined by the Benedictine Rule, which allowed retention of personal property and the possibility of leaving in order to be married.[34] However, the term 'canoness' is not one that has been generally applied to Anglo-Saxon female religious either within the Anglo-Saxon period or in later literature.[35] Another result of the recognition of religious diversity in the early middle ages is that it has become increasingly difficult for any individual study to do justice to all its forms.[36] There has been a trend towards individual studies of the different types of religious experience available to early medieval religious women. This is one of the contexts in which this work on royal nunneries may be viewed, though there are also other developments in the study of early medieval women that support the examination of the royal nunneries as a significant grouping.

Nunneries and the study of women in the early middle ages

It is no coincidence that the two periods in which there has been most interest and research on Anglo-Saxon female religious – the turn of the nineteenth and twentieth centuries, and the period from *c.* 1970 onwards – have been concerned with much broader questions about the position and rights of women. In the earlier stage the emphasis was predominantly on collecting and organizing data to demonstrate that early medieval women had a religious history. In the 1970s and 1980s those data came under more vigorous analysis, particularly from a feminist perspective. The decline in the role of women in the church, between the late Antique period when they might be ordained as deaconesses,[37] and the period from the ninth century onwards when strict claustration was imposed and any public religious role apparently denied, became a paradigm of the oppression caused by the increasing patriarchalism of Germanic society fed by androcentric interpretations of the Bible in which the fall of Eve left a baleful inheritance for all womankind.[38] In the face of this oppression, it was argued, women formed their own religious identities and culture in which a distinctive female spirituality was developed and promoted in hagiographical literature.[39]

However, it has gradually become appreciated, in early medieval studies as elsewhere, that there is a danger that androcentric biases will merely be replaced by gynocentric ones. Increasingly in the 1990s the emphasis has been placed on a gendered reading of the early medieval past – 'the social construction of difference between men and women', which will be 'socially created and historically specific' rather than simply biological.[40] There has also been criticism of the tendency to assign a universal, timeless patriarchy to the early middle ages,[41] and of feminist readings of texts, such as hagiographies, which do not take sufficiently into account the audiences for which they were intended and the conventions and models that lay behind their composition.[42] Religious texts including, or perhaps even particularly, in their presentation of women were not necessarily aiming to represent the contemporary status or opinion of women, but could be written from a metaphorical perspective to elucidate such matters as the doctrine of salvation.[43] The *Lives* of female saints were not necessarily written for a female audience, or might be interpreted differently by male and female receptors. For instance, it has been proposed that one potential reading of late Antique female *Lives* was to encourage men to greater spirituality on the grounds that, if even women could achieve grace, there was hope for the greatest male sinner.[44] When a gendered reading of texts is made, there is therefore a problem in deciding how far the theoretical constructs that lay behind them were 'socially actualized', and how far the conclusions presented by one class of texts should be preferred to another when they appear to offer conflicting perspectives.[45]

When attempting gendered readings of past societies, it is essential to try to understand how those societies constructed gender, or else one will be merely projecting modern preoccupations on to the past. On a superficial examination, the early Germanic world might seem to represent a model binary division into separate male and female spheres that could, for instance, be represented in the pre-Christian period by different choices of grave goods for men and women.[46] However, Carol Clover has proposed from her study of Scandinavian evidence a gender system in early Northern Europe in which 'there was one sex and it was male, one "gender", one standard by which persons were judged adequate or inadequate, and it was something like masculine'.[47] The contrast she draws is between those exercising authority, on the one hand, and those who were dependants, on the other. Although the normative of the first category might be the able-bodied man, and women would most typically fall into the dependent category, these male/female boundaries were not impermeable. Men might become dependants in old age, illness or if they were slaves, and alternatively women in the right circumstances could be socially dominant. As Carol Clover puts it, 'the early medieval north was a world in which a physical woman could become a social man, in which a physical man could (and in old age did) become a social woman'.[48] Although due allowance must be made for transferring a theory drawn from Scandinavian sources of the eleventh century and later, to earlier Germanic communities, Clover's observations seem likely to be generally valid for the early Anglo-Saxon world as well, in which a woman could be the 'lord' of men.[49] Her theories are particularly important for understanding the impact of Christianity on the Anglo-Saxon ruling classes. In the Christian tradition inherited from the late Antique world a holy woman could be seen as a virago, literally 'a female man', by imitating the heroic attributes otherwise associated with the male saint.[50] The concept of 'male' as a normative dominant category, to which on occasion biological women could aspire as honorary men, has important implications for understanding the foundation and status of nunneries in the conversion period, for, by assuming the position of abbess, or being promoted as a saint, a woman took on a role where her powers, in theory, were identical to those of her male counterparts. In terms of traditional Germanic ways of viewing society the woman who became an abbess would have thus enjoyed a significant elevation in status. However, such ideas may be expected to have become subject to further modifications as Anglo-Saxon religious became more familiar with classical and patristic writings and the norms of authority within the church. Although monks and nuns could be seen as living analogous lives, a monk had the potential to become a priest which no nun could ever do. Here was a gendered difference that was ever present in the middle ages with the potential to limit the authority and autonomy of female religious communities.

Though understanding early medieval concepts of gender is important for studying female monasticism, it is essential that other societal norms be considered as well. Class was as significant as gender for structuring an individual's place in society. The distance between the lives of women at the top and bottom ends of early medieval society was arguably greater than any common experiences because of their shared sex – and, indeed, implicit in Clover's discussion of early medieval gender is that women born into influential families are more likely to have had the opportunities to transcend the normative position of female dependence.[51] Even among the relatively privileged women who entered nunneries distinctions emerged between foundations patronized by the ruling houses and those which drew their personnel from the lesser ranks of the nobility. Roberta Gilchrist in her study of the material culture of medieval nunneries found that the majority of post-Conquest foundations, that is, those founded by the gentry in the twelfth and thirteenth centuries, had certain distinctive features which set them apart from contemporary male monastic communities, but that these gendered differences were less apparent in the wealthier nunneries which were mainly royal foundations of the pre-Conquest period.[52] Other studies of later nunneries have pointed in a similar direction. The greater authority and freedom enjoyed by abbesses of the Fontrevault order compared to the prioresses of the Gilbertines, though both were double communities of nuns and canons, can be related to the fact that the former were of a higher social class to the latter.[53] The fact that Petronilla, the influential first abbess of Fontrevault, was the social superior of the founder Robert d'Arbrissel seems to have been a significant element in establishing the relative positions of men and women in the order.

Class made a difference to the experiences of religious women in Anglo-Saxon England as well. The larger and longer surviving foundations that dominate the written sources tended to have been founded by members of the royal house, or by those who enjoyed extensive royal patronage, while noble foundations found it difficult to remain autonomous for longer than two generations. Julia Crick's study of the wealth and patronage of women's houses in late Anglo-Saxon England demonstrates very clearly the different fates of royal and non-royal foundations, even though they shared similar patterns of development and aspirations.[54] As we have seen, non-royal religious women might not live in conventional nunneries at all, but be associated with male foundations or live informally as vowesses in small households or the family home.[55] The contrast between royal and noble foundations is particularly marked in the post-viking period, but similar variations seem also to have been apparent in the eighth and ninth centuries, even if not so well attested.[56]

The status and fortunes of the family into which a woman was born were all-important in deciding the future direction of her life.[57] The men of the family had a responsibility for a kinswoman that lasted throughout her life, including after any marriage they might arrange for her, and a woman took her legal status from the family she was born into rather than that of her husband.[58] Obligations to kin were central to the framework of Anglo-Saxon society, and would have impinged equally strongly upon men and women, even if their responsibilities within the kin-group differed.[59] But although links with more distant kin could be significant, especially for those of high status, it was the nuclear family that was the focal unit in Anglo-Saxon society and an individual's close relatives who played dominant roles in their lives, though these might be from both maternal and paternal kin, and also include in-laws. Such obligations were not laid aside if individuals took positions within the church. Bishops in all periods took advantage of their office to promote the interests of male and female relatives. Leoba owed her unusual opportunities in Germany to the support of her kinsman Boniface and his delegation to her of aspects of his authority.[60] Bishop Oswald of Worcester, one of the leaders of the tenth-century reform movement, provided positions for kinsmen in church and supported kinswomen on lands belonging to his bishopric.[61] Churchmen also looked for assistance from their lay relatives; Bishop Herman of Ramsbury (1058–78) sought to move his see because its revenues were insufficient to support him as he had no relatives to help him.[62] Therefore one might expect that Anglo-Saxon religious women would also have carried family obligations with them into the church, and that their lives as religious would have been affected by the histories of their birth families.

Nunneries and the Anglo-Saxon royal houses

It is possible now to move closer to explaining the rationale of this study which focuses on the royal nunneries of Anglo-Saxon England. In the pre-viking period there is nothing inherently different in the way royal nunneries functioned as religious institutions that would distinguish them from other Anglo-Saxon minsters, and they are not distinguished as a significant subgroup in either Latin or Old English terminology.[63] They would have shared many similarities with other family minsters founded by members of the aristocracy, and as cadet branches of royal houses rose and fell there is not always a clear line to be drawn between families that could be classed as 'royal' and those that were 'noble'. Nevertheless the royal nunneries feature much more prominently in surviving literature, especially in the narrative sources, than do female communities founded by the nobility, and they dominate modern studies of early Anglo-Saxon female monasticism.[64] In the later Anglo-Saxon period the situation is rather different because nearly all the nunneries were royal foundations, and women from noble families who wanted to follow a religious vocation outside them adopted different expedients. The study of Anglo-Saxon royal nunneries is in effect the study of the major female religious institutions of the pre-Conquest period. While there was no institutional continuity between the earlier and later royal nunneries, they shared the common feature of royal patronage.[65] It is the interrelationship of nunneries with the royal houses that supported them, and the consequences of that relationship for their operation as religious communities, that forms the core of this book.

The book follows in the tradition of some other studies of female monasticism which have stressed that patronage was not just an ecclesiastical issue but should be viewed alongside broader political and social developments.[66] Entering the religious life was one of the gendered roles allotted to women within the royal family nexus, and the considerable investment of resources in these nunneries implies that they were considered to have a valuable role in sustaining and promoting the interests of the royal kin-group.[67] These roles may have been primarily religious, but some are also likely to have had political connotations, and it may not have been easy, then or now, to draw a clear distinction between them. Facets of the interrelationship of the royal and religious roles of these women and their communities have been studied. Particularly important have been Pauline Stafford's studies of the lives and status of Anglo-Saxon royal women,[68] and Susan Ridyard's detailed studies of Anglo-Saxon royal cults.[69] Marc Meyer has also made a number of studies of later Anglo-Saxon nunneries and the religious roles of queens.[70] However, the royal nunneries have not yet been the focus of a single study that aims to cover the entire Anglo-Saxon period.

The theme of the series 'Women, Power and Politics' is thus very relevant to this volume on a number of different levels. Queens and princesses who entered the church may be seen as having responsibilities to two of the main powers of Anglo-Saxon England: those of church and state, the latter embodied by rulers who were their kinsmen. But the word 'power' may be interpreted in several different ways, and in recent years there has been a particular interest in how it should be understood in the context of the position of women in the past.[71] A distinction has been drawn between 'authority', which is seen as an attribute of a position that was socially sanctioned or 'public', such as the position of abbess, and 'power', which has been interpreted as a more informal influence over the lives of others that, in the case of medieval women, is often seen as channelled through the family.[72] Anglo-Saxon royal abbesses could therefore be said to have exercised authority through their ecclesiastical roles that not only included responsibility for male and female religious under them, but also for a much wider group of people who lived on the lands which they administered. That authority would have helped strengthen the rather more intangible power in family affairs they would already have enjoyed by virtue of their birth. As royal patronage must often have been the deciding factor in their appointment, it may be suggested that they may have been given abbatial authority on the understanding that they would use it to help underpin the interests of the family group, and so their office had the potential to enhance their power within the family nexus.

Some feminist anthropologists would prefer to define 'power' rather differently as the ability of individuals to direct the course of their lives and follow a chosen strategy. It is, of course, a fundamental principle of the Christian doctrine concerning the taking of religious vows that they represent a personal commitment to God, and in hagiographical literature for princessly saints this factor is stressed. How such actions were actually perceived by early medieval individuals is one of the most difficult things for a modern historian to discover, but it is arguable that many members of early medieval royal and noble houses, both male and female, had severe restrictions on how they could order their lives which might be subjugated to the broader interests of the family group.[73] In a period when the rights of the individual are often seen as paramount, it is easy to forget that even in relatively recent times people readily accepted that 'duty' should have priority over personal preferences and so constructed their self-worth from the correct performance of it. Clearly the freedom of action royal abbesses enjoyed in directing the affairs of their communities is an aspect that will need to be considered. The course they had to steer cannot always have been an easy one, since there was the potential for conflicting expectations from the two powers of church and state to which they had to answer and from which their own authority derived.

A major part of the study will consist in tracing the histories of the royal nunneries, paying particular attention to the role of royal patronage and wider political events in their histories, and the interrelationship of nunneries with the two powers of church and state. This will be done by dividing the timespan from the conversion of the Anglo-Saxons to the eleventh century into three main periods that were times of both major political and religious change: (1) the conversion period *c.* 600–750; (2) the period coinciding with viking attacks in the later eighth and ninth centuries; and (3) the later Saxon period of the tenth and eleventh centuries, and each will form one of the first three chapters of the book. Chapter 4 will look at the roles of nunneries as religious institutions, and Chapter 5 will examine how membership of a royal house affected the lives of royal abbesses and nuns. The Conclusion will revisit some of the issues raised here about the dual roles of royal nunneries and the lives and status of royal religious women. Many of the developments to which the royal nunneries were subject were not peculiar to them alone and were experienced by all male and female foundations.[74] The aim here is to consider the particular ramifications for a distinctive group of nunneries that were subject not only to broader developments within the church, but also to the varying fortunes of different royal houses and to political change.

Terminology

Finally, there needs to be a brief explanation of the terminology adopted in this study. The vocabulary applied to religious women in the early middle ages has been elucidated by the work of Sarah Foot.[75] Before the middle years of the tenth century, Anglo-Saxon texts did not distinguish between different types of female or male religious houses. All might be described as *monasterium* or *coenobium* in Latin, and in Old English as *mynster*, and these terms are usually translated into modern

English as 'monastery' or 'minster'. Female religious were most commonly referred to as *sanctimoniales* in Latin, though a number of synonyms also existed, and as *nunne* in Old English. From the latter part of the tenth century there was for the first time an attempt to distinguish in vernacular texts between two different classes of religious, the *mynecena* and the *nunnan*, translated by Sarah Foot as 'cloistered women' and 'vowesses' respectively. However, no such distinction can be seen in Latin texts which appear to use words like *nonnae* and *moniales* for all female religious; nor were there specific terms for the houses of different classes of religious women – suggesting perhaps that such distinctions were of less account, or less apparent, in the late Anglo-Saxon world than modern historians would like to believe. Trying to find an equivalent modern terminology for that used in the Anglo-Saxon period is therefore no easy matter, and probably no solution will satisfy all experts. In this study neutral terms like 'female religious' and 'female religious community' are regularly employed, especially when general statements are being made that might apply to all Anglo-Saxon religious women. The word 'nunnery' is applied to religious institutions that were commanded by an abbess, but with no stronger implication than that about the exact nature of their organization. 'Nuns' are taken to be those women who lived in nunneries. 'Double house' is retained for the joint communities of male and female religious under the authority of an abbess that characterized the seventh and early eighth centuries and which feature so prominently in the *Historia Ecclesiastica*. The term is used in particular when it is necessary to distinguish the double houses from later female religious communities, but in other instances they may also be covered by the general term 'nunnery'. Neutral terms such as 'minster' or 'religious community' refer to all religious foundations, both male and female, with 'monastery' reserved for those male houses that followed a monastic rule. The distinction between male secular and monastic communities is not always clear-cut, and it would appear that some foundations could, especially in certain periods, contain both secular clergy and men following a monastic rule. The potential for considerable variation within male and female communities that might be portrayed as a single group in sources such as ecclesiastical legislation is something that needs to be constantly kept in mind and cannot be adequately conveyed in existing terminology. Royal nunneries as a group may share certain features, especially as the result of royal patronage, but it is not the intention to suggest that they were completely uniform in all facets of their existence as religious communities, or even that all those who lived in any one community conformed to the same standards.

Notes

1. An author who qualifies on both counts is John Milner, who included the history of Nunnaminster/St Mary's Abbey in his work on Winchester first published 1798–99; J. Milner, *The History and Survey of the Antiquities of Winchester*, 2 vols, 3rd edn (London, 1839), II, 219–23.

2.   L. Eckenstein, *Woman under Monasticism: Chapters on Saint-Lore and Convent Life between A.D. 500 and A.D. 1500* (Cambridge, 1896), vii and ix.

3.   D. M. Stenton, *The English Woman in History* (London, 1957), esp. 28–9.

4.   S. C. Dietrich, 'An introduction to women in Anglo-Saxon society (c. 600–1066)', in B. Kanner (ed.), *The Women of England from Anglo-Saxon Times to the Present* (Hamden, CT, 1979), 32–56; C. Fell, C. Clark and E. Williams, *Women in Anglo-Saxon England and the Impact of 1066* (London, 1984), esp. 7–14.

5.   A. Klinck, 'Anglo-Saxon women and the law', *Journal of Medieval History*, 8 (1982), 107–21; S. Hollis, *Anglo-Saxon Women and the Church* (Woodbridge, 1992).

6.   C. Wybourne, 'Leoba: a study in humanity and holiness', in *Medieval Women Monastics*, ed. M. Schmitt and L. Kulzer (Collegeville, MN, 1996), 81–96, at 93.

7.   It cannot be demonstrated that all early Anglo-Saxon foundations for women were double houses, but neither is there sufficient evidence to prove that any of the houses containing women did not have a male element as well. Dagmar Schneider identified sixty-five pre-viking communities for women, of which nineteen had definite evidence for being double communities: D. B. Baltrusch-Schneider, 'Die Angelsächsen Doppelklöster', in K. Elm and M. Parisse (eds), *Doppelklöster und andere Formen der Symbiose männlicher und weiblicher Religiosen im Mittelalter*, Berliner Historische Studien, 18.8 (Berlin, 1992), 57–79, at 59, n. 12.

8.   M. Bateson, 'Origin and early history of double monasteries', *TRHS*, 1st series, 13 (1899), 137–98.

9.   M. Varin, *Mémoire sur les causes de la dissidence entre l'Eglise bretonne et l'Eglise romaine* (Paris, 1858), 165–205.

10. A. Dierkens, 'Prolégomènes à une historie des relationes culturelles entre les Îles Britanniques et le continent pendant le haut moyen âge', in H. Atsma (ed.), *La Neustrie: les pays au nord de la Loire de 650 à 850*, 2 vols (Sigmaringen, 1989), II, 371–94. For further references and discussion, see Chapter 1. A forceful case for female communities being well established in Ireland before the end of the sixth century is made in C. Harrington, 'Women of the Church in Early Medieval Ireland c. A.D. 450–1150', unpublished Ph.D. thesis (University College, London, 1997).

11. S. Hilpisch, *Die Doppelklöster: Entstehung und Organisation* (Munster, 1928); K. Elm and M. Parisse, *Doppelklöster und andere Formen der Symbiose männlicher und weiblicher Religiosen im Mittelalter*, Berliner Historische Studien, 18.8 (Berlin, 1992); B. J. Golding, *Gilbert of Sempringham and the Gilbertine Order c. 1130–c. 1300* (Oxford, 1995), 71–136.

12. Bateson, 'Double monasteries', 197.

13. A point stressed in B. L. Venarde, *Women's Monasticism and Medieval Society: Nunneries in France and England, 890–1215* (Ithaca, NY, 1997).

14. J. Blair, 'Minster churches in the landscape', in D. Hooke (ed.), *Anglo-Saxon Settlements* (Oxford, 1988), 35–58; *idem, The Church in Anglo-Saxon Society* (Oxford, forthcoming).

15. For example, the nuns who had to flee because of an enemy army (perhaps from land regained by the Picts) and who were given an estate near Melrose by Bishop Cuthbert (Bede, *VC*, ch. 30, 254–5).

16. As Heiu, the first abbess of Hartlepool may have done when she retired to *Kaelcacaestir* (*HE*, IV, 23); the form of the religious life of Pega, the sister of St Guthlac, is obscure, but she seems to have lived for a period as a solitary religious near his hermitage after his death (though her major preoccupation was managing his shrine and cult) (*V. Guthlaci*, ch. 53, 167–71).

17. The mixing of lay and religious was one of the evils of family monasteries denounced by Bede in his *Letter to Ecgbert* (Plummer, I, 405–23), and was denounced at the Council of *Clofesho* in 747 (C. Cubitt, *Anglo-Saxon Church Councils c. 650–c.850* (Leicester, 1995), 100–21). Cuthbert's foster mother is probably an early example of a widow who had taken vows staying in her own house (Anon., *VC*, ch. 7, 89–91; Bede, *VC*, ch. 14, 201–2). S. Foot, in *Veiled Women*, 2 vols (Aldershot, 2000), I, 56–9, stresses the problems in detecting women living outside the cloister in the pre-viking period.

18. J. Nelson, 'The wary widow', in W. Davies and P. Fouracre (eds), *Property and Power in the Early Middle Ages* (Cambridge, 1995), 54–82.

19. Foot, *Veiled Women*, I, 148–56; see also ch. 3.

20. D. N. Dumville, *Wessex and England from Alfred to Edgar* (Woodbridge, 1992); Blair, *Church in Anglo-Saxon Society*.

21. A. Gransden, 'Traditionalism and continuity during the last century of Anglo-Saxon monasticism', *Journal of Ecclesiastical History*, 40 (1989), 159–207; S. Coupland, 'The rod of God's wrath? The Carolingian theology of the Viking invasions', *Journal of Ecclesiastical History*, 42 (1991), 535–54.

22. S. Foot, 'Violence against Christians? The vikings and the church in ninth-century England', *Medieval History*, 1.3 (1991), 3–16; Foot, *Veiled Women*, I, 71–84; D. N. Dumville, *The Churches of North Britain in the First Viking Age* (Whithorn, 1997). See further in Chapter 2.

23. S. Wemple, *Women in Frankish Society: Marriage and the Cloister 500–900* (Philadelphia, 1981); J. T. Schulenburg, 'Strict active enclosure and its effects on the female monastic experience (*ca.* 500–1100)', in J. A. Nichols and L. T. Shank (eds), *Medieval Religious Women. I: Distant Echoes* (Kalamazoo, 1984), 51–86.

24. D. Knowles, *The Monastic Order in England 940–1216*, 2nd edn (Cambridge, 1963); D. Knowles, C. N. L. Brooke and V. C. M. London, *The Heads of Religious Houses: England and Wales, 940–1216* (Cambridge, 1972); D. Knowles and R. N. Hadcock, *Medieval Religious Houses: England and Wales*, 2nd edn (London, 1971); Venarde, *Women's Monasticism*.

25. P. Halpin, 'Women religious in late Anglo-Saxon England', *Haskins Society Journal*, 6 (1994), 97–110; J. Crick, 'The wealth, patronage and connections of women's houses in late Anglo-Saxon England', *Revue Bénédictine*, 109 (1999), 154–85; Foot, *Veiled Women*.

26. Halpin, 'Women religious'; Foot, *Veiled Women*, I, 172–9. For similar arrangements after the Norman Conquest see S. Thompson, 'Why English nunneries had no history; a study of the problems of the English nunneries founded after the Conquest', in J. A. Nichols and L. T. Shank (ed.), *Medieval Religious Women. I: Distant Echoes* (Kalamazoo, 1984), 131–49; S. K. Elkins, *Holy Women of the Twelfth Century* (Chapel Hill, NC, 1988), 46–64.

27. J. Crick, 'Men, women and widows; widowhood in pre-Conquest England', in S. Cavallo and L. Warner (eds), *Widowhood in Medieval and Early Modern Europe* (Harlow, 1999), 24–36; Crick, 'Wealth, patronage and connections'; Foot, *Veiled Women*, I, 179–88.

28. S. Foot, 'Language and method: the Dictionary of Old English and the historian', in M. J. Toswell (ed.), *The Dictionary of Old English: Retrospects and Prospects*, Old English Newsletter Subsidia, 26 (1998), 73–87; Foot, *Veiled Women, passim*.

29. The number of double houses cannot be calculated absolutely as there are several

cases of problematical interpretations, nuns whose communities have not been identified and so on. For a list of thirty-three double houses with royal connections founded in the late seventh and early eighth centuries, see the Appendix. To these must be added non-royal foundations made in the course of the eighth century. Eight is the number of nunneries listed as ecclesiastical tenants-in-chief in Domesday Book [Amesbury, Barking, Chatteris, Nunnaminster, Romsey, Shaftesbury, Wherwell and Wilton]. As will emerge in Chapter 3 there were other places with abbesses and nuns in the tenth and eleventh centuries, but these either failed to become established as nunneries or may have been intended only as temporary expedients for particular family members.

30.   Foot, *Veiled Women*, I, 111–44.

31.   T. Symons (ed.), *Regularis Concordia Anglicae nationis monachorum sanctimonialiumque* (London, 1953). See Chapter 3.

32.   *Epistola Bede ad Ecgbertum Episcopum*, in Plummer, I, 405–23. See Chapter 2.

33.   Wemple, *Women in Frankish Society*, 155–74.

34.   M. Parisse, 'Les chanoinesses dans l'empire Germanique (ix–xi siècles)', *Francia*, 6 (1978), 107–28; K. Leyser, *Rule and Conflict in an Early Medieval Society: Ottonian Saxony* (London, 1979), 49–73.

35.   Foot, *Veiled Women*, I, 96–110. The apparent pairing of *nunnan* (vowesses) with *canonicas* (canons) in laws of Æthelred and Cnut has suggested to some authors that it was the vowesses who could be described as canonesses, but, as Sarah Foot has shown, the Anglo-Saxon vowesses lived singly or in small ephemeral communities that were very different from the great Saxon houses of canonesses studied by Karl Leyser and Michele Parisse.

36.   The last major study to attempt to do so for Anglo-Saxon England was D. B. Schneider, 'Anglo-Saxon women in the religious life; a study of the status and position of women in an early medieval society', unpublished Ph.D. thesis (University of Cambridge, 1985), an excellent study with many important observations, but unfortunately unpublished, though, through citations in the work of various scholars, it has made important contributions to the study of Anglo-Saxon nunneries, for instance, in recognizing the dynastic role of many of the major foundations.

37.   Although it is far from clear that deaconesses ever exercised a ministry in the early Western church; see R. Gryson, *The Ministry of Women in the Early Church*, trans. J. Laporte and M. L. Hall (Collegeville, MN, 1976), esp. 100–8.

38.   Wemple, *Women in Frankish Society*; Schulenburg, 'Strict active enclosure'; Hollis, *Anglo-Saxon Women and the Church*.

39.   S. Wemple, 'Female spirituality and mysticism in Frankish monasticism: Radegund, Balthild and Aldegund', in J. A. Nichols and L. T. Shank (eds), *Medieval Religious Women. II: Peace Weavers* (Kalamazoo, 1987), 39–54; J. A. McNamara, 'The need to give: suffering and female sanctity in the Middle Ages', in R. Blumenfeld-Kosinski and T. Szell (eds), *Images of Sainthood in Medieval Europe* (Ithaca, NY, 1991), 199–221; J. Salisbury, *Church Fathers and Independent Virgins* (London, 1991); J. A. McNamara, J. E. Halborg and E. G. Whatley (eds and trans.), 'Introduction', in *Sainted Women of the Dark Ages* (Durham, NC, 1992), 1–15; J. T. Schulenberg, *Forgetful of Their Sex: Female Sanctity and Society ca. 500–1100* (Chicago, 1998).

40.   R. Gilchrist, *Gender and Material Culture: The Archaeology of Religious Women* (London, 1994), 2; see also A. Frantzen, 'When women aren't enough', *Speculum*, 68 (1993), 445–77.

41. J. Nelson, 'Women and the word in the earlier middle ages', in W. J. Shiels and D. Wood (eds), *Women in the Church*, Studies in Church History, 27 (Oxford, 1990), 53–78.

42. J. Smith, 'The problem of female sanctity in Carolingian Europe c. 780–920', *Past and Present*, 146 (1995), 3–37; L. Coon, *Sacred Fictions: Holy Women and Hagiography in Late Antiquity* (Philadelphia, 1997); S. Coates, 'Regendering Radegund? Fortunatus, Baudonivia and the problem of female sanctity in Merovingian Gaul', in R. N. Swanson (ed.), *Studies in Church History*, 35 (Woodbridge, 1998), 37–50.

43. Coon, *Sacred Fictions*, xvi–xvii. See also Lévi-Strauss's famous maxim of women as *bonnes à penser* ('goods/good to think') (Nelson, 'Women and the word').

44. K. Cooper, *The Virgin and the Bride: Idealized Womanhood in Late Antiquity* (Cambridge, MA, 1996); Coon, *Sacred Fictions*.

45. Hollis, *Anglo-Saxon Women and the Church*, 4–7.

46. N. Stoodley, *The Spindle and the Spear: A Critical Enquiry into the Construction and Meaning of Gender in the Early Anglo-Saxon Inhumation Burial Rite*, BAR, 288 (Oxford, 1999). For further critique of traditional methods of analysis see S. Lucy, 'Housewives, warriors and slaves? Sex and gender in Anglo-Saxon burials', in J. M. Moore and E. Scott (eds), *Invisible People and Processes: Writing Gender and Childhood into European Archaeology* (London, 1997), 150–68; D. M. Hadley and J. M. Moore, '"Death makes the man"? Burial rite and the construction of masculinities in the early middle ages', in D. M. Hadley (ed.), *Masculinity in Medieval Europe* (Harlow, 1999), 21–38.

47. C. Clover, 'Regardless of sex: men, women and power in early northern Europe', *Speculum*, 69 (1993), 363–87.

48. Clover, 'Regardless of sex', 385.

49. See, e.g., Tangl no. 135, a letter from Denehard, Lull and Burghard to a West Saxon abbess Cyneburh, or Imma the thegn of Queen Æthelthryth of Northumbria, in *HE*, IV, 22.

50. J. Smith, 'Gender and ideology in the early middle ages', in R. N. Swanson (ed.), *Studies in Church History*, 34 (1998), 51–73.

51. Clover, 'Regardless of sex'.

52. Gilchrist, *Gender and Material Culture*, esp. 188–91.

53. Golding, *Gilbert of Sempringham*, 91–126; Venarde, *Women's Monasticism*, 57–62; 76–82.

54. Crick, 'Wealth, patronage and connections'.

55. Halpin, 'Women religious'; Foot, *Veiled Women*.

56. See Chapter 2.

57. Fell *et al.*, *Women in Anglo-Saxon England*, 74–88.

58. Klinck, 'Anglo-Saxon women and the law'.

59. L. Lancaster, 'Kinship in Anglo-Saxon society; parts I and II', *British Journal of Sociology*, 9 (1958), 230–50, 359–77; H. Loyn, 'Kinship in Anglo-Saxon England', *A-SE*, 3 (1974), 197–209.

60. Y. Hen, '*Milites Christi Utriusque Sexus*, Gender and the politics of conversion in the circle of Boniface', *Revue Bénédictine*, 109 (1999), 17–31, and see further in Chapter 4.

61. A. Wareham, 'St Oswald's family and kin', in N. Brooks and C. Cubitt (eds), *St Oswald of Worcester: Life and Influence* (London, 1996), 117–28.

62. F. Barlow, *The English Church 1000–1066*, 2nd edn (London, 1979), 21–4, 220–1.

63. Foot, 'Language and method'; *Veiled Women*, I, 26–30, 96–110.

64. As is apparent from Schneider, 'Anglo-Saxon women in the religious life'.

65. B. A. E. Yorke, '"Sisters under the skin"? Anglo-Saxon nuns and nunneries in southern England', *Medieval Women in Southern England*, Reading Medieval Studies, 15 (1989), 95–117, was a preliminary examination of some of the issues.

66. See, e.g., Leyser, *Rule and Conflict*; Venarde, *Women's Monasticism*.

67. As demonstrated for the Ottonian royal house in Leyser, *Rule and Conflict*, 50–73, and in P. Corbet, *Les Saints ottoniens; sainteté dynastique, sainteté royale et sainteté féminine autour de l'an Mil*, Beihefte von *Francia*, bd 15 (Sigmaringen, 1986).

68. P. Stafford, 'Sons and mothers: family politics in the early middle ages', in D. Baker (ed.), *Medieval Women*, Studies in Church History Subsidia, 1 (1978), 79–100; *idem*, 'The king's wife in Wessex 800–1066', *Past and Present*, 91 (1981), 3–27; *idem*, *Queens, Concubines and Dowagers: The King's Wife in the Early Middle Ages* (London, 1983); *idem*, *Queen Emma and Queen Edith: Queenship and Women's Power in Eleventh-Century England* (Oxford, 1997); *idem*, 'Queens, nunneries and reforming churchmen: gender, religious status and reform in tenth- and eleventh-century England', *Past and Present*, 163 (1999), 3–35.

69. S. Ridyard, *The Royal Saints of Anglo-Saxon England: A Study of West Saxon and East Anglian Cults* (Cambridge, 1988); *idem*, 'Monk-kings and the Anglo-Saxon hagiographic tradition', *Haskins Society Journal*, 6 (1994), 13–27.

70. M. A. Meyer, 'Patronage of the West Saxon nunneries in late Anglo-Saxon England', *Revue Bénédictine*, 91 (1981), 332–58; *idem*, 'Women and the tenth-century English monastic reform', *Revue Bénédictine*, 87 (1977), 34–61; *idem*, 'Queens, converts and conversion in early Anglo-Saxon England', *Revue Bénédictine*, 109 (1999), 90–116.

71. M. Erler and M. Kowaleski (eds), *Women and Power in the Middle Ages* (Athens, Georgia, 1988); P. Stafford, 'Emma, "The powers of the queen in the eleventh century"', in A. J. Duggan (ed.), *Queens and Queenship in Medieval Europe* (Woodbridge, 1997), 3–26.

72. J. A. McNamara and S. Wemple, 'The power of women through the family in medieval Europe, 500–1100', in Erler and Kowaleski (eds), *Women and Power*, 83–101.

73. For some examples of princes feeling such restriction see J. Nelson, 'Family, gender and sexuality in the middle ages', in M. Bentley (ed.), *Companion to Historiography* (London, 1997), 153–76; W. Aird, 'Frustrated masculinity: the relationship between William the Conqueror and his eldest son', and J. Nelson, 'Monks, secular men and masculinity c. 900', in D. M. Hadley (ed.), *Masculinity in Medieval Europe* (Harlow, 1999), 39–55 and 121–42 respectively.

74. Blair, *Church in Anglo-Saxon Society*.

75. S. Foot, 'Anglo-Saxon minsters: a review of terminology', in J. Blair and R. Sharpe (eds), *Pastoral Care before the Parish* (Leicester, 1992), 212–25; *idem*, 'Language and method'; *idem*, *Veiled Women*, I, ix–iv, 26–30, 96–110.

1   Foundation in the Conversion Period

It is impossible to give definitive figures for the numbers of nunneries founded by members of the royal house, or for the numbers of royal women who entered nunneries, in the seventh and early eighth centuries. The surviving records are too fragmentary, and there are variations in degree of survival both between kingdoms and between different religious houses within kingdoms. What does emerge from a survey of the evidence is that in the period following the conversion of the royal courts, patronage of nunneries was a major concern of all the Anglo-Saxon royal houses for which adequate written records have survived.[1]

The earliest narratives concerning the foundation of royal nunneries are those provided by Bede in his *Historia Ecclesiastica*, and, not surprisingly, these have played a large part in previous studies of the early Anglo-Saxon nunneries. Bede was best placed to gather information on his own province of Northumbria. He provides the most detail for the career of Hild, a member of the Deiran royal house, including her first monastery at Hartlepool,[2] and her more significant foundation of *Streanæshalch*/Whitby,[3] with its daughter house at Hackness.[4] Whitby, both in the time of Hild and that of her successor and kinswoman Ælfflaed, features prominently as well in various hagiographic works written in early Christian Northumbria, including Bede's *Life of St Cuthbert*, the Anonymous *Life of St Cuthbert* and Stephens' *Life of St Wilfrid*,[5] not to mention the *Life of St Gregory the Great* written at Whitby itself.[6] The domination of Whitby in the Northumbrian sources does seem to reflect the importance of the foundation, but other Northumbrian nunneries with royal connections included Coldingham, founded by King Oswiu's sister Æbbe,[7] and Carlisle where the former Queen Iurminburh (wife of King Ecgfrith) and her sister were abbesses.[8]

Outside Northumbria, Bede paid special attention to the nunneries at Ely and Barking. The former was a foundation of the East Anglian princess Æthelthryth, who had been Queen of Northumbria previously as the first wife of King Ecgfrith (670–685).[9] Bede's evidence on East Anglia is particularly valuable because of the lack of native sources surviving for this province.[10] The only other nunnery recorded for the kingdom was at Dereham (Norfolk), where Wihtburh, claimed in later sources as a sister of Æthelthryth, was culted, but this is virtually all that is known of her or the foundation.[11] The shortage of surviving evidence is all the more frustrating because East Anglian princesses seem to have been the first Anglo-Saxon royal women to enter the religious life, and East Anglia seems to have been important for dissemination of ideas regarding royal female monasticism.[12] For Barking, on the other hand, Bede's evidence, which was drawn largely from an otherwise lost *libellus* of miracles,[13] is complemented by charters recording gifts of lands from rulers to the foundation.[14] Barking is one of the few prominent early nunneries whose foundress is not recorded as a member of a royal house. Bede records that Barking was founded by Eorcenwald, before he became bishop of London in 675, for his sister Æthelburh.[15] However, the charters reveal that the initial grant of land came ultimately from King Swithfrith of the East Saxons, and that the nunnery received several other benefactions from East Saxon rulers in its early years. It therefore seems justified to regard Barking as a nunnery that was closely linked with the East Saxon royal house, irrespective of the ancestry of Æthelburh and Eorcenwald, for whom some connection with the East Saxon royal line cannot be ruled out.[16] A recent discovery of charters which had come into the possession of the Hospital of St Mary and St Thomas at Ilford has revealed two hitherto unknown grants from King Swaefred (floruit *c.* 700) of the East Saxons to a woman called *Fymme* to found a religious house at Nazeing, which is presumed to be the foundation whose cemetery was excavated in the 1970s.[17]

Charters are the main source of evidence for several provinces where Bede provides no information on female religious communities. He barely acknowledges the existence of the western provinces of the Hwicce and the Magonsaetan as Christianized communities, but the charter evidence reveals nunneries founded in the late seventh or early eighth centuries, and in a number of cases commanded, by members of the Hwiccian royal house at Bath,[18] Fladbury (Worcs.),[19] Glouces-ter,[20] Inkberrow (Worcs.),[21] Twyning (Glos.)[22] and Withington (Glos.),[23] and a major Magonsaetan foundation at Much Wenlock.[24] Many of the charters for these and other early foundations are not without their problems, since most survive only as copies in later medieval cartularies. Although many were faithfully copied, unfamiliar names or difficult handwriting might be wrongly understood and some features, such as witness-lists, abbreviated. Most problematical of all, charters might be partly rewritten or adapted to suit later claims or changing circumstances, and such tamperings are often more difficult to evaluate than out-and-out forgery which often betrays itself by use of anachronistic forms. For instance, the found-ation charters for Gloucester and Much Wenlock do not survive in their original form, but in later medieval edited versions where excerpts have been taken from several early grants and joined together somewhat awkwardly (Eorcenwald's so-called grant of privileges to Barking is also of this type[25]). Distinctive early spellings and formulae help with the identification of authentic elements, but there are inevitably problems in interpretation of the excerpted material.

Kent is another province for which charters survive for early royal nunneries not mentioned by Bede, though in this case, the failure to mention any of the kingdom's female communities is more surprising because some other aspects of the establishment of the church in Kent are discussed in detail. A meeting in 699 at which grants of privileges were confirmed to Kentish religious houses was attended by four abbesses,[26] and a further synod, probably in 716, was witnessed by five.[27] Charters survive for Minster-in-Thanet,[28] and for Lyminge,[29] which at the end of the eighth century was ruled jointly with Minster-in-Thanet. Further information on the Kentish nunneries is provided by the *Mildrith Legend*, which it is presumed was written at Minster-in-Thanet, where Mildrith, the daughter of King Merewalh of the Magonsaetan and Æbbe of Kent, was abbess in the mid-eighth century.[30] The *Mildrith Legend* seems to have been widely circulated in the late Saxon and post-Conquest periods and adapted to serve a number of different purposes, but the original is likely to have been composed in the latter part of the eighth century, though no surviving witnesses preserve its exact form. In addition to an account of the life of Mildrith, the *Legend* includes the story of the foundation of Minster-in-Thanet in the reign of King Ecgbert of Kent (664–673), and information on the marriages and saintly careers of other members of the Kentish royal house and their East Anglian, Magonsaetan and Mercian in-laws. The *Mildrith Legend* is therefore a potentially valuable source for several nunneries and royal abbesses that are otherwise poorly recorded, but its evidence, particularly for the seventh century, cannot be assumed to be completely accurate. The account of the foundation of Minster-in-Thanet, for instance, includes a number of traditional story-telling elements, such as the extent of the Minster estate being delineated by the circuit of a deer and the wicked royal adviser Thunor being swallowed by the earth, and appears (in some of the forms in which it has come down to us) to equate 'Domne Eafe', the first abbess (Æbbe) with her sister Eormenburh.[31]

Among the West Saxons, it is the royal nunnery of Wimborne about which we are best informed. The foundation of the nunnery by Cuthburh, the sister of King Ine and former wife of King Aldfrith of Northumbria, is acknowledged in an *Anglo-Saxon Chronicle* entry for 718, recording the death of a second brother, but the actual date of foundation is not known. It was the nunnery's connection with Bishop Boniface, rather than its royal links, which was responsible for its being relatively well recorded. Boniface's correspondent Eadburh was probably based at Wimborne, rather than Thanet as has often been supposed,[32] and among her pupils was Boniface's kinswoman Leoba who was destined to join Boniface as a missionary in Germany and become abbess of a nunnery at Bischofsheim in Hesse.[33] Her *Vita*, written in *c.* 836 by Rudolf, a monk of the monastery of Fulda where she was buried, records her upbringing at Wimborne by Abbess Tetta, who, like the foundress Cuthburh, was apparently of royal descent.[34] Rudolf made use of the recollections of some of Leoba's Anglo-Saxon nuns, especially her kinswoman Thecla who had probably also been at Wimborne,[35] but his seductive portrait of the West Saxon nunnery in the early eighth century should be used with care, since it may have been influenced by Carolingian reformist ideals of what a nunnery should be like, current at the time he wrote, and may not be an exact reflection of how it was in Leoba's youth.[36] The oldest of the royal nunneries in Wessex may have been that founded some time after 688 by Princess Bugga, the daughter of King Centwine (675–685), for which we have Aldhelm's dedication poem for the church but not its exact location.[37] We also do not know the site of the double monastery, probably in the northern part of Wessex, of which Lull was a member before he joined Boniface in Germany; his letter to his 'lord', Abbess Cyneburh, implies that she was of royal descent.[38] Another nunnery with royal associations was located at Wareham, where King Beorhtric of Wessex was buried in 802, but we do not know when it was founded or the circumstances of its foundation.[39] The names of several other West Saxon abbesses or nuns are known through letters of Aldhelm and the Boniface-Lull collections and the occasional charter, but they cannot be related to specific foundations, or their relationship (if any) to the royal house established,[40] so that we do not know the full extent of royal patronage of early nunneries in Wessex. The situation in the adjoining province of the South Saxons is even more obscure. The only documented foundation by a member of the royal house is the nunnery founded by Nothgyth, the sister of King Nothhelm in *c.* 692, though the relevant charter falls into the category of those based on authentic material which has subsequently been reworked.[41]

Royal nunneries in Mercia are also inadequately represented in the surviving written records. Repton (Derbys.) seems to have been of particular significance as a number of members of the Mercian royal house were buried there,[42] and it was the foundation which the Mercian prince Guthlac (d. 716) entered when he wished to become a monk in the time of Abbess Ælfthryth (though it is not clear if she herself was of royal descent).[43] An abbess who definitely was is Werburh, the daughter of King Wulfhere of Mercia and his Kentish Queen Eormenhild, whose maternal connections ensured her inclusion in the *Mildrith Legend* which was partly used as the basis for her own *Vita*, known only from a later medieval version.[44] After an early upbringing at Ely, Werburh was reputedly given authority over all the Mercian monasteries, and can be specifically associated with two: Threekingham (Threckingham) (Lincs.) where she died *c.* 700, and Hanbury (Staffs.) where she was buried and where she was subsequently promoted as a saint on the orders of her cousin King Ceolred (709–716).[45] Two daughters of King Penda of Mercia (d. 655), Cyneswith and Cyneburh, were associated with the monastery of Castor (Northants.) before their translation to Peterborough in the later Saxon period;[46] Cyneburh had been married to Alhfrith, subking of Deira, according to Bede.[47] Another two saintly women who are described as daughters of Penda are Eadburh of Adderbury and Bicester (Oxon.) and Edith of Aylesbury (Bucks.) who are mainly known through the *Vita* of Osyth of Aylesbury, reputedly the daughter of their sister Wilburh and King Frithuwold of Surrey. Studies of the *Vita* of Osyth have revealed the complexities that can arise when churches in the post-Conquest period found themselves in possession of the bodies of Anglo-Saxon saints with feast days recorded, but little else.[48] A shortage of information for Osyth of Aylesbury was in part remedied by assuming she was the same person as Osyth of Chich (Essex) whose separate identity is vouchsafed by having a different feast day and an entry in the oldest part of the *Secgan*, an Anglo-Saxon list of saints' resting places.[49] Osyth of Aylesbury's *Vita* was developed still further by incorporation of elements of the story of St Modwenna of Burton-on-Trent who had herself been wrongly equated with an Irish saint called Monenna.[50] It is in one of the stories derived ultimately from the *Vita* of St Monenna that Osyth's aunts Edith and Eadburh make their appearance. But for Eadburh at least we are not solely dependent on the testimony of the *Vita* of Osyth; during the middle ages her cult is well attested at Bicester (where her relics were enshrined from at least the twelfth century) and at Adderbury whose name is derived from 'Eadburh's *byrig*'.[51]

In addition to these possible saintly descendants of the main Mercian line of Penda and his son Wulfhere, there are other abbesses and female saints of the late seventh and early eighth centuries who were, or were claimed to be, members of dependent rulers on the periphery of the main Mercian kingdom. These include St Frideswide (d. 727), who was venerated at Oxford by the late Saxon period, but seems to have been associated originally with Bampton and Binsey, though versions of her *Vita* survive only in post-Conquest accounts and make use of some stock hagiographical elements.[52] Frideswide was reputedly the daughter of Didan, 'King of Oxford', but more in favour of her being an authentic member of an early ruling house is that the first element of her name 'Frid/Frith' connects her with two important seventh-century individuals, Frithuric *princeps* (who was buried at Repton) and Frithuwold, subking of Surrey (reputedly the father of St Osyth of Aylesbury).[53] A surviving charter of Frithuwold (672–674) was witnessed by Æbbe, perhaps, as Susan Kelly has suggested, the same woman who gave her name to Abingdon, which was probably the site of an early nunnery, and who is commemorated in St Ebbe's church in Oxford.[54]

The surviving evidence for early Mercian royal nunneries is far from ideal, and many of the hagiographical details for their princessly saints appear highly suspect. On the other hand, many of the cults are attested as being in existence in the late Saxon period, and the houses with which they are associated may be identified as minster churches – that is, churches with a large dependent parish that are often of early foundation.[55] Many of these churches in the post-Conquest period came under the control of Augustinian canons who were responsible for commissioning the surviving *Vitae*. It would appear that names and feast days for these otherwise obscure Anglo-Saxon saints were known, but little else. One of the crucial questions for identification of royal foundations is whether the descent from the Mercian royal house claimed for many of them was one of the few things that had been kept on record, or whether claims to royal descent should be seen as a hagiographical topos and the result of a desire to relate an otherwise unknown saint to individuals named by Bede. It is possible that a Mercian equivalent to the 'saintly' genealogical list incorporated in the *Mildrith Legend* was in circulation in the middle ages and used in several of the surviving hagiographies.[56] However, one must also be aware that bodies of saints could be translated from one foundation to another, and new foundations of the tenth and eleventh centuries not infrequently translated the relics of established saints from what had become lesser churches into their own foundations;[57] the transfer of Cyneburh and Cyneswith from Castor to Peterborough is one example. This could lead to some confusion about where the saints had been based originally, and some of the surviving accounts, where saints are associated with more than one place, may in fact be evidence for later transfers of either the body or relics. Therefore, for a certain community to claim to have the body of an early Anglo-Saxon female saint in the later middle ages, or even in the later Anglo-Saxon period, is no guarantee that it was the site of a nunnery founded by that saint if there is no earlier supporting evidence. A definitive answer cannot be given about the validity of the claims for many of these early nunneries supposedly founded by women alleged to be Mercian princesses, though it can reasonably be expected, by analogy with kingdoms with better documentation such as Northumbria and Kent, that princesses of the Mercian royal house would have founded and entered nunneries as the traditions claim they did. The female monastic descendants of the Mercian royal house may already appear to be legion, but it should be noted that there are a number of local cults of female saints in Mercia for whom no traditions survive at all. It is possible that some of these were also Mercian princesses of the conversion period. They included Eadburh of Southwell and Edith of Polesworth in the *Secgan*;[58] and Ealdgyth of Bishop's Stortford and Osburh of Coventry in the list of Hugh Candidus.[59]

One conclusion that may be drawn from this survey, which is summarized in the Appendix, is that we are unlikely to have a full record of all the royal nunneries founded in the late seventh and early eighth centuries. Survival of different types of record from the various kingdoms is extremely variable and individual results may be misleading; some of the largest and politically dominant kingdoms are the least well represented in the lists. For instance, no charters survive from Northumbria and East Anglia, where wealthy and influential female communities are well attested in other sources. Where charters do survive in any number, this tends to be because a nunnery's archive was acquired subsequently by another religious community. We have an exceptionally good survival rate for the kingdom of the Hwicce because many of the lands once held by its nunneries were acquired by the bishopric of Worcester. The result is that the relatively small kingdom of the Hwicce appears to have been one of the best endowed with royal nunneries which may be a misleading impression. Mercia has some compensation for the poor survival of contemporary evidence for its early nunneries in its good preservation in later centuries of evidence for localized saints' cults.[60] Wessex largely lacks this type of evidence, but it is not clear whether this reflects a genuine variation in practice between the Mercian and West Saxon kingdoms, or if Wessex once had a similar network of early cults which were swept away by changes to ecclesiastical provision in the later Saxon period.[61] Hints of an even greater provision of royal nunneries come from scattered references to individual nuns and foundations which cannot be precisely localized and so have not been included in the survey. In other cases, nunneries have been omitted because it is not clear whether or not they were royal foundations. Noble families also began to found nunneries in the eighth century or even before, and, although it is sometimes difficult to define whether a family should be classed as royal or aristocratic, the aim has been here to concentrate on those foundations which are definitely connected with a ruling house. Bearing all these caveats in mind, one is still left with a surprisingly high total of twenty-five to thirty nunneries that we can say with some certainty were founded, patronized and, generally, commanded by members of royal houses in the late seventh and early eighth centuries. The actual number founded may be presumed to have been even higher. The foundation of royal nunneries was a substantial trend, which went well beyond being the result of individual royal women discovering a vocation, and, to be better understood, it needs to be viewed within the context of the responses of the royal houses to conversion.

The chronology of foundation

The bulk of the known Anglo-Saxon royal nunneries were founded, as far as we can tell, since specific foundation dates are rare, in the latter part of the seventh century between *c.* 670 and 700 (Appendix). We can therefore equate them with the phase of Christianization, when Christianity was adapted and absorbed into Anglo-Saxon society, and not with the initial periods of conversion. The earliest claim for the foundation of a royal nunnery is the statement in some versions of the *Mildrith Legend* that Lyminge was founded by Queen Æthelburh when she returned to Kent after the death of her husband King Edwin of Deira in 633.[62] The flight of Æthelburh to Kent is recorded in Bede's *Historia Ecclesiastica*, but he says nothing of her entering the religious life.[63] The pattern of a widowed queen retiring to a nunnery was one which became commonplace in Anglo-Saxon England, but, of course, that pattern had not been established by the 630s. The association of Æthelburh with Lyminge is not to be found in the earliest surviving versions of the *Mildrith Legend*,[64] even those which include her flight to Kent, and it seems unwise to accept its validity without some additional supporting evidence. It may be that Lyminge had a connection with a Queen Æthelburh, but that she was not the widow of Edwin. One of the surviving charters of the nunnery was a grant from King Wihtred and his wife Queen Æthelburh made in 697;[65] once memories of seventh-century Kentish history became remote, the confusion of two Queen Æthelburhs may have been made in the interests of creating an early foundation date for Lyminge and a link with Bede's *Historia*. Equally obscure are the circumstances surrounding the foundation of the Kentish royal nunnery at Folkestone, said to have been founded by Eanswith, the daughter of King Eadbald (616–640), who was buried there.[66] It is possible that Folkestone was the earliest Kentish foundation, though the obscurity of its history makes this difficult to believe. On the other hand, even with an association with Eanswith, it need not necessarily pre-date the other Kentish foundations, discussed later, as it could have been founded at any point in Eanswith's life (of which nothing else is known).

If we put the problematical Kentish houses aside, the royal house to be identi-fied as the first to embrace the concept of placing female members in nunneries was that of the East Angles. Bede records that Saethryth and Æthelburh, stepdaughter and daughter of King Anna (d. 654), entered the nunnery of Faremoutiers in Brie, where they both became abbesses, and were joined by their niece Eorcengota, daughter of their sister Seaxburh and King Eorcenbert of Kent (640–664).[67] Fare-moutiers had been founded *c.* 620 on a family estate for Burgondofara by her father Chagneric, an important official at the court of King Theudebert.[68] It was one of a series of monastic houses founded by leading Neustrian nobility on their family lands, under the influence of the Irish missionary Columbanus and his foundation at Luxeuil.[69] Bede does not explain how the association of the East Anglian royal house with the Neustrian foundations came about, but the connec-tion may have been made through Anna's predecessor King Sigebert (acc. *c.* 630) who had been in exile in Francia, and appointed a Burgundian bishop, Felix, who, it has been plausibly proposed, may have come from Luxeuil.[70] Sigebert also patronized an Irish monk Fursey,[71] who either already had, or went on to establish, links with the same group of Neustrian nobility and, with the aid of the Neustrian mayor of the palace Eorcenwald, founded a monastery at Lagny, not far from Fare-moutiers, when he left East Anglia, probably in the 640s.[72]

The entry of Saethryth and Æthelburh into a Frankish nunnery could be taken to imply that no nunneries were founded in East Anglia until a later date, but con-tinental traditions concerning Fursey claim that he founded monasteries in England for both monks and nuns.[73] The experiences of Fursey and his brother Foillan show that the time was not propitious for the permanent foundation of religious houses in East Anglia in the second quarter of the seventh century. Fursey had established a monastery at Burgh Castle through the gift of King Sigebert when he came to the kingdom from Ireland.[74] Fursey subsequently retired to live as a hermit and entrusted Burgh to his brother Foillan, but, because 'the kingdom was disturbed by heathen invasions and monasteries were in danger', Fursey left for Gaul and founded Lagny. Plummer discusses the evidence that dates his departure to between 641 and 644.[75] A vivid account of the dangers faced by Foillan after Fursey's departure is given in a document written at Nivelles (to which Fursey had moved when he fell out with Eorcenwald, the Neustrian mayor of the palace) in 655–656.[76] King Anna was expelled, the monastery looted by the pagans and many monks taken away. Foillan would have suffered this fate himself, but for the sudden flight of the enemy on the news that King Anna was returning. However, Foillan had had enough; he packed his bags and left for Nivelles. These events probably occurred in about 649; in 650 Foillan was murdered by Frankish enemies.[77] The heathen king who caused all the trouble was presumably Penda of Mercia, who is consistently portrayed by Bede as an aggressive pagan who was responsible for the deaths of both King Sigebert and King Anna (654).[78] We can therefore see that even if Anna's daughters had wished to live as nuns in East Anglia, circumstances were against them, and one may conjecture that they left for Faremoutiers at some point in the 640s, and perhaps even travelled with either Fursey or Foillan.[79]

Anna's sister-in-law the Deiran princess Hereswith also travelled from the East Anglian court to Francia to become a nun.[80] Hereswith had left for Francia by 647, when her sister Hild arrived in the province intending to follow her.[81] Her choice was not Faremoutiers, but the nearby nunnery of Chelles, which had been founded by Queen Clothild (wife of Clovis I) in the sixth century.[82] Hereswith's selection of Chelles was possibly influenced by the connection with the Frankish royal house which the Deiran royal family enjoyed following the marriage of King Edwin, Hereswith's uncle, with Æthelburh of Kent, whose mother Bertha was the daughter of the Frankish king Charibert I (561–567).[83] When Æthelburh fled from Northumbria after the death of Edwin in 633, she sent an infant son and grandson to be under the protection of King Dagobert I *amicus illius*.[84] Hild, of course, never reached Chelles, as Bishop Aidan persuaded her to return to Northumbria and take control of the religious house at Hartlepool; in 657 she founded Whitby.[85] The grave-markers used in its monastic cemetery have parallels in Francia and may show the influence of Hild's contacts with Chelles.[86]

The nexus of links between East Anglia, Northumbria and the Frankish nunneries to the east of Paris[87] was important in the spread of female monasticism to other Anglo-Saxon kingdoms, many of whose early nunneries may be associated with foundations in one or more of these provinces. Although exact foundation dates are often hard to establish, the great period of expansion seems to have occurred after the major outbreak of plague in 663 to 664, when mortality among the clergy seems to have been particularly high,[88] and continued apace during the archepiscopate of Theodore (669–690). That Theodore's archepiscopate should be the period of major expansion in female monasticism in England could be seen as rather surprising, because in the Penitential attributed to him reservations are expressed about the double house as a monastic institution: 'It is not permissible for men to have monastic women nor women, men; nevertheless we shall not overthrow that which is the custom in this region.'[89] The only region of Anglo-Saxon England (if the Kentish traditions are discounted) where the double community, headed by an abbess, could possibly be considered as customary when Theodore became Archbishop was Northumbria, where Hartlepool, Whitby and probably Coldingham[90] had been founded by 669, though East Anglian princesses, as we have seen, had also become nuns, but in northern Francia, where double houses could be described as 'customary' among certain Neustrian aristocratic families. By the time of Theodore's death in 690, the royal double community had become something of a *sine qua non* in all the Southumbrian kingdoms.

In Kent, the first houses which may be dated with some certainty seem to have been founded either during the reigns of king Ecgbert (664–673) or that of his brother Hlothere (673–685), while their mother Seaxburh, another daughter of King Anna of the East Angles, was an important influence in the province. Their father King Eorcenbert had died in the plague outbreak of 664, and Seaxburh had remained in the kingdom, perhaps initially as regent for Ecgbert and to oversee the upbringing of Hlothere and his sister Eormenhild,[91] before retiring to Ely on the death of her sister Æthelthryth in 679/80.[92] Probably, before any nunneries had been constructed in Kent, Seaxburh's daughter Eorcengota was sent to join her aunts at Faremoutiers and, after an early death, was apparently regarded there as a saint.[93] The first community for women in Kent may have been that which Seaxburh founded for herself and her daughter Eormenhild at Milton, subsequently supplemented by a new church at Minster-in-Sheppey which eventually seems to have become the senior partner in their nexus. Unfortunately the sources that record this information are very imprecise, and at best allow foundation to be dated only to her widowhood. The earlier text is a fragmentary version of the *Mildrith Legend*, written in the late eleventh century, perhaps at Minster-in-Sheppey, which stresses the role of Hlothere as benefactor of his mother's foundations,[94] while the twelfth-century *Vita beatae Seaxburgae reginae*, written at Ely, but possibly using a version of the *Mildrith Legend* from Sheppey, substitutes Ecgbert.[95] According to the traditions of the *Mildrith Legend*, it was during the reign of Ecgbert that Minster-in-Thanet was founded for his cousin Æbbe in expiation for his murder of her brothers Æthelred and Æthelbert,[96] but the earliest of the Minster-in-Thanet charters to survive claims the land was first granted by Hlothere (673–685) and his nephew and co-ruler Eadric.[97] The father of the murdered princes, Eormenred, was a brother of Eorcenbert, and may have ruled with him briefly on the death of their father; Æthelred and Æthelbert were presumably despatched because of their rival claims to the throne. Although the account in the *Mildrith Legend* contains fabulous elements, there is no reason to doubt the light it throws on seventh-century Kentish politics and the circumstances in which a royal nunnery was endowed.[98]

Elsewhere in southern England, Seaxburh's sister Æthelthryth founded Ely on her return from Northumbria in 673.[99] The nunnery of Barking was founded by Eorcenwald for his sister Æthelburh before he became bishop, that is, by 675.[100] Links with Faremoutiers are suggested by parallels between miracles in the Barking *libellus* and those recorded for the Frankish nunnery by Ionas in his *Life of Columbanus*.[101] In Mercia, nunneries are unlikely to have been founded before the reign of Wulfhere, the first Christian king (658–675), whose many reputed sisters are among the putative earliest founders of Mercian royal nunneries. They would perhaps have been aided by the contacts which could have been provided by Wulfhere's Kentish wife Eormenhild, daughter of Seaxburh and Eorcenbert.[102] Among the Hwicce, there are foundation dates for royal nunneries of 675 for Bath and *c.* 679 for Gloucester, though both of these come from somewhat problematical later medieval manuscripts.[103] Oftfor, the first bishop of the Hwicce, came from Whitby, and there are signs of direct links between Whitby and Hwiccian foundations, especially perhaps during the time of Queen Osthryth of Mercia who was of Northumbrian descent and the sister of Abbess Ælfflaed of Whitby.[104] The presence of Frankish nuns in Hwiccian foundations in the early years[105] could have been the result of Whitby's northern Frankish contacts through Hereswith and her East Anglian in-laws. The earliest royal female communities in Wessex seem to have been made in the reign of King Ine (688–725), when Bugga, the daughter of his predecessor Centwine (abdicated 685) founded her unlocated house,[106] and Ine's sister Cuthburh founded Wimborne following her separation from King Aldfrith of Northumbria (686–705).[107] To this same general period in the last quarter of the seventh century may be attributed the foundation of Much Wenlock for Mildburh, daughter of King Merewalh, whose early history clearly reveals the complex nexus of relationships underpinning these early female houses. Mildburh's mother was Æbbe, who had returned from the province of the Magonsaetan to Kent to found Minster-in-Thanet with another daughter Mildrith, who was to succeed her there as abbess after a period at the nunnery of Chelles.[108] Much Wenlock was also in contact with Barking, as an account was sent there of the vision of the after-life experienced by one of the Much Wenlock brothers.[109] But what the so-called 'Testament of St Mildburh' reveals is a primary link with East Anglia, the ultimate starting-point for the trend of Anglo-Saxon royal women entering the church.[110] The foundation of Much Wenlock seems to have been entrusted originally to the abbot of *Icanho* in East Anglia, the foundation of Botulf, an acknowledged authority on monasticism in early Anglo-Saxon England with whom Ceolfrith of Wearmouth and Jarrow had studied.[111] According to his eleventh-century *Vita* by Folcard, Botulf was in contact with two East Anglian princesses in a Frankish monastery – presumably Saethryth and Æthelburh at Faremoutiers – whom he had visited and who helped to secure patronage for him.[112] So when the 'Testament of St Mildburh' reveals that Much Wenlock, before Mildburh ruled it, was in the charge of Abbot Æthelheah of *Icanho* and an abbess with the Frankish name Liobsind, it seems likely that the connection with Faremoutiers may lie behind her presence.[113]

When the chronology of the foundation of the early royal nunneries is viewed in its entirety, we can trace an upsurge in foundation in the last thirty years of the seventh century following initial moves in East Anglia and Deira in the 640s and 650s. The marriages of royal women seem to have been important in spreading ideas of female monasticism, with the marriage of the Deiran Hereswith into the East Anglian royal house and the East Anglian Seaxburh into that of Kent being of seminal importance. The role of the daughters of Anna in making the monastic life an acceptable and desirable vocation for ex-queens and royal princesses was of prime significance, and had probably been aided by the strength of East Anglian connections with Francia.[114] Thus at one level the vogue for female monasticism in the Anglo-Saxon royal houses could be seen as an example of how political alliances spread new ideas through the different kingdoms, aiding the development of a common Anglo-Saxon culture in which emulation of Frankish forms was an important ingredient.[115] However, if one examines more closely the pattern of foundation in the individual kingdoms against the background of each royal house's commitment to Christianity, one can see that the foundation of religious houses for their women was a fundamental aspect of their response to, and adoption of, the new religion. They are part of a dynastic strategy for assimilating Christianity in ways beneficial to royal houses and in accordance with their expectations of the type of religious support that should be received.

Foundation and the conversion of the Anglo-Saxon royal houses

When the foundation of the royal nunneries is viewed in the context of the progress of Christianity among the different royal houses, a clear pattern emerges. The nunneries are founded after Christianity had been accepted as the only religion of each kingdom; that is, after places of pagan worship have been destroyed and no further unbaptized members of the royal house are known.[116] It could be anywhere between thirty and fifty years after the initial introduction of Christianity to a kingdom before this stage was reached. The gap is particularly striking in the case of the West Saxons. The first West Saxon king to be baptized was Cynegils in 633, [117] but the last king to come to the throne unbaptized was Caedwalla in 685.[118] It was only after Caedwalla's abdication in 688, when King Ine came to the throne, that the first nunneries appear to have been founded in Wessex, making it the last of the major kingdoms to sponsor these foundations. The delay in founding nunneries until after a full commitment had been made by a royal house to the new religion (for, while unbaptized members were still coming to the throne, some pagan rites may be presumed to be continuing) is particularly notable in the case of Wessex because it was otherwise ideally placed to receive the trend towards royal female monasticism. Cynegils' son and successor Cenwalh (642–672), who had come to the throne unbaptized, accepted Christianity while in exile at the court of King Anna of the East Angles (645–648), whose daughters were key promoters of monasticism.[119] He had then appointed as bishop of his see at Dorchester-on-Thames the Frank Agilbert (*c.* 650–*c.* 660), whose sister Theodechild was abbess of Jouarre, one of the leading Neustrian double houses in the vicinity of Chelles and Faremoutiers.[120] Theodechild was succeeded by other relatives as abbess of Jouarre, and Agilbert's nephew Leuthere was subsequently bishop of Winchester (670–*c.* 676). Wessex had important trading contacts with the Paris region which almost certainly went back earlier than the foundation of its *wic* at Hamwic,[121] and so we would expect the West Saxon royal house to have been very open to innovations among the leading Neustrian nobility, like their counterparts in East Anglia. But for reasons that cannot now be explained, pre-Christian religious practices seem to have been particularly tenacious in Wessex and, in spite of the existence of several channels of influence towards royal female monasticism, no nunneries were founded until after the West Saxon royal house had renounced them completely.

The relative chronology of foundation in Wessex may be traced in other kingdoms as well, many of which also show another significant pattern whereby royal nunneries were founded only after a king had initiated royal involvement with monasticism by entering a monastery himself.[122] Thus in Wessex, the first member of the royal house known to have entered the monastic life was King Centwine (abdicated 685), the father of Bugga, who was probably the first royal West Saxon nun.[123] In East Anglia, the interest of King Anna's daughters in monasticism had been preceded by that of his predecessor King Sigebert, who had apparently spent a considerable part of his reign in a monastery, leaving the day-to-day business of ruling to a kinsman called Ecgric.[124] Like the West Saxons, East Saxon kings had something of a stop-start relationship with Christianity, but final commitment came in the reign of Saebbi (*c.* 664–694) who, after wishing to do so for many years, was finally able to abdicate to become a monk shortly before his death.[125] Barking had certainly been founded by the time of his abdication and played a significant part in promoting his cult, but the foundation of the East Saxon royal nunnery at Nazeing probably dated from after Saebbi's abdication.[126] Mercia's example of a monk-king Æthelred, who abdicated to enter his own foundation at Bardney in 704,[127] seems to have done so after the entry of several Mercian princesses into the religious life (though the earliest possible examples are those least satisfactorily recorded). Nevertheless, Æthelred was of the first generation of Mercian royals to enter the monastic life and may have been the first Mercian king to have had the opportunity to do so: his father Penda died in battle a pagan (655) and his brother Wulfhere was probably only in his thirties at the time of his death (675).[128] Northumbria did not have an example of a monk-king, but King Oswald (634–642) was recognized as a saint soon after his death in battle against the pagan Penda,[129] and his brother Oswiu (642–670), in whose reign the first Northumbrian royal nunneries were founded, had proposed to abdicate to spend his last days in Rome if he had survived his final illness.[130] Kent also had no monk-kings, but did have two early royal saints in the murdered princes Æthelred and Æthelbert, whose deaths were the occasion for the foundation of the royal nunnery at Minster-in-Thanet.[131] It is possible that cults were also established, or it was intended that they should be established, for the monk-kings as well. Æthelred was certainly culted at Bardney, and Saebbi is presented in terms reminiscent of hagiography in Bede's account that was presumably based on material provided by Barking.[132] Founders of monastic communities were especially likely to come to be regarded as saints in the early medieval world. It may therefore have been saintliness rather than the monastic life *per se* that was the goal of these holy kings, though they may also have been attracted by the idea of combining royal and ecclesiastical office. It may not be too fanciful to suggest that, in this phase when Christianity was finally accepted as the only viable religion in the Anglo-Saxon kingdoms, there was concern to protect the special, sacral status that had been guaranteed previously by descent from the gods, and to demonstrate that the Christian brand of holiness also manifested itself in the royal line.[133]

It would appear that once royal houses had decided to fully support Christianity, kings wished to demonstrate their commitment to the new religion by some action which would mark them out as holy men as well as rulers. Bishop Wilfrid and some other clergy strongly influenced by Irish practices may have encouraged such instances of royal *peregrinatio*,[134] but others are likely to have been alarmed by this potential confusion of royal and ecclesiastical office. Those, like Bede, who had read the *De Excidio Britanniae* of Gildas would have wanted to avoid a recurrence of his example of the sixth-century King Constantine of Dumnonia, who retired to become an abbot and murdered two of his kinsmen in front of his altar.[135] Neither Sigebert nor Æthelred were able to cast off all their former responsibilities as rulers when they became monks.[136] Sigebert was prevailed upon to ride at the head of the East Anglian army for a fatal encounter with Penda of Mercia,[137] and Æthelred ordered his nephew Cenred, whom he had appointed in his place, to reinstate Bishop Wilfrid.[138] Although Anglo-Saxon kings may have expected a close involvement with the Christian church because of the roles they played in pagan religious practices,[139] other considerations may have encouraged them to accept the idea that the kingly and clerical professions were incompatible; an idea promoted by Bede when he reported that King Saebbi's love of prayers, almsgiving and 'religious exercises' caused many to conclude 'that a man of his disposition ought to have been a bishop rather than a king'.[140] In accepting that royal and ecclesiastical life were not compatible, after an initial period of experimentation, Anglo-Saxon kings would have been influenced by Frankish attitudes, for in Francia by the seventh century compulsory retirement to a religious community was a way of removing rivals to the throne and humiliating one's opponents as well as taking them out of circulation.[141] The clerical advisers of Anglo-Saxon kings could also point to the fact that kingship itself was a divinely appointed office and one that could not be relinquished.[142]

The phenomenon of the monk-king was a short-lived one in Anglo-Saxon England, and no kingdom is known to have produced more than one example (though the cult of murdered kings recurred throughout the period and became firmly implanted in lay devotion[143]). Either it was an experiment in the period of accommodation with Christianity which was swiftly crushed by the church, or the very public renunciation of office by a king to serve the new religion was a rite of passage which needed to be performed only once to demonstrate a royal house's sacrality and complete commitment to the change in religion. But if kings and princes were discouraged from compromising their status by entering the church, this left the way clear for widowed queens and princesses to become the highest ranked members of a royal house who were acceptable to churchmen as members and leaders of monastic communities and as potential demonstrators of the sacrality of the royal lines through their personal saintliness.[144] In future the closest kings would get to holding office in the church was vicariously through their kinswomen who became abbesses and nuns.

Circumstances of foundation

One essential point for understanding the foundation of Anglo-Saxon double houses is that formerly married women retired into houses in their home provinces, not those of the province into which they had married. There might be a temporary withdrawal to a nunnery in the husband's province, but, in accordance with what appears to have been Anglo-Saxon custom as represented in the lawcodes, a married woman remained primarily the responsibility of her paternal kin.[145] Well-recorded examples include the sisters Æthelthryth and Seaxburh who returned from Northumbria and Kent respectively to end their days at Ely, Æbbe who was summoned back from the province of the Magonsaetan to found Minster-in-Thanet in her native Kent as compensation for the murder of her two brothers, and Cuthburh of Wessex who founded Wimborne after her separation from King Aldfrith of Northumbria. In some other instances where the provincial origin is not so immediately obvious, there are indications that the rule applied. Iurminburh, the second wife of King Ecgfrith of Northumbria, retired to Carlisle to become a nun after his death in battle in 685. Although the first element of her name is cognate with 'Eormen', a name-element otherwise associated with Kent, and exogamous marriage was the norm in Anglo-Saxon kingdoms in the conversion period, in this case it seems likely that Iurminburh was herself a Northumbrian, because her sister was abbess of Carlisle.[146] If this was the same (unnamed) sister who had been married to King Centwine of Wessex, she would be another example of a woman who returned home after separation from her husband.[147] Such separations seem to have been envisaged as an accepted occurrence under Anglo-Saxon law,[148] and although retirement to a nunnery came to be the expected vocation of separated women, the practice of separation by mutual agreement seems likely to have pre-dated Christian influence on the Anglo-Saxon kingdoms.[149]

For princesses born to such unions the situation was more complex, as they had ties to both maternal and paternal kin, and the question of to which they would most closely relate could be the subject of negotiation when the marriages were dissolved.[150] Thus, when Æbbe of Kent and Merewalh of the Magonsaetan went their separate ways, Mildrith seems to have gone to Kent with her mother and followed her as abbess of Minster-in-Thanet, but her sister Mildburh stayed in the Magonsaetan province and became abbess of Much Wenlock. Eormenhild, the daughter of Seaxburh of the East Angles and King Eorcenbert of Kent, seems to have inherited interests in the provinces of both her mother and her father. She may have been raised initially at Minster-in-Sheppey, founded by her mother in Kent,[151] and perhaps returned there after the end of her marriage to King Wulfhere of Mercia (658–675) if she was the abbess Eormenhild who attested a grant of privileges to the Kentish churches in 699.[152] However, in Ely tradition she took over that monastery after the death of her mother Seaxburh, and is recorded as being buried there.[153]

The one kingdom with which she does not seem to have had a monastic association was her marital province of Mercia. On the other hand, her daughter by Wulfhere, Werburh, was linked with a number of religious houses in her paternal homeland of Mercia.[154] Once we are into the period when many monasteries have been founded, one cannot provide a hard-and-fast rule about whether princesses would command monasteries in their paternal or maternal kingdom. No doubt individual circumstances and personal choice played a part. Eanflaed, wife of her cousin Oswiu of Northumbria and the daughter of a former Northumbrian king (though from a rival dynasty of her husband), was brought up in her mother's home province of Kent. One might have expected her to return to Kent on being widowed (670), but Northumbria was her paternal home, and she entered the nunnery of Whitby where her daughter Ælfflaed was already a nun and being brought up by her cousin Hild who was abbess.

In a period of complex intermarriage between dynasties, many royal women were spoilt for choice when it came to entering a religious community, but one point remains clear: the responsibility for providing for them lay with blood relatives, whether of paternal or maternal kin, and not with their in-laws. Where we have evidence for the circumstances of foundation, the nunnery is generally stated to have been founded for the woman by a king or bishop.[155] It would in fact be unlikely that any other scenario was possible in the late seventh century, since it would appear that private landownership with rights of free alienation, as understood in late Roman land law, was a concept unfamiliar to the Anglo-Saxons, and was re-introduced by the church in the post-conversion period to ensure its own landed endowment.[156] Previously, land seems to have been regarded as family land, inalienable from the kin. Royal lands were probably also interpreted in this way, but could be granted out on a temporary tenure to those who had been in royal service. However, interpretation of traditional forms of tenure is hampered by there being very little recorded about them. The new tenure, known as bookland, was initially only granted for ecclesiastical purposes, and only a king with the consent of his councillors could issue a charter (*boc*) which could transform land into bookland with rights of permanent ownership and free alienation; thus Eorecenwald, having acquired various lands for ecclesiastical purposes from the East Saxon kings, was able to use some of them to endow a monastery at Barking for his sister.[157]

Therefore any claims that royal women in the seventh century were in a position to found nunneries, in the sense that they already 'owned' the land on which they were founded, need careful scrutiny, because at that time the concept of individuals having private ownership and rights of free disposition of land did not exist. It is a claim that has been made for Ely. Bede merely says that Æthelthryth, after separating from her husband King Ecgfrith of Northumbria in 672 or 673, withdrew to the Northumbrian nunnery of Coldingham, and after a year was made (*facta*) abbess *in regione vocatur Elge* where she built (*constructa*) her nunnery.[158] Bede does not commit himself on how Æthelthryth acquired the land. An additional explanation is to be found in the first book of the twelfth-century *Liber Eliensis*, which draws upon hagiographical traditions about Æthelthryth extant in the late Saxon period, and says that Æthelthryth received Ely as dower from her first husband, Tondbert, *princeps* of the South Gyrwe.[159] The information about Æthelthryth's marriage to Tondbert comes from Bede, but although he describes Peterborough (*Medehamstede*) as being in the territory of the Gyrwe, he refers to Ely as being a *regio* of the province of the East Angles, and specifically states that Æthelthryth 'wished to have her monastery here because . . . she sprang from the race of the East Angles'.[160] Although it is not impossible that Ely had once been Gyrwan – but by 673 or 674 had become East Anglian – that Æthelthryth's marriage had been significant in allowing the take-over, and that a former association with the province explains why she became abbess there rather than somewhere in the heart of the East Anglian kingdom, such claims can only be hypotheses, and receive no direct support from Bede's text. We may suspect that the author of the *Liber Eliensis*, upon reading of Æthelthryth's marriage to Tondbert at the beginning of the chapter of the *Historia Ecclesiastica* which describes the foundation of Ely, decided to make his own connection,[161] and certainly his explanation of dower is anachronistic, and reflects late Saxon or Norman expectations of the arrangements to be made on marriage. Bede's stress is on how Æthelthryth, like other separated Anglo-Saxon royal women, returned to her home province, and that provision for her to become an abbess was made there. Nevertheless, one cannot rule out the possibility that some royal women commanded sufficient resources to be able to initiate foundation. Seaxburh, as dowager queen of Kent, is said to have purchased the land on which to found Sheppey from her son,[162] but unfortunately there is once again the problem of the information only being recorded in a relatively late text.[163]

Few foundation charters have survived for the early nunneries, and those which we have often show signs of later interference, for instance to strengthen the terms on which the initial grant was made or the extent of the lands granted. According to the foundation charter for Gloucester (674–679) (whose text is one of those about which reservations must be expressed),[164] the brothers Osric and Oswald of the Hwicce purchased the land and right to found the monastery from King Æthlelred of Mercia *in perpetuam hereditatem possidendum & abhabendum & post se in suam genelogiam qualicunque manu voluerit donandam*. In other words, a family monastery for the Hwiccian royal house was created, to be passed by the founders to whichever of their relatives they chose to nominate. The foundation charter goes on to reveal that the brothers made their sister Cyneburh the first abbess, and that she was succeeded by a kinswoman called Eadburh;[165] the third abbess Eafe may also have been a member of the royal house.[166] Even if the Latin text of the Gloucester foundation charter often appears corrupt, the succession of royal abbesses shows that a family monastery had indeed been created. As the conciliar legislation of the eighth and ninth centuries makes clear, founding families retained rights of lordship over monasteries which might include the claim to appoint the heads of houses.[167]

If more foundation charters had survived, we could expect to have more unambiguous statements of the intentions to found a proprietary house by their royal patrons. As it is, we can point to several instances of succession to the headship of royal nunneries passing between female relatives: Hild, Eanflaed and Ælfflaed at Whitby; Æthelthryth, Seaxburh and Eormenhild at Ely; Æbbe and Mildrith at Minster-in-Thanet. The first abbess seems to have been able to appoint her own heir, but was probably expected to choose a member of the same kin-group. Succession may be shown to have worked in a similar way in early all-male communities; Benedict Biscop, founder of Wearmouth and Jarrow, obtained a papal privilege to exclude his brother (his 'natural' heir) from succeeding him, but still appointed a relative, his cousin Eosterwine.[168] Some insight into how matters may have worked is provided by an account of a dispute over the Hwiccian family monastery at Withington (Glos.) which was adjudicated at a synod in 736 or 737.[169] The nunnery was founded originally by King Æthelred of Mercia, at the request of King Oshere of the Hwicce, for Dunne and her daughter Bugga. It would appear that Bugga predeceased her mother, and Dunne nominated her granddaughter Hrothwaru to succeed her, but, because Hrothwaru was too young at the time of Dunne's death, the estate was administered by a second daughter, Hrothwaru's mother, a married woman. It was the unwillingness of the mother to hand over the estate when Hrothwaru came of age that occasioned the synod, which found in favour of Dunne's arrangements. Subsequently, Withington came under the control of Abbess Æthelburh, who also commanded the Hwiccian royal nunneries of Twyning and Fladbury. She was undoubtedly a member of the Hwiccian royal house, and so it is probable that Dunne was too, though this is nowhere explicitly stated.

In other instances, the dynastic context is suggested by the circumstances of foundation which might be to resolve the tensions caused by a family murder, as in the case of Minster-in-Thanet, or in fulfilment of a vow, as when Oswiu pledged his infant daughter Ælfflaed to the religious life should God grant him victory at the battle of the river Winwaed; the vow led to her being placed in the care of Hild and helps to explain the subsequent importance of the double house of Whitby.[170] Although Bede writes persuasively of the commitment to the religious life of Hild and Æthelthryth, neither in his writings nor in other contemporary texts is the vocation of individual women seen to be at odds with the broader dynastic aims of their families. There are no instances in these texts of that hagiographical topos of the religious woman who heroically resisted attempts by her relatives to make her marry.[171] The absence of this motif is striking, because it had been used in late Antique hagiographical accounts and was regularly used in the *Lives* of Merovingian religious women;[172] it also occurs in the *Lives* of conversion period Anglo-Saxon female saints like Frideswide, which were written in the eleventh century or later. In contrast, Bede chose as his particular monastic heroine Æthelthryth who had been married twice, and although marriage was presumably, in some respects at least, unwelcome to her, since she is reputed to have remained a virgin through both unions, there is no indication in his account that she resisted being wed and no hint of criticism of her father Anna who arranged them; instead he is described as 'a good man and blessed with a good and saintly family'.[173] Royal female monasticism was not in opposition to the dynastic role of royal women in our early texts, but a facet of it.

Exemplification of how Anglo-Saxon royal nunneries aided dynastic interests will be provided in later chapters, but at a simple level they may be seen as providing what was perceived as essential Christian cultic underpinning for their families. But why should it have been felt desirable to have members of the family providing such support, particularly when there were bishops, abbots and priests, who were also patronized by rulers, to provide it? In part, the answer may come from a pre-Christian royal involvement in cults that cannot now be recovered. One should also remember that royal families were not monolithic and stable entities, but, by the end of the seventh century, were composed of a number of different branches which were rivals for power.[174] One branch of a royal house might manage to rule for several generations but still be vulnerable to rival kindred at any sign of weakness. The rulers of smaller kingdoms, like that of the Hwicce which was subject to Mercian overlordship, were in danger of being ousted from power altogether, as indeed did happen to the Hwiccian royal house in the course of the eighth century. The different royal kin-groups were therefore anxious to underpin their authority by any means possible, including the spiritual, and interests were expected to be most reliably nurtured by one's immediate family, a role that could be filled most appropriately by women of the royal house, as we have seen. It may also have been thought desirable to lay down reserves in case of hard times if ousted from power.[175] The acquisition of bookland which could be bequeathed as the holder wished, rather than being regarded as belonging to the royal house in its entirety, and used to found proprietary religious houses, offered the possibility of some future security for vulnerable family members. There was probably no distinction between the aims of royal branches and those of noble families in wishing to acquire bookland,[176] a trend deplored by Bede who felt that some were attracted by the idea of possession of the land and neglected the religious duties which were supposed to go with it.[177] Nobles receiving such grants might also delegate the establishment of religious communities on the land to their female relatives. For instance, in the second quarter of the eighth century, King Æthelbert of the South Saxons granted land to his noble Diosza to found a minster at Wittering which he promptly transferred to his sister.[178]

The link between monastic foundation and cultivation of dynastic identity is something the Anglo-Saxon royal houses may have learned from the Columban-inspired northern Frankish foundations which played such an important role in the development of the Anglo-Saxon double houses. Faremoutiers and Jouarre are both good examples of religious communities founded by Frankish noble houses seeking to establish themselves as landowners and as significant influences at the Neustrian court. The sons of these houses might move away from the patrimonial

estates to become court officials, bishops or monks at one of Columbanus' foundations, but a daughter could remain on them and create a spiritual core for the
family in a monastery. In the words of Patrick Geary, 'Columbanus and his
monastic tradition provided the common ground around which networks of
northern aristocrats could unite, finding a religious basis for their social and
political standing'.[179] Through the foundation of their own double houses, Anglo-
Saxon dynasties joined the network as well, with many of their foundations having
direct links with their Frankish counterparts. No doubt such connections were
another aspect of why foundation of these female-led communities became so
desirable in all the Anglo-Saxon kingdoms. Frankish examples may have helped
establish the idea that it was appropriate and acceptable for women to head these
foundations, and it may also have been the case that royal and noble women had
played a prominent role from the start in the acceptance of Christianity in Anglo-
Saxon England, since elite female burials of the seventh century are more likely to
include overt Christian symbolism than those of men.[180] It is often difficult, at this
remove, and with limited, often formalized sources, to unpick the bundle of
reasons which made the foundation of double houses so attractive to Anglo-Saxon
rulers in the late seventh century. Genuine enthusiasm for the new religion, vouchsafed by the sources for the Frankish foundations as well as the Anglo-Saxon,
should not be ignored. Dynastic interests can be only part of the explanation of the
great interest in female monasticism at that time, but they were very significant in
providing the context in which it developed, as well as causing some of the
problems which many of the houses encountered during the later eighth and ninth
centuries.

Notes

1. The only kingdoms identified by Bede which cannot definitely be shown to have
   royal nunneries are two which vanished at an early date, Wight and Lindsey –
   though, given the weight of evidence assembled here for major early nunneries being
   royal foundations, it is possible that the nunnery of Partney in Lindsey and its abbess
   Æthelhild were connected with the province's royal house; *HE*, III, 11; B. A. E.
   Yorke, 'Lindsey: the lost kingdom found?', in A. Vince (ed.), *Pre-Viking Lindsey*
   (Lincoln, 1993), 141–50, at 145.
2. *HE*, III, 24; IV, 23. Hartlepool was originally founded by Bishop Aidan for Heiu, the
   first woman to be ordained a nun in Northumbria, but it was bestowed on Hild when
   she returned to Northumbria in *c.* 648.
3. *HE*, III, 24–5; IV, 23–6. P. Hunter Blair, 'Whitby as a centre of learning in the
   seventh century', in M. Lapidge and H. Gneuss (eds), *Learning and Literature in
   Anglo-Saxon England* (Cambridge, 1985), 3–32, and P. Rahtz, 'Anglo-Saxon and later
   Whitby', in L. Hoey (ed.), *Yorkshire Monasticism: Archaeology, Art and Architecture,
   from the Seventh to the Sixteenth Century*, British Archaeological Association Transactions, 16 (London, 1995), 1–11 for the problems of equating *Streanæshalch* and
   Whitby, which is considered in more detail in Chapter 5. For convenience, the foundation is referred to as 'Whitby' in the rest of this chapter.

4. *HE,* IV, 23.
5. Bede, *VC,* chs 23–4, 34; Anon., *VC,* ch. III, 6; IV, 10; *VW,* ch. 2, 10, 43–4, 59–60.
6. B. Colgrave (ed.), *The Earliest Life of Gregory the Great* (Cambridge, 1968).
7. *HE,* IV, 19 and 26; Anon., *VC,* ch. 3; Bede, *VC,* ch. 10; *VW,* ch. 39.
8. Bede, *VC,* chs 27–8; *VW,* ch. 24.
9. *HE,* IV, 19–20.
10. D. Whitelock, 'The pre-Viking age church in East Anglia', *A-SE,* 1 (1972), 1–22.
11. *A-SC,* 798 records the recovery of her incorrupt body at Dereham fifty-five years after her death, which would place it *c.* 743. If this is correct she could not possibly be a sister of Æthelthryth, who died in 679. S. Ridyard, *The Royal Saints of Anglo-Saxon England: A Study of West Saxon and East Anglian Cults* (Cambridge, 1988), p. 59; J. Blair, 'A handlist of Anglo-Saxon saints', in A. Thacker and R. Sharpe (eds), *Local Saints and Local Churches in the Early Medieval West* (Oxford, 2002), 495–565, at 559.
12. *HE,* III, 8; and see further below.
13. *HE,* IV, 7–11.
14. S 1171, 1246 and 1248; C. R. Hart, 'The early charters of Barking Abbey', in *The Early Charters of Eastern England* (Leicester, 1966), 117–45.
15. *HE,* IV, 6.
16. The first element of Eorcenwald's name is rare in Anglo-Saxon England and may be Frankish in origin. Its use is attested only in the Kentish and East Saxon royal houses; in the case of the latter, the father of King Saebert (d. *c.* 616) was, according to some versions of his descent, called Eorcenwine (B. A. E. Yorke, 'The kingdom of the East Saxons', *A-SE,* 14 (1985), 1–36, at 10–16).
17. K. Bascombe, 'Two charters of King Suebred of Essex', in K. Neale (ed.), *An Essex Tribute: Essays Presented to F. G. Emmison* (Cambridge, 1987), 85–96; P. J. Huggins, 'Excavations of a Belgic and Romano-British farm with Middle Saxon cemetery and churches at Nazeingbury, Essex, 1975–6', *Essex Archaeology and History,* 10 (1978), 3rd series, 29–117. For another possible East Saxon royal nunnery at Chich and its foundress St Osyth, see below.
18. S 51, B 43; S 1167, B 57.
19. S 76, B 76; S 62, B 234. The early history of this minster is somewhat difficult to unravel, but it was definitely a proprietary house of the Hwiccian royal line in the eighth century, and in S 76 (697–699) King Æthelheard of the Hwicce seems to have been asserting a prior claim to the foundation which had come under the control of King Æthelred of Mercia and his wife Osthryth. The first abbess may have been the 'Flaede' who gave her name to the foundation (*Fledanburg*). See further H. P. R. Finberg, *Early Charters of the West Midlands,* 2nd edn (Leicester, 1972), 168–72, and P. Sims-Williams, *Religion and Literature in Western England, 600–800* (Cambridge, 1990), 92–3.
20. S 70, B 60; S 74, B 535; Finberg, *West Midlands,* 153–66; Sims-Williams, *Religion and Literature,* 122–5.
21. S 53, B 85; S 1177, B 122; S 95, B 153.
22. S 1255, B 217. The circumstances of foundation are not recorded, but as the charter seems to indicate that this was one of the proprietary houses which the survivors of the Hwiccian royal house were trying to retain against claims of the Bishop of Worcester in the mid-eighth century, there is a good case for seeing it as an older Hwiccian royal foundation; see Finberg, *West Midlands,* 178–9.

23. S 1429, B 156; S 1255, B 217.
24. S 1798–1802; Finberg, *West Midlands*, 197–216.
25. S 1246, B 87; Hart, *Early Charters of Eastern England*, 122–7.
26. Eormenhilda, Eormenburga, Æbba and Nerienda; S 25, B 99; S. Kelly (ed.), *Charters of St Augustine's Abbey, Canterbury and Minster-in-Thanet*, British Academy, Anglo-Saxon Charters, IV (Oxford, 1995), 38–44.
27. S 22, B 99; Mildrith, Ætheldrith, Ætte, Wilnoth and Hereswith; the foundations they commanded, as named in the text, were Southminster (Minster-in-Thanet), Folkestone, Lyminge, Sheppey and Hoo. It is not clear if the two lists are in the same order, but Mildrith who leads the attesting abbesses was abbess of Minster-in-Thanet, the first of the nunneries to be listed. Hoo was probably the newest nunnery and not represented in S 25. According to S 233 (B 89) it had been founded by Caedwalla during his brief intervention in Kent (686) and granted to Peterborough. Presumably it was reclaimed when King Wihtred (690–725) re-established control and became one of the Kentish royal nunneries. The Werburh who was apparently culted there may have been Wihtred's queen, rather than the Mercian saint (Kelly, *Charters of Minster-in-Thanet*, 103).
28. Kelly, *Charters of Minster-in-Thanet*, 139–82.
29. S 19, B 97; S 21, B 98; S 23, B 148; S 24, B 160; S 160, B 317.
30. D. Rollason, *The Mildrith Legend: A Study in Early Medieval Hagiography in England* (Leicester, 1982); S. Hollis, 'The Minster-in-Thanet foundation story', *A-SE*, 27 (1998), 41–74.
31. B 99, S 20 included both Æbbe and Eormenburh as abbesses; possibly the nunnery of which Eormenburh became abbess after her return from the province of the Magonsaetan was Lyminge, as later abbesses of Minster were also abbesses of Lyminge.
32. Tangl, nos 10, 30 and 35; B. A. E. Yorke, 'The Bonifacian mission and female religious in Wessex', *Early Medieval Europe*, 7 (1998), 145–72.
33. Tangl, nos 29, 67, 96 and 100.
34. G. Waitz (ed.), *Vitae Leobae Abbatissae Biscofesheimensis auctore Rudolfo Fuldensi, MGH Scriptores*, XV (Hanover, 1887), 118–31, at 122–5; a translation can be found in C. H. Talbot, *The Anglo-Saxon Missionaries in Germany* (London, 1954), 204–26.
35. *V. Leobae*, 122.
36. J. T. Schulenberg, 'Strict active enclosure and its effects on the female monastic experience (500–1100)', in J. A. Nichols and L. T. Shank (eds), *Medieval Religious Women. I: Distant Echoes* (Kalamazoo, 1984), 51–86; S. Hollis, *Anglo-Saxon Women and the Church* (Woodbridge, 1992), 271–300.
37. R. Ehwald (ed.), *Aldhelmi Opera Omnia, MGH Auctores Antiquissimi*, XV (Berlin, 1919), 14–18; M. Lapidge and J. Rosier, *Aldhelm: The Poetic Works* (Woodbridge, 1985), 40–9; for a Latin verse epitaph on Bugga, see M. Lapidge, 'Some remnants of Bede's lost *Liber Epigrammatum*', *EHR*, 90 (1975), 798–820, at 815–7.
38. Tangl, no. 49; see Sims-Williams, *Religion and Literature*, 239–42; Hollis, *Anglo-Saxon Women and the Church*, 162–3; Yorke, 'Bonifacian mission', 155–7.
39. *A-SC*, 786, though specific reference to a nunnery at Wareham is first recorded in W. H. Stevenson (ed.), *Asser's Life of King Alfred* (Oxford, 1904, repr. 1959), ch. 49, 36–7, which indicates there was a nunnery in the settlement by 876. That there was a nunnery in Wareham in the time of Beorhtric and that it was the place of his burial can only be an inference which not everyone would accept (see S. Foot, *Veiled Women*, 2 vols (Aldershot, 2000), II, 197–204).

40. Yorke, 'Bonifacian mission', 146–72.

41. S 45, B 78; S. Kelly (ed.), *Charters of Selsey*, British Academy, Anglo-Saxon Charters, VI (Oxford, 1998), no. 2, 13–22.

42. M. Biddle and B. Kjølbye-Biddle, 'The Repton stone', *A-SE*, 14 (1985), 233–92.

43. B. Colgrave (ed.), *Felix's Life of Saint Guthlac* (Cambridge, 1956), ch. 20.

44. Rollason, *The Mildrith Legend*, 26–7; *Vita S. Werburgae*, ed. *AA SS* (1 February) (1658), 386–90; Ridyard, *Royal Saints*, 60.

45. A. Thacker, 'Kings, saints and monasteries in pre-viking Mercia', *Midland History*, 10 (1985), 1–25, at 4; Blair, 'Handlist', 557.

46. D. Rollason, 'Lists of saints' resting-places in Anglo-Saxon England', *A-SE*, 7 (1978), 63–4, 90; *Vita SS. Kyneburgae et Kineswidae*, ed. *AA SS* (1 March) (1668), 441–7; Blair, 'Handlist', 523–4. They were translated to Peterborough in 963 and according to some of the *Mildrith Legend* texts a kinswoman called Tibba was also associated with them at Peterborough: Rollason, *Mildrith Legend*, 77, 80, 81 and 85.

47. *HE*, III, 21.

48. C. Hohler, 'St Osyth and Aylesbury', *Records of Buckinghamshire*, 18 (1966), 61–72; D. Bethell, 'The Lives of St. Osyth of Essex and St. Osyth of Aylesbury', *Analecta Bollandiana*, 88 (1980), 75–127.

49. Rollason, 'Lists of saints' resting-places', 62, 90; she is supposed to have been the wife of King Sigehere of the East Saxons (ruling 664), to have founded Chich in 653 and to have been beheaded by vikings, after which she picked up her head and walked back with it to the church.

50. Hohler, 'St. Osyth', 64–6; Bethell, 'St. Osyth', 79–80.

51. Thacker, 'Monasteries in pre-viking Mercia', 7; Blair, 'Handlist', 525.

52. J. Blair, 'Saint Frideswide reconsidered', *Oxoniensia*, 52 (1987), 71–127; *idem*, 'St Frideswide's monastery: problems and possibilities', *Oxoniensia*, 53 (1988), 221–58.

53. J. Blair, 'Frithuwold's kingdom and the origins of Surrey', in S. Bassett (ed.), *The Origins of Anglo-Saxon Kingdoms* (Leicester, 1989), 97–107.

54. S 1165, B 34. S. Kelly (ed.), *Charters of Abingdon Abbey, Part I*, British Academy, Anglo-Saxon Charters, VII (Oxford, 2000), cxcvii–viii; J. Blair, *Anglo-Saxon Oxfordshire* (Stroud, 1994), 64–5.

55. Thacker, 'Kings, saints and monasteries'; Blair, *Anglo-Saxon Oxfordshire*, 55–68; J. Blair, 'A saint for every minster?', in A. Thacker and R. Sharpe (eds), *Local Saints and Local Churches in the Early Medieval West* (Oxford, 2002), 455–94.

56. Bethell, 'St. Osyth', 80–3.

57. D. Rollason, 'The shrines of saints in later Anglo-Saxon England: distribution and significance', in L. Butler and R. Morris (eds), *The Anglo-Saxon Church* (London, 1986), 32–43.

58. Rollason, 'Lists of saints' resting-places', 63, 89–90. Edith (or Eadgyth) of Polesworth (who may also be the saint of the same name associated with Tamworth) was identified by post-Conquest writers as a tenth-century member of the West Saxon royal house; A. T. Thacker, 'Dynastic monasteries and family cults: Edward the Elder's sainted kindred', in N. Higham and D. Hill (eds), *Edward the Elder 899–924* (London, 2001), 248–63. But contradictory information is given (see Hohler, 'St. Osyth', 65–6). Reasons for thinking that Edith of Polesworth may have been an earlier Mercian saint include her appearance in the first part of the *Secgan* where all the other saints lived pre-900, and the fact that the numerous female saints and nuns of the later West Saxon royal house were all associated with West Saxon houses.

59. W. T. Mellows (ed.), *The Peterborough Chronicle of Hugh Candidus* (Peterborough, 1941), 30–2; for commentary on the list see Rollason, 'Lists of saints' resting-places', 70–2, and Blair, 'A saint for every minster?', 463–7.

60. Thacker, 'Monasteries in pre-viking Mercia'. The early Mercian cults, of course, also include those of a number of men, including some of royal birth, who are not being considered here.

61. Blair, 'A saint for every minster?', 467.

62. Rollason, *Mildrith Legend*, 80–6.

63. *HE*, II, 20.

64. M. Swanton, 'A fragmentary life of St Mildred and other Kentish royal saints', *Archaeologia Cantiana*, 91 (1975), 15–27; Rollason, *Mildrith Legend*, 73–80.

65. S 19, B 97. For Wihtred's queens see Kelly, *Charters of Minster-in-Thanet*, 37–8. As Wihtred had moved on to his third queen by 716, Æthelburh must have either been dead or separated from him; if the latter, it may be suggested that she retired to the nunnery of Lyminge and was buried there. In the late eleventh century the tomb of an Æthelburh was displayed in the north porticus at Lyminge; M. Biddle, 'Archaeology, architecture and the cult of saints in Anglo-Saxon England', in L. Butler and R. Morris (eds), *The Anglo-Saxon Church: Papers on History, Architecture and Archaeology in Honour of Dr H. M. Taylor* (London, 1986), 1–31, at 8.

66. Rollason, *Mildrith Legend*, 75.

67. *HE*, III, 8; S. Robertson, 'St Eanswith's reliquary in Folkestone church', *Archaeologia Cantiana*, 16 (1886), 322–6.

68. F. Prinz, *Frühes Mönchtum in Frankenreich*, 2nd edn (Munich, 1988), 142–3; S. Wemple, *Women in Frankish Society: Marriage and the Cloister 500–900* (Philadelphia, 1981), 158–65.

69. P. J. Geary, *Before France and Germany: The Creation and Transformation of the Merovingian World* (Oxford, 1988), 171–6; A. Dierkens, 'Prolégomènes à une historie des relationes culturelles entre les Îles Britanniques et le continent pendant le haut moyen âge', in H. Atsma (ed.), *La Neustrie: les pays au nord de la Loire de 650 à 850*, 2 vols (Sigmaringen, 1989), II, 371–94, at 373–8.

70. *HE*, II, 15 and III, 18: Bede is careful to stress that Felix went to East Anglia via Kent and had the approval of Archbishop Honorious, but notes that he had been consecrated as bishop in Burgundy. For Felix's probable link with Luxeuil, see J. M. Wallace-Hadrill, *Bede's Ecclesiastical History of the English People: A Historical Commentary* (Oxford, 1988), 77–8, 223. However, Anna's daughters may not have been the first Anglo-Saxon women to become nuns at Faremoutiers, since Ionas in his *Vita S. Columbani* refers to a Saxon (presumably from England) there in the lifetime of Fara (d. 645); B. Krusch (ed.), *Ionas, Vitae Columbani Discipulorumque eius*, MGH *Scriptores Rerum Merovingicarum*, IV (Hanover, 1902), II, 136–8 (ch. 17).

71. *HE*, III, 19. Bede (*HE*, III, 8) records that Anglo-Saxon women entered Frankish houses in the period before nunneries had been established in England.

72. Prinz, *Frühes Mönchtum*, 128–9; Geary, *Before France and Germany*, 183–5.

73. The claim comes in the ninth-century *Virtutes Fursei Abbatis Latiniacensis*, ed. B. Krusch, MGH *Scriptores Rerum Merovingicarum*, IV (Hanover, 1902), 440–9; Whitelock, 'Pre-Viking age church in East Anglia', p. 5, n. 7.

74. *HE*, III, 19. According to the *Annals of Ulster*, Fursey left Ireland in 636 or 637 (Plummer, II, 173).

75. *Op. cit.*

76. B. Krusch (ed.), *Additamentum Nivialense de Fuliano*, *MGH Scriptores Rerum Merovingicarum*, IV (Hanover, 1902), 449–51; P. Fouracre and R. Gerberding, *Late Merovingian France: History and Hagiography 640–720* (Manchester, 1996), 307–8, 327–9.

77. Plummer, II, 123–4; Fouracre and Gerberding, *Late Merovingian France*, 317, 327–9.

78. *HE*, III, 18; for Penda's paganism, see II, 20; III, 12.

79. According to Bede (*HE*, III, 19), Fursey was received at the court of King Clovis II where Abbess Fara's brother Burgundofaro was a referendary.

80. *HE*, IV, 23; Bede says that Hereswith was the mother of King Aldwulf (663 or 664–713), but does not name her husband. The East Anglian genealogy in the Anglian collection names him as Æthelric, son of Eni, which would make him a brother of King Anna. Æthelric is otherwise unknown and presumably predeceased Anna (who was succeeded by another brother), as Hereswith's decision to enter a nunnery could be taken to imply; see F. M. Stenton, 'The East Anglian kings of the seventh century', in D. M. Stenton (ed.), *Preparatory to Anglo-Saxon England* (Oxford, 1970), 394–402.

81. *HE*, IV, 23; Plummer, II, 244.

82. Although it has been doubted that Chelles remained an active nunnery between the time of its foundation and its revamping by Queen Balthild after 657 (to the extent that in Wallace-Hadrill, *Historical Commentary on Bede*, 232, it is proposed that Bede must have been mistaken in thinking Hereswith had gone there), the excavators of Chelles make a convincing case for its continuity as a religious community into the time of Hereswith; see J. Ajot and A. Bulard, 'Chelles durant le Haut Moyen Age', in P. Périn and L.-C. Feffer (eds), *La Neustrie: les pays au nord de la Loire de Dagobert à Charles le Chauve (vii–ix siècles)* (Seine-Maritime, 1985), 160–4; J.-P. Laporte and R. Boyer, *Trésors de Chelles: sépultures et reliques de la Reine Bathilde et de l'Abbesse Bertille* (Chelles, 1991), 3–4.

83. *HE*, I, 25 and II, 9.

84. *HE*, II, 20. The subsequent marriage of Æthelburh's brother Eadbald to the Frank Emma may have reinforced these links. Although Karl Werner (in Périn and Feffer (eds), *La Neustrie*, 42) has suggested she was the daughter of the mayor of the palace Erchinoald, E. Ewig (*Die Merowinger und das Frankenreich* (Stuttgart, 1988)), suggests she was the daughter of Chlotar II, which would make her the sister of King Dagobert I. The texts of the *Mildrith Legend* support the identification of her as a Frankish princess (Rollason, *Mildrith Legend*, 92, 114).

85. *HE*, IV, 23.

86. R. Cramp, *Corpus of Anglo-Saxon Stone Sculpture, Vol. I: County Durham and Northumberland* (London, 1984), 7, 97–101.

87. To Chelles and Faremoutiers must be added their near neighbour Jouarre founded by Ado *c.* 630, another member of a powerful Neustrian noble family with positions at court; when Balthild refounded Chelles she installed Bertilla from Jouarre as its abbess (Geary, *Before France and Germany*, 171–6 and n. 120 below).

88. J. Maddicott, 'Plague in seventh-century England', *Past and Present*, 156 (1997), 7–54.

89. Theodore, *Penitential*, II: vi, 8; J. T. McNeill and H. A. Gamer (eds), *Medieval Handbooks of Penance* (Columbia, NY, 1979), 204.

90. Coldingham had been founded by 672 or 673 when Queen Æthelthryth withdrew

there on her separation from King Ecgfrith; *HE,* IV, 19.

91. Rollason, *Mildrith Legend,* 30–1; D. Kirby, *The Earliest English Kings* (London, 1991), 43–4.

92. *HE,* IV, 19.

93. *HE,* III, 8; Bede provides no help with dating Earcongota's period at Brie.

94. Swanton, 'A fragmentary life of St Mildred', 15–27; Rollason, *Mildrith Legend,* 30–1, 86–7 ['the Lambeth Fragment']. This version rather improbably claims that Seaxburh was regent for thirty years before the succession of her son Hlothere, and completely ignores the intervening reign of Ecgbert.

95. Ridyard, *Royal Saints,* 56–8, 180–1.

96. Rollason, *Mildrith Legend,* 33–51, 90–104 (Oxford, Bodleian Library, MS Bodley, 285, fos 116–21).

97. S 34; Kelly, *Charters of St Augustine's,* no. 40, 139–46. Perhaps Ecgbert was responsible for the murder, and his brother and son for making retribution.

98. There are interesting parallels with the foundation of the male minster at Gilling (Yorks.) by King Oswiu of Bernicia in atonement for the murder of King Oswine of Deira in 651. Oswiu's wife Queen Eanflaed, a cousin of Oswine and on her mother's side of Kentish royal descent, was instrumental in arranging the foundation and a kinsman Trumhere took charge of it; *HE,* III, 14 and 24.

99. *HE,* IV, 19; for the chronology of Æthelthryth's life see Plummer, II, 234–5. Coincidentally or not, 673 was the year of Hlothere's accession in Kent when, according to the somewhat garbled account in the 'Lambeth Fragment' of the *Mildrith Legend,* Seaxburh received a major endowment for Minster-in-Sheppey; Swanton, 'A fragmentary life of St Mildred'; Rollason, *Mildrith Legend,* 87.

100. *HE,* IV, 6.

101. See further below, p. 118.

102. Recorded only in some texts of the *Mildrith Legend;* Rollason, *Mildrith Legend,* 77, 80, 81–4.

103. For discussion of these, and other possible early Hwiccian female houses, see above, p. 18.

104. Sims-Williams, *Religion and Literature,* 92–3, 102–3.

105. P. Sims-Williams, 'Continental influence at Bath monastery in the seventh century', *A-SE,* 4 (1975), 1–10; *idem,* 'Cuthswith, seventh-century abbess of Inkberrow, near Worcester, and the Wurzburg manuscript of Jerome on Ecclesiastes', *A-SE,* 5 (1976), 1–21.

106. Ehwald (ed.), *Aldhelmi Opera Omnia,* 14–18; Lapidge and Rosier, *Aldhelm: The Poetic Works,* 40–1, 47–9. The dedication poem reveals that Ine was ruling when it was written, and it must have been completed by 709 when Aldhelm died. Bugga's mother was a sister of Iurminburh, the second wife of King Ecgfrith of Northumbria (*V. Wilfredi,* ch. 40) and possibly the same sister who was abbess of Carlisle before Ecgfrith's death in 685 (Bede, *VC,* ch. 27).

107. *A-SC,* 718; J. M. J. Fletcher, 'The marriage of St Cuthburga, who was afterwards foundress of the monastery at Wimborne', *Dorset Natural History and Antiquarian Field Club,* 34 (1931), 167–85. For influences on the development of West Saxon female monasticism in Wessex, see Yorke, 'Bonifacian mission', 161–4, and below.

108. Rollason, *Mildrith Legend, passim.*

109. Tangl, no. 10; Sims-Williams, *Religion and Literature,* 243–72.

110. Finberg, *Early Charters of the West Midlands,* 197–216.

111. *Vita Ceolfrithi,* ch. 4, in Plummer, I, 389; Whitelock, 'Pre-Viking age church in East Anglia', 10–12.

112. J. Mabillon (ed.), *Acta Sanctorum Ordinis Sancti Benedicti,* 6 vols (Paris, 1668–1701), III, pt. 1 (1672), 3–7 (ch. 2). However, the content of this *Vita* is at best garbled, since Botulf is made to study monasticism in Old Saxony, which had yet to be converted to Christianity, and the brother of Æthelburh and Saethryth is wrongly named as Æthelmund.

113. Sims-Williams, *Religion and Literature,* 111.

114. I. N. Wood, 'The Franks and Sutton Hoo', in I. N. Wood and N. Lund (eds), *People and Places in Northern Europe 500–1600: Essays in Honour of Peter Sawyer* (Woodbridge, 1991), 1–14.

115. Seen, for example, in the vogue for gold and garnet jewellery or the adoption of sceatta coinage; see L. Webster and J. Backhouse (eds), *The Making of England: Anglo-Saxon Art and Culture AD 600–900* (London, 1991) for useful assemblage of relevant material.

116. B. A. E. Yorke, 'The reception of Christianity at the Anglo-Saxon royal courts', in R. Gameson (ed.), *St Augustine and the Conversion of England* (Stroud, 1999), 152–73.

117. *HE,* III, 7.

118. *HE,* IV, 16.

119. *HE,* III, 7; Cenwalh's wife, who ruled briefly after him (672–643), was called Seaxburh, and it has been suggested that she could have been Anna's daughter of that name who had been married to King Eorcenbert of Kent (640–664); see C. Fell, 'Saint Æthelthryth: a historical-hagiographical dichotomy revisited', *Nottingham Medieval Studies,* 38 (1994), 18–34, at 27. The name is not otherwise recorded among Anglo-Saxon royal women and the chronology is possible, but the theory runs counter to the claims in *The Mildrith Legend,* and the associated *Vita of S. Seaxburga,* whereby Seaxburh remained in Kent, initially as guardian for her sons, until she moved to Ely on the death of her sister in 679 or 680.

120. Prinz, *Frühes Mönchtum,* 125; M. de Maillé, *Les Cryptes de Jouarre* (Paris, 1971); Geary, *Before France and Germany,* 173–4.

121. A. Morton, *Excavations in Hamwic: Volume I,* CBA Research Report, 84 (London, 1992), 59–68.

122. C. Stancliffe, 'Kings who opted out', in P. Wormald (ed.), *Ideal and Reality in Frankish and Anglo-Saxon Society* (Oxford, 1983), 154–76; S. Ridyard, 'Monk-kings and the Anglo-Saxon hagiographic tradition', *Haskins Society Journal,* 6 (1994), 13–27. Aspects of the phenomenon of the early kingly saints and martyrs are explored further in Chapter 4.

123. Lapidge and Rosier, *Aldhelm: The Poetic Works,* 40–1, 47–9.

124. *HE,* II, 15; III, 18.

125. *HE,* IV, 11.

126. Bascombe, 'Two charters of King Suebred'.

127. *HE,* IV, 12; V, 19.

128. Kirby, *Earliest English Kings,* 116.

129. C. Stancliffe and E. Cambridge (eds), *Oswald: Northumbrian King to European Saint* (Stamford, 1995).

130. *HE,* IV, 5. Caedwalla of Wessex in 688 and his successor Ine in 726 both managed what Oswiu had failed to achieve, to travel to Rome to die, and in 709 Cenred of

Mercia and Offa of the East Saxons both abdicated to go to Rome and died soon after their arrival; see Stancliffe, 'Kings who opted out', 156–7.

131. Rollason, *Mildrith Legend*; the legend implies, but does not state categorically, that their cult was promoted at Minster soon after its foundation.

132. Ridyard, 'Monk-kings'.

133. B. A. E. Yorke, 'The acceptance of Christianity at the Anglo-Saxon royal courts', in M. Carver (ed.), *The Age of Conversion in Northern Europe* (forthcoming), and see further in Chapter 4.

134. Stancliffe, 'Kings who opted out', 160–72.

135. M. Winterbottom (ed.), *Gildas: The Ruin of Britain and Other Documents* (Chichester, 1978), 29–30, 99–100 (ch. 28).

136. Ridyard, 'Monk-kings', 26.

137. *HE*, III, 18.

138. *V. Wilfredi*, ch. 57.

139. I. N. Wood, 'Pagan religions and superstitions east of the Rhine from the fifth to the ninth century', in G. Ausenda (ed.), *After Empire: Towards an Ethnology of Europe's Barbarians* (Woodbridge, 1995), 253–79; Yorke, 'Reception of Christianity'; R. North, *Heathen Gods and Old English Literature* (Cambridge, 1997), *passim*.

140. *HE*, IV, 11.

141. See, for instance, the fate of the sons of Chlodomer (B. Krusch and W. Levison (eds), *Gregory of Tours, Decem Libri Historiarum, MGH Scriptores Rerum Merovingicarum* (Hanover, 1902), I, 1; III, 18; L. Thorpe (trans.), *Gregory of Tours: The History of the Franks* (Harmondsworth, 1974), 180–1), or seventh-century examples discussed in P. Fouracre and R. A. Gerberding, *Late Merovingian France: History and Hagiography 640–720* (Manchester, 1996), 21–3, 197–9.

142. Stancliffe, 'Kings who opted out', 172–5; Ridyard, 'Monk-kings', 21–7.

143. C. Cubitt, 'Sites and sanctity: revisiting the cult of murdered and martyred Anglo-Saxon royal saints', *Early Medieval Europe*, 9 (2000), 53–84.

144. The issue of royal women as saints is explored further in Chapter 4.

145. See, for instance, laws of King Æthelbert of Kent, chs 77–81; F. L. Attenborough, *The Laws of the Earliest English Kings* (Cambridge, 1922), 14–15; T. J. Rivers, 'Widows' rights in Anglo-Saxon law', *American Journal of Legal History*, 19 (1975), 208–15.

146. Bede, *VC*, chs 27–8.

147. *V. Wilfredi*, ch. 40. Centwine abdicated and entered a monastery in 685, the year of Ecgfrith's death, by which time his ex-wife was already installed as abbess of Carlisle according to Bede, *VC*, ch. 27. The royal marriage and the position as abbess imply that Iurminburh and her sister are likely to have been of royal descent.

148. See n. 106.

149. Archbishop Theodore in his *Penitential* (ch. XII, 13) recognized the desire of one partner to enter a religious community as grounds for separation, but presumably not for remarriage. As the examples of Ecgfrith and Iuminburh, and the tenth-century King Edgar of Wessex (for whom see Chapter 5), demonstrate, such separation was taken as sufficient grounds for remarriage in Anglo-Saxon England.

150. See n. 145.

151. Swanton, 'A fragmentary life of St Mildred', 23–4, 27; Rollason, *Mildrith Legend*, 86–7.

152. S 20; Kelly, *Charters of St Augustine's*, 38–44.

153. Ridyard, *Royal Saints*, 60, 89–92; for a sceptical view of Eormenhild's supposed connection with Ely see Fell, 'Saint Æthelthryth', 29–34.

154. Ridyard, *Royal Saints*, 60, 89–92, 179–80; the late tradition associating Werburh with Ely is suspect; see also above n. 44–5.

155. Thus Swaefred founded Nazeing for *ffymme*, Eorcenwald Barking for his sister Æthelburh and Aidan installed Hild in her first foundation.

156. E. Levy, *West-Roman Vulgar Law: The Law of Property* (Philadelphia, 1954); P. Wormald, *Bede and the Conversion of England: The Charter Evidence*, Jarrow Lecture, 1984 (Newcastle, 1985).

157. *HE*, IV, 7; Hart, *Early Charters of Eastern England*, 117–45.

158. *HE*, IV, 19.

159. E. O. Blake (ed.), *Liber Eliensis*, Royal Historical Society, Camden Third Series, 92 (London, 1962), I, 4 – *insula Elge ab eodem sponso eius accepit in dotem*.

160. *HE*, IV, 19; IV, 6 (*Medehamstede*).

161. E. Miller, *The Abbey and Bishopric of Ely: The Social History of an Ecclesiastical Estate from the Tenth Century to the Early Fourteenth Century* (Cambridge, 1951), 8–15; Ridyard, *Royal Saints*, 177–8.

162. Hollis, 'Minster-in-Thanet', 47 and 61.

163. The text appears to include an anachronistic reference to viking raids; Rollason, *Mildrith Legend*, 29–31, 87.

164. S 70; Finberg, *Early Charters of the West Midlands*, 158–66; Sims-Williams, *Religion and Literature*, 122–4. The text as we have it may have been compiled in the ninth century, but is only known from a transcript in Abbot Walter Frocester's register of *c.* 1400. The Latin is obviously corrupt in places, presumably as the result of poor transcription, but, as Finberg and Sims-Williams have argued, it seems to contain valuable traditions about the early history of the community.

165. Eadburh is described as the wife of King Wulfhere of Mercia, who is recorded in the *Mildrith Legend* as being married to Eormenhild of Kent (who also retired to a monastery). It is quite plausible that he could have remarried when whichever of these was his first wife separated from him and withdrew into a nunnery. For a parallel see Ecgfrith of Northumbria, whose two wives, Æthelthryth and Iurminburh, both became abbesses.

166. Sims-Williams (*Religion and Literature*, 123–4) rehearses the problems with the suggestion that she be equated with the Hwiccian princess Eaba who married King Æthelwalh of the South Saxons.

167. See Chapter 2.

168. Plummer, I, 364–87. As will be explored further in Chapter 2 the Anglo-Saxon expectation of hereditary succession clashed with that of Benedictine and other monastic rules that the community should elect their own abbot or abbess.

169. S 1429; *EHD*, no. 68; Sims-Williams, *Religion and Literature*, 130–2.

170. *HE*, III, 24. Whitby was an estate of ten hides, the same size as each of the twelve estates on which minsters were to be founded in thanks for Oswiu's victory. However, it is not clear whether Whitby was one of the twelve. Bede merely says that Hild gained possession of the estate of Whitby two years after the battle and the exact circumstances are not explained. See C. Fell, 'Hild, abbess of *Streonaeshalch*', in H. Bekker-Nielsen (ed.), *Hagiography and Medieval Literature* (Odense, 1981), 76–99, at 83–6, which also discusses the question of the identification of *Streonaeshalch* with Whitby.

171. Fell, 'Saint Æthelthryth', 19–21.

172. P. A. Thompson, 'St Æthelthryth: the making of history from hagiography', in M. J. Toswell and E. M. Tyler (eds), *Studies in English Language and Literature: 'Doubt Wisely': Papers in Honour of E. G. Stanley* (London, 1996), 475–92, suggests Æthelthryth herself was influenced in her behaviour by these literary ideals.

173. *HE*, III, 7.

174. B. A. E. Yorke, *Kings and Kingdoms of Early Anglo-Saxon England* (London, 1990), esp. 167–72.

175. See Chapter 2 for the problem of kings and other lay members of the family laying claim to monastery lands.

176. If, indeed, it is possible to distinguish between them – men who came to power in the eighth and ninth centuries claimed to be of royal descent, but to be only distantly related to recent rulers, and some had been filling 'noble' positions such as that of ealdorman.

177. Bede, 'Letter to Ecgbert', Plummer, I, 405–23; *EHD*, I.

178. S 46; Kelly, *Charters of Selsey*, no. 7, 37–40.

179. Geary, *Before France and Germany*, 171; see also 172–6.

180. Though this may also have something to do with different traditions of how men and women were buried in early Anglo-Saxon England; H. Geake, *The Use of Grave-Goods in Conversion Period England, c. 600–c. 850*, BAR, 261 (1997).

2 The Late Eighth and Ninth Centuries

Nearly all the early nunneries had ceased to function, at least as predominantly female communities in the charge of an abbess, by the end of the ninth century. There is usually no record of the exact date or circumstances in which this occurred, and often one simply becomes aware that what had been a nunnery seems to have become a church served only by secular clergy, or has passed into the control of another religious community or into lay hands. But for a few houses where good charter evidence survives one can understand something more of what happened, for charters, or comparable documents recording the resolution of disputes over land, are the best source of evidence for individual communities in the late eighth and ninth centuries, when we lack an overview from a narrative source of the type provided by the *Historia Ecclesiastica* of Bede, or the insight into monastic life given by contemporary saints' *Lives*. The contrast between the degree of documentation surviving from the 'golden age' of the seventh and early eighth centuries and from the succeeding period should not be seen as evidence for a dramatic decline in standards of learning and literacy. The comparative wealth of narrative sources from early eighth-century Northumbria, in particular, was in part the result of tensions within the church of that province to which the controversial career of Bishop Wilfrid made a substantial contribution.[1] Although many of the Northumbrian nunneries disappear from the documentary record after the middle of the eighth century there are other types of evidence, such as the stone inscriptions from Hackness, Hartlepool and Whitby, which imply continuation as female religious institutions with a literate culture into the ninth century,[2] and Southumbrian houses have left positive indications of a thriving ecclesiastical culture as well.[3]

There were a number of forces for change within the later eighth and ninth centuries which need to be viewed in conjunction to discover the fates of the early female foundations. Many of these factors affected male minsters as well,[4] but it is possible to draw out particular consequences for the royal nunneries because, in the first place they were female foundations, and in the second because their fates were bound up with those of the royal houses which supported them. The early minsters had flourished and achieved considerable economic wealth and influence as central places;[5] as the eighth and ninth centuries progressed, both episcopal and secular powers sought to curb their independence and to seize their assets. From the archepiscopate of Archbishop Theodore (669–690), there had been regular synods of the church which sought to bring order to the variant practices introduced in the conversion period and to strengthen episcopal control over monasteries.[6] The records which survive from the Southumbrian province show that nunneries were included in their legislation, and that the bishops became more confident in asserting their rights under influence from reform in the Carolingian church around the turn of the ninth century. In the same period there were also major political changes as smaller kingdoms south of the Humber became absorbed into either Mercia or Wessex, and the fate of former royal monasteries in the subjected provinces became an issue between the dominant dynasties and local bishops. Nor must the role of the traditional suspects, the vikings, be ignored. Some nunnery sites were attacked or occupied by invading armies, and the viking 'great army' was responsible for defeating and killing or exiling the rulers of East Anglia, Mercia and Northumbria, paving the way for West Saxon ascendancy at the end of the ninth century. The contribution of all these factors to the demise of nunneries needs to be weighed carefully.

But the history of nunneries in the late eighth and ninth centuries is not simply a matter of tracing the fates of existing foundations. New houses were also founded, and these need to be viewed in the context of the changing political context within kingdoms. Although no new kingdoms were founded in this period, there were changes within the ruling dynasties with men from obscure cadet lines (or who at least claimed descent from a distant royal ancestor) coming to the fore. The establishment of nunneries for female relatives seems to have been part of their consolidation of power, just as it had been for their predecessors in the late seventh century, though they would also have been spurred on to do so in emulation of contemporary Frankish, Italian and continental Saxon exemplars. Nunneries made an important contribution to the court culture sponsored by Offa of Mercia, which can be glimpsed in the letters of Alcuin and in surviving manuscripts, and had a part to play in Alfred's revival in Wessex.

Nunneries and the church councils

As Bede recorded, Archbishop Theodore (669–690) was the first Archbishop of Canterbury whose authority was recognized in all the Anglo-Saxon provinces,[7] and one of his priorities, in which he was followed by his successors, was to establish the authority of church councils and common standards within the Anglo-Saxon church in accordance with established canon law.[8] In the surviving records of the eighth- and early ninth-century councils, which give only a partial view of all the business transacted at them, no distinction is drawn between male and female monastic communities. Any distinction is rather between laity and religious on the one hand, and priests and non-priests among the religious, on the other. Obviously nuns could not be priests, but a significant number of male religious never acquired that status either. Abbots and abbesses were expected to exercise comparable control over their communities, but whereas some abbots, particularly from Mercian monasteries, seem to have been regular attendees of the provincial synods in the eighth century, abbesses seem to have been present only if directly involved in cases that were being adjudicated.[9] There is no overt discrimination against female communities, nor any apparent attempt to see them as functioning differently from predominantly male houses. However, the legislation of synods would have affected particularly some of the practices of the earliest nunneries, and as the period progressed the links between the royal nunneries and their royal kinsmen would have become increasingly problematical and, indeed, a major bone of contention between bishops and kings which provoked some of the synodal legislation.

The priority of Theodore's first council at Hertford in 672 was to establish the supremacy of the bishop within his own diocese, at least in theory.[10] Succeeding conciliar legislation, most fully articulated in the Council of *Clofesho* of 747,[11] stressed rights of episcopal supervision and jurisdiction over all members of the church and their property in their diocese, and sought to impose common practices within the churches.[12] How far bishops were able to enforce such claims in all minsters is not known, but the legislation had the potential to affect many of the early nunneries which often had links that crossed diocesan boundaries and customs at variance with what was defined as the norm in episcopal legislation. In the conversion period, when monasticism had been introduced through a variety of different channels and founders could write their own Rules, many disparate customs had been established within England. Although bishops had founded the earliest communities in England, they had not always been closely involved with those of the second wave, including many of those founded by royal and leading noble families. In the period immediately following the plague epidemic of 663, when the founding of double houses began in earnest, there was a notable shortage of bishops, and it may not have been established *ab initio* what form the relationship between monasteries and bishops should take. Charismatic leaders, including some who were bishops, were able to found daughter houses which looked to them for leadership across kingdom and diocesan boundaries. The best known, or perhaps one should say notorious, of these early founders was Bishop Wilfrid of Northumbria. His biographer Stephen recorded how 'almost all the abbots and abbesses of the monasteries dedicated their substance to him by vow, either keeping it themselves in his name or intending him to be their heir after their death'.[13] Some of the canons of the council of Hertford, which forbade bishops from interfering in another's diocese and laying claim to monastic property, may have been framed with Wilfrid's activities in mind.[14] We do not know if any of the Northumbrian royal nunneries were drawn into Wilfrid's monastic consortium, and the only abbess named in close association with Wilfrid is a certain abbess Cynethryth, who was given charge of the robe which Wilfrid had been wearing when he died.[15] She was possibly an abbess in Mercia, where Wilfrid had supervision of a number of houses, for Wilfrid died at Oundle. The name 'Cynethryth' was one which was favoured by the Mercian royal house, but we are told nothing about the origins of Wilfrid's abbess. Two royal nunneries which seem to have been part of an early monastic confederation were Much Wenlock which, according to the *Testament of St Mildburg*, was founded under the aegis of Abbot Botulf of *Icanho* in East Anglia,[16] and Repton, one of several Mercian religious houses founded from *Medehamstede* (Peterborough).[17]

Although it would be going too far to say that some of the southern nunneries were daughter houses of Chelles or one of the other northern Frankish nunneries, nevertheless they may have looked to them for guidance rather than to local bishops. Abbess Bertilla of Chelles is portrayed as assisting English houses, and Bath, where the first abbess Bertha and another prominent nun Folcburg appear to have Frankish names, has been proposed as a house that may have been strongly indebted to her intervention.[18] It is possible that some of the great seventh-century abbesses had daughter houses outside their home provinces.[19] The best case can be made for Æthelthryth of Ely, though unfortunately none of the sources are particularly early in date and the evidence is not conclusive. According to the *Liber Eliensis*, Æthelthryth founded two monasteries in what is now Lincolnshire, one in West Halton in the West Riding of Lindsey,[20] the other at a place called *Ætheldredestowe*, which is possibly identical with the monastery at Threckingham where her niece Werburh is said to have died.[21] The tradition inspires some confidence as they do not seem to be estates claimed subsequently by Ely, and the information may have come from earlier hagiographical material about Æthelthryth that seems to have been used by the compiler of *Liber Eliensis*.[22] There is also a post-Conquest record of a church in Herefordshire, the territory of the Magonsaetan, reputedly founded by Æthelthryth and where her cult was active in the twelfth century,[23] but cults and dedications could be spread by various means and then viewed in retrospect as evidence for a personal connection with the sainted individual.

It is not known that any of the early nunneries acquired papal privileges exempting them from episcopal intervention, but a number of the Columbanian foundations with which some of the English nunneries had close links had done so.[24] It would appear that some of the early royal nunneries did not expect close episcopal supervision of all their affairs. When Seaxburh, abbess of Ely, arranged the translation of the remains of her sister Æthelthryth, she did so without involving the local bishop.[25] Seaxburh stage-managed the entire proceedings, and the ceremony was probably based on northern Frankish precedents of which she could have acquired knowledge through her sisters at Faremoutiers.[26] Ælfflaed of Whitby may have in effect obviated the need to call in the diocesan for certain necessary functions, such as the ordaining of priests, by having her own in-house bishop, for Bishop Trumwine settled in the nunnery after having to leave his see at Abercorn following the defeat of King Ecgfrith of Northumbria at the battle of Nechtansmere in 685. Bede comments that Ælfflaed found the bishop 'a very great help in the government of the monastery as well as a comfort in her own life'.[27] In the time of her predecessor Hild, Whitby could be said to have performed one of the functions that might normally be associated with a diocesan, for it was a major training place for priests and bishops – no fewer than five of its male members became bishops.[28]

The bishops who dominated the synods of the eighth century were concerned to impose common standards (though not a common monastic rule) and to establish rights of visitation which would enable them to ensure they were being met in the religious houses of their dioceses.[29] The rights claimed by the bishops were, of course, in accordance with canons of the early church and with the reform programme of the Carolingian church, but may not have been the norm in England in the late seventh and early eighth centuries. For instance, the *Penitential* of Theodore makes a number of judgements on the ministry of women in the church, including forbidding them from prescribing penance, that is, hearing confession,[30] which implies that some Anglo-Saxon women, presumably abbesses, had been doing so. There is no specific record of an English abbess hearing confession or prescribing penance, but the *Vita S. Columbani* shows Burgundofara doing both at Faremoutiers apparently on a regular basis,[31] and it is not unlikely that those in control of English nunneries which were influenced by Faremoutiers would have followed her example. The legislation of the councils also sought to protect religious houses, including nunneries, from undue lay interference and no doubt some facets of that protection would have been welcomed by the communities. The appetite for sex with nuns shown by some kings such as Æthelbald of Mercia was no doubt an unwanted by-product of the type of visiting by laity forbidden by Chapter 20 of the council of *Clofesho*.[32] Many nunneries may also have welcomed the decrees that the *familia* should nominate the new head of a house, not the lay patron,[33] and the restrictions on alienating property for longer than the lease of one life.[34] But bishops were probably not always seen as benign protectors of monastic interests. At the synod of Hertford of 672 it had been the threat that bishops could pose to monastic property which had come under regulation, and the *Dialogus* of Archbishop Ecgbert of York refers to both monks and nuns using force to recover property that had come under episcopal jurisdiction.[35] Successive bishops of Worcester seem to have been successful in asserting their rights to the reversion of land granted in *ius ecclesiasticum*, and in this way acquired several of the nunneries which had been founded by members of the royal family of the Hwicce.[36] Their charters were thus preserved for posterity, and their churches served local communities, but none of them continued as nunneries under the bishop's care. In the council of Chelsea of 816, bishops were legislating that in cases of impoverishment monastic property could be taken directly under episcopal control.[37] Presumably in such circumstances bishops would have been under no obligation to continue a house specifically as a monastic community. Their motives were to prevent land which had been granted to a religious house from coming under lay control, something expressly forbidden in the same council, but the result was one of the factors which contributed to the disappearance of the nunneries. Nunneries are not specifically mentioned in the legislation, but behind it lay a series of clashes between bishops and kings over the ultimate ownership of the lands of royal nunneries. Before looking more closely at some of these issues, political developments, and changing patterns of patronage towards nunneries, need to be considered.

Kings and nunneries in the eighth and ninth centuries

We have seen kings as apparently generous and enthusiastic founders of early nunneries, but their gifts did not mean that they had given up all rights over the land that they had donated. A grant of privileges by King Wihtred to the churches of Kent at the synod of Bapchild in 699, when four abbesses – three of whom can be identified as Kentish princesses – were present, freed them from the payment of public tribute, but reserved *honorem et oboedientiam* to himself and his successors.[38] That such 'honour and obedience' might involve monetary payments, as well as other potentially onerous obligations, is strongly suggested by a letter from the Kentish abbess Eangyth to Boniface, in which she complains of the poverty of the house and the draining *servitium* owed to the king and queen, as well as to the bishops and royal officials.[39] Subsequent correspondence makes clear that Eangyth and her daughter Haeaburg were related to the royal house, and they presumably commanded one of the royal double houses of Kent, but unfortunately we do not know which one.[40] Immunities which certain Hwiccian houses and the Bishop of Worcester purchased from Mercian rulers in the ninth century reveal extensive obligations to render *feorm* and entertain royal officials.[41] The question of exactly what royal rights could be demanded from lands held by churches was one of the great issues of the eighth century. In 745 Boniface and seven other bishops of the Frankish church had sent a strongly worded letter to King Æthelbald of Mercia, in which they complained, among other things, of the severity of royal exactions and demands of service.[42] These criticisms seem to have been met by Æthelbald in the synod of Gumley of 749, in which the Mercian monasteries were guaranteed freedom from all royal exactions apart from bridge-work and the defence of fortresses, to which military service was added subsequently.[43] The Mercian arrangements were spread eventually to, or independently adopted in, other kingdoms.

Royal nunneries, like other religious houses, were bound to rulers by these obligations, but had an additional tie arising from the fact that they had been founded by members of the royal house so that kings could claim lordship over them in that respect as well. One of the other major causes of dispute involving church lands in the late eighth and early ninth centuries was over the rights which lay founders could claim over religious houses. Royal foundations are not distinguished from those of their nobility, but problems of royal lordship are likely to lie behind the provisions of the council of Chelsea of 816, which contain the most uncompromising statements to date against lay control,[44] since it followed bitter disputes between archbishops of Canterbury, kings of Mercia and their female heirs. The outlawing of lay lordship and, specifically, the ability of laymen to appoint the heads of religious houses, were major aims of the council,[45] and these provisions had been anticipated in charters forged by Archbishop Wulfred at the height of his dispute with King Coenwulf of Mercia and his daughter Cwoenthryth.[46]

Royal nunneries could obviously benefit considerably from being royal foundations, and received generous grants of land from royal kinsmen, as was seen in Chapter 1. But changes in the political situation could leave them vulnerable if their influential lay protectors disappeared. It was not just foreign invasion that might be a threat; internal politics could also have severe repercussions if one branch of a royal house was removed from power and replaced with another. One of the major causes of Abbess Eangyth's worries of which she complained to Boniface was that she belonged to a segment of the royal house which had fallen from favour with the dominant kin-group: 'The king [probably Wihtred, 690–725] has a great hatred for our line (*gentem*).'[47] Among her greatest concerns was the loss of most of her male kinsmen, apart from one cousin who had the king's disfavour, and she was feeling the pressure to follow other relatives into exile abroad.

When cadet lines came to power they were not necessarily opposed to nunneries as such; rather, like their predecessors, they saw links with nunneries as a way of reinforcing their newly acquired power. This observation is exemplified by Mercia in the eighth and early ninth centuries when it was the dominant Southumbrian kingdom for most of this period, but with the throne passing between several subgroups of the royal house.[48] Several kinswomen of Offa of Mercia (757–796), who claimed descent from a brother of King Penda (d. 655), but had no direct male ancestors who had ruled since his time, went into the church. One of his daughters Æthelburh, as far as we can tell, was a nun all her life,[49] while two others – Ælfflaed, who married Æthelred I of Northumbria,[50] and Eadburh, who married King Beorhtric of Wessex[51] – retired to religious houses on being widowed, as did Offa's own wife Cynethryth, who is described as abbess after his death.[52] A *propinqua* of Offa called Eanburh was also an abbess.[53] Offa was succeeded by Coenwulf, a distant relative whose daughter Cwoenthryth was abbess of Winchcombe and other foundations.[54] Possibly a second daughter Burghild and another kinswomen were associated with a royal minster at Culham or at Abingdon where they were buried.[55] Cwoenthryth may have been succeeded at Winchcombe by her first cousin Ælfflaed, the daughter of King Ceolwulf, after the latter was widowed.[56] Nunneries were an important element of the confederations of religious houses for which both Offa and Coenwulf obtained papal privileges confirming they were under their authority (*dicio*), especially as their immediate heirs in both cases were royal women with the position of abbess.[57] In neither case has a full list of the houses covered by the privileges survived, and only a partial reconstruction is possible from the records of the disputes which ensued. Offa's privilege placed 'all the numerous monasteries built and justly acquired, established and dedicated in honour of your protector St Peter' directly under the authority of himself and his wife Queen Cynethryth and their heirs.[58] It presumably included Cookham, to which after Offa's death Cynethryth had to defend her right against counter-claims of the Archbishop of Canterbury.[59] She did so as abbess of *Bedeford*, which may well be Bedford where reputedly Offa was buried,[60] and so presumably the heart of the confederation from which some administrative overview of the other houses would have been made. The group probably also included Winch-combe, where Offa was remembered in the annals of the twelfth century as the founder of a nunnery in 787,[61] and Eanburh's nunnery at or near Hampton Lucy.[62] It is not necessary to assume that all the houses were nunneries, even when they were under the supervision of Cynethryth following Offa's death; Bath, which also seems to have been part of the group, had been, but seems to have become an all-male community before Offa acquired it.[63] Ultimately, King Coenwulf may have succeeded in 'inheriting' at least some of the monasteries included in Offa's privilege, for the nunnery at Winchcombe seems to have become the favoured house of his kin-group where their archives were kept, and where Coenwulf and his son Cynehelm were buried.[64] His daughter Cwoenthryth as abbess may have exercised an authority analogous to that of Cynethryth over the houses covered by the papal privileges that Coenwulf had obtained.[65]

The enthusiasm for monastic life among the new Mercian royal lines may have been in part a continuation of the tradition of close connection between royalty and nunneries already noted in Anglo-Saxon England, but is also likely to have been reinforced by contemporary practice in Francia. The Carolingians too were patrons of royal nunneries.[66] Charlemagne's sister Gisela was abbess of Chelles, that important Merovingian nunnery to which Queen Balthild had retired and which had forged links with many early Anglo-Saxon nunneries, and his daughter Rotrud was first a nun and eventually her successor there.[67] A link between Chelles and the Mercian nunneries was provided by Charlemagne's Northumbrian adviser Alcuin, who was the correspondent of both the Frankish and the Mercian royal nuns.[68] He also wrote to Hundrada, 'a woman devoted to God', who apparently lived at the royal court, perhaps as a tutor to some of the princesses.[69] When Offa's daughter Eadburh fled from Wessex on the death of her husband in 802, it was Charle-magne's patronage which apparently secured her a position as abbess in northern Italy (which was by that time part of his dominions).[70] But female monasticism may not have been such a priority with all new royal dynasties. None of the West Saxon royal women before the time of Alfred went into the church, with the possible exception of a sister of King Ecgbert for whom Wilton may have been founded.[71] It is tempting to link this with the apparent low status of the king's wife in Wessex who, unlike her Mercian counterparts, was not styled as queen,[72] but it may simply reflect paucity of evidence. The ninth-century West Saxon kings did, however, continue the patronage of Wimborne founded for Cuthburh and Cwenburh, the sisters of Ine and Ingeld from whom Ecgbert's line claimed descent;[73] Ecgbert's grandson King Æthelred (865–871) was buried there.[74]

Dynastic change within kingdoms did not have to mean the loss of patronage for existing nunneries if they were able to establish links with the new dynasties, or were felt to offer useful continuity with earlier reigns. Æthelbald of Mercia (716–755), for instance, was buried at the nunnery of Repton,[75] which had associations with earlier princes of the royal house,[76] and with which Guthlac, himself a member of the Mercian royal house and apparent supporter of Æthelbald, had been associated.[77] In the ninth century Repton was linked with another line claiming to be of royal descent, that of King Wiglaf (827–840) who was also buried there. His grandson Wigstan, who was murdered in 849 as a result of rivalry with competing lines, was taken to Repton for burial and was subsequently culted as a saint;[78] the surviving crypt at Repton can be linked with his cult.[79] Repton continued to be commanded by abbesses in the ninth century,[80] but we do not know if there were kinship links with the royal house or if its reputation as a royal burial place was a sufficient reason for it to continue to be favoured as a place of royal patronage. However, though Repton continued to thrive, it may have been an exception, since many royal kin-groups coming to power wanted to establish new nunneries, as Offa and Coenwulf did with Bedford and Winchcombe, and had neither the resources nor probably (though this cannot be easily substantiated) the inclination to patronize nunneries that might have close links with rival lines they had deposed. None of the Mercian nunneries, besides Repton, reputedly associated with the family of Penda is known to have been supported by eighth- and ninth-century successors from different segments of the royal house.

The problems caused for nunneries by internal political change would also have been encountered when one kingdom was conquered by another, leading to loss of power for the native royal house. One reason why Offa and Coenwulf could afford to be patrons of religious houses was the successful political expansion of Mercia in the eighth century in which the wide-ranging overlordship of Æthelbald was converted into direct political control. By 800 the kingdoms of the Hwicce, Magonsaetan, South Saxons and Kent had come under Mercian control and their royal houses disappear from view; that of the East Saxons lingered for only a short while longer.[81] In the ninth century the East Saxons and all the former kingdoms south of the Thames passed to the West Saxons. There were two main issues for the controllers of nunneries in conquered territories: first, could they survive as nunneries, that is, as female-dominated institutions; second, could they remain under the control of members of the former ruling dynasties. These two aims were not necessarily compatible. Minster-in-Thanet provides an example of a nunnery where the ruling house lost control, but the nunnery itself survived through establishing links with the new regime, while in the kingdom of the Hwicce measures taken to keep various nunneries under family control in the short term meant loss of control in the long term. The eventual result in both cases was the same; the nunneries came under episcopal control and ceased to be female-led communities.

In the initial stages of conquest a nunnery might be helped by the patterns of intermarriage between dynasties which could mean that a royal abbess was related to several royal houses. Minster-in-Thanet may have benefited, at the height of Æthelbald of Mercia's overlordship of southern England, from its abbess Mildrith, a Kentish princess of her mother's side, being able to claim, through her Magonsaetan father, to be of Mercian descent as well.[82] She was certainly able to obtain advantageous trading privileges for some of her ships from Æthelbald.[83] Was it the potential advantages of this connection that encouraged her successor Eadburh to promote the cult of Mildrith (rather than that of Mildrith's mother Æbbe who was the actual foundress of the nunnery)?[84] The genealogical material connected with her cult celebrates both her Kentish and her Mercian royal connections, and could fit a political context in which the Kentish dynasty was still in control, but where cultivation of Mercian links was becoming advisable.[85] What we can see is that Minster made the transition from being closely linked to the Kentish dynasty to having a similar association with the Mercian, and perhaps other, regimes. In the early 760s Sigeburh was abbess during the period when Sigered was ruling in West Kent, and their shared first-name-element could mean that they were related.[86] Sigered was one of several short-lived rulers in this rather disturbed period, and his name could suggest that he was a member of the East Saxon royal house that had tried to take control of part of Kent in the previous century.[87] Offa established complete control of the province after 785, and Minster and the nunnery of Lyminge are found under the command of Selethryth,[88] who, together with her brother Ealdberht who may have controlled some of the male minsters, seems to have been an important agent of the Mercian regime in Kent.[89] Selethryth continued in her position in the reign of Coenwulf when her *propinquus* Oswulf was ealdorman and probably leader of the Kentish nobility. Minster and other Kentish houses may have been included by Coenwulf's papal privileges and so were ultimately under the control of Coenwulf, and then of Cwoenthyrth as his heir.[90] Archbishop Wulfred was determined to recover Minster and Reculver, probably the two richest Kentish minsters under Mercian lordship, and initiated a long and complex campaign with the king and his heiress which included the archbishop's temporary suspension from office in 817. Eventually in 825 Wulfred seems to have triumphed over Cwoenthryth, and no doubt it was significant for the way the decision went that the presiding king Beornwulf had supplanted her uncle Ceolwulf as ruler of Mercia.[91] Although the terms of the agreement do not explicitly state it, Wulfred seems to have acquired lordship over the Kentish minsters for himself, since in the following year he is found disposing of Minster property and styling himself 'archbishop of the community of Minster-in-Thanet'.[92] It is not clear if any female element remained in the community after this date.[93] Minster had been successful in surviving as a nunnery during the years of Mercian ascendancy in Kent, though not as a centre for the old Kentish royal house, but changes in political control within Mercia probably saw an end of its life as a female-led community under a determined onslaught from the Archbishop of Canterbury. In spite of the stand against Mercian royal privatization of the Minster estates, they, and those of some other Kentish minsters, including the nunneries of Hoo and

Lyminge, seem subsequently to have come under control of the West Saxon kings whose lordship and protection of the Kentish monasteries was recognized in 839, though St Augustine's, Canterbury, eventually acquired the Minster lands by the gift of Cnut.[94]

The royal house of the Hwicce was also deposed by the Mercians in the course of the eighth century after a long period of overlordship. The family had founded a number of nunneries in the late seventh and early eighth centuries which were controlled by female members of the dynasty.[95] Mercian overlords were sometimes patrons of these communities as well,[96] though one of these gifts shows something of the less benign side of the relationship, for Abbess Eafe of Gloucester received one grant from Æthelbald in compensation for his slaying of her kinsman Æthelmund, son of Oswald.[97] In the last generation in which the family was in power, though already with some reduction in status, their monastic inheritance was concentrated in the hands of the last known royal abbess, Æthelburh, daughter of Alfred.[98] Æthelburh commanded three Hwiccian royal houses which had previously each had its own abbess – Fladbury, Twyning and Withington – but with the proviso that all three should revert to the see of Worcester on her death,[99] and this seems to have occurred, because all three can be shown to have become Worcester estates.[100] We can see here the fruits of a policy of asserting lordship over all the monasteries in the diocese which bishops of Worcester had been pursuing since the late seventh century and which was in accordance with the aims of the synods of the archdiocese of Canterbury.[101] The former royal nunnery and burial place of many of the Hwiccian princes at Gloucester may already have been acquired for the see before the time of Abbess Æthelburh.[102] However, although the bishops of Worcester benefited in the long run, the arrangements between them and the Hwiccian abbesses also met the latters' shorter-term aims. Worcester had been able to assert claims to Withington when a dispute over the inheritance of the nunnery was adjudicated by the Archbishop of Canterbury. The synod upheld the testamentary aims of the former Abbess Dunne, allowing her granddaughter Hrothwaru to take charge of the nunnery, but with the proviso that it should revert on her death to the see of Worcester, presumably with the implication that the Bishop of Worcester would protect her rights during her lifetime.[103] Æthelburh would appear to have asserted hereditary rights to the house on her death, and, as often happened in such cases, Bishop Milred of Worcester allowed her to lease the land for her lifetime.[104] Under the protection of the bishop, who had reversion of the houses of Fladbury and Twyning as well, Æthelburh was able to command three well-endowed nunneries, anticipating the monastic empires of the Mercian abbesses Cynethryth and Cwoenthryth. But her actions did nothing to ensure the continuation of these sites as nunneries. When the houses reverted to Worcester, the bulk of the estates would go to the support of the bishopric, and a small team of clergy, at best, would have been maintained at the churches to provide necessary pastoral care. But what was the alternative? It is probably demonstrated by the fate of another Hwiccian royal nunnery, Inkberrow, which came into the hands of King

Æthelbald, who granted out the estates to thegns (though Worcester subsequently reacquired them).[105] Neither bishops nor conquering kings had any incentive to continue to serve as patrons of nunneries of a vanquished royal house.[106]

Anglo-Saxon nunneries and the vikings

What of the role of those traditionally blamed for destroying early Anglo-Saxon monastic foundations, the vikings? Knowles and Hadcock listed forty-one Anglo-Saxon nunneries destroyed in viking attacks, which would seem to make an overwhelming case for their intervention being decisive in the disappearance of the early nunneries,[107] but doubts come in when one looks more closely at the sources of their information. The viking reputation tended to worsen with the passage of time, and all the spectacular accounts of viking rape, pillage and mayhem come a considerable time after the events were supposed to have occurred, usually in texts written after the Norman Conquest.[108] The St Albans historians, Roger of Wendover and Matthew Paris, drawing upon traditions of 'heathen' races and their alleged bad behaviour that had been sharpened by crusading propaganda, provided some of the most melodramatic accounts. St Æbbe the younger of Coldingham is said to have preserved her virtue in the face of viking attack by cutting open her nose and lips with a razor, an action which was imitated by her fellow nuns. The ruse was successful in deflecting the vikings from rape, but only encouraged them to burn down the nunnery with its disfigured inmates inside.[109] The fact that an almost identical story was told of Eusebia and her virgins in Marseilles does nothing to encourage belief in the historical validity of this account,[110] which must also be undermined by the suspicion that Æbbe the younger is a mere duplicate of the older Æbbe, who is known from Bede's *Historia Ecclesiastica*,[111] transferred to a later century. Roger rather gives the game away by making the younger Æbbe, like her older counterpart, the daughter of King Æthelfrith of Northumbria (d. 616). Excavations on the sites of the Northumbrian nunneries of Hartlepool and Whitby – traditionally seen as destroyed by viking raids – have not produced evidence to substantiate such claims.[112]

Æbbe is not the only royal abbess who was born in the seventh century, but was apparently massacred by the vikings in the ninth. Osyth of Chich was said to be both the wife of King Sigehere of the East Saxons (accession *c.* 664) and the victim of Scandinavian aggression in the ninth century, when she was beheaded for refusing to make a sacrifice to their gods.[113] The vikings became very useful for spicing up the stories of obscure saints, and also for explaining away various lacunae in the history of cults. The clergy of Hanbury were able to account for the unfortunate absence of the body of St Werburh from their foundation by claiming that she had made her own incorrupt body dissolve so that it would not fall into the hands of the heathen, when, in fact, it had been transferred to Gloucester by Æthelflaed, lady of the Mercians, in the early tenth century.[114] The canons of St Gregory's Priory in Canterbury supported the claim that they, not St Augustine's, had the body of St Mildrith, which they had inherited with that of Eadburh from Lyminge, with a story that Mildrith and Eadburh had fled to Lyminge because of viking attacks. As Goscelin, writing on behalf of St Augustine's, was able to demonstrate, their account is full of historical inaccuracies.[115] All late accounts of viking activity being responsible for the destruction of nunneries need to be treated with the greatest suspicion, and the widespread topos in later hagiography of the vikings as agents of destruction acknowledged.

On the other hand, it would be equally mistaken to deny the vikings any responsibility for adding to the problems which led to the disappearance of some religious communities as nunneries.[116] Viking attacks may not have destroyed any nunneries outright, but a number of nunnery sites were raided or occupied by invading armies which must, at best, have disrupted life in the communities. Recorded attacks or periods of occupation include Thanet (851; 853; 865), Sheppey (855), Repton (874) and Wareham (876).[117] The excavations at Repton have shown how the church was used as part of a defence built by the overwintering army, and it is impossible to believe that conventual life was able to continue during the occupation.[118] But these accounts may tell only part of the story, and there may have been further viking harassment which has not been recorded. Raids in Kent began in the late eighth century and prompted King Offa to begin the building of fortifications in the province to counteract them.[119] In 804 Abbess Selethryth was granted an estate inside the walls of Canterbury as a refuge for the community of Lyminge,[120] and a nearby church dedicated to St Mildrith, in which Anglo-Saxon stonework is still visible, may be evidence that Minster-in-Thanet (also under the direction of Selethryth) was granted similar sanctuary.[121] At the Council of Chelsea of 816 devastation by an army and the need to purchase freedom were acknowledged as circumstances in which it was permissible to alienate church property.[122] The need to buy off armies and retrieve hostages is something that is associated more often with the later raids of the reign of Æthelred Unraed when, for instance, Abbess Leofrun was taken prisoner in a raid on Canterbury in 1011,[123] but it is suspected that similar incidents occurred in the ninth century as well. A rare example is the agreement by the people of Kent to purchase peace from the 'great army' in 865.[124] No doubt, as in the reign of Æthelred, minsters would have to contribute to such payments which could be a heavy drain for the less well-endowed houses.[125]

Perhaps even more significant for the fate of nunneries would have been the impact of the campaigns of the 'great army' between 865 and 872. Its activities in these years saw the effective end of the rule of the royal houses of Northumbria, Mercia and East Anglia, and paved the way for the future domination of the whole of England by the royal house of Wessex.[126] The loss of patronage of the royal houses would have been disastrous for the surviving royal nunneries in the conquered provinces of the Danelaw, and, like their Mercian and West Saxon counterparts, victorious viking leaders may have claimed former royal holdings, which could include nunnery lands, as their right; the royal estates may have formed the basis for settlement of the armies.[127] The suspension of episcopal succession in the Danelaw would have aided the privatization of church lands, a process which was not necessarily limited to the activities of Scandinavian incomers but probably benefited native landowners as well.[128] Clergy may have survived to serve local communities on former nunnery sites, such as Ely and Repton,[129] but there would not necessarily have been anyone with the means or inclination to continue them as nunneries. The circumstances of the viking wars would also have given the rulers of Wessex the opportunity, in time of national emergency, to privatize former church lands to provide for defence.[130] It is likely that some former nunnery lands passed into the control of the house of Ecgbert, for it is notable that the disappearance of early nunneries was just as much a feature of Wessex, where there was relatively little viking raiding and no settlement, as it was in Kent or the Danelaw. Discussion of the West Saxon evidence is hindered by the fact that the location of only a few of its early Anglo-Saxon nunneries is known.[131] However, one former nunnery site that seems to have been the centre of a royal estate in the tenth century was Abingdon, where Alfred was remembered as a Judas who had seized the abbey site and its appurtenances.[132] A reference in King Alfred's will to the community of Cheddar, which in the tenth century included both men and women, apparently choosing Alfred's son Edward as their lord, may catch a West Saxon double monastery on the point of being absorbed into the royal demesne.[133] Another such house referred to in the same document could be the community at Damerham associated with a woman called Ælfflaed that was apparently being given the opportunity to free itself from royal lordship and reclaim its charters.[134] In fact there is reason to believe that many of the lands acquired by Alfred and his brothers which feature in his will are former minster sites and that 'to a significant extent, the royal administration had achieved territorial stability by battening on to minsters'.[135] Although surviving charters allow us to plot most clearly episcopal appropriation of minsters, it is likely that it was royal and other lay appropriation that provided the greatest threat in the long run.

Conclusion

The number of early nunneries which can be shown to be still in existence under the command of an abbess in 900 is pitifully small, and, where there is any evidence to suggest survival, it is often ambiguous. Take the case, for instance, of the nunnery of Barking, reputedly destroyed by the vikings in 870,[136] but which reappears as a significant nunnery in the mid-tenth century.[137] The case for survival in the ninth and early tenth centuries is strengthened by the preservation of its archive of land charters,[138] though to have survived as a nunnery it would have needed powerful protectors, with the bishops of London[139] or the ealdormen of Essex[140] as the most likely candidates. However, one cannot rule out the possibility of refoundation in the mid-tenth century when there was a movement towards revival of monasteries of the age of Bede – though it must be stated that none of the leaders of monastic reform were apparently interested in reviving the sites of Bedan double houses as nunneries.[141] Similar problems of interpretation occur in other cases where a reference in the latter part of the tenth century to an abbess at the site of a pre-viking nunnery comes some years after it last appeared in records as a female-led community. Thus there is a single reference to an abbess of St Mildrith's taken from Canterbury by the Danish army in 1011, and the death of Abbess Wulfwyn of Wareham is recorded in 982.[142] Either could be an example of continuity or refoundation in the reform period, but, unlike Barking which is the third richest nunnery, neither house appears in *Domesday Book* (though nuns are recorded in Canterbury).[143] It is also the case that several of the later West Saxon nunneries were either founded on the sites of minsters or endowed with nearby minsters and their lands.[144] Some of these minsters could have been former female houses, so there may be more continuity between the early and later nunneries in Wessex than is at first apparent.

What is more frequently found is that an early nunnery site has continued as the site of a church of minster status served by a priest or a small group of secular clergy, and it is at such sites that the cults of early female saints, often originally the founders of the community and of royal birth, were preserved.[145] It seems reasonable to conclude continuity of use as an ecclesiastical centre, sometimes with religious women associated, but not as a nunnery commanded by an abbess. The reason the early royal nunneries were not able to sustain their existence as female-led communities may be found by setting the concerns of the church councils against an evolving political situation in which the families which had originally supported the foundations fell from power. Some nunneries, such as Repton with its established reputation as a burial place of the kingdom's rulers, were able to attract support from the new regime, though abbesses were likely to be recruited from the family of the new ruling house, as may be seen in the history of Minster-in-Thanet. The loss of patronage and continuing gifts of royal land would have been a serious blow to the spurned nunneries,[146] and even if a nunnery had been careful to build up an archive of charters, it is clear from the concerns of the church councils that they would not necessarily be able to retain control of their lands under lay lordship. Royal nunneries in such circumstances might be subject to attempts both from descendants of the founding family to reclaim 'family land' (a desire that would have become more acute after a fall from power with accompanying loss of wealth), and from the new rulers who might claim the same lands as the inheritance they should receive from their predecessors.[147] In addition, bishops might step in to try to prevent ecclesiastical lands from being secularized and claim they should come under their own control; by the early ninth century episcopal annexation of impoverished monasteries had apparently become official policy.[148] In such circumstances the new controller of the land, whether king, noble family or bishop, would have been expected to provide for basic continuity of pastoral care, but the bulk of the former estates would be absorbed into holdings of family or bishopric. There was no incentive to keep alive a nunnery which would have been a much more expensive religious institution to maintain than a small community of priests.

When the great double houses were founded, the religious role had fallen to the women of the royal house; apart from in the early years of conversion, kings and princes did not as a rule enter the church, but when a royal line fell from power it is likely that attitudes to gendered roles changed. A career in the church would have provided a substitute for lost secular status; it may even have been desirable to seek such a role to reassure the new regime that one was not a threat, and defeated rulers and princes may have been obliged to enter the church for the same reason.[149] In other words, as dynasties fell from power, abbesses of royal family minsters are likely to have been replaced by kinsmen as abbots – for, as church councils complained, it was the lay patrons who generally chose the head of the community rather than the *familia*. Nunneries founded by noble houses had probably always been subject to these tendencies; in fact it may be more accurate to think of all noble foundations as family minsters where headship might devolve on either men or women of the house as inclination of individual members or family circumstances dictated. Many such foundations which had begun under female control, perhaps influenced by the same factors which had led to the foundation of royal nunneries, may have subsequently passed to male members of the family. A letter from Pope Paul I to King Eadbert and Archbishop Ecgbert of York in 757 or 758 seems to be concerned with just such a transfer of communities which had been headed by an abbess to the control of an abbot.[150] It records the complaint of Abbot Forthred that three religious communities granted to him by an abbess had been forcibly taken from his control by Eadbert and Ecgbert, and transferred to his brother, the 'patrician' Moll, who can probably be identified with Æthelwald Moll who became king in 758.[151] A number of themes seem to be illustrated by this document, in particular a king and bishop intervening to overrule a decision made by an abbess, and minsters moving from control of an abbess to that of an abbot. The latter may have been much commoner than our records suggest, but transfer could go the other way as well; one of the rulings in Archbishop Ecgbert's *Dialogus* apparently envisages that any monastery might be inherited by a man or a woman.[152] One example is the monastery of Berkeley which seems to have been controlled by abbots in the late eighth and late ninth centuries, but had an abbess in 807.[153] In this case and, for instance, when Abbess Cwoenthryth controlled Reculver, the communities under their control may have been predominantly, or even entirely, male, but it was perhaps more usual for family minsters to have both male and female members whether under male or female headship. Both Much Wenlock and Winchcombe had mixed communities in 901 and 897 respectively, on the evidence of the witness-lists of charters, but do not seem to have been headed by abbesses. Much Wenlock had a *senior*,[154] and Winchcombe had a lay lord who intervened in their affairs, possibly in the capacity of lay abbot, Æthelwulf, the brother of Queen Ealhswith of Wessex, who seems to have inherited control of the foundation from the heirs of Coenwulf.[155] Although these mixed communities are generally considered a feature of the pre-viking age, what are probably family minsters containing both men and women may still be found in the tenth century. Cheddar (Som.), for instance, is recorded as possessing a mixed community in the tenth century.[156] Such traditions may also explain isolated references in the tenth century to abbesses at foundations which otherwise seem to have been predominantly male minsters. These places need not be seen so much as failed nunneries, but as minsters with a strong association with a particular lay family and which had came under female headship, perhaps when a female member wished to live a monastic life in a period when there was an increasing revival of interest in the monastic way of life.[157]

In conclusion, one could say that the problem for many royal nunneries in the late eighth and ninth centuries was that they did not remain 'royal' in the sense, as defined in Chapter 1, of being controlled by close female relatives of a ruler. When former royal lines were reduced to the ranks of the nobility, many of the nunneries they had founded lost wealth and status as well, and came to resemble the 'family monasteries' of the nobility which drew Bede's ire.[158] In particular, abbesses might be replaced by kinsmen as abbots, or the nunnery's estates might be absorbed back into the family's lands. However, they also have to be seen as part of a wider pattern of social and economic change which saw the diminution of most of the major monasteries of the Bedan period with a number becoming more significant as centres of royal control.[159] There was no campaign to extinguish nunneries as such, but when minsters became merely parochial centres, whether through royal, episcopal or noble intervention, there was no incentive to retain them as communities of women. A few priests and other secular clergy were all that was required, and they needed only a modest landed endowment to sustain them. Nunneries required a substantial investment with the risk that family lands might come ultimately under the control of the church; better to make a temporary provision for female relatives with a vocation in the family home or a male minster.[160] Ruling families did not have to take into account such financial restraints, and the established pattern of what was expected of the women of a royal house acted as an incentive for continuing patronage towards royal nunneries. New dynasties of the eighth and ninth centuries seemed just as eager to found religious houses under the supervision of wives and daughters as their predecessors of the seventh century had been. Abbesses such as Cynethryth and Cwoenthryth rivalled the powerful abbesses of the conversion period, though both became vulnerable when rival lines came to power. The competition between rival groups for the throne in ninth-century Mercia hindered any of the newly founded Mercian royal nunneries from establishing an inviolate base, and none of them survived, at least as nunneries, into the tenth century when royal nunneries were concentrated in Wessex, the homeland of the only surviving Anglo-Saxon dynasty.

Notes

1. W. Goffart, *The Narrators of Barbarian History* (Princeton, NJ, 1988); D. Rollason, 'Hagiography and politics in early Northumbria', in P. Szarmach (ed.), *Holy Men and Holy Women: Old English Prose Saints' Lives and Their Contexts* (Albany, NY, 1996), 95–114.

2. J. Higgitt, 'Monasteries and inscriptions in early Northumbria, the evidence of Whitby', in C. Bourke (ed.), *From the Isles of the North: Early Medieval Art in Ireland and Britain* (Belfast, 1995), 229–36; C. Neuman de Vegvar, 'Saints and companions to saints: Anglo-Saxon royal women monastics in context', in P. Szarmach (ed.), *Holy Men and Holy Women: Old English Prose Saints' Lives and Their Contexts* (Albany, NY, 1996), 51–94.

3. See e.g., M. Biddle and B. Kjølbye-Biddle, 'The Repton stone', *A-SE*, 14 (1985), 233–92; S. Hollis, 'The Minster-in-Thanet foundation story', *A-SE*, 27 (1998), 41–74.

4. J. Blair, *The Church in Anglo-Saxon Society* (Oxford, forthcoming), chs 5 and 6.

5. *Ibid.*, chs 3 and 4.

6. C. Cubitt, *Anglo-Saxon Church Councils c. 650–c. 850* (Leicester, 1995).

7. *HE*, IV, 2.

8. *HE*, IV, 5 (Synod of Hertford 672); IV, 17 (Synod of Hatfield 679); Cubitt, *Church Councils*. The section which follows draws extensively on Dr Cubitt's work.

9. Cubitt, *Church Councils*, 42–4.

10. *HE*, IV, 5.

11. *HS*, 362–76; Cubitt, *Church Councils*, 100–52.

12. See Cubitt (*Church Councils*, 65–74) for other evidence for claims of episcopal jurisdiction in this period.

13. *V. Wilfredi*, ch. 21, 42–5.

14. *HE*, IV, 5.

15. *V. Wilfredi*, ch. 56, 142–5.

16. H. P. R. Finberg, *Early Charters of the West Midlands*, 2nd edn (Leicester, 1972), 197–216.

17. F. M. Stenton, '*Medehamstede* and its colonies', in D. Stenton (ed.), *Preparatory to Anglo-Saxon England* (Oxford, 1970), 179–92.

18. P. Sims-Williams, 'Continental influence at Bath monastery in the seventh century', *A-SE*, 4 (1975), 1–10, and see Chapter 1, p. 18.

19. For Fladbury in Worcestershire as a possible daughter house of Whitby, see P. Sims-Williams, *Religion and Literature in Western England, 600–800* (Cambridge, 1990), 92–3.

20. E. O. Blake (ed.), *Liber Eliensis*, Royal Historical Society, Camden Third Series, 92 (London, 1962), 30; P. Sawyer, *Anglo-Saxon Lincolnshire* (Lincoln, 1998), 64–6. Sawyer raises the question of whether this was the site excavated at Flixborough, six miles south of West Halton.

21. The location may actually have been at nearby Stow Green where there was formerly a church dedicated to Æthelthryth (D. Roffe, 'The seventh-century monastery of Stow Green, Lincolnshire', *Lincolnshire History and Archaeology,* 21 (1986), 31–2).

22. S. Ridyard, *The Royal Saints of Anglo-Saxon England: A Study of West Saxon and East Anglian Cults* (Cambridge, 1988), 54–6.

23. In which context see above for links between *Icanho* and Much Wenlock, in Blake,

Liber Eliensis, 281–3; D. Whitelock, 'The pre-Viking age church in East Anglia', *A-SE*, 1 (1972), 12; Sims-Williams, *Religion and Literature*, 99–100.

24. E. Ewig, 'Beobachtungen zu den Klosterprivilegien des 7. und frühen 8. Jahrhunderts', in J. Fleckenstein and K. Schmid (eds), *Adel und Kirche: Gerd Tellenbach zum 65ten Geburtstag* (Freiburg, 1968), 52–65; A. Dierkens, 'Prolégomènes à une histoire des relations culturelles entre les Îles Britanniques et le continent pendant le haut moyen âge', in H. Atsma (ed.), *La Neustrie: les pays au Nord de la Loire de 650 à 850*, 2 vols (Sigmaringen, 1989), II, 371–94.

25. *HE*, IV, 19.

26. A. T. Thacker, 'The making of a local saint', in A. Thacker and R. Sharpe (eds), *Local Saints and Local Churches in the Early Medieval West* (Oxford, 2002).

27. *HE*, IV, 26.

28. *HE*, IV, 23.

29. *HS*, 360–76; 447–62; Cubitt, *Church Councils*, 100–21, 153–90. See Bede, *Letter to Ecgbert*, implying that bishops had not been as active as they might have been in this respect.

30. J. T. McNeill and H. A. Gamer (eds), *Medieval Handbooks of Penance* (Columbia, NY, 1979), II, 8, 205.

31. B. Krusch (ed.), *Vita S. Columbani*, ch. 13 (where penance is said to have been prescribed), 17 and 22.

32. For Æthelbald's unhealthy interest in nuns see Tangl, no. 73, and for this aspect of royal involvement with nunneries, see further below, in Chapter 5.

33. Council of Chelsea, ch. 4; *HS*, 364. The bishop had to confirm the appointment and invest with office.

34. Council of Chelsea, ch. 7; *HS*, 364–5.

35. *HS*, 407–8.

36. Sims-Williams, *Religion and Literature*, 144–76.

37. *HS*, ch. 8, 582–3; Cubitt, *Church Councils*, 194–202.

38. B 99; S. Kelly (ed.), *Charters of St Augustine's Abbey, Canterbury and Minster-in-Thanet*, British Academy, Anglo-Saxon Charters, IV (Oxford, 1995), no. 10, 38–44. The three royal abbesses were Æbba, foundress of Minster-in-Thanet, her sister Eormenburh, and Eormenhild, the daughter of King Eorcenbert.

39. Tangl, no. 14.

40. B. A. E. Yorke, 'The Bonifacian mission and female religious in Wessex', *Early Medieval Europe*, 7 (1998), 145–72, at 148–9.

41. Sims-Williams, *Religion and Literature*, 135–7.

42. Tangl, no. 73; *EHD*, I, no. 177.

43. N. Brooks, 'The development of military obligations in eighth- and ninth-century England', in P. Clemoes and K. Hughes (eds), *England before the Conquest: Studies in Primary Sources Presented to Dorothy Whitelock* (Cambridge, 1971), 69–84.

44. The *Dialogus* of Archbishop Ecgbert also refers in passing to *monasterii* under lay control; *HS*, 406, ch. 7.

45. *HS*, 580–5, especially chs 4 and 8; Cubitt, *Church Councils*, 191–203.

46. S 22 and 90; N. Brooks, *The Early History of the Church of Canterbury* (Leicester, 1984), 191–7.

47. Tangl, no. 14. Eangyth and her daughter cannot be located in the Kentish royal genealogy, but the succession of the descendants of Æthelbert, which included Wihtred, had been maintained only by suppressing the claims of the descendants of

some sons to rule. One of these excluded members, Oswine, had ruled briefly from 688–689 and 690–692; see Kelly, *Charters of Minster-in-Thanet*, 195–203.

48. B. A. E. Yorke, *Kings and Kingdoms of Early Anglo-Saxon England* (London, 1990), . 111–27. It has been doubted whether all those who claimed the throne of Mercia in this period were actually of royal descent, but one can at least say that they maintained they were.

49. She was a correspondent of Alcuin who addressed her as 'Eugenia'; Dümmler, 36, 102, 103 and 300 (for translation, see S. Allott, *Alcuin of York* (York, 1974), nos 42–5). She witnessed S 127, a grant of King Offa to Chertsey, as abbess. Unfortunately the identity of her nunnery is not known, and W. Levison (*England and the Continent in the Eighth Century* (Oxford, 1946), 251, n. 2) was wrong to identify her with the Abbess of Fladbury of that name, since S 1255 makes it clear that Æthelburh of Fladbury was the daughter of Alfred and probably a member of the Hwiccian royal house.

50. *A-SC*, 792; we cannot be completely certain that she retired to a religious house, but at the time she was widowed moral pressure to do so was applied by Alcuin via her sister Æthelburh; Dümmler, 102.

51. See Asser (chs 14–15) for a very prejudiced account of Eadburh's career as queen of Wessex and abbess. H. Becher ('Das königliche Frauenkloster San Salvatore/Santa Giulia in Brescia im Spiegel seiner Memorialüberlieferung', *Frühmittelalterliche Studien*, 17 (1983), 299–392, at 380–1) has proposed that she could be Abbess Eadburh who appears in the *liber memorialis* of Reichenau abbey at the head of a list of fifty-eight nuns with Lombardic-Italian names.

52. S 1258; Levison, *England and the Continent*, 251–2; see further below.

53. S 120; she leased land from Bishop Hathored of Worcester at Hampton Lucy (War.), and Sims-Williams (*Religion and Literature*, 163–4) suggests her monastery was situated there.

54. Levison, *England and the Continent*, 251–2, and see further below.

55. S. Kelly (ed.), *Charters of Abingdon Abbey, Part I*, British Academy, Anglo-Saxon Charters, VII (Oxford, 2000), ccv and charter no. 10, 45–9 (S 184).

56. Levison, *England and the Continent*, 251–2. Ælfflaed appears as heir to Winchcombe in S 1142, B 575, and the suggestion she became an abbess is inferred from that.

57. Levison, *England and the Continent*, 249–59; Brooks, *Church of Canterbury*, 183–6.

58. H. Foerster (ed.), *Liber Diurnus Romanorum Pontificum* (Bern, 1958), no. 93, 172–3; Cubitt, *Church Councils*, 226.

59. S 1258, B 291; *EHD*, no. 79. According to the settlement reached at the Synod of *Clofesho* in 798 King Æthelbald had granted the minster and its estate to Canterbury, but Offa, after retrieving the site from King Cynewulf of Wessex, kept it for himself and his heirs. Although judgement was in favour of the archbishop, Cynethryth was able to retain Cookham by swapping it for land she owned in Kent. It is not directly stated that this Cynethryth was Offa's widow, but the context makes the supposition likely and it has been widely accepted by later commentators.

60. '*Vitae Offa Secundae*', in W. Watts (ed.), *Matthei Paris Monachi Albanensis Angli, Historia Maior* (Paris, 1644), 20; Cubitt, *Church Councils*, 226.

61. Levison, *England and the Continent*, 249.

62. Offa had tried to reclaim this estate from the Bishop of Worcester as part of his inheritance from King Æthelbald; he had been forced to relinquish this and other claims at the Synod of Brentford in 781 (S 1257, B 241), but in the same year Eanburh acquired the lease of Hampton Lucy for her lifetime (S 120, B 239).

63. Sims-Williams, *Religion and Literature*, 160–1; by conceding the other estates at the Synod of Brentford, Offa was able to retain Bath.

64. Levison, *England and the Continent*, 249–59; Thacker, 'Kings, saints and monasteries', 8–12.

65. Cwoenthryth is not stated directly in any document to have been Abbess of Winchcombe. S 1442, B 575 refers to Coenwulf's heir at Winchcombe as being 'Cynethryth', but most commentators have followed Levison (*England and the Continent*, 252) in assuming an error for Cwoenthryth, though Sims-Williams (*Religion and Literature*, 165–6) is sceptical. This 'Cynethryth' is unlikely to be Offa's queen as she is referred to as an heir of Coenwulf. S 1436, B 384, the settlement of the dispute between the Archbishopric of Canterbury and Cwoenthryth over the minsters of Reculver and Minster-in-Thanet, makes it clear that Cwoenthryth was Coenwulf's main heir and that the family's diplomas were kept at Winchcombe. The accounts of her brother's death also associate her with Winchcombe.

66. S. Wemple, *Women in Frankish Society: Marriage and the Cloister 500–900* (Philadelphia, 1981), 165–74.

67. J.-P. Laporte, *Le Trésor des Saints de Chelles* (Chelles, 1998), 115–60; J. Nelson, 'Women and the word in the earlier middle ages', in W. J. Shiels and D. Wood (eds), *Women in the Church*, Studies in Church History, 27 (Oxford, 1990), 64–5.

68. See Dümmler (nos 15, 152, 154, 159, 164, 195, 216, 228 and 255) for letters from Alcuin and Gisela and Rotrud; see n. 49 above for his correspondence with Æthelburh.

69. Dümmler, no. 62.

70. Asser, ch. 15.

71. Discussed in Chapter 3, pp. 75–6.

72. P. Stafford, 'The king's wife in Wessex 800–1066', *Past and Present*, 91 (1981), 3–27.

73. *A-SC*, 718; P. Coulstock, *The Collegiate Church of Wimborne Minster* (Woodbridge, 1993).

74. *A-SC*, 871.

75. *A-SC*, 757; Æthelbald was murdered at Seckington about twelve miles south-west of Repton. We do not know if burial was in accordance with his wishes or those of whoever arranged his funeral. For the sculpture which may have been erected as a memorial to Æthelbald at Repton see Biddle and Kjølbye-Biddle, 'The Repton stone'.

76. Repton had reputedly been founded by the *subregulus* Frithuric, and is said to have been the burial place of King Merewalh of the Magonsaetan claimed in some accounts as a son of King Penda (see n. 82): see Stenton, '*Medehamstede* and its colonies', 179–92; A. Dornier, 'The Anglo-Saxon monastery at Breedon-on-the-Hill, Leicestershire', in A. Dornier (ed.), *Mercian Studies* (Leicester, 1997), 155–68; D. Rollason, *The Mildrith Legend: A Study in Early Medieval Hagiography in England* (Leicester, 1982), 25–6, 81.

77. *V. Guthlaci*, chs 20–4 (Repton); 40, 49, 51 (for links with Æthelbald); Thacker, 'Kings, saints and monasteries in pre-viking Mercia', 5–6.

78. D. Rollason, *The Search for St Wigstan*, Vaughan Paper, 27 (Leicester, 1981); *idem*, 'Cults of murdered royal saints in Anglo-Saxon England', *A-SE*, 11 (1983), 1–22, at 6–9; Thacker, 'Kings, saints and monasteries', 12–14.

79. M. Biddle, 'Archaeology, architecture and the cult of saints in Anglo-Saxon England', in L. Butler and R. Morris (eds), *The Anglo-Saxon Church: Papers on History, Architecture and Archaeology in Honour of Dr H. M. Taylor* (London, 1986), 1–31, at

14–22; H. M. Taylor, 'St Wystan's church, Repton, Derbyshire: a reconstruction essay', *Archaeological Journal*, 144 (1987), 205–45.

80. S 1624, B 414.

81. Yorke, *Kings and Kingdoms*, 111–17.

82. According to the genealogical material associated with the 'Mildrith Legend', her father Merewalh was a son of Penda of Mercia (D. Rollason, *The Mildrith Legend: A Study in Early Medieval Hagiography in England* (Leicester, 1982), 73–87). The claim receives possible support from the 'Testament' of her sister Mildburh which refers to King Æthelred of Mercia, son of King Penda, as her uncle (Finberg, *Early Charters of the West Midlands*, 197–216).

83. Kelly (*Charters of Minster-in-Thanet*, nos 49 and 50); in no. 51 Æthelbald made a similar grant of toll to her successor Eadburh, which is said to be out of love for his kinswoman Mildrith, and in no. 52 Offa made one to Eadburh's successor Sigeburh. See also S. Kelly, 'Trading privileges from eighth-century England', *Early Medieval Europe*, 1 (1992), 3–27.

84. Kelly, *Charters of Minster-in-Thanet*, no. 51; 'Goscelin, *Vitae Mildrethae*', ch. 28, in Rollason, *Mildrith Legend*, 142–3.

85. Rollason, *Mildrith Legend, passim*; Hollis, 'The Minster-in-Thanet foundation story'.

86. Kelly, *Charters of Minster-in-Thanet*, nos. 52–3.

87. S 32 and 33; B. A. E. Yorke, 'The kingdom of the East Saxons', *A-SE*, 14 (1985), 1–36; Kelly, *Charters of Minster-in-Thanet*, 201.

88. Kelly, *Charters of Minster-in-Thanet*, xxvii–xxviii; Selethryth emphasized the link between the two foundations by transferring the body of Eadburh to Lyminge and initiating her cult (S 160).

89. Brooks, *Church of Canterbury*, 184–5; J. Crick, 'Church, land and nobility in early ninth-century Kent', *Bulletin of the Institute of Historical Research*, 61 (1988), 251–69; S. Keynes, 'The control of Kent in the ninth century', *Early Medieval Europe*, 2 (1993), 111–31, at 115–19; B. Brooks, 'Archbishop Wulfred (825–32) and the lordship of Minster-in-Thanet in the early ninth century', *Downside Review*, 111 (1994), 211–27.

90. Brooks, *Church of Canterbury*, 183–6.

91. S 1436, B 384; Brooks, *Church of Canterbury*, 180–3.

92. S 1267, B 1337.

93. See Rollason, *Mildrith Legend*, 22–5, for a dubious late account of the nuns of Minster fleeing to Lyminge because of viking attacks. For a later possible abbess of Minster, see S. Foot, *Veiled Women*, 2 vols (Aldershot, 2000), II, 125–32.

94. Brooks, *Church of Canterbury*, 197–206.

95. Chapter 2, p. 18.

96. For example, S 95 and 1429.

97. S 209; Sims-Williams, *Religion and Literature*, 35, 145.

98. Her kinship with the Hwiccian royal house is revealed in S 62, where she is referred to by Ealdred, *subregulus* of the Hwicce, as *propinqua*.

99. S 62 and 1255; Finberg, *Early Charters of the West Midlands*, 38–9.

100. Sims-Williams, *Religion and Literature*, 144–76, S 172 and 185 show that King Coenwulf subsequently acquired control of Twyning and Fladbury, but Worcester seems eventually to have won these estates back again.

101. See above; Brooks, *Church of Canterbury*, 175–80.

102. Eafe seems to have been the last abbess; Finberg, *Early Charters of the West Midlands*,

153–66. Bath had also been lost, perhaps because of its border position. In S 265, 757–8 it is under the patronage of King Cynewulf of Wessex and has become a male minster.

103. S 1429, B 156; *EHD*, I, no. 68. Hrothwaru's claim was against her own mother who, by the terms of Dunne's deathbed bequest, was to have managed, as a lay supervisor, the monastery and its lands until Hrothwaru came of age, but had then proved unwilling to relinquish them.

104. S 1255.

105. S 1430; Sims-Williams, *Religion and Literature*, 237–9.

106. Instead Offa and Coenwulf supported a new nunnery in former Hwiccian territory, Winchcombe. S. Bassett, 'In search of the origins of Anglo-Saxon kingdoms', in *idem* (ed.), *The Origins of Anglo-Saxon Kingdoms* (London, 1989), 3–27, at 8–17, argues that the area around Winchcombe formed the core of the patrimony of the Hwiccian royal house.

107. D. Knowles and R. N. Hadcock, *Medieval Religious Houses: England and Wales*, 2nd edn (London, 1971), 463–87; J. T. Schulenberg, *Forgetful of Their Sex: Female Sanctity and Society ca. 500–1100* (Chicago, 1998), 143–7.

108. R. Page, '*A Most Vile People': Early English Historians on the Vikings*, Viking Society for Northern Research (London, 1987).

109. H. O. Coxe (ed.), *Roger of Wendover, Flores Historiarum* (London, 1841–44); H. R. Luard (ed.), *Matthew Paris, Chronica Majora*, Rolls Series (London, 1872–83), I, 391.

110. Schulenburg, *Forgetful of Their Sex*, 143.

111. *HE*, IV, 25.

112. R. Daniels, 'The Anglo-Saxon monastery at Hartlepool, England', in J. Hawkes and S. Mills (eds), *Northumbria's Golden Age* (Stroud, 1999), 105–12; P. Rahtz, 'Anglo-Saxon and later Whitby', in L. Hoey (ed.), *Yorkshire Monasticism: Archaeology, Art and Architecture, from the Seventh to the Sixteenth Century*, British Archaeological Association Transactions, 16 (London, 1995), 1–11.

113. D. Bethell, 'The Lives of St. Osyth of Essex and St. Osyth of Aylesbury', *Analecta Bollandiana*, 88 (1980), 75–127.

114. Rollason, *Mildrith Legend*, 26–7.

115. *Ibid.*, 59–68.

116. S. Foot, 'Remembering, forgetting and inventing; attitudes to the past in England at the end of the first viking age', *TRHS*, 6th series, 9 (1999), 185–200; *idem, Veiled Women*, I, 71–84; Blair, *The Church in Anglo-Saxon Society*, ch. 6.

117. All are events recorded in the *A-SC*.

118. M. Biddle and B. Kjølbye-Biddle, 'Repton and the Vikings', *Antiquity*, 66 (1992), 36–51.

119. Brooks, 'Development of military obligations', 78–80.

120. S 160, B 317.

121. Brooks, *Church of Canterbury*, 35–6, 201; Kelly, *Charters of Minster-in-Thanet*, xxviii–xxix.

122. *HS*, 582, ch. 7.

123. *Worcester*, 468–9; Leofrun is described as 'abbess of the monastery of St Mildrith'; see further below for problems of identification.

124. *A-SC*, 865, though the offer does not seem to have been successful in preventing east Kent from being ravaged.

125. M. K. Lawson, 'The collection of danegeld and heregeld in the reigns of Æthelred II and Cnut', *EHR*, 99 (1984), 721–38.
126. A. Smyth, *Scandinavian Kings in the British Isles, 850–880* (Oxford, 1977).
127. D. M. Hadley, '"And they proceeded to plough and support themselves"; the Scandinavian settlement of England', *Anglo-Norman England,* 19 (1997), 69–96; *idem, The Northern Danelaw: Its Social Structure c. 800–1100* (London, 2000); L. Abrams, 'Edward the Elder's Danelaw', in N. Higham and D. Hill (eds), *Edward the Elder 899–924* (Manchester, 2001), 128–43.
128. D. N. Dumville, *Wessex and England from Alfred to Edgar* (Woodbridge, 1992), 31–3; D. M. Hadley, 'Conquest, colonisation and the church. Ecclesiastical organisation in the Danelaw', *Historical Research,* 69 (1996), 109–28.
129. Whitelock, 'Pre-Viking age church in East Anglia', 20–2; Taylor, 'St Wystan's church, Repton'.
130. R. Fleming, 'Monastic lands and England's defence in the viking age', *EHR*, 100 (1985), 247–65, to be read in conjunction with Dumville, *Wessex and England,* 29–54.
131. Yorke, 'Bonifacian mission'; some early West Saxon royal nunneries may have suffered from being too close to other branches of the royal houses which disappear from view after Ecgbert and his descendants came to power. However, it should be noted that a number of the late West Saxon nunneries were either founded on the sites of existing minsters or endowed with minsters and their property, and some of these minsters may have originated as female communities (see Chapter 3).
132. A. T. Thacker, 'Æthelwold and Abingdon', in B. A. E. Yorke (ed.), *Bishop Æthelwold: His Career and Influence* (Woodbridge, 1988), 43–64, at 45–6; see Chapter 1 for early history of Abingdon, in origin a Mercian rather than West Saxon foundation.
133. S. Keynes and M. Lapidge (eds), *Alfred the Great: Asser's Life of King Alfred and Other Contemporary Sources* (Harmondsworth, 1983), 174–8; S 806; J. Blair, 'Palaces or minsters? Northampton and Cheddar reconsidered', *A-SE,* 25 (1996), 97–122.
134. A. Smyth, *King Alfred the Great* (Oxford, 1995), 264–5.
135. Blair, *The Church in Anglo-Saxon Society*, ch. 6.
136. Knowles and Hadcock, *Medieval Religious Houses,* 256 and 457.
137. S 1483, 946–51; and see Foot, *Veiled Women*, II, 27–33, and Chapter 3 for later history of Barking.
138. C. R. Hart, *The Early Charters of Eastern England* (Leicester, 1966), 117–45; K. Bascombe, 'Two charters of King Suebred of Essex', in K. Neale (ed.), *An Essex Tribute: Essays Presented to F. G. Emmison* (Cambridge, 1987), 85–96; the latter implies that Barking had acquired the lands of the former East Saxon nunnery of Nazeing.
139. *HE*, IV, 6 records how Bishop Eorcenwald of London founded Barking for his sister Æthelburh.
140. Ealdorman Ælfgar of Essex was a major patron of Barking in the tenth century; C. R. Hart, 'The ealdordom of Essex', in K. Neale (ed.), *An Essex Tribute: Essays Presented to F. G. Emmison* (Cambridge, 1987), 57–81.
141. P. Stafford, 'Queens, nunneries and reforming churchmen: gender, religious status and reform in tenth- and eleventh-century England', *Past and Present*, 163 (1999), 3–35; see further Chapter 3.
142. Both recorded in *A-SC* under these years; for the abbess of St Mildrith being the

remnant of the Thanet community see above, and for Wareham's later history see Chapter 3.

143. J. Crick, 'The wealth, patronage, and connections of women's houses in late Anglo-Saxon England', *Revue Bénédictine*, 109 (1999), 154–85, esp. Table 1, 162–3.

144. See Chapter 4.

145. J. Blair, 'A saint for every minster?', in A. Thacker and R. Sharpe (eds), *Local Saints and Local Churches in the Early Medieval West* (Oxford, 2002), 455–94 *passim*.

146. Ch. 7 of the Council of Chelsea in 816 (*HS*, III, 582) assumes that bishops, abbots and abbesses are likely to have their own property to distribute, in other words that private wealth might be necessary for the independent existence of a religious community. Cf. Wilfrid's will where one-third of his wealth was left to his monasteries 'to purchase the friendship of kings and bishops'; *V. Wilfredi*, ch. 63, 136–7.

147. As Offa did when he claimed that the Bishop of Worcester was holding various estates 'without hereditary right [that were] the inheritance of his kinsman, to wit King Æthelbald'; *EHD*, I, no. 77; S 1257.

148. Council of Chelsea, ch. 8; *HS*, 582–3. In the eleventh century Abbess Selethryth was praised at St Augustine's, Canterbury (which had acquired former Minster estates) for attempting to regain nunnery lands from Archbishop Wulfred; see Kelly, *Charters of Minster-in-Thanet*, xxvii.

149. For instance, this was the fate imposed on a number of the deposed Northumbrian kings in the eighth century; Yorke, *Kings and Kingdoms*, 86–94.

150. *EHD*, I, no. 184; *HS*, 394–6. M. Parker, 'An Anglo-Saxon monastery in the Lower Don valley', *Northern History*, 21 (1985), 19–32.

151. Opinions differ on whether all those who came to the Northumbrian throne in the eighth century were actually of royal descent, however loosely that might be defined. Perhaps the best one can say is that many of them claimed to be, though Æthelwald Moll is not known to have done so; Yorke, *Kings and Kingdoms*, 86–94.

152. *HS*, 408, ch. 11; however, the main concern of this chapter is what should happen if a monastery was left to two individuals jointly, who might be a man and a woman – the recommendation was that they should rule successively.

153. C. S. Taylor, 'Berkeley minster', *Transactions of the Bristol and Gloucestershire Archaeological Society*, 19 (1894–5), 70–84; Sims-Williams, *Religion and Literature*, 118, 172–6.

154. S 221, B 587.

155. S 1442, B 575. Eadburh, the mother of Æthelwulf and Ealhswith, was of Mercian royal descent according to Asser, ch. 29; Levison, *England and the Continent*, 252–3.

156. S 806, B 1219 – '*famulis famlabusque Domini on Ceodre degentibus*'; and see n. 133 above.

157. See, e.g., Dumville, *Wessex and England*, 177–8; P. Halpin, 'Women religious in late Anglo-Saxon England', *Haskins Society Journal*, 6 (1994), 97–110; Foot, *Veiled Women*, II, 1–14, who cautions making too much of the limited evidence for the association of religious women with male minsters in this period. See further in Chapter 3.

158. Bede, 'Letter to Bishop Ecgbert', Plummer, I, 405–23; *EHD*, I, no. 170. These might be controlled by a married couple and literally be the abode of a family.

159. Blair, *The Church in Anglo-Saxon Society*, ch. 6.

160. Foot, *Veiled Women*, I, 62–6.

3   The Later Nunneries of the West Saxon Royal House

In 825 King Ecgbert of Wessex (802–839) won a decisive victory over King Beornwulf of Mercia at *Ellendun* which resulted in his house gaining control of the East Saxons, South Saxons, Kent and Surrey. During the reign of his grandson Alfred (871–899), thanks to the impact of the 'great army', Wessex was left as the only Anglo-Saxon kingdom still controlled by its own dynasty. By the end of his reign, in co-operation with the remnants of Mercia, Alfred was promoting himself as 'king of the Anglo-Saxons',[1] and in the tenth century his successors had conquered the Danelaw and become kings of England. It was Alfred who initiated a new intensive phase in the foundation of royal nunneries, though all the royally sponsored new foundations lay within the confines of pre-ninth-century Wessex. Earlier foundations for women did not enjoy evident support from the new dynasty, with the exception of Barking in Essex, though unfortunately the history of the foundation from the time of its inclusion in Bede's *Ecclesiastical History* to around the mid-tenth century is a blank.[2] The impetus towards supporting new foundations may in part have come from the continuing importance of nunneries to many of the ruling houses of Europe, but is also likely to have owed much to Mercian practices following intermarriage between the West Saxon and Mercian dynasties. The close connections between certain nunneries and the royal house were subject to minor modification in the period of monastic reform. The whole question of the role of nunneries in the reform movement needs careful elucidation, for the attitudes of the reformers to female monasticism were often ambiguous and the degree of 'Benedictianization' they experienced should not be overstated.[3] After the Norman Conquest many survivors of the old regime retreated to Anglo-Saxon royal nunneries which therefore retained for a while their particular association with the former ruling house. Changes in patterns of patronage ultimately caused them to become less royal and aristocratic than previously,[4] though the wealth accumulated during the tenth and eleventh centuries meant that the nunneries supported by the Anglo-Saxon royal house – Amesbury, Barking, Romsey, Shaftesbury, Wherwell, Wilton and Winchester (Nunnaminster) – were not only the wealthiest in England at the time of Domesday Book, but retained that position at the Dissolution.[5]

The long history of these later royal nunneries has ensured a better survival of documentation than for many of the earlier foundations, though inevitably there are still major gaps. Not only do more sources survive from the tenth and eleventh centuries than for earlier periods, but they are also more varied in type, with new forms such as wills appearing.[6] The range of references to nunneries in contemporary sources reflects the variety of material, and also the involvement of nunneries and their inhabitants in many different facets of contemporary life, but records of land transactions remain a dominant source. Charters from the tenth or eleventh centuries survive for all the royal foundations, with the exception of Amesbury,[7] but only in substantial numbers for Shaftesbury[8] and Wilton.[9] However, the long survival of the nunneries also meant that key sources were rewritten to suit changing situations, or because of the necessity of replacing Old English texts with Latin. Hagiographies, which provide the main narratives in which nunneries play a part, were particularly prone to revision. Post-Conquest *Lives* survive for Edith (and Wulfthryth) of Wilton[10] and for Wulfhild of Barking by Goscelin,[11] who may also have been the author of the *Passio* of King Edward the Martyr, the most significant of Shaftesbury's pre-Conquest saints.[12] From the twelfth century there is the *Vita* of Eadburh of Nunnaminster by Osbert of Clare,[13] while the *Vitae* of Æthelflaed and Maerwynn of Romsey survive in their earliest form in a manuscript of the early fourteenth century.[14] Although these accounts show signs of the concerns and expectations of the periods in which they were written,[15] their authors used both oral and written sources preserved at their foundations or other houses with which they were associated.[16] Goscelin himself refers to earlier written sources available to him at Wilton,[17] and refers specifically to a vernacular account of the visit of the epileptic dancers of Colebek which Abbess Brihtgifu had ordered to be recorded in the early eleventh century.[18] Other information he received about Edith at Wilton was linked with objects associated with her such as items she had embroidered, or her clothes chest which had survived a fire unscathed.[19] The author of the *Passio Edwardi* also refers to using earlier written material, by which he may well have meant an earlier *Life* written at Shaftesbury, as well as oral testimony of the nuns for some of the miracles following translation of the body in 1001.[20] Susan Ridyard has brought together the evidence which suggests that Osbert, and others writing on Eadburh after the Norman Conquest, were able to draw on earlier written material for her life which had probably been produced at Nunnaminster in the pre-Conquest period.[21] Anglo-Norman historians seeking to record the pre-Conquest history of England also provide information on these and other Anglo-Saxon royal saints associated with the later nunneries. The *Gesta* of William of Malmesbury are particularly important, but similar problems arise about the nature of his sources and the degree of authorial adaptation of the material.[22] The promotion of saints and production of written material concerning them is also evidence, of course, for a vibrant ecclesiastical culture of the later nunneries, for which other types of evidence can be adduced such as the surviving chapel at Bradford-on-Avon, which was probably built by the nuns of Shaftesbury to house the relics of Edward the

Martyr, the two roods from Romsey or the pre-Conquest prayer-book that may have been assembled at Nunnaminster.[23]

From Ecgbert to Alfred

One of the ways in which the West Saxon conquest of Kent contrasted with that of the Mercians is that the West Saxon rulers do not seem to have tried to put their female relatives in charge of Kentish minsters. That may be seen as an example of the more diplomatic policies which enabled West Saxon kings to remain in control of Kent[24] – though their conquest nevertheless seems to have involved some annexation of former minster estates[25] – but may also be viewed in conjunction with Asser's statement that 'the West Saxons did not allow the queen to sit beside the king, nor indeed did they allow her to be called "queen", but only "king's wife"',[26] to suggest that in ninth-century Wessex traditional ways of enhancing the royal line through promotion of royal women as queens and abbesses were abandoned temporarily. According to Asser the change in policy was occasioned by the reign of Ecgbert's predecessor Beorhtric during which his wicked wife Eadburh, the daughter of Offa of Mercia, had been allowed too much influence and, in the act of poisoning those who opposed her, had accidentally killed Beorhtric himself. Perhaps significantly in the light of this evidence for female power at court, Beorhtric may have been the first West Saxon king known to have been buried in a nunnery, and he (and perhaps Eadburh) may have been responsible for the fine basilican church of St Mary's at his burial site in Wareham which is known from nineteenth-century descriptions and paintings.[27] Eadburh herself became an abbess after she was widowed, though under Carolingian protection for Asser says that she was obliged to flee to Frankia after Beorhtric's death.[28]

Asser's account of Eadburh and the West Saxon aversion to queens is not only prejudiced but also highly selective in its references to ninth-century practice in Wessex. Not only was Judith, who married first Alfred's father Æthelwulf and then Alfred's brother Æthelbald, crowned as queen[29] – reference to this occasioned Asser's explanation of why it was contrary to the kingdom's practice – but so probably was Wulfthryth the wife of Æthelred, the brother whose reign immediately preceded Alfred's, for she was designated as *regina* in the only charter where she appears.[30] The link between elevation of the position of queen and the patronage of nunneries, suggested for Beorhtric, may also be applicable to Æthelred, because he was buried in the nunnery at Wimborne which had been founded by Cuthburh, sister of King Ine and a distant ancestress.[31] When Æthelwold, the son of Æthelred and Wulfthryth, attempted to claim the throne on the death of King Alfred in 899, Wimborne was one of the two estates he seized, and he is said to have removed one of the nuns when he did so.[32] We are not told her identity, nor whether she was removed as a demonstration of Æthelwold's authority over the nunnery,[33] or because she was a kinswoman, or someone he wished to marry, perhaps to strengthen his claim to the throne. What does emerge is the importance of the nunnery where his father was buried as a means of enhancing Æthelwold's own status and throne-worthiness. Æthelwold's coup may help to explain why King Alfred was apparently keen to stress to Asser that it was not normal in Wessex for a king's wife to be a queen, for he may have been sensitive to the fact that Æthelwold was the son of a *regina*, whereas his own son Edward was not, since Alfred's wife Ealhswith appears not to have been endowed with this title.[34]

The involvement of Wimborne in Æthelwold's attempt to claim the West Saxon throne may also provide an explanation of why it ceased to be favoured as a royal nunnery after Æthelwold was defeated. The account of Æthelwold's coup in the *Anglo-Saxon Chronicle* is the last reference we have to Wimborne as a nunnery, and no charters for the foundation survive, nor is it the recipient of gifts in royal or aristocratic wills. In 962 the church was used for what may have been a politically sensitive burial, that of King Sigeferth who had committed suicide,[35] but it is not clear whether it was still in the charge of an abbess at this time. By Domesday Book it appears to have become a small community of secular priests, presumably a remnant of those who had originally served the nuns.[36] Wimborne's fate may be paralleled by that of Wareham which may also have declined as a royal nunnery since it had too close an association with a vanquished royal line (that of Beorhtric). The only reference to a nunnery at Wareham after the ninth century is the record of the death of Abbess Wulfwynn of Wareham in the *Anglo-Saxon Chronicle* for 982. However, it is impossible to say if Wareham nunnery had had a continuous history from the ninth century until the time of Wulfwyn, or whether we should see Wareham as an example of a short-lived attempt to refound an earlier West Saxon nunnery during a period of monastic revival, for Wulfwyn may have been the woman of that name who was a kinswoman of Æthelmaer, the founder of Cerne Abbey, and thus a member of a leading noble line (descended from King Æthelred I) who were patrons of monastic reform.[37] There is no certain reference to a nunnery in Wareham after Wulfwyn's tenure as abbess.[38]

Although the West Saxon royal house was the only one to survive to the end of the ninth century, its early nunneries scarcely had a better survival rate than those of other kingdoms, partly perhaps because they were associated with rival lines of the royal house. Nor is there much evidence for a wave of new nunnery founding before the reign of Alfred, though there is a tradition recorded in verse in the fifteenth-century *Chronicon Wilodunense* that King Ecgbert was the founder of the nunnery at Wilton which, in spite of the many unsatisfactory features of this work, must be allowed some credence.[39] According to the *Chronicon* the church at Wilton was founded in 800 by 'Erle Wolstonus', who is identified in the poem with Ealdorman Weohstan of Wiltshire who died in battle against the Hwicce in 802,[40] but was converted to a nunnery by King Ecgbert in 830 at the request of his sister 'Elburga', the widow of 'Wolstonus'.[41] A subsequent reorganization and rebuilding of the nunnery by Alfred is recorded.[42] The pattern of a king founding a nunnery for a widowed sister is certainly one that is compatible with Anglo-

Saxon practice, but the poem as a whole does not inspire confidence in its historical accuracy, and one is left with the suspicion that its author was making creative
use of the *Anglo-Saxon Chronicle* entry for 802 in which the first reference to the
Wilsaetan appears. Ecgbert's father Ealhmund is wrongly identified as St
Alhmund, a Northumbrian prince murdered in 800 and culted in Mercia,[43] and
there is no corroboration of the existence of 'Elburga', or of Abbess Radegund and
her father Earl Æthelstan of Wiltshire of the refoundation of Alfred's time (though
there was an Ealdorman Æthelhelm of Wiltshire in the latter part of Alfred's
reign).[44] The alternative tradition, one that can scarcely be regarded as more
reliable, is that Wilton was founded by Edward the Elder as recorded in a forged
charter in the Wilton cartulary.[45] According to William of Malmesbury, King
Edward the Elder's second wife Ælfflaed (daughter of Ealdorman Æthelhelm of
Wiltshire) was buried there, together with two of their daughters, Eadflaed and
Æthelhild, who were perhaps members of the community.[46] The association with
Wilton of Edward's daughter Eadflaed seems to be confirmed by a grant of 937
from King Athelstan to the *collegio Christicolarum* of Wilton said to have been
made for her sake,[47] and it is probably safe to assume that the Wilton community
was in existence by the reign of Athelstan.[48] The memory of Ælfflaed and her
daughters was eclipsed later in the tenth century when Queen Wulfthryth
separated from her husband King Edgar in 963 or 964 to become abbess of
Wilton. Their daughter Edith was brought up at Wilton and became Wilton's
most significant saint after the translation of her remains some time between 997
and 1000.[49]

Royal foundations in the late ninth and tenth centuries

A pattern of royal foundation and support for nunneries identified with the ruling
house can be traced with greater confidence from the reign of Alfred who founded
the nunnery of Shaftesbury for his daughter Æthelgifu in *c.* 888.[50] Æthelgifu may
have been consecrated to God in childhood, as Asser's words perhaps imply,[51] in
which case she must have been raised in another West Saxon nunnery – Wimborne
still seems to have been a nunnery at this time, and Wareham and Wilton are other
possible candidates. The tradition later recorded at Shaftesbury in a forged foundation charter of the late eleventh or twelfth century was that Æthelgifu had been
vowed to the church because of ill-health.[52] The tradition may be valid, but her
health was evidently sufficiently robust for her to be abbess of the new foundation,
as Asser makes clear.[53] What we know of the chronology of the lives of the siblings
on either side of her, Edward and Ælfthryth, suggests she may have been only in
her mid-teens at the time of her appointment.[54] Shaftesbury was subsequently
favoured by other members of the royal house.[55] Eadgifu, the third wife of Edward
the Elder, may have entered the community at some point after her husband's
death in 925. The Shaftesbury cartulary contains a grant of land at Felpham in
Sussex to her in 953 from her son King Eadred in which she is described as *famulus*

dei, and this estate was part of the Shaftesbury holdings in Domesday Book.[56] Queen Ælfgifu, the wife of King Edmund and the mother of kings Eadwig and Edgar, was buried in the abbey after her death in 944.[57] It was Æflgifu, rather than Æthelgifu, who became the patron saint of the community. Her cult seems to have been well established by the 970s when Æthelweard and Lantfred both record that many miracles and cures had been effected at her tomb.[58] But her cult was ultimately to be eclipsed at Shaftesbury by that of her murdered grandson Edward the Martyr, whose remains were transferred from Wareham to Shaftesbury in 979, and translated in order for him to become a saint in 1001.[59]

The second new foundation with Alfredian associations was the Nunnaminster of Winchester, later known as St Mary's Abbey, which was founded by Alfred's widow Ealhswith following his death in 899.[60] Ealhswith died in 902,[61] before work on Nunnaminster was completed, and was buried in New Minster which had been founded, at least in part, as a burial place for Alfred and his family.[62] It is therefore not surprising that the memory of Ealhswith was eclipsed at Nunnaminster by the reputation of her granddaughter Eadburh, the daughter of Edward the Elder and his third wife Eadgifu,[63] who entered the community at the age of three before her father's death in 924.[64] Eadburh is said to have died in her thirtieth year, and her translation and cult may date from the episcopate of Bishop Æthelwold of Winchester (963–984).[65] There was possibly one further royal abbess of Nunnaminster. Eadgifu, who was Abbess of Nunnaminster in the second half of the tenth century, is identified in one document as king's daughter,[66] but unless this is an allusion to Edgar's daughter Edith whom Goscelin believed was given control of Nunnaminster,[67] it is not clear whose daughter she might have been.

Nunnaminster, Shaftesbury and Wilton are the only three new nunneries which can be said with some certainty to have been established before the reign of King Edgar (959–975). All three were left gifts in the will of King Eadred, and are the only female communities mentioned in it.[68] Claims for other nunneries as royal foundations of the first half of the tenth century appear dubious on close examination and are dependent on post-Conquest evidence alone. One of these is Polesworth (War.) where, according to the Anglo-Saxon list of saints' resting-places known as *Secgan,* a St Edith (Eadgyth) was buried.[69] Matthew Paris appears to be the first of the later historians to identify this Edith as the sister of King Athelstan who had been married to King Sihtric, and says that she ended her days there as a widow.[70] The identification can be doubted on a number of grounds. First, William of Malmesbury, who seems to have had access to detailed genealogical information on the children of Edward the Elder (though his source is unfortunately not known), says that he was unable to discover the name of his daughter by Ecgwynn who married Sihtric.[71] He does show though that one of Edward's six daughters by Ælfflaed was called Edith/Eadgyth and, although Edward had an exceptionally large number of daughters, it is unlikely that he gave two of them the same name. Therefore the name of his daughter who married Sihtric is not likely to have been Edith. An alternative version connects the supposed Edith, widow of

Sihtric, with Tamworth rather than Polesworth,[72] while others make Edith a daughter of King Ecgbert of Wessex and connect her with the legends involving the much earlier St Edith of Aylesbury and her associates St Osyth and St Modwenna; the latter is said to have cured Ecgbert's son Æthelwulf of leprosy.[73] In Chapter 1 it was suggested that St Edith of Polesworth was more likely to have been in origin a Mercian saint of the seventh or eighth centuries,[74] and this would better suit the positioning of her entry in the first half of the *Secgan* with other early saints whose burial places are identified as being on rivers.[75] It is possible that relics of an earlier St Edith were acquired for Polesworth in the tenth century, and then subsequently moved to Tamworth.[76] The issue of Edith and Polesworth needs to be separated from the question of whether there were nuns at Polesworth before the Norman Conquest. Dugdale preserves an account of their expulsion to Oldbury and subsequent return to Polesworth under new patronage,[77] but there is no confirmation of this in earlier sources or in Domesday Book.[78]

The other nunnery often claimed wrongly as a pre-Edgarian foundation of the West Saxon house is Romsey (Hants). The claim is one that is frequently repeated in secondary literature,[79] but appears to rest on misreading and a misidentification of the name of Æthelflaed, the 'royal' saint of Romsey, as Ælfflaed, in spite of the correct version of her name appearing in *Secgan*,[80] the *Liber Vitae* of Hyde Abbey[81] and the oldest surviving version of her life.[82] The starting point of the confusion may well have been an entry for 967 in the *Chronicle of John of Worcester* recording that King Edgar 'established nuns in the monastery (*monasterium*) of Romsey, which his grandfather, Edward the Elder . . . had built'.[83] The chronicle does not say that King Edward had founded a nunnery at Romsey, but this was what was subsequently inferred, and William of Malmesbury's account of the daughters of Edward the Elder was subsequently adapted to state that 'Elfleda' the eldest was buried at Romsey[84] – in spite of the fact that William gives her name as Eadflaed and associates her with Wilton, where her mother, who was called Ælfflaed, was also buried.[85] The tradition preserved in the *Lives* of Æthelflaed of Romsey is that she was the daughter of Ealdorman Æthelwold of East Anglia and Brihtgifu/Brihtwine.[86] The death of Æthelwold in *c.* 962 enabled King Edgar to marry his widow Ælfthryth, stepmother of Æthelflaed, as his third wife,[87] and, according to the *Lives*, the foundation of Romsey was by way of discharging their obligations to provide for her stepdaughter.[88] She was brought up there by its first abbess Maerwynn, and subsequently became the nunnery's third abbess.[89] The earliest extant evidence for a nunnery at Romsey, in the form of charters and a reference in the *Anglo-Saxon Chronicle* for 972, is from the reign of Edgar.[90]

Queen Ælfthryth is even more closely associated with the foundation of the two remaining new royal nunneries of the tenth century, Amesbury and Wherwell. A confirmation of privileges from her son King Æthelred II to the community at Wherwell provides the earliest evidence for Ælfthryth's role in 'diligently building up' the nunnery.[91] Narratives purporting to describe the circumstances of foundation date from after the Norman Conquest, and link

Ælfthryth's patronage with her need for expiation following her involvement in the murder of her stepson Edward the Martyr,[92] a tale which had grown in the telling, for Ælfthryth is not explicitly implicated in the earliest accounts of Edward's death.[93] Even the Wherwell cartulary recorded the guilt of the abbey's foundress, while her obituary claims that she founded the house 'to beg Christ's pardon for the death of her wounded step-son Edward and the shedding of his blood'.[94] However, as Diana Coldicott has shown, another entry in the Wherwell cartulary casts rather a different light on the circumstances of foundation.[95] It dates the house's origins to 962 and names the founder as Alfred, son of Osgar, ealdorman of Devon, who is said to have been buried in the church.[96] No ealdorman by the name of Osgar is known, but Ælfthryth's father was called Ordgar and was ealdorman in the west country. Was Alfred therefore an otherwise recorded brother of Ælfthryth and the original founder of the nunnery, or, at least, of a significant church on the site? Ælfthryth is said to have spent her last years at Wherwell and is presumed to have died there, but it is not claimed that she took any specific vows.[97] Less evidence survives about her involvement with Amesbury, but she is described as founder of the nunnery in the *Chronicle* of John of Worcester.[98] Finberg drew attention to similarities between Æthelred's confirmation of privileges to Wherwell and what seems to have been a similar grant to Amesbury, partly excerpted in fifteenth-century Exchequer records.[99] Furthermore, both grants seem to have been to the same abbess, called 'Heanfled' in the Wherwell charter and 'Heahpled' in the Amesbury document,[100] supporting the idea that the two houses had a common founder in Ælfthryth who had entrusted their supervision to one individual. A daughter or stepdaughter of Ælfthryth who may have been raised in Wherwell nunnery as an abbess in the reign of Edward the Confessor is described as his sister, though she is not named.[101] The Domesday Book entries show Amesbury and Wherwell to have been significantly poorer than the other nunneries patronized by the royal house in the tenth and eleventh centuries. Their modest holdings may be attributed to relatively late foundation towards the end of the period in which the royal houses were most active in their support for nunneries.[102]

Connections and comparisons

In founding and supporting six new nunneries in the late ninth and tenth centuries for daughters and ex-queens, the family of Alfred was conforming to an established aspect of court culture in the West in the ninth and tenth centuries. West Saxon links with the Carolingian and Ottonian courts would have provided reinforcement for the idea of entry into the religious life as appropriate for royal women. Some members of the West Saxon royal house had even had the opportunity to visit continental nunneries. As Simon Keynes has demonstrated, the entry of the names of Alfred and his father Æthelwulf in the *Liber Vitae* of San Salvatore in Brescia suggests that they visited this aristocratic nunnery while travelling to Rome in the 850s, as on another occasion did Æthelwulf's sister and brother-in-law Queen Æthelswith and King Burgred of Mercia accompanied by men and women of their court.[103] San Salvatore provides an excellent example of a nunnery which was supported by, and perhaps was considered to provide support for, successive regimes in northern Italy. It had been founded in the 750s by King Desiderius and Queen Ansa of the Lombards for their daughter Ansilperga.[104] In the ninth century the nunnery was granted in succession to women of the Carolingian royal house. It belonged first to Judith, wife of Louis the Pious, and then to Ermengard, wife of Lothair I from whom it passed to her daughter Gisela, who, unlike her immediate predecessors, actually seems to have taken religious vows there. Most of the Carolingian women had the position of *rectrix*, while an abbess oversaw the religious life of the convent; for a period Gisela was both abbess and *rectrix*. Headship passed from Gisela to her two nieces Gisela and Ermengard, and then to Angilberga, wife of Louis II and sister of Charles the Fat under whom many of the dispersed Carolingian principalities were controlled briefly by one ruler again. In the early tenth century control of the nunnery passed to a new regime and was in the hands of Berta, daughter of Berengar I.[105]

Support for royal nunneries was also an integral part of Ottonian court culture, and had its roots in the ninth century when, following conversion, leading Saxon families, including the Liudolfings who were the ancestors of the Ottonians, founded convents for family members with an enthusiasm echoing that of Anglo-Saxon dynasties in the late seventh century.[106] Gandersheim and Quedlinburg, in particular, were major cultural centres controlled by daughters of the imperial house, and concerned not only with memorializing its members, but with the history of the family. Widukind dedicated his *History of the Saxons* to Abbess Matilda of Quedlinburg, daughter of Otto I (912–973), while Abbess Gerberga of Gandersheim, Otto's niece, commissioned a biography of her uncle from Hrostwitha, who was a member of the community at Gandersheim.[107] These powerful royal abbesses might also have had political roles. Abbess Matilda of Quedlinburg, together with her mother Adelheid and sister-in-law Theophanu, took over the regency of the young Otto III in 984, and when he came of age his sister Sophie, a canonness of Gandersheim, kept him company at court for two years, carrying out many of the duties of a consort.[108] The West Saxon dynasty had direct links with the Ottonians.[109] Edward the Elder's daughter Edith married the future Otto I at Quedlinburg in 929, an occasion for the exchange of gifts and embassies on a lavish scale. Edith's granddaughter, Abbess Matilda of Essen, was in contact with Ealdorman Æthelweard, a descendant of King Æthelred I, who dedicated his Latin version of the *Anglo-Saxon Chronicle* to her, and in his Preface traced their common descent and what he knew of the foreign marriages of his family, as he had done for her previously in a letter.[110] Of the English nunneries, there is direct evidence of links between Wilton and continental houses, albeit male ones. King Edgar recruited Radbod from Rheims and Benno from Trier as tutors for his daughter Edith.[111] The cycle of wall-paintings on the Life of Christ which Benno executed at Wilton were seen and recorded by Goscelin, but it also seems that Benno may have taken influences from Anglo-Saxon art back with him to Germany.[112]

Important though these foreign links and exemplars were, we should not forget that the West Saxons were subject also to influences closer to home. Alfred's wife Ealhswith was descended through her mother Eadburh from the Mercian royal house,[113] among whom a tradition of royal women entering royal nunneries had remained significant throughout the eighth and ninth centuries, and in particular had been used to underpin cadet lines when they came to power.[114] It was probably through their mother that Ealhswith's brother Ealdorman Æthelwulf had inherited the lordship of Winchcombe Abbey, a former royal nunnery of great significance for the families of kings Coenwulf and Ceolwulf.[115] Asser says that Eadburh lived after her husband's death as a 'chaste widow', perhaps implying the taking of a religious vow.[116] Ealhswith herself when widowed founded Nunnaminster in Winchester, and it may have been her expectations as a Mercian woman of royal descent that were a significant factor in the entry of her daughter Æthelgifu into the church and in the foundation of Shaftesbury nunnery for her. Another feature of importance in Wessex in the tenth century which may have owed something to Mercian connections was the cult of the royal saint.[117] As far as we know, none of the early West Saxon rulers were culted, and the only known early West Saxon royal saints were Cuthburh and Cwenburh of Wimborne, and we cannot be certain that their cults existed before the late Saxon period, as they are first recorded in the *Secgan*.[118] The Mercians, on the other hand, had many royal saints from the seventh to the ninth centuries.[119] The first West Saxon to demonstrate a comprehensive use of saints' cults for political purposes was Alfred's daughter Æthelflaed, who as 'Lady of the Mercians' transferred a number of earlier Mercian and Northumbrian saints to new centres, such as Gloucester and Chester, associated with herself and her husband Ealdorman Æthelred.[120] Her activities included the transfer from Bardney to the New Minster at Gloucester of the remains of St Oswald,[121] who in the tenth century was apparently being promoted as a kinsman by the West Saxon royal house,[122] perhaps because he had been godfather to King Cynegils. The cult of Edward the Martyr at the end of the tenth century stands at the end of an Anglo-Saxon tradition of cults of murdered princes in which St Wigstan at Repton and St Cynehelm at Winchcombe (both royal Mercian nunneries) played conspicuous parts.[123]

But although there are broad parallels between the later West Saxon patronage of royal nunneries and that of the earlier Anglo-Saxon royal houses and of the Ottonians, there are also some significant contrasts. A leading role had been played in the early Anglo-Saxon double houses by royal daughters moving back to their home provinces after their marriages had ended. But in the tenth and eleventh centuries princesses often no longer returned home in such circumstances, but stayed in their husbands' provinces and took their dower there. None of Edward the Elder's daughters who married abroad returned to die at home (at least two predeceased their husbands), and Æthelweard was forced to admit that the family had lost track of one of them.[124] At least one of them, Eadgifu, is known to have ended her days in a foreign convent that had been a wedding gift from her first husband Charles the Simple.[125] Nor did Emma of Normandy return to her home province after the death of Cnut, and she died in Winchester in 1051.[126] The princesses who went into the church in later Anglo-Saxon England tended to have been entered at a young age, like Eadburh of Nunnaminster and Edith of Wilton. Perhaps it is just chance that none of them seem to have lived to a ripe old age and become the equivalent of Matilda of Quedlinburg or Sophie of Gandersheim, although Edith as presented in her *Vita* shows signs of potential in that direction.[127] But the early deaths of Eadburh and Edith, and the reputed illness of Æthelgifu of Shaftesbury, who may also have died young, does raise the question of whether the later princesses who went into the church were sent there because they showed early signs of debility, leaving more robust sisters for diplomatic marriages.[128] One of the surprising features of the later Saxon nunneries is how few princesses who went into the church became abbesses. Only Æthelgifu of Shaftesbury and the unnamed sister of Edward the Confessor at Wherwell are known to have done so,[129] unless the royal stepdaughter Æthelflaed of Romsey is included, or the single reference to Eadgifu, Abbess of Nunnaminster, as a king's daughter be allowed.[130]

Earlier Anglo-Saxon kings had married princesses from other Anglo-Saxon kingdoms, but the success of the West Saxon dynasty meant that by the tenth century this resource was no longer available. Nor, with the exception of Æthelred II's marriage to Emma of Normandy, did they seek brides from foreign ruling houses. Instead, they married daughters of leading aristocratic houses and thus cemented important alliances with the nobility. Thus whereas in the seventh and eighth centuries the widowed queens who became abbesses were of royal birth (and had returned to their home provinces), their tenth-century successors had achieved royal status only through marriage. These queens from the nobility, together with their families, were important patrons of the later Saxon nunneries even if few of them became abbesses. Succession disputes and noble factions in the tenth century did not involve rival branches of the royal house, as it seems to have been accepted that only sons of kings were eligible for the throne.[131] Instead they were centred around the rival claims of kings' sons by different queens.[132] Patronage of individual nunneries can sometimes be associated with particular queens and their families, and the nunneries may be seen as supporting these women and the claims of their sons in ways analogous to that given earlier to rival royal lines. The royal associations must also have helped enhance the prestige of their families, as they sought to establish themselves in key positions within the kingdom. Shaftesbury, for instance, became closely associated with the family of Queen Ælfgifu, wife of King Edmund, a connection that seems to have been made before Ælfgifu's burial there in 944. Ælfgifu's mother Wynflaed was a benefactress of Shaftesbury and is identified in a charter, confirming a gift of land from her, as the maternal grandmother of King Edgar.[133] She has usually been identified with the *religiosa femina* Wynflaed, who was granted an adjoining estate by King Edmund in 942 that subsequently came into the nunnery's possession.[134] Her designation as 'a religious woman' implies some association with the community, perhaps as a vowed widow. She may also have been the Wynflaed for whom a will survives, for the testatrix seems to have had a similar religious status,[135] and was a beneficiary of Shaftesbury, but the identification is not certain.[136] Wynflaed of the will had a mother called Beorhtwyn, and an estate granted to a woman of this name also became part of Shaftesbury's holdings.[137] The cult of Ælfgifu at Shaftesbury may be seen as supporting the status of the royal family, and particularly the claims of Ælfgifu's sons by King Edmund, Eadwig and Edgar, and that context may explain why their paternal grandmother and supporter, the former Queen Eadgifu, had chosen to be associated with the nunnery. But the cult may also be read as enhancing the status of Ælfgifu's own family, and her mother may have played a significant role in promoting her claims to sainthood. Dual royal and noble interests may explain why Ælfgifu and not its foundress Æthelgifu, daughter of Alfred, was recognized as a saint at Shaftesbury.

The link between Wilton and the ealdormanry of Wiltshire, epitomized in the tradition of its foundation by Ealdorman Weohstan in the *Chronicon Vilodunense*, may explain the involvement of both Queen Ælfflaed and her daughters, and Queen Wulfthryth and her daughter Edith with Wilton nunnery. According to William of Malmesbury, Ælfflaed was the daughter of Ealdorman Æthelhelm of Wiltshire, and he may be the Ealdorman 'Æthelstan' of the *Chronicon Vilodunense* associated with major patronage of the house in the reign of Alfred.[138] Such a connection may explain the choice of Wilton as Ælfflaed's place of burial and that of two of her daughters who may have been members of the community. Æthelstan's predecessor as ealdorman of Wiltshire was Wulfhere, who may have been the brother of Queen Wulfthryth, the wife of Æthelred I.[139] His grandson Wulfgar was later ealdorman of eastern Wessex which included Wiltshire.[140] It will be noted that these three individuals have names beginning with 'Wulf', like several of the relatives of the second Queen Wulfthryth, the wife of King Edgar, who retired to Wilton; all her other known kin had names alliterating on 'W', presumably indicating a deliberate choice of nomenclature and leading names in this family. Members included her cousin Wulfhild (who narrowly escaped seduction by Edgar), whose father was Wulfhelm, and an aunt called Wenflaed.[141] Another kinswoman 'Wulwenna' (Wulfwaen?) was also a member of the Wilton community,[142] where both Wulfthryth and Wulfhild were living when Edgar developed his desire to marry one of them. Traditionally, Wilton was believed to have been founded by Ealdorman Weohstan of Wiltshire, or possibly by a man called Wulfstan.[143] It cannot be proven that all these individuals with names beginning with 'W', and a connection with the ealdormanry of Wiltshire or Wilton, were related, but that could be a plausible hypothesis. Wilton Nunnery may have been not just a 'royal' foundation, but one closely connected with leading aristocratic families of the shire for which Wilton was the shire town.[144] It is not surprising that the ambitious Earl Godwin of Wessex saw Wilton as an appropriate place for the education of his daughter Edith, who bore (or acquired) the name of its most significant saint who was both a princess and a descendant of this key aristocratic house.[145]

Ælfthryth who supplanted Wulfthryth of Wilton as queen and wife of King Edgar had her own nexus of nunneries. In patronizing the nunnery at Wherwell she may have been developing a religious house that had been founded by one of her family,[146] but intriguingly, in the early 960s Wherwell appears to have been the residence of Wenflaed, aunt of Wulfthryth and Wulfhild, and the place of Edgar's attempted seduction of the latter.[147] Wulfhild was compensated with the position of Abbess of Barking, but, according to her *Vita*, Ælfthryth subsequently plotted to have her expelled and she withdrew to Horton (Dorset), described as *hereditarium monasterium suum*, presumably a minster belonging to her family.[148] However, Horton appears subsequently as connected with the family of Ælfthryth, for her brother Ordulf is described as patron and is said to have died there, though the information comes from what seems to have been a rather garbled account by William of Malmesbury of the family of Ordulf and their foundation at Tavistock.[149] The interrelationship of these lands and associated nunneries among the families of Wulfthryth and Ælfthryth is hard to unravel completely, but the explanation must lie in the peculiar circumstances in which Wulfthryth, after a marriage of little more than a year to Edgar, withdrew to become Abbess of Wilton and thus allowed Edgar to marry the recently widowed Ælfthryth with whom reputedly he had been infatuated for some time.[150] Subsequently the issue of which of the children of Edgar should rule in the disturbed years following his death was one in which his two former queens were actively involved. The expulsion of Wulfhild from Barking is likely to have been one result of the hostility between them, and the traditions preserved at Wilton concerning Edith, the daughter of Wulfthryth and Edgar, seem to have been shaped by the politics of these years.[151] It was identification with particular noble houses, in the context of factionalism around a disputed succession, that drew these nunneries into the political events of the 970s.

Wulfthryth was exceptional among the group of ex-queens from the ranks of nobility in becoming an abbess. Eadgifu may have had an association as a vowed widow with Shaftesbury; Ælfthryth and Edith, widow of Edward the Confessor, seem to have spent part of their later years in retirement at the two nunneries Wherwell and Wilton, with which they had close associations, but without any evidence that they took religious vows.[152] Ælfflaed, the second wife of King Edward the Elder, is sometimes stated to have separated from him to enter a religious community, but this rests on an uncertain identification.[153] Not even Ælfgifu, who was separated from her husband King Eadwig by Archbishop Odo on the grounds that they were too closely related,[154] seems to have been obliged to enter a religious community. If she can be identified with the Ælfgifu who left a will,[155] it would seem that she lived in retirement as an independent widow on extensive estates which had no doubt been provided by way of compensation. Emma too lived independently as a widow during the reigns of her two sons Hathacnut and Edward the Confessor.[156] By the later Anglo-Saxon period it had long been accepted that women could hold land in their own right, even if it was often entailed, so that wealthy widows could enjoy greater independence than in the period of the double houses, especially if protected by their relationship with the royal family.[157] There had also been an enhancement of the position of queen.[158] Widowed queens who had been consecrated had no need of further sacralization as abbesses to continue their status, and both Eadgifu and Ælfthryth seem to have dominated their daughters-in-law and been the major queens at court even after the deaths of their husbands.[159] Queenship may have been seen as coming to parallel kingship as an office sanctioned by God that was normally ended only by death. The active roles played by Eadgifu and Ælfthryth at court in early widowhood could have been seen as incompatible with roles as abbesses, especially as the movement towards purer monastic standards developed in strength in the course of the tenth century.[160] Instead, Ælfthryth became a lay protector of the nunneries in the *Regularis Concordia*,[161] and was thus a *rectrix* of nunneries like many of the Carolingian queens,[162] who may indeed have provided a model for the new definitions of queenship in her time.[163] Entry into a nunnery could come to have demeaning associations for queens as it had done for kings and princes at an earlier date; Edward the Confessor's desire to place his queen Edith in a nunnery was meant to signal her withdrawal from active political involvement and was part of an attempt to humiliate her family.[164] Monastic reform ushered in other changes as well. One of the expectations of the reform movement was that abbesses would be elected from within their communities,[165] and it is probable that the majority of abbesses of the later tenth and eleventh centuries, whose family backgrounds are largely unknown, can be accounted for in this way.[166] Royal patronage remained essential for the successful late nunneries, but royal personnel increasingly became a less significant element within the foundations.

Nunneries and the monastic reform movement

By the mid-ninth century, England, which had once been so rich in monasteries, seems to have possessed few religious houses, either male or female, which would have qualified for that title, even allowing for a broad definition of the term 'monastic'.[167] The threat had come from two major directions. On the one hand, from bishops eager to turn proprietary monasteries into secular, male communities under their supervision, and on the other, from kings and nobles eager to absorb or reabsorb lands held by religious communities into their own landholdings, a process aided by the disruption of viking attacks.[168] One must also allow for noble houses wishing to keep a firm hold of minsters on their family estates, and being reluctant to tie up family lands in permanent monastic foundations,[169] though isolated references to abbesses of minster churches, like Wulfwyn of Wareham, may indicate either attempts to found or refound nunneries on noble estates or the type of temporary female headship of a family minster that may be occasionally glimpsed in pre-viking sources.[170] By the end of the ninth century a movement to reverse some of these trends had begun, spearheaded by Alfred's foundations at Athelney and Shaftesbury, and the number of royal grants to *religiosae feminae* suggest a continuing enthusiasm in aristocratic as well as royal circles for women living by religious vows, even if not all of them lived in formal nunneries.[171] In the first half of the tenth century nunneries must have formed a major part of the communities which could be described as 'monastic', even if in continental terms they probably would have been categorized as convents of canonesses, like the great Ottonian foundations such as Quedlinburg and Gandersheim.[172] One of the characteristics of these communities was that individual canonesses could retain private wealth,[173] something which seems to have been a feature of Anglo-Saxon royal nunneries for much of the tenth century as well. Eadburh of Nunnaminster enjoyed an estate provided for her by her half-brother Athelstan, which does not seem to have passed to the community,[174] and Wulfthryth and her daughter Edith used their private wealth to endow Wilton with relics, a new church and ecclesiastical art.[175] However, the distinction between nuns and canonesses is not found in Anglo-Saxon England, though a distinction was drawn in the later Anglo-Saxon period between nuns and vowesses, who lived in their own homes or in small, temporary communities.[176] These two different categories may be referred to in William of Malmesbury's careful contrast between the two daughters of Edward the Elder as *deo voventes Edfleda in sacrato Ethelhilda in laico tegimine*, 'vowed to God, Eadflaed taking the veil and Æthelhild in lay attire'.[177] According to William, both princesses were buried at Wilton and so both may have been associated with the community, but with only Eadflaed living a communal life and presumably following a stricter personal regime than her sister. Varieties of religious practice within the same institution may not have been that unusual in the first half of the tenth century. Something perhaps not dissimilar is attested in the same period in some male communities such as Glastonbury, where the young Æthelwold and Dunstan followed personal monastic ways of life in what seems to have been a mixed community of monks, secular clerks and lay youths receiving an education.[178] In addition, male and female communities might have had vowed women associated who lived in their own houses, such as Wynflaed at Shaftesbury and Æthelflaed, niece of Athelstan, at Glastonbury.[179] Both Wilton and Glastonbury were also used for the education of noble girls and boys respectively, who would leave to follow secular careers.[180]

Patronage of nunneries, and of individual vowed women (who might dwell in their own homes or in small communities),[181] was only one manifestation of royal support for greater investment in monasticism. Both men and women of the royal house were also generous in their support for the monastic reformers Æthelwold and Dunstan, and these charismatic men seem ultimately to have been more successful than the nunneries in the amount of royal patronage they acquired.[182] At the time of Domesday Book, Wilton, the richest of the royal nunneries, was only the thirteenth wealthiest religious community when male and female houses are grouped together.[183] Nevertheless, the nunneries were involved in the reform movement. Abbesses attended the council of 970 to 973 which resulted in the production of the new reformed Rule for Anglo-Saxon religious houses, the *Regularis Concordia*, in which nuns were treated equally with male religious,[184] and a translation of the *Rule of St Benedict* into Old English was made specifically for use in nunneries.[185] However, of the royal nunneries only Nunnaminster is specifically said to have been reformed,[186] and it is difficult to know how strictly all the provisions of the Benedictine Rule were followed within them. We can say that at least three features of reformed monasticism – corporate ownership of property, election of abbesses by the community and strict enclosure – can be found more in evidence among the main Anglo-Saxon nunneries in the period following 970, and can arguably be seen as the result of the reform movement.

The most significant element for the future survival of the West Saxon nunneries was the recognition of corporate ownership of lands as opposed to estates being regarded as private property of individual abbesses and nuns, perhaps granted for life only. Insecurity of tenure, and the threat of repossession of lands by the founding family, had been a major problem for nunneries throughout the Anglo-Saxon period, and had continued into the tenth century when many of the nunneries were endowed from royal estates that could apparently be subject to recall.[187] In 968 Wilton convent obtained confirmation of its ownership of the lands previously granted *temporaliter* to Abbess Wulfthryth, presumably as part of her settlement on separation from King Edgar.[188] Wherwell received a comparable confirmation of its lands in 1002, significantly not long after the death of its patroness Queen Ælfthryth.[189] Its sister foundation of Amesbury may have received a similar confirmation at about the same time, but only a brief summary of the text survives.[190] Whether the other nunneries acquired similar grants of confirmation is not known; Shaftesbury's foundation charter is a forgery probably of post-Conquest date, perhaps implying that no suitable charter or later confirmation of privileges existed.[191] However, grants to Shaftesbury from the 960s onwards are made explicitly to the community as a whole,[192] whereas earlier grants had often been to individual members.

The confirmations to Wherwell and Amesbury both included the right of the communities to elect their own abbesses, subject to diocesan approval. The recent past had contained examples of abbesses being imposed upon communities when Wulfthryth and Wulfhild had been created abbesses of Wilton and Barking respectively, apparently through royal patronage. Presumably both replaced existing abbesses whose identities are not known. Wulfhild was subsequently herself expelled from Barking through the intervention of Queen Ælfthryth, who had been given supervisory powers over the nunneries in the *Regularis Concordia*, and the clergy of her community.[193] However, there are indications in the *Lives* of Wulfhild and Edith that later abbesses at Barking and Wilton had been members of the community before their elevations to office. Wulfhild had foreseen that

Leofflaed, a member of the community, would one day be Abbess of Barking,[194] while the dead St Edith appeared to foretell the appointments of both Brihtgifu and her successor Ælfgifu, who were members of the community.[195] These accounts suggest that the idea of election of abbess by the communities was sufficiently novel as to require saintly endorsement. The *Lives* of Æthelflaed of Romsey also emphasize that both Æthelflaed and her predecessor were chosen from the community as abbesses,[196] and one of the *Orthodoxorum* group of charters, which were particularly concerned with establishing principles of free election, survives for Romsey.[197]

The best evidence for the reform period bringing new concepts of strict enclosure to one of the nunneries is for Nunnaminster in Winchester, where a combination of charter, excavation and later topographical evidence shows a replanning of the urban estate on which Nunnaminster was situated so that the nunnery was firmly separated from the tenements of its tenants and provided with a substantial enclosure wall.[198] There was an adjustment of the bounds of all the Winchester minsters so that each could have its own discrete enclosure, with Nunnaminster compensated for the loss of a watercourse with two mills from the Abbot of New Minster.[199] Passing references imply a substantial enclosure wall was also a feature of Wilton nunnery.[200] Rebuilding or the foundation of new churches was also a characteristic of the tenth-century reform movement.[201] The chapel at Bradford-on-Avon built by the nunnery at Shaftesbury to house the remains of Edward the Martyr is one of the most sophisticated buildings of the period to survive,[202] while the great stone rood of Romsey is testimony to the high standards in its church, parts of which have been recovered in excavation.[203] Excavations have also shown that the main church of Nunnaminster was rebuilt as a fine stone building with a western apse to replace the earlier timber structure.[204] However, the chapel of St Denys, with its wall-paintings on the Life of Christ by Benno of Trier, commissioned by St Edith for Wilton, and the stone church which Queen Edith had built to replace the earlier timber structure are known only from written descriptions.[205]

The reform movement enabled the royal nunneries to establish greater independence from intervention by the royal house, though perhaps inevitably one price of that distancing was an apparent decline in royal interest and support for the communities, reflected, for instance, in the relatively poor endowments for Amesbury and Wherwell in Domesday Book compared to those of the longer established nunneries.[206] Nunnaminster also seems to have been significantly poorer than the other royal nunneries founded in the ninth or early tenth centuries,[207] and its interests may have been adversely affected by the two great male minsters of Winchester and by the close interest in its affairs by the acquisitive Bishop Æthelwold of Winchester, who was responsible for its reorganization in the later tenth century.[208] There were also limits to the independence that the communities could win within the church, for in writings of the reform period there are indications of a misogynistic assumption of the superiority of male celibates, with a concomitant suspicion of the threat women might pose towards their purity, that was to restrict the roles of religious women in succeeding centuries.[209] However, behind the reform there was a rhetoric of desire to return to the monasticized church of Bede's day that did not, as far as the main reformers were concerned, extend to a revival of the prominent female communities in that period. Their vision and ideal was purely male celibate communities controlled by monastic bishops, and they attracted substantial royal patronage in its pursuit. One of Bishop Æthelwold's major refoundations was the former double monastery of Ely. St Æthelthryth and her saintly kinswomen were honoured in the revived foundation,[210] and Æthelthryth received the accolade of a full-page miniature in the *Benedictional of St Æthelwold*,[211] but there was apparently no question of its being refounded as a community of women. None of the major reformers is known to have founded a nunnery, and the only new foundation sponsored by a leading ecclesiastic was Chatteris (Cambs.) founded between 1006 and 1016 by Eadnoth, Abbot of Ramsey and Bishop of Dorchester, for his sister Ælfwen.[212] Chatteris is the only nunnery, in addition to the seven whose histories have already been considered, to appear in Domesday Book as an ecclesiastical tenant-in-chief, though with an endowment of only thirty hides it was by far the poorest, which presumably explains its early demise.[213] The impetus of monastic revival may have stimulated interest among the nobility in reviving former nunneries, and this may account for the references to individual abbesses at Berkeley (Glos.),[214] St Mildrith's (Canterbury)[215] and Wareham.[216] These are places recorded in earlier centuries as having been ruled by an abbess, but where continuity as female communities cannot be demonstrated. In addition, the presence of abbesses at Reading and Leominster appears to have been short-lived. The two minsters probably had a continuous history from the seventh or eighth centuries, but they cannot be shown to have had women associated with them before the later Saxon period.[217] Abbess Leofrun of Reading is recorded in the *Liber Vitae* of Hyde Abbey,[218] and in Domesday Book Reading is said to have been held by Abbess 'Leveva' in the time of King Edward.[219] An abbess of Leominster was the subject of scandal when abducted by Swein in 1046,[220] but nuns were still present at Leominster in 1086, though subsequently its lands were used to endow Henry I's new foundation in Reading.[221] There are also examples from the later period of vowesses and female religious associated with male communities that suggest the desire for a religious life for women was widespread, but it was not to be met by a major foundation of new nunneries until the twelfth century.[222]

The Norman Conquest and after

The reigns of Cnut and Harthacnut disrupted the pattern of patronage of nunneries by the West Saxon royal house, but the link was restored in the reign of Edward the Confessor when one of his sisters can be found as Abbess of Wherwell, one of the nunneries founded by their grandmother Ælfthryth.[223] The ambitious

Earl Godwin had his daughter Edith educated at Wilton where she was seen as receiving the type of education to equip her for her future role as King Edward's consort.[224] After the Norman Conquest the 'royal' connotations of the West Saxon nunneries still seem to have beeen significant. In the aftermath of the Battle of Hastings and the subsequent rebellions, the Anglo-Saxon royal nunneries became safe havens for the female survivors of the old regime whose menfolk had been killed or exiled.[225] Wilton and Romsey seem to have been particularly favoured. Wilton may have benefited from the protection of Queen Edith, who had been educated at the nunnery and seems to have spent part of her widowhood there.[226] It may have been Edith's influence that ensured that when Abbess Ælfgifu died, probably in 1067, she was succeeded by her sister Godgifu rather than by a Norman appointee.[227] Among those who sought refuge at Wilton was Gunnhild, the daughter of Harold Godwinson.[228] On the other hand, Romsey was chosen by Christina, the sister of Edgar Aetheling, the true heir of the West Saxon royal line, and she may eventually have become abbess there. Romsey's identification with the Anglo-Saxon regime is confirmed by the attempt to develop a cult of Earl Waltheof who had been executed at Winchester in 1086. Anselm forbade any honour of oblation to be made for him and ordered the expulsion of his son from the nunnery.[229] Christina's sister Margaret, wife of King Malcolm Canmore, sent her daughters Mary and Edith-Matilda to be educated by their aunt at Romsey, and Edith-Matilda subsequently transferred to Wilton.[230] A number of the Anglo-Saxon women who had retreated to nunneries in the unsettled years immediately following King William's victory subsequently wished to come out again, and were allowed to do so by Lanfranc, who recognized that it had been fear of the French rather than love of God that had caused their temporary vocations.[231] His successor Anselm was faced with a greater dilemma when both Gunnhild and Edith-Matilda wished to leave Wilton to get married in spite of the fact that both had apparently taken monastic vows.[232] Gunnhild had hoped to be chosen as abbess, and when she was passed over eloped with Count Alan of Brittany who had gone to Wilton with a view to marrying Edith-Matilda. The latter argued that she had been veiled against her will, and William Rufus seems to have insisted upon it to remove her from the marriage market. Anselm was persuaded to release her which left her free to marry Rufus' brother Henry I. The Norman Conquest was an exceptional event with exceptional results, but one does wonder if the earlier conquest of Cnut had also resulted in a rush for the cloister. Cnut's take-over was of a very different nature to William's which had resulted in the virtual annihilation of the leading Anglo-Saxon noble families, but the long-drawn-out war with the Danish kings had resulted in a considerable loss of life among the nobility that would have left many widows and daughters without close male kin. The cloister may therefore have seemed an attractive haven for many women earlier in the eleventh century as well, which may explain the foundation of a number of apparently new but ultimately short-lived nunneries, such as Reading, and also account for the concern in the laws of Cnut's reign with women leaving the cloister to marry or have other sexual liaisons.[233] Gunnhild's and Edith-Matilda's expectations that they could easily withdraw from Wilton to marry may give us an insight into what may have been a not infrequent practice in the pre-Conquest houses in the tenth and eleventh centuries, when it had been regarded as possible for the apparently vowed Wulfhild to leave Wilton to marry Edgar; the status of her cousin Wulfthryth who did do both of these things is more ambiguous.[234] In the continental houses of canonesses it had apparently been accepted that members might withdraw to be married,[235] though such women had not necessarily made formal professions. Anselm's expectations of the English communities which he assumed to be regular Benedictine convents would have been rather different.

At the other royal nunneries, women with Norman names appear to have been appointed abbesses after the deaths of the last Anglo-Saxon incumbents, reflecting the pattern found in male communities as well.[236] At Shaftesbury a list of properties donated as dowries with new entrants reveals that daughters of the lesser Norman nobility, many of whom were landowners in the abbey's vicinity, were entering the community within a few years of the Norman Conquest.[237] This entry of girls from the ranks of the lesser nobility does not necessarily represent a distinct change in practice. Although we know about the women of the royal house who entered religious communities we know very little about the backgrounds of other nuns in the foundations they patronized. We cannot identify the families of any of the fifty-four nuns of Romsey in the eleventh century who are listed in New Minster's *Liber Vitae*.[238] A number of those whose daughters entered Shaftesbury after the Norman Conquest were royal officials and administrators in the south-west. Families in royal service are one of the groups who are very likely to have had access to the royal nunneries in the pre-Conquest period as well. Lands came into the possession of nunneries which had previously been granted to royal servants, and which might be granted out again to officials.[239] In 1066 many royal servants of both king and queen held land which had been granted out to nunneries or other religious houses in the past, and the cartularies of Wilton and Shaftesbury contain many charters to men in royal service which they had subsequently come to own,[240] such as the grants to the *ministri* Sigestan and Agemund by Kings Edgar and Cnut respectively which were among Shaftesbury's possessions in Domesday Book.[241] From such evidence one could suggest that in the pre-Conquest period, as well as after the Norman Conquest, the daughters and widows of royal officials were among the groups likely to have entered royal nunneries and that they might bring with them estates that had been granted originally to support their office-holder kinsmen in their official positions. The nunneries were sometimes successful in retaining control of the land, but in other cases the estates were reclaimed by the crown and subsequently granted out to others in royal service. As nunneries were also endowed with royal estates, some of which at one time had been held by royal officials, it is not surprising that there was sometimes confusion about a nunnery's right to certain lands.

What ultimately brought about a diminution of the Anglo-Saxon royal nunneries was failure to attract comparable support from the new regime and its successors. Neglect was not absolute, as some rulers valued the links the nunneries could provide with royal and saintly ancestors. Henry I stayed at least twice at the nunnery of Romsey where his wife Edith-Matilda had spent part of her childhood under the direction of her aunt Christina, and was a generous patron.[242] King Stephen's daughter Mary of Blois became abbess of Romsey for a short period, although she had not been a member of the community previously, but resigned her position in order to get married.[243] Other abbesses although not of royal birth might have had strong connections with the royal court. Cecily who became Abbess of Shaftesbury sometime after 1107 and her sister Hawise who became Abbess of Wilton were the sisters-in-law of Robert, Earl of Gloucester.[244] But many leading Normans and their successors preferred to sponsor their own foundations, many of which were outside England. William and his wife Matilda did not favour the Anglo-Saxon nunneries at all, but preferred their own foundations at Caen, where their daughter Matilda was abbess of the nunnery they had founded. The Anglo-Saxon royal nunneries continued to profit from the lands amassed in the pre-Conquest period, and their prestigious saints' cults for saintly patrons such as Edith at Wilton, Eadburh at Nunnaminster and Edward the Martyr at Shaftesbury continued to attract pilgrims and miracle-seekers up to the Reformation, but they did not add significantly to the landed endowments that had been established before the Conquest.

Conclusion

The endowment of nunneries for womenfolk of the royal house was important to the West Saxon royal house from the time of Alfred, if not the time of Ecgbert, as it had been for earlier royal dynasties. However, by the end of the Anglo-Saxon period, nunneries had ceased to be so significant either to kings as patrons or to women of the royal house as places where they would spend part of their lives. A number of factors contributed here. As the kings of Wessex became kings of England they ceased to have any Anglo-Saxon rivals, and as no major dynastic divisions occurred within the royal house there was no need to consolidate status and landholdings against prospective rivals. The sacral nature of kingship was emphasized in new ways, with development of the coronation service in particular stressing the quasi-sacerdotal powers of the king as God's representative on earth.[245] Queenship benefited as well, and a consecrated queen through that ceremony had status and powers that did not cease with the death of the king.[246] Like kings and princes in the earlier period, ex-queens did not want to prejudice their continuing influence in worldly affairs by retreating to nunneries in a period of reform that sought to emphasize the segregation of monastic communities from secular concerns. As women could inherit bookland, and widows hold it in their own right, there was less incentive for ex-queens to enter the church, as their prominent secular positions would usually guarantee that they could hold their lands unmolested.[247] Princesses who married out to other families no longer necessarily returned to their birth family on widowhood, and few of the princesses who did enter the church seem to have lived to an old age which might have brought them greater influence in the family circle. None of the leaders of tenth-century monastic reform championed nunneries, and the refoundation of the former double monastery of Ely as a male monastic community may be seen to typify the prejudices in favour of male over female monasticism that lay not far beneath the surface of the male leadership of the monastic reform movement and attracted royal patronage away from nunneries. Nevertheless, royal connections remained important to nunneries, which did not miss opportunities to draw such links to the attention of potential royal patrons,[248] but it was queens and their noble families who were key players in the promotion of the later nunneries. As Abbess of Wilton, ex-queen Wulfthryth was both a major patron of the monastic arts and a formidable opponent of the woman who had ousted her from the throne, Queen Ælfthryth, who founded her own network of nunneries. In many ways we can see a continuation of earlier rivalries between different royal kin-groups, in which nunneries had played an active role, in the factions that grew up around the offspring of rival queens and their families in the latter part of the tenth century. Although the monastic reformers wished to separate nunneries from the affairs of the world, this was not a realistic hope when nunneries were closely linked with the most powerful families in the kingdom. Events like the disputed succession after the death of Edgar, culminating in the murder of Edward the Martyr, saw nunneries directly involved in the politics of the period, but a more detailed examination of such topics is reserved for the final chapter (Chapter 5).

Notes

1. S. Keynes, 'King Alfred and the Mercians', in M. Blackburn and D. N. Dumville (eds), *Kings, Currency and Alliances* (Woodbridge, 1998), 1–45.
2. S. Foot, *Veiled Women*, 2 vols (Aldershot, 2000), II, 27–33; and see Chapter 2.
3. P. Stafford, 'Queens, nunneries and reforming churchmen: gender, religious status and reform in tenth- and eleventh-century England', *Past and Present*, 163 (1999), 3–35.
4. K. Cooke, 'Donors and daughters: Shaftesbury Abbey's benefactors, endowments and nuns c. 1086–1130', *Anglo-Norman Studies*, 12 (1989), 29–45.
5. D. Knowles and R. N. Hadcock, *Medieval Religious Houses: England and Wales*, 2nd edn (London, 1971), 253–5; J. Crick, 'The wealth, patronage and connections of women's houses in late Anglo-Saxon England', *Revue Bénédictine*, 109 (1999), 154–85. Nunnaminster/St Mary's Abbey seems to have underestimated its wealth in the *Valor Ecclesiasticus* of 1535, as it confessed the following year; see D. K. Coldicott, *Hampshire Nunneries before and after the Norman Conquest* (Chichester, 1989), 114.
6. Wills begin to appear from the mid-ninth century. For a recent study bringing out their relevance to the study of Anglo-Saxon women, see J. Crick, 'Women, post-humous benefaction and family strategy in pre-conquest England', *Journal of British Studies*, 38 (1999), 399–422.

7. Though for a reference to a lost Amesbury charter see n. 99 below.

8. S. Kelly (ed.), *Charters of Shaftesbury Abbey*, British Academy, Anglo-Saxon Charters, V (Oxford, 1996).

9. R. C. Hoare (ed.), *Registrum Wiltunense* (London, 1827); a new edition is being prepared by Simon Keynes.

10. A. Wilmart, 'La légende de Ste Edith en prose et vers par le moine Goscelin', *Analecta Bollandiana*, 56 (1938), 5–101, 265–307; two versions of the *Life* exist and the revised version was completed before 1087.

11. M. Esposito, 'La vie de Saint Wulfilda par Goscelin de Cantorbery', *Analecta Bollandiana*, 32 (1913), 10–26. The work was probably composed between 1080 and 1082 when Goscelin is known to have visited Barking (F. Barlow (ed.), *The Life of King Edward Who Rests at Westminster*, 2nd edn (Oxford, 1992), Appendix C, 91–111, at 101).

12. C. Fell, *Edward King and Martyr*, Leeds Texts and Monographs, New Series, 3 (Leeds, 1971). However, a significant amount of contemporary material also survives for the events surrounding the development of Edward's cult; see *idem*, 'Edward King and Martyr and the Anglo-Saxon hagiographic tradition', in D. Hill (ed.), *Ethelred the Unready: Papers from the Millenary Conference*, BAR, 59 (Oxford, 1978), 1–13, and discussion in Chapter 5.

13. S. Ridyard, *The Royal Saints of Anglo-Saxon England: A Study of West Saxon and East Anglian Cults* (Cambridge, 1988), Appendix 1, 255–308. The composition of the work cannot be dated precisely, but probably lies between *c.* 1120 and 1140; Ridyard, *Royal Saints*, 17–18, n. 19.

14. London, BL MS Landsdowne 436, fol. 43b; another version, which would appear to draw independently from the same source as Landsdowne 436, but in certain respects, such as the rendering of names, appears more accurate, is to be found in C. Horstmann (ed.), *Nova Legenda Angliae*, 2 vols (Oxford, 1901), I, 379–81. Both are printed in *Acta Sanctorum* (12 October 1867), 918–26.

15. S. Millinger, 'Humility and power: Anglo-Saxon nuns in Anglo-Norman hagiography', in J. Nichols and L. T. Shank (eds), *Medieval Religious Women. I: Distant Echoes* (Kalamazoo, 1984), 115–30; G. Whalen, 'Patronage engendered: how Goscelin allayed the concerns of nuns' discriminatory publics', in L. Smith and J. H. M. Taylor (eds), *Women, the Book and the Godly* (Woodbridge, 1995), 123–35.

16. However, R. Love (*Three Eleventh-Century Anglo-Latin Saints' Lives* (Oxford, 1996), xxxiv–xxix) argues for a gap in composition of hagiography between the late tenth and early eleventh centuries, with the implication that only oral traditions would have survived from this period.

17. *V. Edithae*, 39.

18. *Ibid.*, 292.

19. *Ibid.*, 68–9, 71–2. On the importance of objects as pegs for memory, see E. van Houts, *Memory and Gender in Medieval Europe 900–1200* (Basingstoke, 1999), 93–120.

20. Fell, *Edward*, xvii–xx; Ridyard, *Royal Saints*, 48–50.

21. Ridyard, *Royal Saints*, 23–37; see also L. Braswell, 'St Edburga of Winchester; a study of her cult a.d. 950–1500, with an edition of the fourteenth-century Middle English and Latin Lives', *Medieval Studies*, 33 (1971), 292–333.

22. R. M. Thomson, *William of Malmesbury* (Woodbridge, 1987).

23. B. J. Muir (ed.), *A Pre-Conquest English Prayer-Book (BL MSS Cotton Galba Axiv and Nero Aii (ff. 3–13)*, Henry Bradshaw Society, 103 (Woodbridge, 1988). For Bradford and the Romsey roods see further below, p. 88.

24. S. Keynes, 'The control of Kent in the ninth century', *Early Medieval Europe*, 2 (1993), 111–31.
25. N. Brooks, *The Early History of the Church of Canterbury* (Leicester, 1984), 197–203.
26. Asser, ch. 13; P. Stafford, 'The king's wife in Wessex 800–1066', *Past and Present*, 91 (1981), 3–27.
27. H. M. and J. Taylor, *Anglo-Saxon Church Architecture*, 2 vols (Cambridge, 1965), II, 634–7 and fig. 602. *A-SC*, 786 for Beorhtric's burial at Wareham in 802, but as Foot (*Veiled Women*, II, 197–204) rightly stresses, one cannot be certain that Wareham possessed a nunnery before Asser's reference in ch. 45 to a community of nuns there in 876, nor that the church of St Mary's was the site of the nunnery.
28. Asser, ch. 70. One might have expected her to return to Mercia where her mother and at least one sister were in nunneries. For her possible identification as abbess of an Italian nunnery see Chapter 2.
29. J. Nelson, 'The earliest surviving royal *ordo*: some liturgical and historical aspects', in *Politics and Ritual in Early Medieval Europe* (London, 1986), 341–60; J. A. Smith, 'The earliest queen-making rites', *Church History*, 66 (1997), 18–35.
30. S 340; J. Nelson, 'Reconstructing a royal family: reflections on Alfred from Asser, chapter 2', in I. Wood and N. Lund (eds), *People and Places in Northern Europe, 500–1000* (Woodbridge, 1991), 47–66, at 55.
31. *A-SC*, 718; P. Coulstock, *The Collegiate Church of Wimborne Minster* (Woodbridge, 1993), 43–68.
32. *A-SC*, 900.
33. M. Clunies Ross, 'Concubinage in Anglo-Saxon England', *Past and Present*, 108 (1985), 3–34, at 31–2.
34. B. A. E. Yorke, 'Edward as Ætheling', in N. J. Higham and D. H. Hill (eds), *Edward the Elder 899–924* (London, 2001), 25–39.
35. *A-SC*, 962; the name is probably an Anglicized version of a Scandinavian one and he may be the man who attested S 566 of 955. Should one see him by 962 as a political prisoner, perhaps housed at Wimborne?
36. Coulstock, *Wimborne*, 94–7.
37. L. Whitbread, 'Æthelweard and the Anglo-Saxon Chronicle', *EHR*, 74 (1959), 577–89, esp. 583–4.
38. Foot (*Veiled Women*, II, 199–204) assesses the later evidence; it is possible that the nunnery at Wareham came into the possession of Abbess Wulfhild of Barking and Horton.
39. C. Horstmann (ed.), *S. Edithe sive Chronicon Vilodunense* (Heilbronn, 1883); S. Keynes, 'Wilton', in *Anglo-Saxon Charters: Archives and Single Sheets*, British Academy (Oxford, forthcoming).
40. *A-SC*, 802; the form 'Wolston' would seem rather to suggest the name 'Wulfstan'.
41. Horstmann, *Chronicon Vilodunense*, lines 130–53, 318–57.
42. *Ibid.*, lines 598–629.
43. A. T. Thacker, 'Kings, saints and monasteries in pre-viking Mercia', *Midland History*, 10 (1985), 1–25, at 16–17.
44. The death of Ealdorman Æthelhelm of Wiltshire is recorded in the *A-SC* for 897.
45. S 799; it is difficult to know at what date the claim was first made, but the cartulary, BL Harley 436, was written at the beginning of the fourteenth century.
46. *Gesta Regum*, II, ch. 126, 198–201.
47. S 438, B 714.

48. See also S 424, B 699; Foot (*Veiled Women*, II, 222–4) urges caution and points out that the first explicit reference to nuns at Wilton is from 955 in the reign of Eadwig, a grant that is witnessed by Ælfgyth *magistra prefati monasterii* (S 563, B 903).
49. Ridyard, *Royal Saints*, 140–75; B. A. E. Yorke, 'The legitimacy of St Edith', *Haskins Society Journal* (forthcoming).
50. Asser, ch. 98; he places the foundation after 887 and describes it as fully functioning at the time he was writing, i.e. 893. S. Keynes, 'King Alfred the Great and Shaftesbury Abbey', in L. Keen (ed.), *Studies in the Early History of Shaftesbury Abbey* (Dorchester, 1999), 17–72, at 18.
51. Asser, ch. 90; Keynes, 'Alfred and Shaftesbury Abbey', 41.
52. S 357; Kelly, *Charters of Shaftesbury*, no. 7, 28–30.
53. Asser, ch. 98.
54. Yorke, 'Edward as Ætheling', 25–6.
55. For discussion of its many grants of land and other marks of royal favour see Foot, *Veiled Women*, II, 165–80.
56. S 562; Kelly, *Charters of Shaftesbury*, no. 17, 70–2
57. Æthelweard, 54.
58. Keynes, 'Alfred and Shaftesbury Abbey', 45–6; see also D. Rollason, 'Lists of saints' resting-places in Anglo-Saxon England', *A-SE*, 7 (1978), 61–94, at 92; A. T. Thacker, 'Dynastic monasteries and family cults: Edward the Elder's sainted kindred', in N. Higham and D. Hill (eds), *Edward the Elder 899–924* (London, 2001), 248–63, at 258–9.
59. Ridyard, *Royal Saints*, 154–71.
60. 'The Book of Nunnaminster' (London, BL Harley MS 2965), a Mercian prayer-book which may have belonged to Ealhswith contains the bounds of Ealhswith's estate in Winchester that can be identified with the area of Winchester that contained Nunnaminster (W. de Gray Birch (ed.), *An Ancient Manuscript of the Eighth or Ninth Century* (London, 1889), 96). Ealhswith is recorded as *monialum aedificatrix monasterii* in the Preface to the *Liber Vitae* of Hyde Abbey (W. de Gray Birch (ed.), *Liber Vitae: Register and Martyrology of New Minster and Hyde Abbey, Winchester* (London, 1892), 5); S. Keynes (ed.), *The Liber Vitae of the New Minster and Hyde Abbey, Winchester* (Copenhagen, 1995), 6.
61. *A-SC* (Mercian Register), *s.a.* 903
62. Keynes, *Liber Vitae*, 'Introduction', 2–5.
63. *Gesta Regum*, ch. 126, 201.
64. *V. Eadburgae*, ch. 2, 264–6.
65. *Ibid.*, ch. 12, 283; Ridyard, *Royal Saints*, 103–14.
66. S 1449; A. J. Robertson, *Anglo-Saxon Charters*, 2nd edn (Cambridge, 1956), no. 49, 102–5, a record of adjustment of bounds between the three Winchester minsters. It appears to date from the reign of Edgar, but it is possible that final settlement was reached and recorded slightly later (but before the death of Bishop Æthelwold in 984). Abbess Eadgifu probably also appears in S 1454, the record of a dispute between Wynflaed and Leofwine in 990 to 992 (by which time Edith of Wilton was dead).
67. *V. Edithae*, ch. 16; Foot, *Veiled Women*, II, 249–50.
68. S 1515; Nunnaminster is the most favourably treated as it was left estates, whereas the other two received only money.
69. Rollason, 'Lists of saints' resting-places', 90; Thacker ('Dynastic monasteries', 257–8) puts the case for the traditional identification.

70. H. R. Luard (ed.), *Matthew Paris, Chronica Majora*, Rolls Series (London, 1872–83), I, 446–7.

71. *Gesta Regum,* ch. 126, 198–202.

72. See e.g., E. Edwards (ed.), *Liber Monasterii de Hyde*, Rolls Series (London, 1866), 111.

73. J. Cox, 'Religious houses', in *VCH Warwickshire*, Vol. II (London, 1908), 62–5; Knowles and Hadcock, *Medieval Religious Houses*, 263. Yet another version, in John of Tynemouth, makes her the daughter of King Edmund.

74. Chapter 1, pp. 21–2; C. Hohler, 'St Osyth and Aylesbury', *Records of Buckinghamshire*, 18 (1966), 61–72; J. Blair, 'A handlist of Anglo-Saxon saints', in R. Sharpe and A. T. Thacker (eds), *Local Saints and Local Churches in the Early Medieval West* (Oxford, 2002), 527–8.

75. Rollason, 'Lists of saints' resting-places', 62–3.

76. Hohler, 'St Osyth and Aylesbury', 72, n. 27.

77. *VCH Warwickshire*, II, 62–5.

78. S. Thompson, 'Why English nunneries had no history; a study of the problems of the English nunneries founded after the Conquest,' in J. A. Nichols and L. T. Shank (eds), *Distant Echoes: Medieval Religious Women I* (Kalamazoo, 1984), 131–49; S. K. Elkins, *Holy Women of the Twelfth Century* (Chapel Hill, NC, 1988), 46–60; Foot (*Veiled Women*, II, 139–42) doubts if there was a community of female religious at Polesworth at any point before the Norman Conquest.

79. H. G. Liveing, *Records of Romsey Abbey 907–1558* (Winchester, 1906) has probably been particularly instrumental in perpetuating the confusion.

80. Rollason, 'Lists of saints' resting-places', 92.

81. Birch (ed.), *Liber Vitae*, 58; Keynes (ed.), *Liber Vitae*, 95.

82. BL MS Landsdowne 436, fol. 43b; the version of John Capgrave has 'Elfleda'; *Acta Sanctorum*, 12 October, 918–26.

83. *Worcester, s.a.* 967, 416–19. Edward may merely have been establishing a minster at Romsey; for recent work on the early history of town and church see I. R. Scott, *Romsey Abbey: Report on the Excavations 1973–1991*, Hampshire Field Club Monograph, 8 (Stroud, 1996).

84. See e.g., *Liber de Hyda*, 112.

85. *Gesta Regum,* ch. 126, 198–202.

86. The marriage does not seem to be otherwise recorded, but it is not implausible that Æthelwold could have been married before he married Ælfthryth, especially as we do not know the date of their marriage or its duration. M. A. Meyer ('Patronage of the West Saxon nunneries in late Anglo-Saxon England', *Revue Bénédictine*, 91 (1981), 332–58, at 340), however, suggests that Brihtgifu/Brihtwine may have been Æthelwold's mistress. For what is known of Æthelwold, see C. R. Hart, 'Æthelstan "Half King" and his family', *A-SE*, 2 (1973), 115–44, esp. 127–31.

87. In later tradition, for instance, *Gesta Regum*, ch. 157, 256–9, Edgar was said to have murdered Æthelwold while out hunting so that he could marry Ælfthryth.

88. In the *Lives* Æthelflaed is merely described as related to Ælfthryth, and the latter's marriage to Æthelwold is not mentioned.

89. As recorded in the *Lives*, see n. 82. Æthelflaed is recorded as Abbess of Romsey in the *Liber Vitae* of Hyde Abbey; Birch (ed.), *Liber Vitae*, 58; Keynes (ed.), *Liber Vitae*, 95.

90. S 765 and 812; the Chronicle reference was originally in A, but was apparently erased; it survives in G; see Foot, *Veiled Women*, II, 151–2.

91. S 904; J. M. Kemble, *Codex Diplomaticus Aevi Saxonici*, 6 vols (1839–48), 707.

92. See e.g., *Gesta Regum*, ch. 162, 264–7.

93. Fell, 'Edward King and Martyr'; B. A. E. Yorke, 'Edward King and Martyr; a Saxon murder mystery', in L. Keen (ed.), *Studies in the Early History of Shaftesbury Abbey* (Dorchester, 1999), 99–116. However, the murder did occur when Edward was visiting his stepmother at Corfe.

94. BL MS Egerton, 2104a, 43 and 45. I am very grateful to Rhoda Bucknell for making available to me her work on the Wherwell cartulary in preparation for a University of London Ph.D. thesis.

95. Coldicott, *Hampshire Nunneries*, 17–19.

96. BL MS Egerton, 2104a, f. 152v–53; 962 is the date on which Ealdorman Æthelwold is said to have been killed by King Edgar in Harewood Forest while hunting from the royal estate at Wherwell.

97. *Gesta Regum*, II, 163, 266–7 (which refers to her penitential regime); BL Egerton 2104a, f. 43.

98. *Worcester*, 538–9.

99. H. P. R. Finberg, *Early Charters of Wessex* (Leicester, 1964), no. 331, 103–4.

100. *Op cit*. In the mortuary roll of Matilda of 1113 the first abbess of Amesbury is called 'Hehalfleda'.

101. *A-SC*, E, s.a. 1048; alternatively this abbess could be one of the known married daughters of King Æthelred Unraed by his first wife who retired to Wherwell on being widowed.

102. Crick, 'Wealth, patronage and connections', Table 1, 162–3.

103. S. Keynes, 'Anglo-Saxon entries in the "Liber Vitae" of Brescia', in J. Roberts and J. L. Nelson (eds), *Alfred the Wise: Studies in Honour of Janet Bately* (Woodbridge, 1997), 99–119; H. Becher, 'Das königliche Frauenkloster San Salvatore/Santa Giulia in Brescia im Spiegel seiner Memorialüberlieferung', *Frühmittelalterliche Studien*, 17 (1983), 299–392, esp. 377–82.

104. J. Nelson, 'Making a difference in eighth-century politics; the daughters of Desiderius', in A. C. Murray (ed.), *After Rome's Fall: Narrators and Sources of Early Medieval History. Essays Presented to Walter Goffart* (Toronto, 1998), 171–90.

105. K. F. Drew, 'The Italian monasteries of Nonantola, San Salvatore and Santa Maria Teodata in the eighth and ninth centuries', *Manuscripta*, 9 (1965), 131–54, at 134–8; S. Wemple, 'S.Salvatore/S.Guilia; a case study in the endowment and patronage of a major female monastery in northern Italy', in J. Kirschner and S. Wemple (eds), *Women of the Medieval World* (Oxford, 1985), 85–102.

106. K. Leyser, *Rule and Conflict in an Early Medieval Society: Ottonian Saxony* (London, 1979), 63–73.

107. Van Houts, *Memory and Gender*, 68–9.

108. Leyser, *Rule and Conflict*, 49–62; J. W. Bernhardt, *Itinerant Kingship and Royal Monasteries in Early Medieval Germany, c. 936–1075* (Cambridge, 1993), 142–4, 149–51.

109. K. Leyser, 'The Ottonians and Wessex', repr. and trans. in T. Reuter (ed.), *Communications and Power in Medieval Europe: The Carolingian and Ottonian Centuries* (London, 1994), 73–104; M. Wood, 'The making of King Athelstan's empire: an English Charlemagne?', in P. Wormald (ed.), *Ideal and Reality in Frankish and Anglo-Saxon Society* (Oxford, 1983), 250–72.

110. Æthelweard, 1–2; E. van Houts, 'Women and the writing of history in the early

middle ages: the case of Abbess Matilda of Essen and Æthelweard', *Early Medieval Europe*, 1 (1992), 53–68; *idem, Memory and Gender,* 69–71, Appendix 1.

111. *V. Edithae,* ch. 7, 49–51.

112. T. Kempf, 'Benna Treverensis Canonicus de Sancti Paulini Patrocino', in *Mainz und der Mittelrhein in der europäischen Kunstgeschichte* (Mainz, 1966), 179–84; R. Deshman, '"Christus rex and magi reges": Kingship and Christology in Anglo-Saxon and Ottonian art', *Frühmittelalterliche Studien*, 10 (1986), 367–405; V. Ortenberg, *The English Church and the Continent in the Tenth and Eleventh Centuries: Cultural, Spiritual and Artistic Changes* (Oxford, 1992), 79–90.

113. Asser, ch. 29; this cannot be the same woman as Eadburh, the daughter of Offa, who married King Beorhtric of Wessex.

114. See Chapter 2.

115. W. Levison, *England and the Continent in the Eighth Century* (Oxford, 1946), 249–57.

116. Asser, ch. 29; such a vow may explain why Asser writes so favourably of her. It is possible that Eadburh was the woman of that name recorded with the Mercian party in the *Liber Vitae* of Brescia: Becher, 'San Salvatore', 380–1.

117. Thacker, 'Dynastic monasteries'.

118. Rollason, 'Lists of saints' resting-places', 93. The saints appear only in the latter part of the list, not in the first part where saints with cults established pre-ninth century are to be found.

119. Thacker, 'Kings, saints and monasteries', and see Chapters 1 and 2.

120. Thacker, 'Kings, saints and monasteries', 18–19; *idem,* Dynastic monasteries', 255–6.

121. C. Heighway and R. Bryant, *The Golden Minster: The Anglo-Saxon Minster and Later Medieval Priory of St Oswald at Gloucester*, CBA Report, 117 (York, 1999). It was in this church that Æthelred and Æthelflaed were buried.

122. So Hrostwitha of Gandersheim believed, for she wrote of Edith, wife of Otto I, that 'she was born of the blessed lineage of St Oswald' (H. Homeyer (ed.), *Hrotsvithae Opera* (Munich, 1970), 409 (lines 95–6)).

123. D. Rollason, 'Cults of murdered royal saints in Anglo-Saxon England', *A-SE*, 11 (1983), 1–22.

124. Æthelweard 2; Edith who married Otto I predeceased him and died in 946; Eadgifu married as her first husband Charles the Simple and as her second Herbert of Vermandois, later Count of Troyes; Eadhild married Hugh, Duke of the Franks, and died before him, and Ælfgifu, probably a brother of Rudolf II of Burgundy (it was the whereabouts of Ælfgifu of which Æthelweard was uncertain): see R. M. Thomson and M. Winterbottom, *William of Malmesbury, Gesta Regum Anglorum: General Introduction and Commentary* (Oxford, 1999), 109–10.

125. The nunnery was at Laon and had been part of the endowment of previous Carolingian queens; in 936 she received an English delegation there led by Bishop Odo of Ramsbury concerning support for her son Louis d'Outremer. Previously Eadgifu had returned to England, but perhaps her decision to retire to Laon was linked with enforcing Louis' claims; D. Ó Cróinín, 'The Salaberga Psalter', in C. Bourke (ed.), *From the Isles of the North: Early Medieval Art in Ireland and Britain* (Belfast, 1995), 127–35.

126. *A-SC,* 1051. For her career as widow see P. Stafford, *Queen Emma and Queen Edith: Queenship and Women's Power in Eleventh-Century England* (Oxford, 1997), 236–54.

127. Yorke, 'Legitimacy of St Edith'.

128. This is perhaps less likely to apply to Edith, who entered Wilton because of particular circumstances arising from her mother's separation from her father, King Edgar.
129. The known later abbesses are conveniently presented in Crick, 'Wealth, patronage and connections', Table III, 171–2. The *V. Edithae* (ch. 16) claimed that Edgar wanted to make Edith abbess of three nunneries, but she preferred to remain under the jurisdiction of her mother at Wilton.
130. See n. 66.
131. A. Williams, 'Some notes and considerations on problems connected with the English royal succession, 800–1066', *Anglo-Norman Studies*, 1 (1978), 144–67.
132. B. A. E. Yorke, 'Æthelwold and the politics of the tenth century', in *idem* (ed.), *Bishop Æthelwold: His Career and Influence* (Woodbridge, 1988), 65–88.
133. Kelly, *Charters of Shaftesbury*, no. 26, 102–6; S 744.
134. Kelly, *Charters of Shaftesbury*, no. 13, 53–9; S 485.
135. The status is implied by her possession of a nun's clothing and veil while apparently living on her own estate; G. Owen, 'Wynflaed's wardrobe', *A-SE*, 8 (1979), 195–22.
136. S 1539; D. Whitelock, *Anglo-Saxon Wills* (Cambridge, 1930), no. 3, 10–15, 108–14. Professor Whitelock favoured the identification of Wynflaed the testatrix with Wynflaed, mother of Ælfgifu and benefactress of Shaftesbury, but this has been called into question because Wynflaed's will contains no references to the royal house or anything that would identify her as the mother-in-law of one king and grandmother of two others; see Keynes, 'Alfred and Shaftesbury Abbey', 43–5, for discussion.
137. Kelly, *Charters of Shaftesbury*, no. 10, 39–43; Beorhtwyn appears to have been daughter of Wulfhelm and sister-in-law of Bishop Ælfred of Sherborne.
138. Nn. 42 and 46 above. The abbess Radegund of Wilton in this account would be Ælfflaed's sister, but it is doubtful how much reliance can be placed upon this source.
139. J. Nelson, ' "A king across the sea": Alfred in continental perspective', *TRHS*, 5th series, 36 (1986), 45–68, at 54–5; Yorke, 'Edward as Ætheling', 35–6.
140. S 1533; Robertson, *Anglo-Saxon Charters*, no. 26, 52–3, 307–9.
141. *V. Wulfhildae*, chs 1 and 2.
142. *V. Edithae*, ch. 10.
143. See n. 41 above.
144. J. Haslam, 'The towns of Wiltshire', in *Anglo-Saxon Towns in Southern England* (Chichester, 1984), 87–148, at 122–8 for topographical and archaeological evidence for the town of Wilton in the early middle ages.
145. Stafford, *Queen Emma and Queen Edith*, 257–9. Edith, of course, went on to become queen as the result of her marriage to King Edward the Confessor.
146. Nn. 94 and 95 above.
147. *V. Wulfhildae*, ch. 2.
148. *Ibid.*, ch. 9. She appears as Abbess of Horton in the *Liber Vitae* of Hyde Abbey (ed. Birch, 57; ed. Keynes, 94). There is no evidence that Horton was a nunnery before or after the time of Wulfhild.
149. *Gesta Pontificum*, I, 202–4; H. P. R. Finberg, 'The house of Ordgar and the foundation of Tavistock Abbey', *EHR*, 58 (1943), 190–201; M. A. O'Donovan (ed.), *Charters of Sherborne*, British Academy, Anglo-Saxon Charters, III (Oxford, 1988), lx–lxi.
150. *Gesta Regum* (ch. 157, 256–9) claims Edgar murdered Ælfthryth's husband, Ealdorman Æthelwold.
151. Yorke, 'Legitimacy of St Edith'; see further in Chapter 5.

152. For Eadgifu and Ælfthryth see above; for Edith see Stafford, *Queen Emma and Queen Edith*, 274–9.

153. L. Abrams, *Anglo-Saxon Glastonbury* (Woodbridge, 1996), 185–6; Foot, *Veiled Women*, I, 180–1.

154. *A-SC*, 'D', 958; Yorke, 'Æthelwold and politics', 76–9.

155. Whitelock, *Wills*, no. 8, 21–3; S 1484.

156. Stafford, *Queen Emma and Queen Edith*, 236–53.

157. T. J. Rivers, 'Widows' rights in Anglo-Saxon law', *American Journal of Legal History*, 19 (1975), 208–15; A. Klinck, 'Anglo-Saxon women and the law', *Journal of Medieval History*, 8 (1982), 107–21; but see reservations in Crick, 'Women and family strategy'. Not even royal women could assume security; Eadgifu had her property confiscated by her grandson Eadwig; Yorke, 'Æthelwold and politics', 74–5.

158. Stafford, *Queen Emma and Queen Edith*, 162–92

159. Stafford, 'King's wife in Wessex'.

160. Stafford, 'Queens, nunneries and reforming churchmen'.

161. T. Symons (ed.), *Regularis Concordia Anglicae nationis monachorum sanctimonialiumque* (London, 1953), 2.

162. Wemple, 'S.Salvatore/S.Guilia', 85–91; see also Queen Matilda, wife of Henry I of Germany, who was regent and founder of several major Ottonian nunneries; P. Corbet, *Les Saints ottoniens: sainteté dynastique, sainteté royale et sainteté féminine autour de l'an Mil*, Beihefte von Francia, bd 15 (Sigmaringen, 1986), 30–40, 208–29.

163. J. Nelson, 'Early medieval rites of queen-making and the shaping of medieval queenship', in A. J. Duggan (ed.), *Queens and Queenship in Medieval Europe* (Woodbridge, 1997), 301–15.

164. Stafford, *Queen Emma and Queen Edith*, 262–6.

165. Symons (ed.), *Regularis Concordia*, 6; see further below.

166. Crick, 'Wealth, patronage and connections', Table III, 171–2.

167. See e.g., Asser, ch. 93, where he complains that at the beginning of Alfred's reign there were no adult male Anglo-Saxons in the monastic life and that former monastic houses no longer followed a rule.

168. See Chapter 2.

169. Foot, *Veiled Women*, I, 64–5.

170. See Chapter 2, and for Wulfwyn n. 37 above.

171. Dumville, *Wessex and England*, 185–205; Foot, *Veiled Women*, I, 85–110.

172. M. Parisse, 'Les chanoinesses dans l'empire Germanique (ix–xi siècles)', *Francia*, 6 (1978), 107–28.

173. Parisse ('Chanoinesses', 109) lists four major characteristics that identify a foundation of canonesses. The other three are the absence of a profession, residence in individual houses and the possibility of leaving the convent to be married. Not enough evidence survives to comment one way or the other on the first two, but leaving a community to get married is a key element in the narratives of Wulfhild and Wulfthryth at Wilton, and a major issue after the Norman Conquest; see further Chapter 5.

174. S 446, B 742, for her charity to the poor which may be evidence for private wealth, see *V. Eadburgae*, ch. 8, 274–5: Osbert comments: 'at that time the nuns of that house were allowed to have an abundance of personal riches.'

175. *V. Edithae*, chs 10. 14, 15 and 20.

176. S. Foot, 'Language and method: the Dictionary of Old English and the historian',

M. J. Toswell (ed.), *The Dictionary of Old English: Retrospects and Prospects*, Old English Newsletter Subsidia, 26 (1998), 73–87, 76–82; Foot, *Veiled Women*, I, 96–107.

177. *Gesta Regum*, ch.126, 198–201.

178. N. Brooks, 'The career of St Dunstan', in N. Ramsay and M. Sparkes (eds), *St Dunstan: His Life, Times and Cult* (Woodbridge, 1992), 1–23, esp. 5 and 13.

179. W. Stubbs (ed.), 'The "B" Life of St Dunstan', in *Memorials of St Dunstan Archbishop of Canterbury*, Rolls Series, 63 (London, 1874), 17; Brooks, 'Career of Dunstan', 6–7. Many examples are discussed in Halpin, 'Women religious in late Anglo-Saxon England', *Haskins Society Journal*, 6 (1994), 92–110, and are more sceptically reviewed in Foot, *Veiled Women*, I, 172–88.

180. See Stafford (*Queen Emma and Queen Edith*, 257–9) for Edith's education at Wilton. The ambiguous status of some of the girls educated at Wilton is discussed in Chapter 5.

181. Halpin, 'Women religious', 103–5; Foot, *Veiled Women*, I, *passim*.

182. M. A. Meyer, 'Women and the tenth-century English monastic reform', *Revue Bénédictine*, 87 (1977), 34–61; Yorke, *Bishop Æthelwold*, 1–12; Brooks, 'Career of Dunstan'.

183. Knowles and Hadcock, *Medieval Religious Houses*, 136 and 702.

184. Symons (ed.), *Regularis Concordia*, 2–3.

185. M. Gretsch, *Die Regula Sancti Benedicti in England und ihre altenglische Übersetzung* (Munich, 1973); *idem*, 'The Benedictine Rule in Old English: a document of Bishop Æthelwold's reform politics', in M. Korhammer (ed.), *Words, Texts and Manuscripts: Studies in Anglo-Saxon Culture Presented to Helmut Gneuss* (Cambridge, 1992), 131–58.

186. M. Lapidge and M. Winterbottom (eds), *Wulfstan of Winchester, Life of St Æthelwold* (Oxford, 1991), ch. 22, 36–9.

187. These issues are discussed more fully in Chapter 5.

188. S 766; Meyer, 'Patronage', 352–4. The Wilton cartulary also contains a grant of privileges and land from King Edgar to Wulfthryth [S 799], but the text does not seem to be genuine as it stands.

189. S 904; Stafford, 'Queens, nunneries and reforming churchmen', 26–8.

190. Finberg, *Charters of Wessex*, no. 331, 103–4.

191. S 357; Kelly, *Charters of Shaftesbury*, no. 7, 28–30.

192. Kelly, *Charters of Shaftesbury*, nos 26, 28, 29.

193. *V. Wulfhildae*, ch. 8.

194. *V. Wulfhildae*, ch. 7, 427; Leofflaed subsequently arranged the translation of Wulfhild's remains (ch. 13, 431–2).

195. *V. Edithae*, I, 26, 99–100 (Brihtgifu); II, 20, 295–6 (Ælfgifu).

196. *AA SS*, 12 October, 923 and 925.

197. S 812, B 1187; S. Kelly ((ed.), *Charters of Abingdon Abbey, Part I*, British Academy, Anglo-Saxon Charters, VII (Oxford, 2000), lxxxv–vi, civ–cvi) argues that the charter is basically genuine, though subject to some editing before inclusion in a cartulary.

198. M. Biddle and D. Keene, 'Winchester in the eleventh and twelfth centuries', in M. Biddle (ed.), *Winchester in the Early Middle Ages*, Winchester Studies, I (Oxford, 1976), 241–448; G. Scobie and K. Qualmann, *Nunnaminster: A Saxon and Medieval Community of Nuns* (Winchester, 1993).

199. Robertson, *Anglo-Saxon Charters*, no. 49, 102–5.

200. *V. Edithae*, I, 10, 64; II, 7, 274.

201. So was the promotion of saints' cults, which was often connected with the rebuilding programmes; the nunneries were active in this area as well, but the cults are discussed in detail in Chapter 4 where some other aspects of religious life in the period of reform are also considered.

202. H. M. Taylor, 'The Anglo-Saxon church at Bradford-on-Avon', *Archaeological Journal*, 130 (1973), 141–71; Kelly, *Charters of Shaftesbury*, no. 29, 114–22.

203. E. Coatsworth, 'Late pre-conquest sculptures with the crucifixion south of the Humber', in B. A. E. Yorke (ed.), *Bishop Æthelwold: His Career and Influence* (Woodbridge, 1988), 161–93, esp. 167–9; D. Tweddle, 'Romsey', in Tweddle *et al.*, *Corpus of Anglo-Saxon Stone Sculpture, Vol. IV, South-East England* (Oxford, 1995), 261–3. For excavations of the church see Scott, *Romsey Abbey.*

204. Scobie and Qualmann, *Nunnaminster.*

205. *V. Edithae*, ch., 7, 50–1; ch., 20, 86–7; F. Barlow (ed.), *The Life of King Edward Who Rests at Westminster*, 2nd edn (Oxford, 1992), 70–5.

206. Crick, 'Wealth, patronage and connections', Table I, 162–3.

207. *Ibid.*, 162–3; Foot, *Veiled Women*, II, 251–2.

208. For instance, the cult of St Swithun, in which Æthelwold seems to have taken a close interest, may have adversely affected the cult of St Eadburh (Ridyard, *Royal Saints*, 105–14).

209. Stafford, 'Queens, nunneries and reforming churchmen'.

210. Ridyard, *Royal Saints*, 181–96.

211. BL MS Add. 49598, fol. 90v; R. Deshman, *The Benedictional of Æthelwold*, Studies in Manuscript Illumination, 9 (Princeton, NJ, 1995), plate 28.

212. C. R. Hart, 'Eadnoth, first abbot of Ramsey and the foundation of Chatteris and St Ives', *Proceedings of the Cambridge Antiquarian Society*, 56–7 (1964), 61–7; *idem*, 'Eadnoth I of Ramsey and Dorchester', in *The Danelaw* (London, 1992), 613–23 (collected and revised essays); Foot, *Veiled Women*, II, 55–8.

213. Crick, 'Wealth, patronage and connections', Table I, 162–3.

214. Berkeley seems to have been predominantly a male minster under command of an abbot, but over which Ceolburh had control as abbess in the early ninth century: C. S. Taylor, 'Berkeley minster', *Transactions of the Bristol and Gloucestershire Archaeological Society*, 19 (1894–5), 70–84. A single reference to an abbess there in the late tenth or early eleventh century comes from the *Liber Vitae* of Hyde Abbey (Birch (ed.), 58; Keynes (ed.), 95). For further discussion see Foot, *Veiled Women*, II, 39–42.

215. *A-SC*, 1011 refers to the capture of Abbess Leofrun in Canterbury, identified in *Worcester Chronicle* (468–9) as Abbess of St Mildred's. However, there was an Abbess Leofrun of Reading at about this date (see n. 218) and one wonders if the identification is mistaken. Foot, *Veiled Women*, II, 125–32.

216. See n. 37.

217. For Reading, see J. Blair, 'The minsters of the Thames', in J. Blair and B. Golding (eds), *The Cloister and the World* (Oxford, 1996), 5–28; for Leominster, see J. Hillaby, 'Early Christian and pre-conquest Leominster: an exploration of the sources', *Transactions of the Woolhope Naturalists Field Club*, 45.ii (1986–87), 557–685, though his case for the prayer-book Cotton Galba A xiv having been produced at Leominster and providing evidence for the nunnery being of greater antiquity has not been generally accepted. See also Foot, *Veiled Women*, II, 103–7, 145–7.

218. '*Liber Vitae*', Birch (ed.), 58; Keynes (ed.), 95.

219. DB, I, 60a; similarity of names could suggest that 'Leveva' was a kinswoman of Leofrun.
220. *A-SC* 'C', 1046.
221. DB, I, 180rv. P. Stafford, '"Cherchez la femme": queens, queens' lands and nunneries: missing links in the foundation of Reading abbey', *History*, 85 (2000), 4–27.
222. Elkins, *Holy Women*; Halpin, 'Women religious'; Foot, *Veiled Women*, I.
223. *A-SC*, E s.a. 1048 (for 1051).
224. Barlow (ed.), *The Life of King Edward*, 70–1.
225. A. Williams, *The English and the Norman Conquest* (Woodbridge, 1995).
226. Stafford, *Queen Emma and Queen Edith*, 275–8.
227. *V. Edithae*, II, ch. 20, 295–6; Ælfgifu's sister is named in the Preface (I, 36).
228. R. W. Southern, *Saint Anselm and His Biographer* (Cambridge, 1966), 185–8.
229. Coldicott, *Hampshire Nunneries*, 29; Williams, *English and Norman Conquest*, 64.
230. M. Rule (ed.), *Eadmer, Historia Novorum in Anglia*, Rolls Series, 81 (London, 1884), 121–6. There is considerable confusion in the secondary literature about whether Edith-Matilda was brought up at Romsey or Wilton, but her own account, cited by Eadmer, suggests that she spent time at both nunneries.
231. E. Searle, 'Women and the succession at the Norman Conquest', *Anglo-Norman Studies*, 3 (1980), 159–70, at 165–6.
232. Southern, *Saint Anselm*, 182–93; Searle, 'Women and succession', 166–9.
233. Cnut, I, 6a, 7.1; Cnut, II, 50.1; F. Liebermann, *Gesetze der Angelsachsen* (Halle, 1903), I, 288, 290, 346.
234. Yorke, 'Legitimacy of St Edith'; see further Chapter 5.
235. Parisse, 'Chanoinesses', 118–24.
236. For instance, Eulalia to Shaftesbury 1074; Beatrice to Nunnaminster (d. 1084).
237. Cooke, 'Donors and daughters'.
238. Birch (ed.), *Liber Vitae*, 62–3; Keynes (ed.), *Liber Vitae*, 96.
239. See R. Lavelle, 'Royal Estates in Wessex', unpublished Ph.D. thesis (University of Southampton, 2002).
240. Meyer, 'Patronage'; Stafford, *Queen Emma and Queen Edith*, 153–5.
241. S 730 and 955; Kelly, *Charters of Shaftesbury*, nos 25 and 30, 101–2 and 122–7.
242. Coldicott, *Hampshire Nunneries*, 30.
243. *Ibid.*, 32.
244. Cooke, 'Donors and daughters', 33.
245. J. Nelson, 'Inauguration rituals', in P. Sawyer and I. N. Wood (eds), *Early Medieval Kingship* (Leeds, 1977), 50–71.
246. P. Stafford, 'Emma: the powers of the queen in the eleventh century', in A. J. Duggan (ed.), *Queens and Queenship in Medieval Europe* (Woodbridge, 1997), 3–26, and *idem, Queen Emma and Queen Edith*, 162–92.
247. Though dowager Queen Eadgifu was deprived of her lands when she fell out with her grandson Eadwig, and for noble women the status of vowed widow and protection provided by the church may have been of continued importance against the machinations of male kin (J. Crick, 'Men, women and widows; widowhood in pre-Conquest England', in S. Cavallo and L. Warner (eds), *Widowhood in Medieval and Early Modern Europe* (Harlow, 1999), 24–36).
248. Ridyard (*Royal Saints*) provides several examples of nunneries taking the initiative in attracting royal patronage; the topic will be explored in greater detail in Chapter 4.

4 Nunneries as Royal Ecclesiastical Foundations

The first three chapters have established that most of the royal dynasties of Anglo-Saxon England founded nunneries in which some of their female members served as nuns and abbesses. The nunneries are a particularly striking feature of the reception of Christianity at the royal courts in the latter part of the seventh century, and the important role played in them by princesses returning to their native provinces from the kingdoms into which they had married helps to emphasize their character as familial foundations. Because there were at least ten Anglo-Saxon kingdoms in existence in the latter part of the seventh century, a greater number of royal nunneries was founded *c.* 670–730 than in any other period. Nevertheless, although the number of new foundations may not have been so striking, as new dynasties came to the fore in subsequent centuries they too founded their own royal nunneries, with notable periods of activity in Mercia in the late eighth and early ninth centuries and Wessex in the late ninth and tenth centuries. A few nunneries that probably had substantial resources, such as Whitby, Repton and Minster-in-Thanet, managed to survive some changes in regime, but generally speaking, when different branches of a royal house came to power, or took over a foreign kingdom, they had a limited interest in supporting the nunneries of rivals. They preferred to found their own new nunneries in their central territories, a tendency particularly well illustrated by the actions of the West Saxon dynasty in the late ninth and tenth centuries who, in spite of claiming to be kings of the Anglo-Saxons and then of England, made all their new nunnery foundations in the central shires of Wessex. Many contemporary European royal dynasties also founded nunneries of which kinswomen became abbesses, and their leading nobles followed their example. Some of the earliest Anglo-Saxon royal nunneries seem to have been directly, or indirectly, influenced by the Columban-inspired nunneries founded by leading Merovingian nobles in northern Francia and which 'provided the common ground around which networks of northern aristocrats could unite, finding a religious basis for their social and political standing'.[1] Once the founding of nunneries, and their staffing by princesses, had been established as appropriate actions for Christian, royal Anglo-Saxons, the pattern would have been reinforced when Carolingian, Lombardic and Ottonian rulers also made the patronage of royal nunneries part of their court culture.

To a certain extent, then, royal nunneries may be seen as a common feature of the Christian royal courts of Western Europe in the early middle ages. They were the appropriate places to which widowed queens could retire, and in which it might be expected that at least one daughter would be placed in infancy. The importance of expected models of royal behaviour should not be underestimated in a period when diplomatic contacts between the different royal courts ensured many common features of court culture throughout Christian Europe. However, it is unlikely to be the whole explanation for the enduring importance of royal nunneries in Anglo-Saxon England between the late seventh and eleventh centuries, and closer examination reveals that though many dynasties of Europe supported female monasticism, distinctive features varied over time and place.[2] Why nunneries were deemed so significant to Anglo-Saxon royal houses is one of the key issues to be explored in the remaining two chapters. This chapter concentrates on nunneries as religious institutions and, in particular, explores, as far as the sources will allow, the ecclesiastical functions performed by nunneries on behalf of the royal families that supported them. It will also consider the wider ecclesiastical roles of royal nunneries and how far they resembled the other ecclesiastical foundations of Anglo-Saxon England, for they were subject to the same trends as other Anglo-Saxon minsters.[3] However, the issue of whether their royal associations compromised their role as religious communities cannot be fully considered until after the final chapter (Chapter 5), which will look at non-ecclesiastical roles nunneries performed for royal houses, their involvement in contemporary politics and their freedom for action within the constraints imposed by church and family duty. Although in this chapter the focus is on nunneries meeting the needs of royal families as a unit, with particular reference to those of the head of the family nexus who was also ruler of a kingdom, the final chapter will concentrate more fully on the powers and status enjoyed by royal women who became nuns and abbesses.

Religious functions of nunneries

Prayers and intercession

One of the main functions of religious houses was the daily round of prayers, which could help ensure God's support for both individuals and for larger concerns such as kingdoms.[4] In his *Ecclesiastical History* Bede frequently stressed the importance of such intercessions for a kingdom's prosperity. Before setting out to meet the larger army of Penda of Mercia at the Battle of the River Winwaed in 655, Oswiu vowed twelve small estates on which *monasteria* could be established if God granted him victory. After his success in the battle, Oswiu fulfilled his vow so that, as Bede explains, 'a site and means might be provided for the *monachi* to wage heavenly warfare and to pray with unceasing devotion that the race might win eternal peace'.[5] One of these estates was at Hartlepool and was given to the king's kinswoman Hild, so Bede's *monachi* must be seen as including both male and female religious. The metaphor of religious waging heavenly warfare, often in opposition to the earthly warfare of the king's warriors, was a favourite one with Bede, but was not matched by a more appropriate epithet for religious women. It recalled the fact that the endowments for the early monasteries came from lands that might otherwise be used to support the warriors in the king's service, as Bede reveals more fully in his *Letter to Ecgbert*.[6] The significance of the prayers of religious communities was stressed at the Council of *Clofesho* of 747 where it was emphasized that they prayed for the welfare of kings and the whole Christian people.[7] An additional lengthy statement to the same effect was made in the final chapter, apparently in response to a view circulating among the laity that religious houses were interested only in acquiring wealth and prayed only for their own benefit.[8] These canons suggest that from the point of view of laymen the main justification for the support of religious houses was the benefits they would receive from their intercessions with God.

As chapters of the Council also make clear, one of the main ways in which religious communities obtained intercession was through the daily office with its fixed hours of prayers, singing of the psalms and other biblical readings.[9] The proceedings of the Council of *Clofesho* applied to all religious communities, whether run by men or women, and there are additional confirmatory references (in the absence of the survival of early service books) that the performance of the monastic office was a feature of the early Anglo-Saxon female houses. The *libellus* of the nuns of Barking, cited by Bede, refers in passing to the sisters visiting the monks' cemetery for extra prayers for the departed after completing *matutinae laudis psalmodiis*,[10] while Æthelthryth of Ely is said to have often remained in the church after matins for extra prayer.[11] Aldhelm's poem for the Church of St Mary in Princess Bugga's double house in Wessex refers to the separate choirs of monks and nuns, to the use of psaltery and lyre to accompany the psalms, and to male and female lectors who read the lessons.[12] At Repton, under Abbess Ælfthryth, Guthlac was instructed in 'canticles, psalms, hymns, prayers, and church routine'.[13] Royal houses were no doubt included in the confraternities of prayer known to have been a feature of Anglo-Saxon nunneries from the eighth century. A letter from eighth-century Wessex refers to such bonds between male and female religious communities,[14] and Abbess Æthelburh, daughter of King Offa of Mercia, was advised by Alcuin to enrol the name of Queen Liutgard of Francia 'with the names of your sisters in the records of the church' after she had sent Æthelburh the gift of a dress.[15] Within the broad framework of adherence to a monastic office, it is likely that there was considerable variation in liturgical practice within the country as a whole, particularly since many different traditions had contributed to conversion and the establishment of the earliest monastic communities; one of the aims of the Council of *Clofesho* of 747 was to achieve greater uniformity with Rome.[16]

In seeking to reassure laymen of the service they received from religious houses, the proceedings of the Council of *Clofesho* emphasized their intercession on behalf of kings, and the implication may be that prayers for the ruler were an integral feature of the daily round from an early date. They may have formed part of the 'honour and obedience' which King Wihtred expected from the major Kentish churches, including the royal nunneries, in return for immunity from other demands,[17] and part of the *servitium regis*, of which Eangyth, who commanded one of the Kentish double houses, complained to Boniface.[18] A clearer statement of such an obligation is provided in one of the lawcodes of Athelstan where it is decreed that fifty psalms should be said in all minsters every Friday on behalf of the king.[19] Standardization of prayers for the royal house was one of the features of the *Regularis Concordia* in which it was decreed that prayers for the king, queen and benefactors were to be said after each office except Prime.[20] The generous provision of prayers for the royal house has no exact parallel in any of the continental customaries which served as models for the *Regularis Concordia*, but it is not certain whether their inclusion reflects traditional English practice, or should be seen as an example of the cultivation of close royal links by Æthelwold and Dunstan, the leaders of monastic reform.[21] The answer may lie somewhere between the two possibilities: some prayers for the royal house may have been normal practice in Anglo-Saxon religious houses, but the leaders of monastic reform may have increased the provision in the reformed communities to strengthen the bonds between them and the ruling house. Although royal nunneries were apparently included among the reformed Benedictine communities, the male houses predominated. By the eleventh century interest in royal nunneries seems to have declined to some extent, and in England we may have a reflection of the European trend whereby male houses, both monastic and secular, became more highly valued for their intercessory powers than those of women. The explanation generally advanced is that the greater number of men in orders in the male houses enabled frequent private masses to be said, often at several altars simultaneously.[22]

However, although some prayers for the ruling house may have been general in Anglo-Saxon England, one might expect that the royal nunneries, founded, patronized and often staffed by members of the royal house, would make greater provision for them than was the norm. Charters to religious communities generally contain only a broad reference for the grant being made for the good of a king's soul, but a group of charters of King Athelstan make a clearer statement of the religious services expected in exchange. A grant of 932 to the nuns of Shaftesbury was made on condition that they would sing fifty psalms after Prime and celebrate a mass for the king's soul during Terce every day until Judgement Day.[23] Not only is this considerably more onerous than Athelstan's requirement for all minsters, and more demanding than the extra royal prayers of the *Regularis Concordia* several reigns later, but it is also more than the additional services that Athelstan required from male communities in return for grants of land. In the following year Sherborne was required only to sing the whole psalter through on All Saints' Day for the sake of the king's soul.[24] The Shaftesbury charter provides evidence that liturgical demands on the royal nunneries could be more onerous than those laid on male religious communities that were not so directly under royal control.

Further insight into the provision of prayers for the royal house in a later Anglo-

Saxon nunnery is provided by the early eleventh-century prayer-book whose contents are divided between BL Cotton Galba Axiv and Nero Aii (ff. 3–13).[25] The language of its texts includes both male and female forms, but with a significant number of references to female servants of God. It has therefore been suggested that it was made in a community containing both men and women, and one that was evidently monastic, since a number of texts relate to the regular life and the *opus dei*. As there is strong internal evidence to connect the prayer-book with Winchester, the Nunnaminster, which in the eleventh century would have contained both the nuns and their chaplains, has been proposed as its place of origin.[26] The prayer-book is an informal collection which drew upon a variety of sources and so seems to be for individual reflection or study rather than communal use, but it is likely to reflect the range of texts available in its place of origin. It includes a number of links with the ruling house, including a poem in honour of Athelstan and special prayers for Æthelred II, Edward the Martyr and St (formerly Queen) Ælfgifu.

Anglo-Saxon kings are likely to have felt the need for intercession through prayers on their behalf. Not only were they subject to the temptations that came with powerful office, but their effective performance as rulers might necessitate behaviour incompatible with keeping the Ten Commandments, such as the murder of rivals. Individuals who experienced visions of the other world reported that former rulers were to be found inhabiting the nether regions. The visionary monk of Much Wenlock was allowed to foresee the torments that awaited King Ceolred of Mercia,[27] and Bishop Boniface reminded his successor Æthelbald, in a letter urging his reform, of the fulfilment of this prophecy in the sudden and terrible fit which led to Ceolred's death 'raging and distracted, conversing with devils and cursing the priests of God'.[28] But although the debauchery of Ceolred and Æthelbald was a personal sin that they could have avoided, churchmen were forced to concede that in the reality of early Anglo-Saxon politics other forms of bad behaviour might be regrettable but unavoidable. Commenting on the saintly King Saebbi of the East Saxons, who eventually retired to become a monk, Bede says, 'many people thought and often said that a man of his disposition ought to have been a bishop rather than a king';[29] in other words, the two offices of king and bishop required different qualities. More typical of early Anglo-Saxon rulers, and more problematic for a churchman like Bede, was King Oswiu of Northumbria who undoubtedly did much to promote church interests, but was also a ruthless and (according to Bede) sinful ruler. Among his crimes was the murder of his Deiran rival King Oswine, a cousin of his own wife, which enabled him to bring the two Northumbrian kingdoms of Bernicia and Deira together again under his joint rule.[30] Fortunately the church could provide the means of atonement for this unfortunate crime, for a monastery was founded at Gilling, where a kinsman of the murdered king was appointed first abbot and 'prayer was continually to be said for the eternal welfare of both kings, for the one who planned the murder and for his victim'.[31] Matters may be said to have been worked out in a way that was very satisfactory for King Oswiu. He had gained the political advantage he wanted through the murder of Oswine, but obviated any dangers of earthly or heavenly revenge by compensating the family of the murdered prince, but in such a way that contributed to Oswiu's own salvation. By such means were early rulers convinced of the value of the Christian church.

The community founded at Gilling was a purely male one – the concept of female monasticism had been introduced only recently to Northumbria when the murder was carried out in 653; however, there are other instances where nunneries were founded or patronized in comparable circumstances. The best recorded example is Minster-in-Thanet.[32] According to its foundation legend, King Ecgbert had his two cousins Æthelbert and Æthelred killed at the royal vill of Eastry because they were rivals for the throne (though the main onus for the crime is ascribed to his chief councillor Thunor).[33] A pillar of light over the spot where the princes were buried made the crime impossible to ignore, and Ecgbert was advised to provide compensation for the killing to the princes' sister Æbbe, who was married to King Merewalh of the Magonsaetan, but took advantage of the offer to return home to found the nunnery on the Isle of Thanet. The Minster foundation account has a number of legendary elements that probably derive from oral tradition, such as Æbbe's request for as much land as her pet hind could delineate,[34] and the involvement of Thunor would appear to have arisen from the need to explain a prominent burial mound called *Thunores hlaew* which is said to have marked the spot where he was swallowed up by the earth as punishment for the murder. Nor is it clear when the legend was first written down, though an account must have been in circulation by the tenth century when the bodies and cult of the princes were moved to Wakering (Essex), and internal evidence suggests the material that lies behind the surviving texts is likely to have been assembled before the collapse of the ruling house of Kent in the eighth century.[35] Æbbe, Minster and the cult of the princes certainly existed, and there seems no reason to reject the claim that Minster-in-Thanet was founded as compensation paid to Princess Æbbe for the murder of her brothers in striking parallel to the circumstances in which Gilling had been founded.[36] Once nunneries had been founded, they might attract additional grants as similar acts of compensation. Gloucester is said to have received one grant from King Æthelbald of Mercia in compensation for his murder of Abbess Eafe's kinsman, Prince Æthelmund of the Hwicce.[37] Several other royal nunneries were to nurture cults of murdered kinsmen, notably those of Cynehelm at Winchcombe, Wigstan at Repton and Edward the Martyr at Shaftesbury, reflecting the fact that not only was the murder of rival kinsman a fact of Anglo-Saxon life, but that it was also one from which a religious house might hope to benefit, as those guilty of the deed recognized the need to absolve their guilt.[38]

Further credit could be gained by the oblation of a daughter into the church; no sons of a reigning monarch are known to have been vowed to the monastic life in this way. The most informative account is that provided by Bede of King Oswiu's vow that if God granted him victory over Penda he would not only grant twelve ten-hide estates to found churches, but also 'dedicate his daughter to the Lord as a holy virgin'.[39] After Penda was defeated he gave Ælfflaed, who was scarcely a year old, into the care of her kinswoman Abbess Hild 'to be consecrated to God as a holy virgin', and she subsequently became abbess of Hild's foundation at Whitby. We do not know if any of the other princesses who entered the church in infancy did so in fulfilment of specific pledges made by their fathers. It is possible that Alfred's foundation of Shaftesbury, and the entry there of his daughter Æthelgifu at what was probably an early age, could be interpreted as an act of thanksgiving for victory over the vikings, for it was founded at about the same time as the monastery at Athelney where Alfred had taken refuge from Guthrum. Asser implies that the two foundations complemented one another as monasteries for women and men respectively.[40] Osbert of Clare and Goscelin follow a hagiographic convention in making the infant princess-saints Eadburh and Edith decide their vocation by rejecting objects of temporal power and wealth for the spiritual.[41] The two-year-old Edith is said to have gone without hesitation to a monastic veil which she placed on her head. Princess Eadburh was apparently three years old at the time of her oblation. This early entry into the monastic life corresponds with Carolingian practice whereby children might be oblated after they had passed the significant threshold from dependent infancy to childhood.[42] Like the entries of Ottonian princesses into the religious life,[43] Edith's oblation is described as a major court occasion that was accompanied by substantial grants of land and other gifts from her father King Edgar to the nunnery of Wilton; it was clearly an act of dedication that brought him credit. The fact that princesses were being entered into nunneries as infants, before they could make their own decisions, underscores that the choice of vocation was being made to benefit those who took the decision on their behalf.

There is no record of an Anglo-Saxon prince having been oblated. Presumably in a period of such high mortality rates among princes, no king, no matter how numerous his sons, wanted to take the risk of having any debarred from succession because they had entered the church.[44] Frankish kings sent princes whom they wished to deprive of rights to the throne into monasteries,[45] and Coenwulf of Mercia seems to have been able to justify the deposition of Eadbert Praen from the throne of Kent on the grounds that he was a priest.[46] But the reasons may go deeper than this. Cemeteries of the sixth and seventh centuries suggest that a military persona, symbolized by burial with weapons, was fundamental to the construction of elite Anglo-Saxon male identity and that roles of men and women were sharply differentiated.[47] There may have been basic concepts in the construction of elite male and female identities in early Anglo-Saxon England that would have made entry into religious houses seem an appropriate gendered role for Anglo-Saxon princesses but not for princes. Existing concepts would have been reinforced by established practice in other areas of Western Europe, with Merovingian attitudes to the significance of sending princes into monasteries likely to have been particularly influential with the Anglo-Saxon royal courts.[48]

Kings had the wealth to employ others to pray on their behalf, but seem to have particularly wanted to establish nunneries where daughters and others kinswomen could serve them in this capacity, and attentively supervise others who were so doing. One implication may be that it was felt that relatives would take greater care of an individual's spiritual needs than non-kin, however devout and well endowed. A high value was placed on kinship obligations in Anglo-Saxon England, with kin-groups, centred on the nuclear family, having a legal and moral responsibility for the welfare of their members.[49] But obligations might be gendered, and within the royal family nexus the duties of expiation, of care for the ruler's soul and of prayer for the benefit of the family fell upon female members, especially daughters of the house either vowed from infancy or returning to their kingdom of birth in widowhood. Such care for relatives was, of course, to be lavished not only during their lifetimes, but was to be continued after their deaths.

Burial and commemoration of the dead

Royal burial had been a matter of conspicuous display before conversion to Christianity. In some cases at least burial had been with elaborate provision of grave goods in specially prepared chambers which when covered with a mound became prominent features in the landscape.[50] No doubt there had also been elaborate funeral ceremonies as well which cannot now be reconstructed. Conspicuous display could continue in Christianized form in association with churches, but there was considerable variation in the exact form of church burial within different kingdoms, reflecting the variety of practice current in mainland Europe at the time.[51] In discussing royal burial choices it should be remembered that we only know the places of burial of a proportion of the kings before 900,[52] and references to burial locations of other members of the royal house are even more random. Burial in the episcopal centre was one of the preferred options. A number of kings of Kent appear to have been buried in Canterbury. Bede describes in some detail the burial of Æthelbert and his wife Bertha in the southern porticus of the Church of St Peter and St Paul in Augustine's monastery outside the walls, and the sites of their burials were subsequently located in excavation.[53] According to traditions recorded after the Norman Conquest, other Kentish kings were buried in a separate church dedicated to St Mary built in alignment with the Church of St Peter and St Paul.[54] The Old Minster in Winchester was the site of burial of a number of West Saxon kings, though not necessarily all those claimed for it in the twelfth-century Winchester annals.[55] King Saebbi of the East Saxons was buried in a stone sarcophagus at St Paul's, London,[56] and King Ceolred at Lichfield,[57] but neither of these episcopal sites is known to have been used for other royal burials. The head of King Edwin was placed in a porticus of St Peter's at York,[58] while that of Oswald went to his see at Lindisfarne.[59] By implication the subking Ælfwine, son of King Oswiu, was also buried in York.[60] Other early rulers preferred burial at church sites with which they had a particular association. Some all-male monastic or minster sites were favoured,[61] and the status of some sites used for royal burial is not known. For instance, Axminster (Devon) where the Ætheling Cyneheard was buried after his unsuccessful attempt to overthrow King Cynewulf of Wessex in 757, could have been either a nunnery or a male minster, for though there were several early nunneries in Wessex the exact location of most of them is not known.[62] Nevertheless, of the non-episcopal sites known to have been used for royal burial in the period up to 900, royal nunneries form a significant category.

Nunneries that can be identified as the burial place of several members of a royal house in the period include Gloucester, Repton, Whitby and Winchcombe. Other sites, including Bedford (Offa), Wimborne (Æthelred) and possibly Wareham (Beorhtric),[63] where only one royal burial is recorded, may have been intended as dynastic mausolea, but the royal lines that favoured them died out before such a tradition could be established. With fuller records the use of nunneries for royal burial might appear greater still. Excavation may provide a means of adding to the list, though identification of specific individuals can only be tentative without supporting written evidence. The earliest timber church of the nunnery of Nazeing, excavated at Nazeingbury (Essex), contained only four burials which were situated at the east end.[64] Two female burials were primary and tentatively identified as founder burials, perhaps those of the first abbesses. They were accompanied by two slightly later burials, one female, the other male.[65] A possible candidate for the latter could be King Swaefred who gave the land on which the nunnery was founded.[66]

As we saw in Chapter 1, the models for the early Anglo-Saxon double houses were foundations of the Merovingian nobility in northern Francia. Burial of members of the founder's family, who generally also provided abbesses for the foundation, were a feature, and arguably an important aspect of establishing the family's group identity in a region.[67] The most notable example is Jouarre, whose crypt survives with a series of stone sarcophagi of early abbesses and of one of their most notable kinsmen Agilbert, who was Bishop of Wessex in the 650s before his appointment as Bishop of Paris.[68] The best surviving remains from an Anglo-Saxon nunnery are from Repton where what was originally a free-standing subterranean structure to the east of the church, which may once have served as a baptistery, was adapted for use as a burial mausoleum, perhaps in the first place for King Æthelbald of Mercia (d. 757) and then for King Wiglaf (d. 840) and his grandson St Wigstan.[69] Subsequently the chamber was incorporated into the church as a crypt. A standing cross found outside the east end of the church has on one face a carving of a Germanic ruler in the stance of a conquering emperor.[70] If the identification of it as a memorial to King Æthelbald can be accepted, it is striking evidence for the promotion of a royal image at a nunnery site, and for the high standards of workmanship that the house could command. Remains of what may have been a mausoleum for King Coenwulf and his son Cynehelm have been identified at another Mercian site, the former nunnery of Winchcombe, the family centre where their archives were kept.[71]

An account of the royal burials at St Peter's, Gloucester, was included in the register compiled in the time of Abbot Walter Frocester (1382–1412).[72] Cyneburh, the first abbess, is said to have been buried beside her brother Osric who made the foundation grant before the altar of St Petronilla. The next two abbesses, Eadburh and Eafe, who were also members of the Hwiccian royal house, were buried next to Cyneburh. This arrangement shares similarities with that of the burial chapel excavated at Nazeingbury, though the Gloucester burials could also have been in a porticus attached to the main church with its own altar and with a separate dedication, as was the case in Canterbury and York. In the latter, Edwin's head was buried in a porticus dedicated to St Gregory,[73] but his body was interred at the nunnery of Whitby, 'together with other of our kings . . . on the south side of the altar which is dedicated in the name of the blessed apostle Peter and east of the altar dedicated to St Gregory',[74] possibly a reference to burial in a southern porticus. Bede implies that Abbess Ælfflaed, who organized the translation of her grandfather Edwin's body to Whitby, regarded Whitby as a family mausoleum where her father Oswiu and mother Eanflaed, as well as *multi nobiles,* were buried.[75] Unfortunately we know nothing of the exact place of burial of any of them besides Edwin, nor that of Hild the first abbess.

Favoured sites for royal burial in the period before 900 seem to have been episcopal centres and royal nunneries, with some variation between kingdoms as to which was preferred. Both could provide burial in special structures devoted to that purpose, generally either in a chapel attached to the main church or in a free-standing mausoleum, close to the church and aligned with it. However, after 900, when only one royal dynasty remained, a clear preference emerged for burial in the churches of male minsters. New Minster in Winchester was founded by King Edward the Elder in 901, perhaps fulfilling the intentions of his father King Alfred to serve as a burial place for himself, his father, mother and other members of his family.[76] When the church was completed the remains of Alfred and his wife Ealhswith were placed in a special chapel.[77] But if the intention was that New Minster should serve as a mausoleum for all King Edward's descendants, it was frustrated by events, and, of subsequent kings, only King Eadwig (d. 959) was buried there. Winchester seems to have been a centre of opposition to Edward's son Athelstan (d. 939), and he was buried in Malmesbury where he had previously arranged for two cousins who died at the battle of *Brunanburh* to be interred.[78] His successor Edmund (d. 946) was buried at Glastonbury; his body seems to have been hijacked by Dunstan for his own foundation after the king's unexpected death.[79] As Edmund's own descendants eventually followed him to the throne, Glastonbury developed as a significant royal mausoleum where his son Edgar (d. 975) was also buried,[80] and Edgar's grandson Edmund Ironside (d. 1016).[81] When Winchester was favoured again, it was the Old Minster, not the New, that was selected. Eadred (brother of Edmund) (d. 955) was buried there,[82] as well as Cnut (d. 1035) and his son Harthacnut (d. 1042).[83] King Æthelred Unraed (d. 1016) and his son Edward the Confessor (d. 1066) were buried outside Wessex, at St Paul's[84] and Westminster Abbey respectively.[85]

In the pattern of royal burials after 900, we can see the continuing importance of the concept of a family mausoleum. Edward the Elder gathered his family together in his new burial church in Winchester, and Dunstan's acquisition of Edmund's body for Glastonbury meant that some of his descendants wished to be buried there as well. But none of the foundations chosen for these royal burials were nunneries, and in royal burial practice we seem to have further evidence for a trend in which male communities of monks (reformed Old Minster; Glastonbury; Westminster) or secular clergy (Malmesbury (?); New Minster; St Paul's) were preferred to female houses. However, some qualifications are necessary. Wessex had not been one of the kingdoms in which royal burial in nunneries had been particularly favoured before 900. The burials of Beorhtric at Wareham and Æthelred at Wimborne had been exceptional rather than the norm,[86] and so the choice of Winchester as the site of several post-900 royal burials may be seen as in accord with a pre-900 tendency for royal burial in an episcopal centre. Nor was it necessarily the case that the place of burial always reflected a king's personal wishes. It may have been Dunstan, not Edmund or his immediate family, who arranged his burial at Glastonbury, while in his will King Eadred made gifts to Old Minster, New Minster and Nunnaminster and a separate donation 'to the place where he wishes his body to rest', which implies that he intended it to be somewhere other than Old Minster where he was in fact buried.[87]

There was, however, one exception to kings being buried in male communities which demonstrates that, in certain circumstances, a royal nunnery might still be seen as the most appropriate place for a royal burial, namely the interment of the murdered Edward the Martyr at the royal nunnery of Shaftesbury. The circumstances of Edward's reburial at Shaftesbury were exceptional in a number of ways. After his murder on 18 March 978, the body of Edward seems to have been hastily buried and concealed, but almost a year later as part of the reconciliation between rival supporters, Ealdorman Ælfhere retrieved the body and placed it first, on 13 February, in the church of the nunnery at Wareham,[88] and then, on 18 February, oversaw its transfer with appropriate ceremonial to the nunnery at Shaftesbury.[89] Miracles and an appearance of Edward himself established his transition to saintliness which was acknowledged formally in the translation of his remains on 20 June 1001. The choice of Shaftesbury for Edward's final place of burial may have been influenced by the fact that his paternal grandmother Ælfgifu was buried there and was already an active saint. The whole issue of Edward's reburial and burgeoning cult was politically very delicate. Even if King Æthelred's own mother Ælfthryth was not directly involved in the murder, as later tradition was to record,[90] members of the faction supporting Æthelred are likely to have been implicated. Any cult of Edward had to be carefully handled to make sure that it was to Æthelred's advantage,[91] and it may have been felt that Shaftesbury with its well-established royal links could be relied upon to provide the necessary sensitivity.[92] The traditional intercessory role of nunneries may also have been invoked. One of the matters of concern to the contemporary commentators Byrhtferth of Ramsey and the author of the northern recension *Anglo-Saxon Chronicle* was that the murder had never been properly expiated and the perpetrators punished.[93] Shaftesbury, like Gilling and Minster-in-Thanet some centuries earlier, may have been charged with praying for both the murdered king and those responsible for the murder. Some of its nuns may have been related to the two brothers, so making it particularly appropriate for compensation for the murder to be paid in the form of gifts to the house.[94] The *coenobium* at Bradford and its substantial estates would have formed part of the expiatory payment Shaftesbury received, and the charter in which it was granted makes frequent reference to the gift being in honour of the martyr Edward and for the salvation of the whole lineage, both past and future.[95] It may also have been at this time that Shaftesbury received the estate at Kingston (Dorset) where the murder had taken place.[96]

The ætheling Edmund, the elder son of King Edgar and Ælfthryth, who died in infancy, was also buried in a nunnery.[97] Romsey may have been chosen for his burial because Ælfthryth's young stepdaughter Æthelflaed was being raised there, and Edgar was the founder of the community.[98] More distant members of the royal house might also be buried in nunneries. The burial of Ælfgar, King Edgar's kinsman, is recorded at Wilton in 962,[99] when it was probably under the control of Abbess Ælfgifu.[100] Was Ælfgar her kinsman as well? If we had more information on burials in nunneries and the family background of abbesses, we might see further evidence for the development of links between nunneries and leading noble houses that was posited in Chapter 3 as one of the reasons for a decline in nunneries as specifically royal institutions by the end of the Anglo-Saxon period.[101] As in other periods, queens who had entered, or were associated with, nunneries tended to be buried in them. Thus Ælfflaed (wife of Edward the Elder) and Wulfthryth (wife of Edgar) were buried at Wilton, Ælfgifu (wife of Edmund) at Shaftesbury[102] and Ælfthryth (wife of Edgar) at Wherwell. Ealhswith, however, was buried in New Minster, Winchester, not the Nunnaminster she had founded, and the two last queens of English kings (excluding Harold Godwinson) were also buried with their husbands – Emma at Old Minster with Cnut and Edith at Westminster with Edward the Confessor.[103]

But even when members of the royal house were buried elsewhere, the royal nunneries might be expected to have provided prayers for the departed as part of their regular round of prayers discussed in the last section.[104] The prayer for King Æthelred in the Cotton Galba prayer-book was for the repose of his soul.[105] Memorial books have not survived from any of the Anglo-Saxon nunneries in the way that they have for some of their continental counterparts;[106] indeed, only two Anglo-Saxon *liber vitae* are known, one probably from either Jarrow or Durham and begun in the seventh century, and the other from New Minster, Winchester, whose contents go back to the tenth century.[107] Both contain names of members of royal houses and of nunneries, and no doubt many of the nunneries would have had similar books to memorialize important patrons and their families, as well as members of other religious communities with which they were in confraternity.

Further evidence for the memory of departed family members being nurtured in nunneries may come in other forms.[108] The texts of the *Mildrith Legend* contain detailed accounts of family history that include not just the Kentish main line, but links with other Anglo-Saxon kingdoms as a result of the marriages of royal women, many of whom subsequently became abbesses.[109] It is quite possible that the individuals recorded here were also liturgically commemorated at Minster. The lost archetype of the *Mildrith Legend* was probably drawn up in the eighth century when the genealogies of kings were also being written down,[110] and largely mythical accounts of the foundation of Kent were being elaborated.[111] The genealogies and foundation myths celebrate matrilineal descent and boost the royal image by tracing descent from gods and heroes; sometimes the choice of these seems to have been influenced by political alliances.[112] It is possible to see the narrative of the *Mildrith Legend* as a counterpart to the genealogies in which the contribution of female members to the prosperity of the line is stressed, both through their matrimonial alliances and the sanctity of their religious careers. Such claims, presumably prepared by the nuns at Thanet, boosted the position of the royal house, but also reminded the men of the family of the value of their female members.

Whitby is another early community whose abbesses may be seen as guardians of family history. It is possible that the very precise details Bede was able to provide about the fates of princes of the Deiran royal line came from records kept at Whitby where King Edwin and other family members were buried.[113] Once again it may be suspected that such records had a liturgical function. Whitby seems to have been seen as embodying Deiran family traditions. King Oswiu by choosing to be buried at Whitby, where his daughter Ælfflaed was abbess, symbolically underpinned the union of the Bernician and Deiran houses which had been in-augurated by his marriage to the Deiran princess Eanflaed – and conveniently reduced the likelihood of Whitby becoming a centre of Deiran opposition. Whitby has also preserved examples of another way in which the dead might be com-memorated at nunneries, and other religious houses, namely through stone monuments. The sculptures of Whitby are simple standing-stone crosses with names inscribed on the head, or plain stone crosses on which names may have been painted. Rosemary Cramp has suggested that an early example of a plain stone cross from Whitby, probably dating to the seventh century, may have been inspired by the wooden cross associated with King Oswald (the uncle of Abbess Ælfflaed) and that Whitby may have pioneered the development of the standing-stone cross.[114]

Only a few other examples of inscribed cross-heads are known. Another comes from Carlisle, a royal nunnery in the time of Ecgfrith, the son of Oswiu,[115] and close to Carlisle is the famous Bewcastle cross which has been described as 'a mon-umental tree of life and death, a Book of the Dead, on which a royal lineage has been recorded'.[116] Unfortunately due to weathering, little can be deciphered now of a large runic inscription on the west face, but it appears to have been set up by three people in memory of a fourth whose name included the letters 'lcfri'.[117] The dedicatee can be identified with the aristocratic figure holding a hawk at the base of the west shaft.[118] It has long been suggested that the individual commemorated was Alcfrith/Alhfrith (d. *c.* 664), son of Oswiu and subking of Deira, especially as the name Cyneburh, which was that of his Mercian wife, occurs elsewhere on the monument. But if that identification is accepted, and it is far from certain, then the ruler was being commemorated sometime after his death, for the Bewcastle cross probably dates to the eighth century. Bewcastle and Repton are the only known sculptures from before 900 to depict lay figures (in the case of Repton certainly a ruler) and they, like other monumental sculptures inscribed with names, may be seen as not only having a commemorative function, but also acting as a focus of prayers and liturgy.[119] Such monuments are not confined to nunneries, but nunneries (even allowing for the problem of what foundation was responsible for Bewcastle) have produced some striking examples that can be placed in the context of their role in family commemoration.[120]

Saints' cults

A particular aspect of the care for the departed, where nunneries can be seen performing an important service for their royal patrons, is in the treatment of the 'special dead', the saints. Nunneries played an innovatory role in the promotion of native Anglo-Saxons of royal birth as saints. Several cults promoted by royal women pre-date the translation of Cuthbert in 697, the first of the native Anglo-Saxon bishops to be elevated to sainthood. Cults of founding abbesses and their male kinsmen were a significant element of the northern Frankish monasteries which provided the models for the Anglo-Saxon royal nunneries. In the words of Patrick Geary, such cults added 'a family tradition of supernatural power and prestige to that of traditional lordship'.[121] The detailed account Bede provides of Seaxburh's translation of her sister Æthelthryth's remains in 695 or 696 at Ely – the erection of a tent over the first burial site in the graveyard, the examination of the remains by the abbess, the vouching for the incorruptibility of the body by expert witnesses including Æthelthryth's doctor, the washing of the body and translation into the church in a sarcophagus – strongly suggests the influence of contemporary Frankish practices.[122] No bishop is recorded as being present, and the translation seems to have been carried out on Seaxburh's own initiative. Knowledge of the appropriate ceremonials may have come via a third sister, Æthelburh, who was abbess of Faremoutiers in Brie where she presided over the establishment of the cult of her niece Eorecengota who was Seaxburh's own daughter.[123] Influence from Faremoutiers is also likely at Barking, where the cult of its founder abbess Æthelburh was promoted in about the same period, because there are striking parallels between miracles recorded at Faremoutiers in Jonas' biography of Columbanus and those taken by Bede from the lost *libellus* of Barking.[124] The establishment of the cult of the founder of a monastery, whose way of life also provided a model for the community, rapidly became established practice in both royal and noble foundations, leading to a plethora of local saints whose origins appear to date to the late seventh or early eighth centuries, though the existence of many is not recorded before the tenth or eleventh centuries.[125]

However, an early characteristic of houses closely associated with the royal house was the promotion of kings and princes as saints. Perhaps even earlier than the elevations of Æthelthryth and Æthelburh to sainthood were the translations organized by royal kinswomen of the bodies of kings Edwin and Oswald of Northumbria.[126] Both kings had died in battle against the pagan Penda of Mercia: Edwin in 633 and Oswald in 642. Oswald's body had been dismembered; the head and arms were displayed on posts from which they were retrieved by his brother Oswiu in 643. The head was sent to the episcopal centre of Lindisfarne and the arms to the royal chapel at Bamburgh.[127] It is possible that Edwin was treated in a similar way, for his head also had a different posthumous history from the rest of his body and was deposited in his episcopal church in York.[128] However, the cults of the two kings only really got under way after the retrieval of their bodies was organized by the sisters Ælfflaed, Abbess of Whitby (Edwin), and Osthryth, Queen of Mercia and patroness of Bardney (Oswald),[129] who as daughters of King Oswiu were granddaughters of Edwin and nieces of Oswald. The formal cult of Oswald developed rapidly after his translation, especially after it was championed by Bishop Acca of Hexham and promoted by Bede, who effectively made Oswald the patron saint of Northumbria.[130] Although Edwin's role in the conversion of Northumbria was fully acknowledged by Bede, he is not presented as a saint in the *Ecclesiastical History*. However, that he was being promoted as such at Whitby is made clear in the monastery's *Vita* of Gregory the Great that refers to miracles attributed to the king.[131]

It must be stressed that these attempts to promote kings as saints were extremely unusual in Europe at this time. The initiative for the formal recognition of the cults seems to have been taken by members of the royal house, and the princesses who commanded double houses seem to have played a particularly significant role, though some male minsters, especially those under royal patronage, were also the sites of early princely cults. Bishops were not involved with these early translations and were slow to support the cults; as Alan Thacker has observed, the Lindisfarne community seems to have been initially reluctant to treat Oswald's head as a relic.[132] Oswald and Edwin are not the only examples of men of the royal house who died violent deaths and who were promoted as saints in the latter part of the seventh century in houses under royal patronage. There was also King Oswine of Deira, who was murdered by Oswiu; Bede does not refer directly to him as a saint, but his entry in the calendar of Willibrord might suggest the early development of a cult, presumably at Gilling, though it did not necessarily pre-date those of Oswald and Edwin.[133] In Kent, the murder of the princes Æthelred and Æthelbert was the occasion for the foundation of the nunnery of Minster-in-Thanet during the reign of King Ecgbert (664–673). The *passio* of the princes is believed to have been in existence by the early eighth century and may have been promoted at the monastery from the time of its foundation.[134] Of considerably more dubious authority are the cults of St Wulfhad and St Ruffin, reputedly the sons of King Wulfhere of Mercia (658–675) and murdered by him because they had converted to Christianity.[135]

One could also consider the case of Sigebert of the East Angles, who lived as a monk for many years before he too was killed in battle with Penda of Mercia. He appears as a saint only in calendars from the twelfth century onwards in association with cults promoted by Ely,[136] but it is possible that his cult had an earlier basis and had been promoted at the royal nunnery of Ely. On the other hand, Sigebert might appear to have more in common with two monk-kings with rather better attested cults: Saebbi of the East Saxons and Æthelred of Mercia. The cult of the latter and his murdered wife Osthryth was promoted at the male minster they had founded at Bardney, as recorded in the late Saxon 'list of saints' resting-places'.[137] Bede knew of Saebbi's reputation of holiness from the Barking *libellus*.[138] He falls short of calling him a saint, but the material he uses is clearly hagiographical in tone and so it could be argued that he was regarded as a saint at Barking. Saebbi was buried in St Paul's, London, but the evidence we have for him apparently being promoted as a saint came from the double house at Barking.[139] It provides support for the hypothesis that, in spite of it not being clear whether Æthelburh, the first Abbess of Barking, was a member of the East Saxon royal house, nevertheless, Barking should be seen as a double house closely linked with the East Saxon dynasty.[140]

Monk-kings were a particular phenomenon of the conversion period in Anglo-Saxon England, when royal families can also be seen to have been actively promoting cults of murdered and martyred kings. It would appear that there was some anxiety in this period to demonstrate the sacrality of royal lines under the new religion and an active cultic role for its rulers. It may not be too fanciful to see this as part of the transition process from paganism to Christianity because, before conversion, royal lines had apparently traced their descent from gods, and kings had had an active role in certain cultic practices.[141] It was not a trend which church leaders seem to have been anxious to encourage at this time, though the tradition of murdered kings and princes being regarded as saints was exploited throughout the period and appears to have had a deep-rooted popular basis which may have had its origins before conversion and been actively utilized by the early impresarios of kingly cults in the royal nunneries.[142] Royal nunneries were certainly involved in the promotion of cults for some of the later murdered or martyred kings, those of Cynehelm at Winchcombe,[143] Wigstan at Repton, Edward the Martyr at Shaftesbury and Waltheof at Romsey being notable examples. But what is more significant in the nunneries after the seventh century is the concentration on the promotion of royal women of the community as saints. These princess-saints could also demonstrate the sacrality of the royal line, but in a way that was much more acceptable to early church leaders such as Bede. Bede's preferences are strongly suggested by the large number of royal female saints who fill the pages of the *Ecclesiastical History* in contrast to a lone male royal saint, the blessed Oswald, whom Bede stresses was not a martyr, but worthy of being a saint because of the good Christian life he led.[144] The contrast is all the more striking because other princely saints were apparently being culted by the time Bede wrote. He acknowledged the Christian lives of some like Oswine and Sigebert of the East Angles, but fell short of referring to them as saints, and other influential cults like that of Æthelbert and Æthelred of Kent have not been included in any form.[145]

That saintly women were seen as adding a sacral lustre to a royal pedigree, is suggested by Hrostwitha's account of the ancestry of Edith, the daughter of Edward the Elder who married the future Otto I in 929 or 930.[146] Hrostwitha saw Edith as bringing a new distinction to the Liudolfng line as she was not only descended from a race of great kings, but from a line of saintly ancestors and was *natam de stirpe beata Oswaldi regis* whose praises were sung throughout the world because he had died in the name of Christ.[147] The West Saxon royal line did not in fact descend directly from Oswald of Northumbria though they could claim less direct kinship. There had been several instances of intermarriage between the Northumbrian and West Saxon royal houses, and Oswald had stood as godfather to King Cynegils of Wessex whose daughter he had married.[148] Relics of important early saints were deliberately transferred to West Saxon centres of power to boost their claims to rule all England,[149] and Oswald had been claimed for the dynasty in 909 when Æthelflaed (sister of Edward the Elder) and her husband Æthelred moved his remains from Bardney to their own New Minster in Gloucester where they were to be buried.[150] It would appear that by the early tenth century Oswald had become an adopted member of the West Saxon royal house, making up for their own lack of any early male royal saints. However, though he added distinction to the royal line, in the early tenth century it was the women of the royal house like Eadburh of Nunnaminster and Edith of Wilton who manifested its inherited saintly qualities. To Hrostwitha – and presumably this is how matters were viewed in England as well – royal saints indicated a *beata stirps*. Widukind also believed that Edith came from a family distinguished by *sancta religio* as well as *regalis potentia*,[151] and it seems to have been hoped that the former would be transmitted to the children of Otto and Edith, and so raise them above rivals within the royal house and among the Saxon nobility.[152] One sign of the sacral qualities of Anglo-Saxon royal blood was that, according to Hrostwitha, Edith had inherited a virtuous personality with a potential for saintliness[153] which was confirmed by miracles after her death.[154]

The saintly princesses of Anglo-Saxon royal houses must have been seen in this way as well, as manifestations of the holiness of their royal lines that predisposed these women towards lives of personal sanctity. The rehearsal of saintly relatives by birth and marriage that forms part of the 'Kentish legend' produced at Minster-in-Thanet provides a hagiographical alternative to the secular pedigrees which traced descent from heroes of the Germanic past.[155] The one exemplified Widukind's *sancta religio* and the other the *regalis potentia* of the Anglo-Saxon royal houses. Thus, although the Anglo-Saxon royal houses may have been predisposed to esteem and desire male royal saints, the profusion of princess-saints implies that their cults also became highly valued, and no doubt the royal nunneries nurtured this view to their own advantage. With the issue of the promotion of royal saints we get close to the heart of why the foundation of nunneries was so significant for successive dynasties in Anglo-Saxon England. Royal princesses who founded them, or who were nurtured within them, were a manifestation of the special status of royal houses as *beatae stirpes* which separated them from the merely noble. Although princess-saints may not have been as dear to popular belief as murdered princes, they nevertheless seem to have formed a significant category. Not all Anglo-Saxon female saints were royal, but the majority do seem to have been, though allowance must be made for those for whom royal status was claimed when little else was known.[156] The fact that royal status became a topos for an Anglo-Saxon female saint in itself reflects the prevalence of the princess-saint.

However, the queenly saints of the tenth century are a rather different matter, since they were not blood descendants of the royal house, but women of the nobility who had married into it. Their personal saintliness helped to further ennoble the families from which they came, but also made their royal children doubly blessed. This latter aspect may have been particularly prominent in the cult at Shaftesbury of St Ælfgifu, wife of King Edmund and mother of King Edgar. Her cult was widely diffused in Wessex on the evidence of calendars and litanies of the saints, and was probably promoted in the reformed monasteries in the reign of Edgar.[157] William of Malmesbury provides the only indication of the contents of the *Vita* that must once have existed for her.[158] The references to her personal charity, clemency and prophetic powers are reminiscent of those attributed to Matilda, the mother of Otto I, another dynastic saint who had devoted her life to being a wife and mother.[159] The case of Wulfthryth of Wilton is rather different, since she had spent a large part of her life as an abbess, but the development of her sanctity may have been aided by the fact that she was the mother of St Edith, whose cult was developed at a time when King Æthelred was particularly keen to stress his possession of two saintly siblings, Edith and Edward the Martyr.[160] The cult of the latter was carefully nurtured at the dynastic centre at Shaftesbury in ways that would continue the tradition of murdered princes manifesting the strength of God's support for an Anglo-Saxon royal house. In all periods nunneries showed a willingness to develop cults of male and female members of the royal house, and this must have been one of the ways in which they demonstrated their usefulness as religious communities to their kingly patrons.

Other religious functions of royal nunneries

Pre c. 850

The ecclesiastical duties described above which royal nunneries performed on behalf of the royal houses that were their patrons were compatible with the contemplative life traditionally associated with monasticism. Bede praises the religious life of several early nunneries, and presented abbesses such as Hild of Whitby and Æthelthryth of Ely not just as models for female religious, but for all who followed the monastic life. However, Anglo-Saxon England possessed no deserts of the type to which the early ascetics of the East had been able to retreat. Few Anglo-Saxon monastic communities were in a position to isolate themselves from secular society and the needs of the broader Christian community. Nor does the legislation of church councils draw a distinction between what was expected of the leader of a religious community on grounds of sex; all had the same general responsibilities.[161] In practice there may have been some variations between the ways abbots and abbesses exercised authority. In spite of Hild and Ælfflaed of Whitby attending Northumbrian church councils, with Hild, of course, hosting a famous synod at her own foundation, after the mid-eighth century abbesses did not usually attend major church councils, while some abbots did, and we seem to have here a differential treatment that is gendered.[162] Contributions from both traditional secular and ecclesiastical strains of thinking probably converged here which stressed how women must guard their reputations by not roaming freely and that nuns should be strictly cloistered.[163] One also has to remember that there were many male heads of religious communities who did not attend synods either, and that attendance of abbots varied in different periods and kingdoms. Representation may sometimes have been delegated to men, but as major landowners and office-holders within the church, abbesses did attend some public meetings, as the Mercian royal abbesses Cynethryth and Cwoenthryth had to do when their claims to various minsters and estates were heard in synods;[164] it would appear that the abbesses were never wholly barred from these predominantly male gatherings.

Recent years have seen a major debate in Anglo-Saxon studies concerning the so-called 'minster hypothesis', of which an important element is the issue of how far monasteries were involved in the provision of pastoral care in the seventh and eighth centuries.[165] Differing conclusions are possible because none of the surviving Anglo-Saxon sources specify exactly how the religious needs of the bulk of the population were met. The most informative sources concentrate on different facets of the complete picture, and while in theory it should be possible to combine them to create a whole, there is room for debate over how far they intersect. Bede's ecclesiastical landscape was filled with *monasteria*, and all his religious, whether monks, nuns or priests, seem to have been members of communities, though no doubt of different sizes and considerable variation in organization.[166] He has relatively few references to other types of church or to interaction of religious, other than bishops, with the lay world. On the other hand, one of the major concerns of the Synod of *Clofesho* of 747 was the provision of pastoral care by priests and their supervision by bishops, but it does not specify where the priests were located, though there is some assumption that they would be living in communities.[167] Therefore one of the key issues is whether the priests providing pastoral care under episcopal supervision were based in their own minsters, or were part of the communities of male and female religious, including the royal nunneries, whose contemplative lives were celebrated by Bede.

As we have seen, provision of pastoral care is unlikely to have been the primary motive for the foundation of royal nunneries, but it may have been a by-product of their endowment with large estates. Excavations at a number of early monastic sites, including Whitby and Hartlepool, appear to have produced evidence that they contained cemeteries for lay communities of men, women and children, as well as for the religious,[168] showing, as Alan Thacker has remarked, that they 'made provision for at least one important pastoral requirement of the surrounding inhabitants'.[169] Monasteries were responsible for many laymen and laywomen who lived on their estates, like the cowman Caedmon who lived and worked as a secular on the Whitby estate before the revelation of his miraculous gift.[170] It is hardly likely that their monastic overseers would leave them to follow non-Christian practices on their doorstep, or without provision to follow Christianity once converted. Hild is specifically said to have been concerned to train the men under her care so that there would be no shortage of priests.[171] The *Lives* of St Cuthbert contain a vignette where the bishop consecrates a church founded by Ælfflaed of Whitby on one of her outlying estates.[172]

In some instances it would appear that a nunnery was founded as the major ecclesiastical centre in one of the administrative districts that can be traced in a number of the early kingdoms. Some of the best evidence comes from Kent where the important royal nunneries of Thanet, Lyminge, Hoo, and probably Minster-in-Sheppey, were the main churches for early *regiones*.[173] Four abbesses are specifically mentioned in the text of Wihtred's grant of privileges to the Kentish churches in terms that suggest they are being ranked alongside the major male foundations,[174] and the proceedings of the Synod of Bapchild that was forged in the ninth century named eight major churches in Kent, of which five were nunneries.[175] Kent may have been exceptional in the degree of parochial supervision concentrated in royal nunneries, but the existence of these large parishes associated with early monastic foundations, including nunneries, has been suggested for many different parts of the country, and is a central plank of the 'minster hypothesis'.[176] The proximity of early minsters to royal vill sites from which the secular administration of the districts would be carried out has been noted as a recurrent feature.[177]

As was argued in Chapter 1, kings may initially have expected that they would have greater authority over the church than in fact they were able to achieve, and the churches delegated to the control of kinswomen would have been one means through which they may have hoped to exercise such authority.[178] Bishops naturally opposed any tendency for well-connected foundations to become independent ecclesiastical fiefs, and in the provisions of the Synod of *Clofesho* of 747 they can be seen exercising their corporate muscle to assert their unquestionable duty to supervise priests providing pastoral care wherever they might be based within their dioceses. Jurisdiction over priests was one of the ways in which bishops could attempt to assert authority over all the religious communities of the diocese. It gave a pretext, and a synodally sanctioned right at the Council of *Clofesho* of 747, for bishops to intervene in monasteries, and at the Council of Chelsea in 816 they were empowered to annex impoverished houses.[179] In this way some former monasteries came into episcopal hands, and so far as the supervision of pastoral care went, the middlemen – the abbots and abbesses – were cut out. In fact the monastic element of the foundations seems to have disappeared altogether in the late eighth and ninth centuries, leaving small groups of secular clergy to carry out pastoral duties under direct episcopal supervision.[180]

Before this stage was reached the dual loyalty which priests (some of whom would also have been monks) would have owed to both their abbatial and episcopal superiors must have caused some strains of which only occasional hints surface in the sources. Such conflicts may have contributed to the problems of which Abbess Eangyth complained to Boniface in having to supervise a mixed community where the monks were fractious.[181] On the other hand, priests or monks, even if they moved away from their original foundations, might still feel strong ties with an abbess who had been their monastic superior. Such a relationship is revealed in the letter from Lull and his two brothers, who were working in the German missions with Boniface, to their former superior, the royal abbess Cyneburh.[182] The letter is couched in terms of the greatest respect, and the brothers assure her that 'if any of us happen to visit the realms of this British land, we will seek out the obedience and government of no man in place of subjection to your benevolence'. It is revealed in the course of the letter that Abbess Cyneburh also appears to be the 'lord' of the brothers' family land, and it may not have been uncommon in the early middle ages for a monastery's inmates to be recruited from subtenants of monastic lands.[183] Monastic overlordship drawing on such deep-rooted ties may not have been as easily overshadowed by episcopal authority as synodal degrees might seem to imply. They present the situation the bishops wanted to achieve, not necessarily what occurred in practice. The desire to present the ideal in the relationship of bishop and monastic head may have influenced the depictions of Bede whose views on pastoral provision may be seen in line with what was propounded at *Clofesho* in 747.[184] Such aims may help to explain what Stephanie Hollis has seen as a derogatory reworking in his *Vita S. Cuthberti* of the portrayal of Abbess Ælfflaed of Whitby in the Anonymous *Life* of the saint.[185] Bede's respect for Abbess Ælfflaed as the leader of a monastic community is made clear in the *Ecclesiastical History*,[186] but in his *Life* of Cuthbert her subordination to the bishop is emphasized. Ælfflaed turns to Cuthbert for advice; the bishop's superior prophetic and healing powers are asserted, and the human frailty of

Ælfflaed's emotions is contrasted with Cuthbert's detachment from such earthly ties.[187] What Bede considered to be the correct balance of authority between bishop and monastic head is demonstrated through the *Vita*, as well as Cuthbert's own sanctity.

It seems likely that the early nunneries, like other contemporary monastic communities, had responsibilities for pastoral care in the districts subject to their authority and, as has been suggested for some time, that one of the reasons they contained both men and women was, at least in part, because of the need to provide priests for parochial duties.[188] There is no suggestion in any of our sources that nuns were involved directly in preaching or ministering to local populations, though Anglo-Saxon nuns who joined the missions in Francia seem to have been more active partly, one presumes, because a shortage of male personnel in this unusual 'colonial' situation meant that these women had to take on roles that their counterparts in England would probably not have considered filling. The position of Leoba was particularly exceptional because of her kinship with Boniface, and a number of other leading female monastics in Germany seem to have been related to him as well so that one could say that the active female missionary role in Germany was a family concern in which all shared.[189] Boniface delegated some of his authority to Leoba, who was apparently his closest surviving relative. His legacy to her was symbolized by his dying gift of his monastic cowl, and she subsequently exercised something of a supervisory role over his foundation of Fulda where he wanted both of them to be buried in the same tomb.[190] Leoba was not just supervisor of the female communities founded as part of the Bonifician mission, but had a broader monastic remit and seems to have been the main representative of Boniface's authority in the region where she was based. Even Rudolf's careful presentation of her life as that of an idealized monastic leader cannot conceal the active role she played as a Christian leader in Tauberbischofsheim and the surrounding area.[191] In England there was probably a readier supply of men to whom all parochial duties from the female minsters could be delegated. However, abbesses as religious heads would inevitably have been drawn into the concerns of local people in a not dissimilar way to Leoba to whom the inhabitants of the area around Bischofsheim are depicted as turning in times of trouble.[192] Bede's belief that an enclosed contemplative life was the most appropriate for religious women may mean that he underplayed their significance as upholders of the new religion in the districts in which they lived.[193] Like the nunneries founded in Germany, those in England may have also been 'facilitators for the creation of new religious allegiances and of new religious patterns of observance . . . a rallying point where the inculcation of Christian ideas and values took place'.[194] As the active role of Leoba and her companions does not seem to have had precedents in existing Merovingian female monasticism, one might suggest that their model came from within England, including from Wimborne, where Leoba and her kinswoman Thecla were trained. Even Bede says of Abbess Hild that not only kings and princes, but ordinary people (*mediocres*) came to seek her advice,[195] and when her cowman

Caedmon received his gift from God her reeve naturally brought him to her attention so that she could decide what should be done.[196]

Only if one believed that an abbess should have a more restricted scope of behaviour than an abbot – and no distinction was made in early Anglo-Saxon church legislation – need the role of nunneries as local pastoral centres have caused concern. Surrounding inhabitants may have come to the nunnery church, but that need not necessarily have involved inappropriate mingling with the nuns. Several early descriptions of double houses are careful to emphasize the segregation of female and male religious,[197] and so presumably nuns and local congregations could be kept separate as well. Excavations are revealing that the sites of nunneries could be spread over substantial areas with zoning of different activities, and so presumably of the various sets of people who made up the communities.[198] Multiple churches were the norm and so could have been designated for separate functions or congregations;[199] the discrete cemeteries at Hartlepool for the religious community and the local population may also imply that each group had its own church.[200] At Lyminge the presence of priest-abbots in the seventh and eighth centuries seems to suggest that the male religious of the community were separately overseen, and such an arrangement may have been connected with their provision of pastoral care.[201]

Post 850

Although a strong case has been made by several authors for double houses as centres from which pastoral care was provided for dependent districts, it has not been so widely appreciated that the later nunneries often had similar responsibilities. The evidence is not so apparent in the sources produced in the Anglo-Saxon or Norman period, though Abbess Wulfthryth of Wilton is reported to have rescued two priests of Wilton from the custody of the sheriff,[202] and it was the *officiarii* of Barking (presumably male clerics) who conspired with Queen Ælfthryth to have Wulfhild replaced as abbess.[203] The text of the Cotton Galba prayer-book, tentatively identified with Nunnaminster, implies that it was produced in a community with male and female religious.[204] But when pre-Conquest charters are viewed in conjunction with later medieval evidence for parochial responsibilities (sources that have played a vital part in the reconstruction of minster parishes), the role of the later nunneries in pastoral care provision becomes more apparent. One of the features that in the post-Conquest period distinguished the nunneries of pre-Conquest origin from the more recent foundations was that the former possessed canons holding freehold benefices as prebends attached to portions of the nunnery estates to which they were presented by the abbess.[205] The canons had stalls in the nunnery churches and were members of the chapter; in the later middle ages they tended to appoint vicars to carry out the pastoral responsibilities in the parishes of which they were rectors. The term 'prebend' is not found in England until the late eleventh century, but the practice of assigning separate estates for priests providing parochial care may go back to the late Saxon period.[206]

The medieval nuns of Wherwell believed that their house had contained such priests from the time of its foundation,[207] and the same was probably true of the other late Saxon royal nunneries. Many were on the sites of existing minsters or were endowed with minster estates in other locations. The nunnery of Romsey, for instance, seems to have been a refoundation on the site of a minster (presumably male) founded by Edward the Elder,[208] and the use of the north aisle of the Norman abbey church by the parish, served by two prebendaries, could be interpreted as a result of the nunnery's inheritance of existing parochial arrangements.[209] A case may be made for Amesbury, Wherwell and Wilton also having been grafted on to existing minsters (though in the absence of information identifying the sites of the early nunneries of Wessex one cannot know whether any of these had been double houses or not; possibly there was greater continuity of female minsters in Wessex than is apparent from the sources).[210] Amesbury is revealed in later medieval documentation as a classic mother church with dependent churches in a compact geographical location corresponding to the hundred that also bore its name;[211] whether the current parish church was originally the site of the Saxon nunnery church and shared by the nuns and their parishioners has long been a topic of debate.[212] At Wherwell a large minster parish seems to have been divided into three prebendaries; the parishioners of Wherwell itself had their own chapel, but the parish font was in the nunnery church and the children of the parish were baptized there.[213] The history of Wilton may be more complex. Wilton was an important early royal centre that gave its name to the shire, and on these grounds alone it is a candidate for an early minster site though none is specifically recorded. However, detailed examination of the later medieval evidence suggests that the foundation of the nunnery may have disrupted earlier arrangements and that part of its endowments included a minster church at South Newton, to the north of Wilton, that became one of its prebends.[214] Something similar may have happened with Shaftesbury. There is no evidence for an early minster at Shaftesbury itself, and a reconstruction of early minster *parochiae* in this part of Dorset has suggested that it lay in a marginal position between two parishes.[215] But these earlier arrangements were probably disrupted when Shaftesbury was endowed with all or part of the lands of one of these, the former monastery of Bectun at Iwerne that became one of its prebends.[216] Shaftesbury was also endowed in 1001 with what had probably been an important early minster church at Bradford-on-Avon, and it seems to have been envisaged originally that the nuns would either move there or at least have a permanent residence at the site (presumably based on the former minster buildings).[217] At Barking it can be presumed that the responsibilities of the seventh-century double house continued into the later Anglo-Saxon period and beyond, though we do not know whether there was an unbroken tradition of nuns living at the site. Nunnaminster never possessed its own *parochia*, that is a dependent parish in its immediate vicinity, but it was endowed with substantial estates at Itchen Abbas and Leckford in Hampshire, and All Cannings and Urchfont in Wiltshire, for which in the post-Conquest period it provided pastoral care through its prebendaries.[218] Shaftesbury, Wherwell and Wilton were also responsible through prebendaries for pastoral care in outlying estates.[219] It would appear that the royal nunneries, like many of the major later monasteries, tended to found their own local churches for parochial care on estates they were granted in the tenth century, and were able to detach them from earlier minster arrangements.[220]

In addition to the prebendaries, the nuns would have had their own chaplains. The names of several of the chaplains of Wilton are known,[221] and they included Radbod, a monk from Saint Remi at Reims, and Benno, a canon at Trier, who provided instruction for King Edgar's daughter Edith,[222] as well as Goscelin from St Bertin's in Flanders who wrote Edith's *Vita* and remembered his time at Wilton with great affection.[223] Post-Conquest accounts record other officials under the authority of the abbess who helped with the administration of the abbey and its estates, and these may also have had their pre-Conquest counterparts, such as the *officiarii* of Barking. Shaftesbury, for instance, had a sacrist who acted as the convent's bailiff and receiver, and Wilton an epistoler on an annual salary,[224] but at Wherwell the canons were expected to assist the nuns in their business affairs.[225] Other arrangements only recorded later in the middle ages may preserve pre-Conquest practices. At Wherwell, where in the fourteenth century it was believed that customs relating to their canons went back to the period of foundation, the canons lived in houses in the village and were supplied daily with food from the nunnery's kitchen,[226] while at Barking in the thirteenth century the chaplains had their own rooms within the precinct.[227] The provision of individual houses within the environs of the main monastic buildings recalls the small timber buildings excavated at the earlier double monasteries of Hartlepool and Whitby that could have housed one or two people,[228] as well as arrangements for secular canons at sites such as Abingdon.[229]

The more rural nunneries with relatively spacious sites could, like their early Anglo-Saxon predecessors, have accommodated nuns and clerics, as well as other dependants of the houses such as servants and tenants, in separate locations, but in towns there would be greater pressure on available space. These problems were most acute at Nunnaminster, and the nunnery's urban estate was reorganized in the monastic reform period so that the nuns could live within a walled precinct, with Colebrook Street laid out beyond the precinct walls for their tenants, and perhaps for the clerical members of the community as well.[230] The tenants had their own parochial church of St Peter's in Colebrook Street,[231] but the nunnery church cannot have been closed to visitors, since it contained the shrine of St Eadburh who apparently rivalled St Swithun in popularity as a worker of miracles.[232] Most of the other nunnery churches contained shrines of active saints as well, as is shown by their entries in the late Saxon 'List of saints' resting-places'.[233] As many nunnery churches were also used in part by local congregations, or as at Bradford-on-Avon, where the nunnery and minster churches were next door to one another,[234] the complete segregation of nuns from the secular world would have been hard to achieve.

Conclusion

Royal nunneries were evidently valued by the families which supported them for their roles as ecclesiastical foundations. The intercessory power of prayer was a prime concern, and it may have seemed particularly desirable that it be carried out, or supervised, by family members. Nunneries nurtured not only spiritual well-being, but also surrounded a royal house with a spiritual aura through the cult of saints. Competition between rival branches of royal houses which was such a feature of political life for much of the Anglo-Saxon period ensured that there was a continual demand for the spiritual services royal nunneries could provide, as no group on reaching the desired heights of royal power wished to risk losing their position by forfeiting divine support, or be seen to be deficient in the behaviour expected of a Christian monarch. But though there was a continual desire for the services of royal nuns, there was not necessarily continual support for the same nunneries, as, although some new dynasties wished to demonstrate continuity with previous reigns by patronage of houses closely associated with past regimes, most preferred to concentrate resources on their own foundations and were not concerned to protect the souls of rivals and enemies. It was only around the beginning of the eleventh century, a period of intense royal support for the male houses of the Benedictine reform movement, that patronage of royal nunneries began to waiver; no further new royal nunneries were founded and fewer royal women entered the church (especially as widows). Whether this trend would have continued if the events of 1066 had turned out differently is impossible to say, but it does fit with what has been perceived as a broader European trend whereby male Benedictine communities attracted patronage away from nunneries.

But few, if any, royal nunneries could be concerned only with the spiritual needs of the families that supported them. As major ecclesiastical foundations, they had obligations to provide pastoral care for the dependants on their vast estates. If these obligations were not inherent from the time of foundation, they would soon be brought to the attention of abbots and abbesses by the bishops who had no alternative but to insist that monasteries recognize their parochial responsibilities if a system of pastoral care was to be provided for the bulk of the population. Even in the later Saxon period when more local churches had been established, the newly founded nunneries might still have parochial responsibilities, especially when they were endowed with, or founded upon, former minster estates. Their ecclesiastical responsibilities towards their families and to the wider populace meant that royal nunneries shared certain characteristics throughout the Anglo-Saxon period. These included the fact that at all periods the foundations contained some men as well as women for whom the abbesses had responsibility. There were, of course, differences as well. The true double monasteries of the conversion period contained substantial numbers of monks as well as nuns, whereas the nunneries founded by the West Saxon house after 850 contained a relatively smaller number of priests and lesser clerics. But what is conceived as the classic double monastery from the pages of the *Historia Ecclesiastica* may not have been the norm up to the end of the ninth century. As more all-male minsters were founded, and as double houses of monks and nuns came to be seen as out of step with forms of monastic provision elsewhere in the Christian world, so the proportion of men in communities commanded by abbesses is likely to have declined. They were also more likely as time progressed to have been priests and clerics rather than monks – part of a general trend in the eighth century away from monasticism which may have been somewhat loosely defined in some early foundations in any case. When Guthlac entered the nunnery of Repton he joined the *clerici* there, and when he wished to follow a more ascetic regime he withdrew to the fens of Crowland. The greater contrast may therefore not have been so much between nunneries of the pre- and post-viking periods (as traditionally conceived), but that between the double houses of the conversion period, on the one hand, and nunneries from the mid-eighth century to the end of the Anglo-Saxon period, on the other.

All Anglo-Saxon abbesses probably had some men as well as women under their control, and nunneries, even after the imposition of the *Regularis Concordia*, were probably never purely contemplative institutions strictly claustered from the concerns of the world. Abbesses not only had to oversee the spiritual lives of the religious subject to them, but also administer large estates and care for spiritual and secular needs of the many people who lived upon them. It is only occasionally that we can glimpse abbesses in narratives as estate managers, as briefly for Hild and Ælfflaed of Whitby, but through charters we can see them acquiring land, and often exercising considerable acumen in arranging additional rights and privileges.[235]

As ecclesiastical foundations, the royal nunneries shared certain features with other major minsters. Some of these, such as Bardney, were also specially favoured by royal patrons, and like the royal nunneries might also serve the royal kin-group through such specialist functions as the promotion of royal saints or as places of burial. In looking at ecclesiastical roles, we cannot point to functions that were *only* performed in royal nunneries, though the concentration of them in the nunneries is often striking. But royal nunneries were interconnected to the families which supported them in more direct ways than the male minsters. Just as women who married remained the responsibility of the family they had been born into, so royal women who went into the church retained strong links with their secular kin. This gave them opportunities to acquire lavish patronage, but also placed them under obligations that sometimes took them away from what church leaders might see as appropriate behaviour for religious women. The roles that abbesses and nuns played within their family networks are the subject of Chapter 5, where it will be seen that many royal nunneries, though they may have performed their religious functions impeccably, remained closely linked with the family circle and were often drawn into the world of secular politics.

Notes

1. P. J. Geary, *Before France and Germany: The Creation and Transformation of the Merovingian World* (Oxford, 1988), 171.
2. See e.g., K. Leyser, *Rule and Conflict in an Early Medieval Society: Ottonian Saxony* (London, 1979), 49–73.
3. J. Blair, *The Church in Anglo-Saxon Society* (Oxford, forthcoming).
4. M. de Jong, 'Carolingian monasticism: the power of prayer', in R. McKitterick (ed.), *The New Cambridge Medieval History, II. c. 700–c. 900* (Cambridge, 1995), 622–53.
5. *HE*, III, 24.
6. Plummer, I, 405–23, esp. 414–15; *EHD*, I, no. 170.
7. *HS*, III, 367, ch. 15.
8. *HS*, III, 375–6, ch. 375; C. Cubitt, *Anglo-Saxon Church Councils c. 650–c. 850* (Leicester, 1995), 101, 111.
9. *HS*, III, 367–8; Cubitt, *Church Councils*, 125–52.
10. *HE*, IV, 7.
11. *HE*, IV, 19.
12. M. Lapidge and J. Rosier, *Aldhelm: The Poetic Works* (Woodbridge, 1985), 47–9.
13. *V. Guthlaci*, ch. 23.
14. Tangl, no. 55; a letter from two abbesses Cuenburh and Coenburh to abbots Coengils and Ingeld agreeing to a proposal for prayers of mutual intercession.
15. Dümmler, no. 102; S. Allott, *Alcuin of York* (York, 1974), no. 42.
16. Cubitt, *Church Councils*, 125–52.
17. S 20; S. Kelly (ed.), *Charters of St Augustine's Abbey, Canterbury and Minster-in-Thanet*, British Academy, Anglo-Saxon Charters, IV (Oxford, 1995), no. 10, 38–44.
18. Tangl, no. 14.
19. *V. Athelstan*, ch. 3 in F. Liebermann, *Gesetze des Angelsachsen*, 3 vols (Halle, 1898–1916), I, 168.
20. T. Symons (ed.), *Regularis Concordia Anglicae nationis monachorum sanctimonialiumque* (London, 1953), esp. xxxii.
21. M. Lapidge and M. Winterbottom (eds), *Wulfstan of Winchester, Life of St Æthelwold* (Oxford, 1991), lx.
22. R. W. Southern, *Western Society and the Church in the Middle Ages* (Harmondsworth, 1970), 310; P. J. Geary, *Phantoms of Remembrance: Memory and Oblivion at the End of the First Millennium* (Princeton, NJ, 1994), esp. 63–9; de Jong, 'Carolingian monasticism', 647–50.
23. S. Kelly (ed.), *Charters of Shaftesbury Abbey*, British Academy, Anglo-Saxon Charters, V (Oxford, 1996), no. 8, 30–5; S 419.
24. M. A. O'Donovan (ed.), *Charters of Sherborne*, British Academy, Anglo-Saxon Charters, III (Oxford, 1988), nos 7 and 8, 25–33; S 422 and 423.
25. B. J. Muir (ed.), *A Pre-Conquest English Prayer-Book* (BL MSS Cotton Galba A xiv and Nero A ii (ff. 3–13)), Henry Bradshaw Society, 103 (Woodbridge, 1988).
26. Muir, *Pre-Conquest Prayer-Book*, ix–xvii; however, M. Lapidge (*Anglo-Saxon Litanies of the Saints*, Henry Bradshaw Society, 106 (London, 1991), 69–70), proposes 'a nunnery in the liturgical ambit of Winchester, perhaps Shaftesbury'. J. Hillaby ('Early Christian and pre-Conquest Leominster: an exploration of the sources', *Transactions of the Woolhope Naturalists Field Club*, 45 (1986–87), 557–685) argued for a Leominster origin as a calendar and litanies include unique references to saints of

Leominster and elsewhere in the West Midlands. Clearly, behind these very long lists of saints there are several contributing sources. If Nunnaminster was the place of origin of the prayer-book it could, for instance, have been endowed with a calendar and other texts from Mercia, the province of origin of its foundress Queen Ealhswith.

27. Tangl, no. 10, 7–15; P. Sims-Williams, *Religion and Literature in Western England, 600–800* (Cambridge, 1990), 243–72.
28. Tangl, no. 73; *EHD*, I, no. 177, at 820.
29. *HE*, IV, 11.
30. *HE*, III, 14.
31. *HE*, III, 24.
32. D. Rollason, *The Mildrith Legend: A Study in Early Medieval Hagiography in England* (Leicester, 1982).
33. Thunor is, of course, the name of an Anglo-Saxon god, and one of the many intriguing aspects of this account is the implication that a pagan cult closely associated with a royal vill was succeeded by the foundation of a royal nunnery.
34. The legend of St Osyth of Chich has an important role for a snow-white stag which appears at an opportune moment to distract King Sigehere from his marital duties; D. Bethell, 'The Lives of St. Osyth of Essex and St. Osyth of Aylesbury', *Analecta Bollandiana*, 88 (1980), 75–127, at 86–7, 112 and 115.
35. Rollason, *Mildrith Legend*, 15–31; S. Hollis, 'The Minster-in-Thanet foundation story', *A-SE*, 27 (1998), 41–74.
36. Rollason, *Mildrith Legend*, 49–51.
37. B 535; Sims-Williams, *Religion and Literature*, 35,123–4
38. D. Rollason, 'Cults of murdered royal saints in Anglo-Saxon England', *A-SE*, 11 (1983), 1–22. However, there are difficulties in dating the inception of the cults of Cynehelm and Wigstan, since the earliest references to their cults date from the eleventh century. See further below.
39. *HE*, III, 24.
40. Asser, chs 92 and 98; S. Keynes, 'King Alfred the Great and Shaftesbury Abbey', in L. Keen (ed.), *Studies in the Early History of Shaftesbury Abbey* (Dorchester, 1999), 17–72, at 39–41.
41. *V. Eadburgae*, ch. 2, 264–6; *V. Edithae*, ch. 5, 43–7.
42. J. Doran, 'Oblation or obligation? A canonical ambiguity', in D. Wood (ed.), *The Church and Childhood*, Studies in Church History, 31 (Oxford, 1994), 127–41; S. Crawford, *Childhood in Anglo-Saxon England* (Stroud, 1999), 53–4.
43. Leyser, *Rule and Conflict*, 49–50, though what was celebrated was not the surrender of infants but a formal veiling at the age of about 11 or 12.
44. King Aldfrith of Northumbria, a son of Oswiu, does seem to have had a monastic career before he became king, but the circumstances were unusual here and belong to the period when Christianity was still being absorbed into Anglo-Saxon society; C. Ireland, 'Aldfrith of Northumbria and the Irish genealogies', *Celtica*, 22 (1991), 64–78.
45. R. Bartlett, 'Symbolic meanings of hair in the middle ages', *TRHS*, 6th Series, 4 (1994), 43–60.
46. N. Brooks, *The Early History of the Church of Canterbury* (Leicester, 1984), 120–5.
47. H. Härke, '"Warrior graves?" The background of the Anglo-Saxon burial rite', *Past and Present*, 126 (1990), 22–43; N. Stoodley, *The Spindle and the Spear: A Critical Enquiry into the Construction and Meaning of Gender in the Early Anglo-Saxon Inhumation Burial Rite*, BAR, 288 (Oxford, 1999).

48. B. A. E. Yorke, 'The acceptance of Christianity at the Anglo-Saxon royal courts', in M. Carver (ed.), *The Cross Goes North* (Woodbridge, forthcoming). See also Chapter 1.

49. L. Lancaster, 'Kinship in Anglo-Saxon society; parts I and II', *British Journal of Sociology*, 9 (1958), 230–50, 359–77; H. Loyn, 'Kinship in Anglo-Saxon England', *A-SE*, 3 (1974), 197–209; C. Fell, *Women in Anglo-Saxon England* (London, 1984), 74–88.

50. J. Shephard, 'The social identity of the individual in isolated barrows and barrow cemeteries in Anglo-Saxon England', in B. C. Burnham and J. Kingsbury (eds), *Space, Hierarchy and Society: Interdisciplinary Studies in Social Area Analysis*, BAR International Series, 59 (1979), 47–79.

51. D. Mauskopf Deliyannis, 'Church burial in Anglo-Saxon England: the pre-rogative of kings', *Frühmittelalterliche Studien*, 29 (1995), 96–119.

52. See Table 1 in Deliyannis, 'Church burial', 117–19, but kings of Hwicce and Magon-saetan are not included.

53. *HE*, II, 3 and 5.

54. R. U. Potts, 'The tombs of the kings and archbishops in St Austin's Abbey, Canterbury', *Archaeologia Cantiana*, 38 (1926), 97–112.

55. Deliyannis, 'Church burial', 101–2. The earliest recorded royal burial at Winchester in an Anglo-Saxon source is that of King Cynewulf (d. 757) from the *Anglo-Saxon Chronicle sub anno* 757. No burials before the ninth century were found within Old Minster when it was excavated, though the southern porticus was not available for excavation.

56. *HE*, IV, 11.

57. *A-SC*, 716.

58. *HE*, II, 20.

59. *HE*, III, 12.

60. *V. Wilfredi*, ch. 24. King Eadbert of Northumbria (d. 768) was probably buried in St Peter's, York, but he had abdicated in 758 in order to enter the community; T. Arnold, '*Historia Regum*', in *idem* (ed.), *Symeonis Monachi Opera Omnia*, Vol. II (London, 1885), 768.

61. These include King Æthelred of Mercia at Bardney (*A-SC*, 716), the arms and hands of King Oswald of Northumbria at Bamburgh (*HE*, III, 12), King Ælfwold I of Northumbria at Hexham (*A-SC*, 788) and King Osred II of Northumbria at Tynemouth (*A-SC*, 792).

62. *A-SC*, 757; see B. A. E. Yorke, 'The Bonifacian mission and female religious in Wessex', *Early Medieval Europe*, 7 (1998), 145–72.

63. See Chapter 3 and S. Foot, *Veiled Women*, 2 vols (Aldershot, 2000), II, 197–204, for uncertainty over whether the church in which Beorhtric was buried at Wareham is to be identified as the site of the nunnery.

64. P. J. Huggins, 'Excavations of a Belgic and Romano-British farm with Middle Saxon cemetery and churches at Nazeingbury, Essex, 1975–6', *Essex Archaeology and History*, 10 (1978), 3rd Series, 29–117. When the first church was replaced by a larger structure burials were made over the site of the former, thus complicating inter-pretation.

65. The male is burial no. 100, a large and robust skeleton, aged between 35 and 45 years, but with stress fractures to the feet as if he had done a lot of walking: G. Putnam, 'Analysis of the skeletal material', in Huggins, 'Nazeingbury', 57.

66. K. Bascombe, 'Two charters of King Suebred of Essex', in K. Neale (ed.), *An Essex Tribute: Essays Presented to F. G. Emmison* (Cambridge, 1987), 85–96.

67. Geary, *Before France and Germany*, 171–6.

68. M. de Maillé, *Les Cryptes de Jouarre* (Paris, 1971).

69. H. M. Taylor, 'St Wystan's church, Repton, Derbyshire: a reconstruction essay', *Archaeological Journal*, 144 (1987), 205–45.

70. M. Biddle and B. Kjølbye-Biddle, 'The Repton stone', *A-SE*, 14 (1985), 233–92.

71. S. Bassett, 'A probable Mercian royal mausoleum at Winchcombe, Gloucestershire', *Antiquaries Journal*, 65 (1985), 82–100.

72. W. H. Hart, *Historia et Cartularium Monasterii Sancti Petri Gloucestriae*, 3 vols, Rolls Series (London, 1863–7), I, 6–7; Sims-Williams, *Religion and Literature*, 125–6.

73. *HE*, II, 20. For the significance of the dedication to Gregory see A. T. Thacker, 'Memorialising Gregory the Great: the origin and transmission of a papal cult in the seventh and early eighth centuries', *Early Medieval Europe*, 7 (1998), 59–84.

74. B. Colgrave (ed.), *The Earliest Life of Gregory the Great* (Cambridge, 1968), ch. 19, 104–5.

75. *HE*, III, 24.

76. B. A. E. Yorke, 'The bishops of Winchester, the kings of Wessex and the development of Winchester in the ninth and early tenth centuries', *Proceedings of Hampshire Field Club and Archaeological Society*, 40 (1984), 61–70; S. Keynes (ed.), *The Liber Vitae of the New Minster and Hyde Abbey, Winchester* (Copenhagen, 1995), 2–5, 81–2; W. de Gray Birch (ed.), *Liber Vitae: Register and Martyrology of New Minster and Hyde Abbey, Winchester* (London, 1892), 3–7.

77. Edward's actions may be compared with those of his sister Æthelflaed and brother-in-law Æthelred in Mercia. They founded their own New Minster in their episcopal centre of Gloucester in which they were buried, but apparently in a separate mausoleum just outside and in alignment with the church that recalls the practice of previous Mercian rulers at Gloucester and Winchcombe; C. Heighway and R. Bryant, *The Golden Minster: The Anglo-Saxon Minster and Later Medieval Priory of St Oswald at Gloucester*, CBA Report, 117 (York, 1999).

78. B. A. E. Yorke, 'Æthelwold and the politics of the tenth century', in *idem* (ed.), *Bishop Æthelwold: His Career and Influence* (Woodbridge, 1988), 65–88, at 70–3. Athelstan also arranged for the burial at Malmesbury of his cousins Ælfwine and Æthelwine who died at the battle of *Brunanburh*.

79. *Worcester, s.a.* 946, 398–9.

80. *Ibid.*, 975, 424–5.

81. *A-SC, s.a.* 1016.

82. *A-SC*, D, *s.a.* 955; S. Keynes, 'The "Dunstan B" charters', *A-SE*, 23 (1994), 165–93, at 188–90, interprets Eadred's will to mean that Eadred had originally intended to be buried somewhere other than Winchester.

83. *A-SC, s.a.* 1035 and 1042 (E).

84. *Worcester, s.a.* 1016, 484–5.

85. *A-SC, s.a.* 1066. King Harold II had also been buried at Westminster, presumably in the church superseded by Edward's new foundation, but his body had been exhumed and dishonoured by Harthacnut (see *Worcester, s.a.* 1040, 528–31).

86. Of course, Æthelred's choice for his burial of Wimborne, founded by the sister of the family's ancestor Ingild, spoilt Wimborne's chances of becoming the mausoleum of the new dynasty, for the succession of Alfred's son Edward involved outmanoeuvring

the claims of his nephew Æthelwold, the son of Æthelred. The politically sensitive nature of Æthelred's burial at Wimborne is shown by the fact that it was one of the places seized by Æthelwold when he made his bid for the throne on the death of Alfred (*A-SC, s.a.* 900).

87. See n. 82; *EHD*, I, no. 107.

88. We know that St Mary's, Wareham was a nunnery at this time as the death of Abbess Wulfwyn of Wareham is recorded in the 'C' text of the *Anglo-Saxon Chronicle* for 982.

89. *Passio Edwardi*, 7–10; *V. Oswaldi*, 448–52; Keynes, 'Alfred and Shaftesbury Abbey', 48–55.

90. C. Fell, 'Edward King and Martyr and the Anglo-Saxon hagiographic tradition', in D. Hill (ed.), *Ethelred the Unready: Papers from the Millenary Conference*, BAR, 59 (Oxford, 1978), 1–13.

91. S. Ridyard, *The Royal Saints of Anglo-Saxon England: A Study of West Saxon and East Anglian Cults* (Cambridge, 1988), 154–71.

92. See further Chapter 5. The *Passio Edwardi* (12) names the abbess at the time of Edward's translation as 'Æthelfreda', but unfortunately we do not know anything of her family background.

93. *A-SC*, D and E, *s.a.* 979; *V. Oswaldi*, 452.

94. If compensation had been paid immediately after the murder it should have gone to Edith of Wilton, the half-sister of the two brothers, but there were various reasons why the nunnery of Wilton would have been seen as a less desirable place for Edward's reburial; see further Chapter 5.

95. S 899; Kelly, *Charters of Shaftesbury*, no. 29, 114–22.

96. See Kelly, *Charters of Shaftesbury*, nos 16, 19 and 20, at 68–9 in particular. Kingston was one of the Shaftesbury holdings in Domesday Book for which it held title through charters granted by King Eadred and Eadwig to two individuals, but it is not known exactly when the estate came into Shaftesbury's ownership.

97. S 812; *A-SC, s.a.* 970 (D, E); 971 (G); 972 (C, B); the entry has been erased in 'A' – why and when this occurred is not known.

98. See Chapter 3.

99. *A-SC*, 962; P. Stafford, *Queen Emma and Queen Edith: Queenship and Women's Power in Eleventh-Century England* (Oxford, 1997), 90–1.

100. Ælfgyth is named as Abbess of Wilton in a charter of 955 (S 582).

101. See Chapter 3.

102. Eadgifu, third wife of Edward the Elder, also seems to have been associated with Shaftesbury in her later years, but it is not specifically stated that she was buried there.

103. Stafford, *Queen Emma and Queen Edith*, 94–6.

104. On the importance placed on prayers for the dead in early medieval Europe, see A. Angenendt, 'Theologie und Liturgie der mittelalterlichen Toten-Memoria', in K. Schmidt and J. Wollasch (eds), *Memoria: Der geschichtliche Zeugniswert des liturgischen Gedenkens im Mittelalter* (Munich, 1984), 79–199; M. McLaughlin, *Consorting with Saints: Prayer for the Dead in Early Medieval France* (Ithaca, NY, 1994); and for the roles of women in commemorating the dead see Geary, *Phantoms of Remembrance*, 49–63.

105. Muir (ed.), *Pre-Conquest Prayer-Book*, 122.

106. O. G. Oexle, 'Memoria und Memorialüberlieferung im frühen Mittelalter', *Frühmittelalterliche Studien*, 10 (1976), 70–95.

107. J. Gerchow, *Gedenküberlieferung der Angelsachsen, mit einem Katalog der libri vitae*

und Necrologien, Arbeiten zur Frühmittelalterforschung, 20 (Berlin, 1988), esp. 109–85; Keynes, *Liber Vitae.*

108. For the importance of women in preserving family memory and history, see Geary, *Phantoms of Remembrance,* 49–62, and E. van Houts, *Memory and Gender in Medieval Europe 900–1200* (Basingstoke, 1999).

109. Rollason, *Mildrith Legend,* esp. 41–51; Hollis, 'Minster-in-Thanet'.

110. D. N. Dumville, 'The Anglian collection of royal genealogies and regnal lists', *A-SE,* 5 (1976), 23–50.

111. N. Brooks, 'The creation and early structure of the kingdom of Kent', in S. Bassett (ed.), *The Origins of Anglo-Saxon Kingdoms* (Leicester, 1989), 55–74.

112. D. N. Dumville, 'Kingship, genealogies and regnal lists', in P. Sawyer and I. N. Wood (eds), *Early Medieval Kingship* (Leeds, 1977), 72–104.

113. M. Miller, 'The dates of Deira', *A-SE,* 8 (1979), 35–61.

114. R. Cramp, 'A reconsideration of the monastic site of Whitby', in R. M. Spearman and J. Higgitt (eds), *The Age of Migrating Ideas* (Edinburgh, 1993), 64–73; J. Higgitt, 'Monasteries and inscriptions in early Northumbria, the evidence of Whitby', in C. Bourke (ed.), *From the Isles of the North: Early Medieval Art in Ireland and Britain* (Belfast, 1995), 229–36.

115. R. N. Bailey and R. Cramp, *Corpus of Saxon Stone Sculpture, Vol. II: Cumberland, Westmorland and Lancashire North-of-the-Sands* (London, 1988), 19–22, 61–76 (Bewcastle), 84–7 (Carlisle). It cannot be demonstrated that Bewcastle, a Roman fort, was linked with the nunnery of Carlisle, but one can at least say that the latter is the nearest known substantial religious house to the monument.

116. C. Karkov, 'The Bewcastle cross. Some iconographic problems', in C. Karkov, R. T. Farrell and M. Ryan (eds), *The Insular Tradition* (Albany, NY, 1997), 9–26, at 19. The description of Bewcastle as a stone *liber vitae* was first made by E. O'Carragain in 'A liturgical interpretation of the Bewcastle cross', in M. Stokes and T. Burton (eds), *Medieval Literature and Antiquities. Studies in Honour of Basil Cottle* (Woodbridge, 1987), 15–42, at 32.

117. R. Page in Bailey and Cramp, *Corpus: Cumberland,* 65.

118. The alternative, favoured by Rosemary Cramp and Eamonn O'Carragain, is that the figure represents St John the Evangelist, but in support of its identification as a secular figure see R. N. Bailey, *England's Earliest Sculptors* (Toronto, 1996), 66–9.

119. R. Cramp, *Corpus of Anglo-Saxon Stone Sculpture, Vol. I: County Durham and Northumberland* (London, 1984), 5.

120. See also the grave-markers from Hartlepool that may show the influence of Hild's Frankish connections: Cramp, *Corpus; Durham and Northumberland,* 7, 97–101.

121. Geary, *Before France and Germany,* 173.

122. *HE,* IV, 19; D. Rollason, *Saints and Relics in Anglo-Saxon England* (Oxford, 1989), 34–5; A. T. Thacker, 'The making of a local saint', in A. Thacker and R. Sharpe (eds), *Local Saints and Local Churches in the Early Medieval West* (Oxford, 2002).

123. *HE,* III, 8. Unfortunately Bede provided no dates for Æthelburh's period as abbess or for the death and translation of Eorcengota, but their positioning in the *Historia Ecclesiastica* could imply that he believed the death of Eorecengota had taken place before the death and translation of Æthelthryth.

124. *HE,* IV, 7–10; B. Krusch (ed.), *Ionas, Vitae Columbani Discipulorumque eius, MGH Scriptores Rerum Merovingicarum,* IV (Hanover, 1902), 130–43. Compare particularly *HE,* IV, 8 and 9 with *Ionas, Vitae Columbani,* II, 13 and 12 respectively. See also Chapter 1.

125. J. Blair, 'A saint for every minster?' and 'A handlist of Anglo-Saxon saints', in A. Thacker and R. Sharpe (eds), *Local Saints and Local Churches in the Early Medieval West* (Oxford, 2002), 455–565. See also Chapter 1.
126. A. T. Thacker, '*Membra disjecta*: the division of the body and the diffusion of the cult', in C. Stancliffe and E. Cambridge (eds), *Oswald: Northumbrian King to European Saint* (Stamford, 1995), 97–127. The translations can only be dated to between 680 and 704 (Edwin) and 679 and 697 (Oswald) (*ibid.*, 106).
127. *HE*, III, 6.
128. *HE*, II, 20.
129. Bardney in the province of Lindsey was a joint foundation of Osthryth and her husband was King Æthelred of Mercia. Osthryth was unusual in being actively involved in the cult of a kinsman in her husband's home province rather than her own, but the situation was complicated by the fact that Oswald had once been ruler of Lindsey. Bardney is a dynastic monastery with many similarities to the Anglo-Saxon double houses. See further A. T. Thacker, 'Kings, saints and monasteries in pre-viking Mercia', *Midland History*, 10 (1985), 1–25, at 2–4.
130. Thacker, '*Membra disjecta*', 107–12.
131. Colgrave (ed.), *The Earliest Life of Gregory the Great*, ch. 18, 100–1.
132. Thacker, '*Membra disjecta*', 101–2. There are signs of a popular cult at the site of Oswald's death soon after his death (*ibid.*, 100).
133. *HE*, III, 14; D. Rollason, 'Cults of murdered royal saints in Anglo-Saxon England', *A-SE*, 11 (1983), 1–22, at 3. In the eleventh century Oswine was believed to be buried at Tynemouth and was translated in 1065; Plummer, II, 164.
134. Rollason, *Mildrith Legend, passim*.
135. They are associated with Stone (Staffs.) and there are traditions implying that Stone had once been a nunnery; Rollason, 'Murdered royal saints', 1, but see also Foot, *Veiled Women*, II, 187–9, for scepticism on this. A. R. Rumble, '*Ad Lapidem* in Bede and a Mercian martyrdom', in A. R. Rumble and A. D. Mills (eds), *Names, Places and People* (Stamford, 1997), 307–19, shows how accounts of their martyrdom appear to have been based on Bede's account of the murder of the princes of Wight in *HE*, IV, 16.
136. S. Ridyard, 'Monk-kings and the Anglo-Saxon hagiographic tradition', *Haskins Society Journal*, 6 (1994), 13–27, at 14–15. The site of Sigebert's monastery is not given by Bede, but a later tradition identified it with Bury (St Edmunds).
137. Thacker, 'Kings, saints and monasteries', 2–4.
138. *HE*, IV, 11; Ridyard, 'Monk-kings', 16–17.
139. Bede's account implies that when Saebbi and his wife separated she too entered a religious community, in which case she may well have become a member of the Barking community.
140. See Chapter 1.
141. I. N. Wood, 'Pagan religions and superstitions east of the Rhine from the fifth to the ninth century', in G. Ausenda (ed.), *After Empire: Towards an Ethnology of Europe's Barbarians* (Woodbridge, 1995), 253–79; Yorke, 'Acceptance of Christianity'.
142. C. Cubitt, 'Sites and sanctity: revisiting the cult of murdered and martyred Anglo-Saxon royal saints', *Early Medieval Europe*, 9 (2000), 53–84.
143. Details come from an eleventh-century *Life* and do not seem to reflect how the cult is likely to have been promoted originally at Winchcombe; indeed, Abbess Cwoenthryth, the murdered prince's sister, who presumably oversaw his burial and

may have originated the cult, is the villain of the piece and responsible for his murder, and Cynehelm/Kenelm who was an adult is presented as a child in accordance with a popular topos in such *Lives* in the period of monastic reform; R. Love, *Three Eleventh-Century Anglo-Latin Saints' Lives* (Oxford, 1996), lxxxix–cxxxix, 50–89; P. Hayward, 'The idea of innocent martyrdom in late tenth- and eleventh-century English hagiography', *Studies in Church History*, 30 (1993), 81–92.

144. V. A. Gunn, 'Bede and the martyrdom of St Oswald', *Studies in Church History*, 30 (1993), 57–66.

145. Bede does not refer to any of the female religious houses in Kent. Abbot Albinus of St Peter and St Paul, Canterbury was a major influence and source for the *Ecclesiastical History*, which is exceptionally detailed on many aspects of the Kentish church, so the exclusion was presumably a deliberate policy on his part, perhaps because he disapproved of their prominent role in the church in Kent.

146. K. Leyser, 'The Ottonians and Wessex', repr. and trans. in T. Reuter (ed.), *Communications and Power in Medieval Europe: The Carolingian and Ottonian Centuries* (London, 1994), 73–104.

147. K. Streckler (ed.), 'Gesta Ottonis', *Hrotsvithae Opera* (Leipzig, 1906), 221–49, vv. 94–7; P. Corbet, *Les Saints ottoniens: sainteté dynastique, sainteté royale et sainteté féminine autour de l'an Mil*, Beihefte von *Francia*, bd 15 (Sigmaringen, 1986), 46–50, 111–14.

148. *HE*, III, 7; see also the marriage of King Aldfrith, son of Oswald's brother Oswiu, and Cuthburh, later Abbess of Wimborne, daughter of King Cenred.

149. D. Rollason, 'Relic-cults as instruments of royal policy *c.* 900–*c.* 1050', *A-SE* 15 (1986), 91–103; *idem*, 'The shrines of saints in later Anglo-Saxon England: distribution and significance', in L. Butler and R. Morris (eds), *The Anglo-Saxon Church* (London, 1986), 32–43.

150. Heighway and Bryant, *Golden Minster*. Offa of Mercia is reported as having richly endowed Oswald's tomb at Bardney, perhaps with the aim of signalling the saint's support for his own power and lineage; P. Goodman (ed.), *Alcuin: The Bishops, Kings and Saints of York* (Oxford, 1982), 34. This is one of several indications that the West Saxons, who had done little to develop traditions of royal saintliness before 900, borrowed practices more strongly established in Mercia.

151. H. E. Lohmann and P. Hirsch (eds), *Widukind of Corvey, Rerum Gestarum Saxonicarum libri tres*, MGH SRG, 5th edn (Hanover, 1935), II, 41.

152. Leyser, 'Ottonians and Wessex'.

153. 'Gesta Ottonis', *Hrotsvithae Opera*, vv. 83–97; Corbet, *Les Saints ottoniens*, 114–17.

154. R. Holtzmann (ed.), *Thietmari Merseburgensis Episcopi Chronicon*, *MGH SRG*, NS 9, 2nd edn (Berlin, 1955), II, 3. Corbet, *Les Saints ottoniens*, 47–9. No doubt the early death of Edith's son Liodolf, which left the succession clear for a son of Otto by his second wife, helps to explain why her cult did not develop further – the political necessity for it had disappeared.

155. Rollason, *Mildrith Legend*. The secular pedigrees, of course, traced royal descent from Woden. Although Woden may have been euhemerized and treated as a Germanic hero after conversion, his presence in the genealogies presumably implies that Anglo-Saxon royal houses claimed originally to be descended from Woden as a god which would have provided further incentive to sacralize the family in a Christian manner through manifestations of saintliness after conversion; see B. A. E. Yorke, 'The reception of Christianity at the Anglo-Saxon royal courts',

in R. Gameson (ed.), *St Augustine and the Conversion of England* (Stroud, 1999), 152–73, at 154–5.

156. Blair, 'Handlist of Anglo-Saxon saints', and see discussion of dubious early Mercian saints in Chapter 1.

157. Lapidge, *Anglo-Saxon Litanies;* F. Wormald (ed.), *English Kalendars before A.D. 1100,* Henry Bradshaw Society, 72 (London, 1934); for detailed listing, see Rollason, *Saints and Relics,* 137–8, and Keynes, 'Alfred and Shaftesbury Abbey', 17–72, 66, nn. 82–3.

158. *Gesta Pontificum,* II, 86, 186–7.

159. Corbet, *Les Saints ottoniens,* 155–230. However, Ælfgifu's interventions on behalf of those who had received severe judicial sentences is not an attribute shared with Matilda, but is a feature shared with other late Anglo-Saxon saints and presumably reflects the rigour of late Anglo-Saxon royal government.

160. Ridyard, *Royal Saints,* 140–75, and see Chapter 5.

161. Cubitt, *Church Councils, passim.*

162. *Ibid.,* 43–4.

163. See, for instance, the sentiments expressed in this Old English maxim: 'It is fitting for a woman to be at her embroidery: a woman who walks about everywhere causes talk, people often defame and blacken her character; men speak of her with contempt; often she is unable to show her face' (T. A. Shippey, *Poems of Wisdom and Learning in Old English* (Cambridge, 1976), 66–7).

164. S 1258 and S 1434. The greater surviving evidence from the later Saxon period shows other ways in which they may have been involved. For instance, an abbess appeared as the oath-helper of Wynflaed in her dispute with Leofwine heard in the Berkshire shire-court recorded in S 1454 *c.* 990.

165. J. Blair and R. Sharpe (eds), *Pastoral Care before the Parish* (Leicester, 1992); E. Cambridge and D. Rollason, 'Debate: the pastoral organization of the Anglo-Saxon church: a review of the "minster hypothesis"', *Early Medieval Europe,* 4 (1995), 87–104; J. Blair, 'Debate: ecclesiastical organization and pastoral care in Anglo-Saxon England', *Early Medieval Europe,* 4 (1995), 193–212; Blair, *The Church in Anglo-Saxon Society,* chs 3 and 5.

166. S. Foot, 'Anglo-Saxon minsters: a review of terminology', in J. Blair and R. Sharpe (eds), *Pastoral Care before the Parish* (Leicester, 1992), 212–25. It is because of this variation that some authorities have preferred the term 'minster', derived from Old English *mynster* that translates *monasterium,* as a collective term for these foundations.

167. C. Cubitt, 'Pastoral care and conciliar canons: the provisions of the 747 council of *Clofesho*', in J. Blair and R. Sharpe (eds), *Pastoral Care before the Parish* (Leicester, 1992), 193–211. Ch. 29 orders *clericos* (as well as monks and nuns) living among the laity to return to the *monasteria* where they made their profession; *HS,* III, 374–5.

168. R. Daniels, 'The Anglo-Saxon monastery at Hartlepool, England', in J. Hawkes and S. Mills (eds), *Northumbria's Golden Age* (Stroud, 1999), 105–12.

169. A. T. Thacker, 'Monks, preaching and pastoral care in early Anglo-Saxon England', in J. Blair and R. Sharpe (eds), *Pastoral Care before the Parish* (Leicester, 1992), 137–70, at 140 (with reference to a similar provision at Wearmouth).

170. *HE,* IV, 24.

171. *HE,* IV, 23.

172. Anon., *VC,* IV, 10; ch. 34 (Bede).

173. Rollason, *Mildrith Legend,* 46–9; see also N. Brooks, 'Creation and early structure of Kent', 55–74, esp. 68–74; Blair, *The Church in Anglo-Saxon Society,* ch. 5.

174. S 20; Kelly, *Charters of St Augustine's*, no. 10, 38–44.
175. S 22; N. Brooks, *Church of Canterbury*, 191–7.
176. J. Blair (ed.), *Minsters and Parish Churches* (Oxford, 1988), and see n. 165 above.
177. J. Blair, 'Minster churches in the landscape', in D. Hooke (ed.), *Anglo-Saxon Settlements* (Oxford, 1988), 35–58.
178. See Chapter 1, pp. 31–6.
179. Cubitt, *Church Councils*, 194–5, and see Chapter 2, pp. 48–52.
180. Sims-Williams, *Religion and Literature*, 144–76, and see Cambridge and Rollason, 'Debate'.
181. Tangl, no. 14.
182. Tangl, no. 49; translated Sims-Williams, *Religion and Literature*, 240. It is not entirely clear if Denehard and Burghard are blood or spiritual brothers, though this letter seems to imply the former. Cyneburh was probably an abbess in Wessex; Yorke, 'The Bonifacian mission',155–7.
183. Bede's parents seem to have been tenants of Monkwearmouth; *HE*, V, 24. For a study of how entry to Cluny was used to create bonds between the monastery and lay families, see B. Rosenwein, *To Be the Neighbor of Saint Peter: The Social Meaning of Cluny's Property, 909–1049* (Ithaca, NY, 1989).
184. Thacker, 'Monks, preaching and pastoral care'.
185. S. Hollis, *Anglo-Saxon Women and the Church* (Woodbridge, 1992), 179–207.
186. *HE*, III, 24 and IV, 26.
187. Anon., *VC*, chs 23, 24 and 34. Hollis (*Anglo-Saxon Women and the Church*, 179–207) sees the misogyny of a male ecclesiastic for a female religious in the depiction of Ælfflaed.
188. A. Hamilton Thompson, 'Double monasteries and the male element in nunneries', in *The Ministry of Women: A Report by a Committee Appointed by His Grace the Lord Archbishop of Canterbury* (London, 1919), Appendix 7, 145–64; M. Deanesly, 'English and Gallic minsters', *TRHS*, 4th Series, 23 (1941), 25–69; J. Godfrey, 'The place of the double monastery in the Anglo-Saxon minster system', in G. Bonner (ed.), *Famulus Christi: Essays in Commemoration of the Thirteenth Centenary of the Birth of the Venerable Bede* (London, 1976), 344–50.
189. Yorke, 'Bonifacian mission'; some of these identifications only appear in relatively late sources and so are not completely secure, but eighth-century sources identify Thecla as a kinswoman of Leoba and kinship between Boniface and the family Willibald and Wynnebald which include the nuns Walburg and Huneburc.
190. *V. Leobae*, ch. 17; the monks of Fulda did not carry out his wishes to the letter and *c.* 836 her body was translated from the monastery to a church on a surrounding hilltop, which was the occasion for the composition of Rudolf's *Vita* of her.
191. Hollis, *Anglo-Saxon Women and the Church*, 271–300; Y. Hen, '*Milites Christi Utriusque Sexus*, Gender and the politics of conversion in the circle of Boniface', *Revue Bénédictine*, 109 (1999), 17–31.
192. For instance, at the time of the great storm recounted in *V. Leobae*, ch. 14, the information was probably provided by her kinswoman Thecla, who was present.
193. In addition to his more historical works, Bede's views may be discerned in the only work he dedicated to a nun, *In Canticum Abacuc Cantica*; see B. Ward, '"To my dearest sister": Bede and the educated woman', in L. Smith and J. Taylor (eds), *Women, the Book and the Godly* (Woodbridge, 1995), 105–11.

194. Hen, 'Gender and politics', 30–1.

195. *HE*, IV, 23.

196. *HE*, IV, 24.

197. For instance, *HE*, III, 11 (house of Æthelhild in Lindsey) and IV, 7 (Barking); *V. Leobae*, ch. 3, though it is difficult to know how far the last work may have been affected by Carolingian ideas of strict claustration.

198. J. Blair, 'Anglo-Saxon minsters: a topographical review', in J. Blair and R. Sharpe (eds), *Pastoral Care before the Parish* (Leicester, 1992), 226–66.

199. Blair, 'Anglo-Saxon minsters', 246–58.

200. R. Daniels, 'The Anglo-Saxon monastery at Hartlepool, England', in J. Hawkes and S. Mills (eds), *Northumbria's Golden Age* (Stroud, 1999), 105–12.

201. S 12 and 23; Deanesly, 'English and Gallic minsters', 25–69; Brooks, *Church of Canterbury*, 187–8. See also the reference to *monasterium clericorum* in *V. Leobae*, ch. 12.

202. *V. Edithae*, II, 4; possibly, as the editor Wilmart suggests, these were chaplains of the nunnery, but Wilton also had priests attached with parochial responsibilities (see below).

203. *V. Wulfhildae*, ch. 8.

204. Muir (ed.), *Pre-Conquest Prayer-Book*; see above, p. 109.

205. Thompson, 'Double monasteries', 149–54.

206. J. Barrow, 'Cathedrals, provosts and prebends: a comparison of twelfth-century German and English practice', *Journal of Ecclesiastical History*, 37 (1986), 536–63, at 552–63.

207. BL Egerton, 2104a, document 54, fos 39–40.

208. *Worcester, s.a.* 967, 416–19; see Chapter 3. See P. Hase ('The mother churches of Hampshire', in J. Blair (ed.), *Minster and Parish Churches: The Local Church in Transition 950–1200* (Oxford, 1988), 45–66, at 46) for an argument that Boniface's monastery *c.* 700 was located at Romsey rather than Nursling, which could mean that the nunnery inherited mother church responsibilities established in the late seventh century.

209. P. Hase, 'The church in the Wessex heartlands', in M. Aston and C. Lewis (eds), *The Medieval Landscape of Wessex* (Oxford, 1994), 47–81, at 62 and n. 60. The arrangement led to the preservation of the abbey church at the Dissolution as it was bought by the parish.

210. From surviving sources it is apparent that there were several congregations of nuns in Middle Saxon Wessex, especially in the diocese of Sherborne, but their exact locations are not known. Presumably like Wimborne, some of these early double houses became male minsters served by a small body of priests. Yorke, 'Bonifacian mission'.

211. D. Hinton, 'Amesbury and the early history of its abbey', in J. Chandler (ed.), *The Amesbury Millennium Lectures* (Amesbury, 1979), 20–31; J. Pitt, 'Wiltshire Minster Parochiae and Ecclesiastical Organisation in Wessex', unpublished Ph.D. thesis (University of Southampton, 2000), ch. 1, 49.

212. C. H. Talbot, 'Amesbury Church. Reasons for thinking that it was not the church of the priory', *Wiltshire Archaeological Magazine*, 31 (1900–1), 8–20; Royal Commission on Historical Monuments (RCHM), *Churches of South-East Wiltshire* (London, 1987), Appendix 1, 233–5.

213. D. K. Coldicott, *Hampshire Nunneries before and after the Norman Conquest*

(Chichester, 1989), 55–61; Hase, 'Church in Wessex heartlands', 70 and n. 61. At Wherwell, as at some of the double monasteries, the cemetery of the local people adjoined the monastic churches they used.

214. Pitt, 'Wiltshire Minster Parochiae', ch. 2, 1–13.

215. T. A. Hall, 'Minster Churches in the Dorset Landscape', unpublished M.Phil. thesis (University of Leicester, 1997), 45–6, 195.

216. E. Murphy, 'Anglo-Saxon Shaftesbury – Bectun's base or Alfred's foundation?', *Proceedings of the Dorset Natural History and Archaeology Society*, 113 (1992), 23–32. However, this land may have come to Shaftesbury when it was endowed with Tisbury Minster and its lands (or part of them); Kelly, *Charters of Shaftesbury*, no. 1 and no. 28, 107–14; R. H. Jackson, 'The Tisbury landholdings granted to Shaftesbury monastery by the Saxon kings', *Wiltshire Archaeological Magazine*, 79 (1985), 164–77.

217. S 899; Kelly, *Charters of Shaftesbury*, no. 29, 114–22; Pitt, 'Wiltshire Minster Parochiae', ch. 2, 48–58.

218. Coldicott, *Hampshire Nunneries*, 55–7.

219. Thompson, 'Double monasteries', 152. The prebends were:
• *Shaftesbury* – Fontmell, Gillingham, Iwerne (Dorset), Liddington (Wilts.)
• *Wherwell* – Goodworth, Middleton, Longparish and Wherwell (Hants.)
• *Wilton* – Chalke, North Newton, South Newton and Stanton St Bernard.

220. Hase, 'Church in Wessex heartlands', 62. Some of these prebendary churches, such as Chalke (Wilts.) and Gillingham (Dorset) may have been minster churches in origin.

221. F. Barlow (ed.), *The Life of King Edward Who Rests at Westminster*, 2nd edn (Oxford, 1992), 138.

222. *V. Edithae*, ch. 7.

223. Barlow, *The Life of King Edward*, 133–49.

224. Thompson, 'Double monasteries', 154–5.

225. BL Egerton, 2104a, document 54, fos 39–40.

226. *Ibid.*

227. Thompson, 'Double monasteries', 158.

228. R. Cramp, 'Monastic sites', in D. Wilson (ed.), *The Archaeology of Anglo-Saxon England* (London, 1976), 201–52; R. Daniels, 'The Anglo-Saxon monastery at Church Close, Hartlepool, Cleveland', *Archaeological Journal*, 145 (1988), 158–210.

229. A. T. Thacker, 'Æthelwold and Abingdon', in B. A. E. Yorke (ed.), *Bishop Æthelwold: His Career and Influence* (Woodbridge, 1988), 43–64, at 47–8.

230. M. Biddle (ed.), *Winchester in the Early Middle Ages*, Winchester Studies, I (Oxford, 1976), 321–3; G. Scobie and K. Qualmann, *Nunnaminster: A Saxon and Medieval Community of Nuns* (Winchester, 1993).

231. This is presumably the Church of St Peter to which Eadburh went to pray 'across the garden' (*V. Eadburgae*, ch. 10), in which case it would date the reorganization of the lands of the Winchester minsters between 963 and 970.

232. Ridyard, *Royal Saints*, 105–14.

233. D. Rollason, 'Lists of saints' resting-places in Anglo-Saxon England', *A-SE*, II (1983), 61–94; the entries for the late Saxon royal nunneries are as follows: *Amesbury* Melorius; *Barking* Æthelburh; *Nunnaminster* Eadburh; *Romsey* Maerwyn, Balthild, Æthelflaed; *Shaftesbury* Ælfgifu, Edward; *Wilton* Iwi, Edith. Wherwell does not feature in the list.

234. H. M. Taylor, 'The Anglo-Saxon church at Bradford-on-Avon', *Archaeological Journal*, 130 (1973), 141–71.
235. See, e.g., S. Kelly, 'Trading privileges from eighth-century England', *Early Medieval Europe*, 1 (1992), 3–27.

5 Abbesses and Nuns as Members of Royal Houses

Women were the religious specialists within the Anglo-Saxon royal houses, but in the early years of Christianization it had not always been the case that the religious role would be so gendered, for in many kingdoms a king was the first member of the royal house to enter a monastery. After this initial period of experimentation it became established that royal women went into the church, while their immediate male relatives tended not to do so except in somewhat adverse circumstances. The question of how new status and responsibilities affected their standing within their family circle is one that needs to be explored. Chapter 4 looked at how royal nunneries supported the kingly families which patronized them in ways that were compatible with their broader religious role and the expectations of how religious houses should conduct themselves. This chapter will start from a somewhat different perspective and look at the status of royal abbesses and nuns within the family nexus, and follow through from that some implications which meant that the lives of royal female religious did not always fit so readily into the idealized patterns of behaviour for monastic communities. It is likely that few Anglo-Saxon religious of either sex succeeded in escaping fully from obligations to their families, or from the patterns of behaviour inherent in the secular aristocratic life into which most were born and spent some of their formative years. But for those abbesses and nuns who came from royal houses, the issues of what were appropriate modes of behaviour were particularly acute because of their closeness to the crown. Involvement in family affairs, when that family was or aspired to be a ruling line meant that royal abbesses and nuns could be drawn into the type of political events from which members of a cloistered community might have expected normally to be immune.

The status of royal religious women in the family nexus

Women of the royal house were not necessarily the first choice to run royal Christian cult centres once royal families had made their final commitment to the new religion.[1] Their role emerged as part of the process of negotiation and compromise during which Christianity was accepted as the new religion of the royal courts in ways that fulfilled the religious expectations of the royal families without damaging basic principles of the faith. It may be that Christianity provided roles which had not existed before for Anglo-Saxon royal women as spiritual leaders within the family group, or at least extended more limited existing practices. Of course, in the absence of adequate written records from the period prior to conversion, it is not possible to say how far royal women had been filling cultic roles that might in some senses be seen as continuing under a Christian guise. Such records that we have for early Germanic religion suggest that the religious roles of women are most likely to have been concentrated in the home, and have been concerned with ensuring its well-being and prosperity.[2] Certain objects from high-status graves such as the crystal balls from Kent or the 'sprinkler' from the bed-burial at Swallowcliffe Down (Wilts.) have been interpreted in this kind of context and may have had a prophylactic function.[3] Women may also have had roles in burial ritual and remembering the dead which could have been continued in and adapted to a Christian milieu.[4] The royal women most likely to have had a more public role in cult were the queens whose duties within the royal household could have had broader implications for the welfare of the kingdom as a whole,[5] especially if, as some early medieval finds from Scandinavia suggest, royal or chiefly halls functioned as foci for religious ritual.[6] However, what more generally linked the positions of queens and abbesses would have been the fact that both had opportunities to transcend the roles normally allotted to women and to become 'honorary men',[7] both within the family circle and on a broader stage. The position of abbess extended the opportunities to enter public life to women of the royal house who might previously have had limited opportunities to do so, such as unmarried daughters and separated wives.[8] To contemporaries, it appeared that the role of abbess had parallels with that of queen.

The roles of queen and abbess were linked together in the so-called '*Liber Vitae Dunelmensis*' under the rubric *nomina reginarum et abbatissarum*.[9] The surviving manuscript was written in the ninth century, but incorporated a *liber vitae* that had originated much earlier, possibly in the reign of King Ecgfrith of Northumbria (670–685). The basic organization of material, and presumably the rubrics that indicate this, seems to go back to this earliest stage. The section for 'queens and abbesses' begins with the names 'Raegnmaeld. Eanflaed. Iurminburg. Æfflaed. Œðilburg'. The first three are Northumbrian queens, of whom the latter two are known to have entered the church when widowed.[10] Ælfflaed was the sister of Ecgfrith who became Abbess of Whitby, but never married, and Œðilburg was probably the *religiosa abbatissa* invoked on a cross from the nunnery of Hackness and was perhaps also a member of the royal house.[11] It was not necessarily the case that queens and abbesses were grouped together simply because a number of queens became abbesses, for while it is true that some members of the list filled both roles, not all its queens are known to have done so; some of its royal abbesses had never married and some of its abbesses may not have been of royal birth. It may be rather that it seemed appropriate to list together an unusual group of women who had public roles and were predominantly of royal birth. Women are conspicuously treated differently from men in the *liber vitae*. The *nomina regum vel ducum* are kept separate from the male ecclesiastical entries, and although a variety of priests, deacons, clerics and monks are included, ordinary nuns are not.

At a practical level, and in terms of a 'public' role, there were ways, especially in this early period, in which parallels could be found between the lives of queens and abbesses. Both, for instance, had control over lands and movable wealth, and commanded mixed households of men and women. They were people of rank and influence whose support was sought by others of lesser birth. In these respects there would have been continuity between Eanflaed's life as Queen of Northumbria and as Abbess of Whitby.[12] As queen, her assistance was sought by the young Wilfrid who was recommended to her by nobles to whom he had ministered in his father's house.[13] She secured a position for him in the monastery of Lindisfarne, and, when he wished to travel to Rome, Eanflaed arranged this as well through her maternal kinsman King Eorcenbert of Kent.[14] As Abbess of Whitby, with her daughter Ælfflaed, Eanflaed would have continued to command men as well as women from the Northumbrian aristocracy, and to have promoted men of her choice within the church. Her cousin Hild, the foundress of Whitby, can be shown exercising this kind of patronage. Five of her monks became bishops, and at least two were able to travel to Kent to study with Theodore and Hadrian.[15] In Stephen's *Life* Wilfrid's career is alternatively helped and hindered by queens and powerful abbesses who are presented as operating in comparable ways.[16] The position of abbess provided opportunities that had probably not existed before for widowed or separated queens, and for unmarried princesses, to exercise the authority and independence that were otherwise the prerogative of a king's wife. The large numbers that took up the position before the end of the tenth century suggest that, in addition to the lure of a religious life, these were attractive propositions.

Conflicting royal and ecclesiastical standards

But how independent were the royal abbesses and nuns, and how free from the customs and demands of the royal courts? It was a frequent complaint among reformers of the Anglo-Saxon church that monks, nuns and other clerics were too closely involved with their lay relatives, and too attached to the dress, pastimes and attitudes of the aristocratic world from which most of them came.[17] Nuns were castigated by Bede and Aldhelm for their elaborate, fashionable clothes and hairstyles,[18] and finds from excavated nunneries such as Whitby and Barking have produced jewellery, dress adornments and personal toilet items.[19] Garments that have survived of Abbess Bertille of Chelles (d. 704) and of the former Merovingian queen Balthild, who may have been of Anglo-Saxon origin and retired to the nunnery, were made from expensive coloured silks,[20] and are probably similar to the clothes worn by their Anglo-Saxon counterparts to which monastic reformers objected. It was the threat to their aristocratic lifestyles, including the prospect of sharing a bath with social inferiors, that fuelled the revolt of the nuns of Holy

Cross in Poitiers.[21] One of the complaints by the revolting nuns was that the abbess had cut up an altar cloth to make a dress for her niece.[22] Keeping up sartorial standards was just as important at the other end of the Anglo-Saxon period, when Edith of Wilton was rebuked by Bishop Æthelwold for the luxuriousness of her dress.[23] Since Edith was the heroine of her own story, as preserved for us by Goscelin, she is presented as trumping the bishop by revealing that she was wearing a hair shirt beneath her fine robes, and she ends by telling him that he should not be misled by outward appearances. Nevertheless, it is apparent that outward appearances mattered at late tenth-century Wilton, and that Edith was remembered there without censure for dressing as befitted a princess.[24]

Dress and jewellery were not only an aspect of aristocratic fashion; they were also symbols of power and status that could not be abandoned easily, particularly perhaps by women who had to assert positions of leadership in what was predominantly a man's world. A jewelled necklace, or collar, was not just a frivolity, but a statement of authority, albeit one that stemmed from the secular world. Their connotations were Christian, as they were modelled on Byzantine court wear, and generally carried Christian symbolism.[25] It was even possible to use the metaphor of a necklace to stand for one of the leading female monastics of the seventh century, and perhaps most surprisingly of all it was Bede, who otherwise championed Benedictine ideals of a modest life and a rejection of worldly wealth for monastics, who provided the comparison. He recounts a dream of Breguswith, the mother of Hild, who while searching for her husband 'found a most precious necklace (*monile*) under her garment and, as she gazed closely at it, it seemed to spread such a blaze of light that it filled all Britain with its gracious splendour'.[26] The gleaming necklace was, of course, a prophecy of Hild and the example she would provide to the whole country by her good, Christian life. Another nun referred to in what may be comparable terms was the Kentish princess Eorcengota who entered the nunnery of Faremoutiers. When close to death she had a vision of angels who said 'that they had been sent to take back with them the golden coin which had been brought thither from Kent'; in other words, Eorcengota herself.[27] In seventh-century Kent the wearing of pierced Roman or Byzantine coins as parts of necklaces is well attested from grave finds, and may be what is alluded to here, though gold coins were produced in Kent in Eorcengota's lifetime.[28] Coins worn in necklaces were sometimes combined with Christianity symbols such as crosses, and may themselves have been considered as signs of Christian affiliation, because Christianity had become the official religion of the late Roman Empire and explicit symbolism of the new religion was incorporated into some of the coinage. Pendants with Christian associations succeeded the wearing of bracteates, which often seem to have had an overt pagan symbolism and were a fashion borrowed from Scandinavia. It may be that more than religious allegiance was being signalled by the wearing of items with religious imagery. Such pendants, like similar ornaments worn in pre-conversion periods, may have been considered to have had an amuletic function that may not only have protected the wearer, but also the household for which she was responsible, and when that household was the royal court the protection may have taken on an even wider significance. We may find some indication of this in a description of Queen Iurminburh of Northumbria, who ostentatiously wore a reliquary she had taken from Bishop Wilfrid 'both in her chamber at home and when riding abroad in her chariot'.[29]

Such interpretations are, of course, speculative and may seem to go further than the sources warrant. But it is important to remember that much of the thought-world of the early Anglo-Saxon period is not overtly stated, and that Christianity was not imposing itself on to a *tabula rasa*, but had to fit itself into a world where there were already established ideas of correct forms of behaviour and dress. Some of the latter may have had a significance that went beyond what would-be Christian reformers characterized as mere vanity and love of wealth. Bede's ideal was the former Queen Æthelthryth of Ely whom he presented as rejecting all the trappings of wealth and status in this world the better to enjoy their spiritual equiv-alents in the next.[30] She is said to have regarded a tumour in her neck as a means of saving herself from the vanity of 'an unnecessary weight of necklaces' (*moniles*) that she used to wear as a girl. Through this unpleasant imagery, Bede may have been addressing issues of dress that were current at the time he wrote. But not all early medieval women dwelling in nunneries were convinced that such necklaces or collars were unnecessary or inappropriate, and there is at least one example of an ingenious compromise. The so-called 'chemise' of Queen Balthild was em-broidered with representations of the magnificent jewelled collars with pendants containing Christian symbolism that she had apparently given away to the poor on the advice of her confessor.[31]

However, while it is not so surprising that elements of the aristocratic life and thought were transferred to the nunneries when they were founded in the seventh century, one might have expected more concessions to have been made to monastic ideals of poverty by the latter part of the tenth century when Edith was power-dressing at Wilton. A revealing story concerning Eadburh of Nunnaminster, discussed by Susan Ridyard, suggests that such matters were not only down to the conscience of the individual princess-nun.[32] The account comes from the *Life* of Eadburh written in the early twelfth century by Osbert of Clare, but is so distinc-tive in its content that one suspects it may derive from a genuine pre-Conquest tradition. Young Eadburh, it appears, had been in the habit of rising in the night and cleaning the shoes of the other sisters. Osbert is full of praise at this act of *humilitas*, but that was not how it was received by her monastic superiors, who were horrified at how such unprincessly behaviour might be received by her father King Edward the Elder. 'It is unseemly,' Osbert has them say, 'for a royal child to bow her neck to such humble service and to set about the work of a common slave; it is harmful to the dignity of her illustrious birth.' Previously the prioress had had to apologize to Eadburh for striking her for a breach of monastic discipline because she had thought her one of the ordinary nuns and not a *principis filiam*. This seems clear testimony to the fact that royal women who entered the church were not necessarily free to embrace the full rigours of a monastic life, even if they had wanted to do so. They remained members of their royal families and were expected by those families and others who had to answer to them to conduct themselves accordingly. Pressure to conform to secular ideals did not necessarily come from the royal nuns themselves but from their lay relatives, though in the revolt of the nuns of Holy Cross, Poitiers, the ringleaders Clotild and Basina were very conscious of the deference that should have been due to them as princesses and were not prepared to be ruled by an abbess whom they took to be their social inferior. They were prepared to hire armed men to take over the nunnery, but ultimately they failed because the Frankish king was not prepared to uphold their claims and let the local bishops decide the case.[33] Dress was but the tip of the iceberg of tensions and contradictions that royal women had to face as a result of having to be both members of a ruling house and of a religious community.

Royal visits

The nuns of Nunnaminster knew that King Edward would discover how Eadburh had been conducting herself because he could be expected to visit the nunnery, and two visits from the king are referred to in the *Vita*.[34] Canons from the Council of *Clofesho* in 747 suggest that inmates of religious houses were not isolated from their families, and might visit them as well as receive visits from them – something that the Council naturally wished to restrict.[35] A few of these visits have found their way into narrative and other sources. The clearest impression of how nunneries might be incorporated into the circuits of king and queens comes from saints' *Lives* written in early eighth-century Northumbria which are particularly informative about the reign of King Ecgfrith (670–685). Ecgfrith and his second wife Iurminburh are said to have included a visit to the nunnery of Coldingham, presided over by Ecgfrith's aunt Æbbe, in their circuit of *civitates*, *castellae* and *vici*.[36] The queen was taken ill in the night, and Abbess Æbbe was able to use the occasion to advise her nephew to free Bishop Wilfrid and restore his confiscated wealth. Queens might also travel on their own. Æbbe had previously received Ecgfrith's first wife Æthelthryth when she separated from her husband (though this cannot, of course, be classed as an ordinary royal visit), and Æthelthryth took the veil at Coldingham before returning to her home province of the East Angles.[37] Queen Iurminburh was staying with her sister at her nunnery in Carlisle when Bishop Cuthbert received intimation of Ecgfrith's defeat at the hands of the Picts.[38] No indication is given of exactly what was involved when a royal visit took place, but presumably it could mean the housing and feeding of a considerable entourage as well. King Æthelbald of Mercia made a grant of relief from seven years' royal refection in Gloucester to Abbess Eafe, and the concession was presumably intended to be a generous one, since it was in compensation for his murder of her kinsman, Prince Æthelmund of the Hwicce.[39]

Carlisle and Gloucester were significant settlements of Roman origin that controlled major routeways, and it is tempting to suggest that kings appointed female relatives to nunneries in such places so that they might help supervise them on their behalf. However, the type of locations favoured for nunneries – enclosed sites, often of Roman or earlier date, with good communications, often riverine or estuarine – apply to minsters as a whole, and there are no locational features that distinguish nunneries (whether royal or not) from other significant churches.[40] Needs and expectations of the church may explain choice of site rather than kingly preferences, though no doubt the requirements of both could play a part. Location on major roads and rivers would have helped the provisioning required not only to run a nunnery in normal circumstances, but to cope with the extra needs of a royal visit. If, as seems increasingly likely from the distribution of coins and other finds, nunneries, like other major minsters, were involved in regional and international trade and served as distributive centres for their regions,[41] the royal nunneries may also have obtained items on behalf of royal courts. Nevertheless, some nunnery sites seem to require a particular explanation. Æbbe's Coldingham, for instance, appears to be a particularly bleak and difficult site, in territory only recently acquired by the Northumbrian kings, even if its coastal location fits a pattern for Northumbrian religious houses. Although the exact location of the early Anglo-Saxon nunnery is uncertain, a case has been made for the fortified site of Kirk Hill which may have been in origin a British fort and centre of authority.[42] Perhaps in this case there was a desire to have a significant, former British centre under the control of a member of a royal house. Æbbe is also associated with the former Roman site of Ebchester (Co. Durham) where the church is dedicated to her and which she is supposed to have received from her brother, King Oswiu.[43] Kings undoubtedly did appoint female relatives to certain nunneries for strategic reasons, as when Coenwulf appointed his daughter Cwoenthryth to Winchcombe and Thanet, though the motive may have been to ensure that the valuable properties of these communities were under control of a member of the royal house rather than because of their immediate geographical location.[44] Another motive for locating nunneries in important, fortified sites could have been to provide protection for the nuns rather than to incorporate the abbesses into royal administration. Carlisle is described as having its own royal reeve, Waga,[45] and Alfred's choice of site for his daughter's nunnery at Shaftesbury may have been influenced by the fact that it had been fortified recently as part of the West Saxon burghal system against the Danes.[46]

Kings undoubtedly visited nunneries on occasion, especially those containing kinswomen to whom they were closely related, and many nunneries shared with other minsters the obligation of providing food and lodging for kings and their officials, even if this appears in our sources only occasionally. But royal itineration seems to have been less formalized and significant than in Ottonian Germany, where the major royal nunneries were important resting-places in regular use and could be the setting of major court ceremonial.[47] Of the later nunneries, the one that comes closest to the great Ottonian centres such as Gandersheim and

Quedlinburg is Wilton. The nunnery at Wilton was probably founded early in the ninth century when Wilton came to prominence as the shire town of Wiltshire, and the nunnery had a long association with prominent ealdormanic families in the shire as well as with the royal house.[48] A number of royal charters were issued from Wilton in the ninth and early tenth centuries, implying visits from the king and his court.[49] In the tenth century, princesses of the royal house were associated with the house: two daughters of Edward the Elder, as well as their mother (daughter of an ealdorman of Wiltshire), were buried there and may have been members of the community,[50] and Edith, daughter of King Edgar, was raised there by her mother Wulfthryth who was abbess of the convent. From the *Life* of Edith we are given an impression of Wilton as a major royal centre where, even when the king was not present, there were frequent visits from royal officials, from petitioners who wanted Edith and Wulfthryth to intervene on their behalf with the king, and from foreign diplomats who were expected to pay their respects to princess Edith and might provide another exotic animal for her menagerie.[51] It is hard to get behind the hyperbole of Goscelin's *Vita S. Edithe*, but a significant characteristic of the work is the conflict between Goscelin's desire to stress Edith's humility and his source material, which appears to have emphasized Edith's position as a princess.[52] Although allowance must be made for Wilton nunnery having its own motives for stressing Edith's princessly status, the picture Goscelin provides is of a late Saxon Wilton where the royal centre and the nunnery are closely interrelated. It is a pity that more is not known for certain about the topography of Wilton in the tenth century. Jeremy Haslam has proposed a possible royal core in the area of Kingsbury Square that is adjacent to the site of St Mary's church, presumed to be the site of one of the nunnery churches.[53] Kingsbury and St Mary's form a discrete area, separated from the main street with its burgage plots and its bank and ditch defences in the manner of other small West Saxon burhs. There could be echoes here of arrangements at Quedlinburg, where in the tenth century the nunnery occupied the site of a former royal fortress on top of the hill and where the king would also stay on his occasional visits.[54]

However, royal itineration does not seem to have been as significant for the kings of England as it was for their Ottonian counterparts, and the later nunneries did not generally feature as major royal stopping-places. England was, of course, smaller, less geographically diverse and more easily encompassed by common forms of royal government. The later royal nunneries were all in Wessex where the kings possessed numerous estates of their own. When formal crown-wearings at major church festivals were introduced into England, probably in imitation of Ottonian practice, they took place in major episcopal and male monastic centres.[55] There was no English counterpart in this respect to the major processional way created at Quedlinburg, a favourite choice for the king's celebration of Easter, when the royal residence was moved from the hilltop to the valley below in about 1000. However, Wilton and Shaftesbury were both significant royal cult centres in the eleventh century, and so likely to attract royal visits, because of the sanctification of the royal siblings Edith and Edward the Martyr.[56]

There were advantages to royal visits in that they were a useful occasion for seeking royal favours and gifts. The nuns of Nunnaminster successfully persuaded Eadburh to ask her father for an estate at All Cannings in Wiltshire, which was to be one of their most valuable possessions, after she had softened him up with her singing.[57] However, apart from the possible expense and disruption, there were other potential disadvantages. The nuns of Gloucester may have breathed a collective sigh of relief when they were freed from visits of King Æthelbald for seven years, not least because of his sexual predatoriness. Sex with nuns was one of the several crimes that earned Æthelbald a major letter of rebuke from Boniface and other missionary bishops safely removed from the Mercian king's sphere of influence.[58] It was, of course, one of the major grounds on which the necessity for strict claustration of religious women, especially from laymen, was argued, even if some churchmen seemed more inclined to blame women for attracting the attention of men than the sexual predators themselves. It is an issue best examined in the wider perspective of marriage and the cloister.

Marriage, sex and the royal nunneries

One of the areas in which we can see compromises between dynastic and ecclesiastical expectations is over issues concerning marriage and the royal nunneries. One of the standard hagiographical topoi for late Antique and medieval religious women was the conflict engendered when a woman who wished to dedicate her life to God came under pressure to marry.[59] The virgin is presented as suffering nobly for her faith, and might find herself imprisoned in a brothel (Lucy) or subjected to hideous torture (Catherine). The harassed late Antique virgins often paid the ultimate penalty of death, though divine intervention might sometimes strike down their main persecutor instead (Barbara). Accounts of this type were produced in the period after the Norman Conquest for saints reputed to have lived during the Anglo-Saxon period (Frideswide, Sidwell), and accounts of late Antique saints were recounted in both Latin and Old English during the Anglo-Saxon period, but there are no accounts of Anglo-Saxon female saints using the topos that are known to have been produced during the Anglo-Saxon period itself. The 'virgin valiantly resisting marriage' motif is conspicuous by its absence from works such as Bede's *Ecclesiastical History*. Instead we have Æthelthryth of Ely who managed to remain a virgin in spite of two marriages. She gets due credit for preferring queenship in heaven and Christ as her bridegroom, but, unlike many of the martyred virgins whom Bede cites in his poem in her honour, there is no suggestion that Æthelthryth made a heroic resistance to marriage, or even that she objected to the unions taking place, and such claims do not form part of the case for her sanctity.[60] There are also no villains in Æthelthryth's story. Neither of her husbands – Tondbert, *princeps* of the South Gyrwe, and King Ecgfrith of Northumbria – is castigated, and the worst that Ecgfrith is portrayed as doing is trying to bribe Bishop Wilfrid to persuade Æthelthryth to consummate the marriage (which lasted for twelve years).[61] Nor is there any criticism of her father, King Anna; rather he is described as 'a very religious man and noble both in mind and deed'. Æthelthryth seems to have represented an ideal compromise for Bede in that she was apparently able to do her dynastic duty by marrying twice and was able to retain the virginity that was most desirable for the monastic life. His enthusiasm for Æthelthryth may be contrasted with his lack of praise for her sister Seaxburh, who also became Abbess of Ely and had been married, for, unlike Æthelthryth, she had several children. However, even Bede may have had his doubts about the viability of combining the roles of virgin and queen, for he had asked Bishop Wilfrid, concerning Æthelthryth's perpetual virginity, 'whether this was true, because certain people doubted it'.[62] There were virgins, like Ælfflaed of Whitby vowed from infancy, in the early Anglo-Saxon royal nunneries, and Bede's bestowal of commendation suggests that this was the preferred state in the monastic life.[63] However, the reality was that many of the powerful abbesses were formerly married women, many of them, like Æthelthryth, separated from husbands who were still living, and so not even decently widowed. This reality of dynastic life in Anglo-Saxon England was accepted by Archbishop Theodore who was able to find justification in Greek practice for the dissolution of a marriage if one partner wished to enter the church, leaving the other free to remarry, and for a formerly married woman being as worthy of becoming an abbess as a virgin.[64] Aldhelm too showed awareness of the realities of the Anglo-Saxon situation when he adapted his sources for his work *De virginitate* by giving greater prominence than Ambrose or Jerome would have allowed to the state of 'chastity' enjoyed by those who had been married, but subsequently opted for the cloister.[65] He goes so far as to suggest in one place that 'chastity' could be preferable to 'virginity', as the formerly married women might strive harder to please God and so surpass in virtue the complacent virgins who were in danger of suffering from spiritual pride.[66]

Pressures leading to sexual liaisons did not necessarily end once a female had entered a nunnery. Letters, penitentials and royal and ecclesiastical legislation demonstrate that women might leave Anglo-Saxon nunneries to be married, and – and these two things might of course be related – that sexual assault on nuns was a continuing problem. Theodore's *Penitential* offers a humane and, it would appear, realistic approach. A nun who left her church to be married was assigned a penance of three years, but one who had sex, but remained in her foundation, had to do penance for seven.[67] Former nuns were discouraged from returning to the religious life after a period of marriage.[68] The scandal of debauched Anglo-Saxon nuns was one that particularly concerned Bishop Boniface, especially as it might lead to additional crime and sin if a nun fell pregnant and killed her child.[69] Perhaps he had in mind an incident which involved his kinswoman Leoba's foundation at Taubersbiscofsheim where the townspeople assumed (wrongly, of course) that a dead baby found in the river which ran through the nunnery and settlement was the offspring of one of the nuns.[70] The legatine councils of 786 seem to have been concerned with the apparent ease with which nuns might leave in order to be married, and decreed that the children from such unions should be barred from inheritance.[71] This was one of the rulings of the councils taken up by Alfred in his legislation.[72] He ruled that a nun who married could not inherit any of her husband's property, nor could it be passed on to their children; if the child was slain the king took the wergild due to the mother's kindred, but the father's kindred could receive their share.[73] His laws are also concerned with the penalties for abducting nuns from nunneries and for seizing them 'lustfully' by the clothes or breast.[74] In the so-called 'Constitutions of Archbishop Oda' from the 940s men are adjured to abstain from marriages with kinswomen and nuns.[75]

The main threat to the purity of nuns does not seem to have come from within their churches, and in spite of the presence of some men in probably all Anglo-Saxon nunneries, the issue of sexual intercourse between nuns and clerics does not seem to have arisen as a major concern. Even at Coldingham, Bede's example of a 'bad' double community, where the nuns are criticized for making themselves elaborate clothes, it is '*externorum virorum*' whose attention they wished to attract, not the resident clerics.[76] This may be an indication that the male element of double monasteries was socially inferior to the royal and aristocratic nuns so that liaisons between them were unlikely to be entertained by either party.[77] The sources make clear that it was laymen who posed the threat, and we return here to the issue raised earlier of the perils of a royal visit to nunneries, and Boniface's explicit criticism of Æthelbald and his rumoured predilection for sex with nuns, a taste which he is said to have shared with his predecessor King Ceolred (709–716) and with King Osred of Northumbria (705/6–716).[78] Osred is said to have been driven by the spirit of wantonness (*luxoria*) 'in his frenzy debauching throughout the nunneries virgins consecrated to God'. In other words, debauchery with nuns was pretty much par for the course with contemporary kings, and Boniface felt he had to spell out in detail to Æthelbald that sexual intercourse with nuns was a worse sin than sex with other unmarried women because the nuns were vowed to God. The implication would seem to be that kings tended to view women at nunneries as they might any other group of royal kinswomen or noble women to whom they expected to have free access and whom they would try to pressurize into a sexual relationship. Royal nunneries might be particularly at risk because of rights of lordship that kings could claim within them. Alfred ruled that a nun should not be removed from a nunnery without the permission of the king or bishop,[79] but such safeguards would not exist if a king, less concerned than Alfred was to maintain sexual purity, gave himself permission to take out a nun. These generalized views are given substance by specific examples of attempted or achieved abduction and seduction of nuns by members of royal or noble houses. Given the infrequency of any narrative references to women in Anglo-Saxon sources, such allusions presumably stand for many more instances in which nuns were removed from their convents either with or without their consent.

In two cases abduction is linked with rebellion. When King Alfred died in 899, his nephew Æthelwold, the son of his brother Æthelred I, made a bid for the throne. Æthelwold seized two major royal centres at Christchurch and Wimborne, and, after he had withdrawn from the latter, a woman was apprehended 'whom he had taken without the king's permission and contrary to the bishops' orders for she had been consecrated a nun'.[80] The implication must be that the woman concerned had been a nun at Wimborne, but it is not clear whether Æthelwold had taken her to demonstrate his lordship as would-be king over the community,[81] or because she was someone politically important to whom he might wish to be married to enhance his claim to the throne. Marriage was apparently the aim of Swein Godwinson when he ordered the Abbess of Leominster to be brought to him on his return from a campaign in Wales in 1046, though he may also have been asserting regalian rights in his earldom which included Herefordshire.[82] Worcester sources maintain that Swein wished to marry Abbess Eadgifu and lived with her for a year, and that the refusal of permission for him to marry her precipitated his withdrawal from the country and fall from favour.[83] Possibly at issue was not just the abduction of an abbess, but Swein's potential marriage to a woman of significant descent, but unfortunately nothing is known of Abbess Eadgifu's background.

The fullest account of the attempted seduction of a nun is that of Wulfhild of Wilton by King Edgar. The account is recorded in the *Vita* of Wulfhild written by Goscelin in the late eleventh century for the nunnery of Barking to which Wulfhild was appointed as abbess after her encounter with the king. A hagiographical source might appear less than ideal, particularly when it has passed through the hands of a specialist such as Goscelin who was writing at a time when there was much interest in the issue of whether a woman could leave a nunnery in order to be married.[84] The 'nun resisting marriage' convention may have influenced the telling of Wulfhild's tale to a certain extent, but the account has a number of unusual circumstantial details that give it credibility. Although Goscelin skilfully embellished his sources, he did need something to embellish – as is suggested by the rest of Wulfhild's short *Vita* where Goscelin has evidently resisted the temptation to spin out the rather thin material with hagiographic convention in order to make a more impressive *Life*.[85] Wulfhild gives a vivid account of her encounter with the king, and one can imagine that this was a tale she recounted many times and that it was well known to Goscelin's informants from Barking.[86] We learn that Edgar had spotted Wulfhild on a visit to Wilton where she was being brought up, was interested in marriage and contacted her aunt Wenflaed to arrange a meeting. Wulfhild was summoned to Wenflaed's villa at Wherwell on the pretext that her aunt was ill, but on arrival found that the king was being entertained and that a place had been laid for her beside him. She became suspicious of the king's intentions, especially when guards were placed at her chamber door, and she used a visit to the privy as an opportunity to escape through the drain-opening.[87] She spent the night in a hut and returned to Wilton the following day, only to be pursued there by the king who attempted to detain her in the cloister. She escaped from him with difficulty to seek sanctuary in the church, leaving Edgar clutching her empty sleeve that was torn off in their struggle. Wulfhild had already made a commitment to the religious life, and when she had convinced the king of this she was compensated with the position of Abbess of Barking.[88] The king instead married her cousin Wulfthryth who had also been brought up at Wilton.

The events involving the two cousins suggest that Edgar had desired a marriage that would link him with an important noble family,[89] even if he seems to have wanted to anticipate the marriage vows – something which would no doubt have helped to circumvent any objection that might have arisen. The family, at least in the person of Wenflaed, seem to have wanted the union as well, and were prepared for either Wulfhild or Wulfthryth to leave Wilton to accomplish it. However, the religious status of the two girls is not entirely clear. Wulfhild is first said to have been educated (*educanda*) at Wilton, but in the account of her attempted seduction she is repeatedly referred to as *virgo Christi* or similar, and so was presumably believed to have taken religious vows. The stories circulating in post-Conquest histories about Edgar's attempted seduction of a nun probably refer to her.[90] Wulfthryth, on the other hand, is said to have been educated at Wilton *in seculari habitu*;[91] that is, she had not taken any vows and so would have been free to leave at any time without incurring any stigma or penance. Nevertheless there may have been some ambiguity in her position, and later writers believed that one of Edgar's marriages had been irregular as it had been contracted with a religious woman.[92]

Events after the Norman Conquest, also involving Wilton, throw light on the somewhat flexible practices at late Anglo-Saxon nunneries that allowed members to leave to marry for dynastic reasons, but could cause confusion about which individuals had been veiled and taken monastic vows. In the aftermath of the Norman Conquest a number of the female survivors of the Anglo-Saxon aristocracy, many of whom would have lost their male protectors, sought refuge in Anglo-Saxon nunneries.[93] Lanfranc recognized the unusual circumstances behind their retreat and many were allowed to re-enter the secular world when circumstances were more propitious. The status of some of these women, however, was politically sensitive as they were related to the rulers of late Anglo-Saxon England. Included in this category was Christina, the sister of Edgar Ætheling, the main Anglo-Saxon claimant for the throne, who became a nun at Romsey.[94] She was joined subsequently by her niece Edith, the daughter of her sister Margaret and the Scottish leader Malcolm Canmore, though Edith seems to have moved later to Wilton.[95] William Rufus was particularly anxious that Edith should take religious vows so that she would not leave to make a marriage that he might find politically inconvenient, and reputedly visited Wilton so that he could check with his own eyes that she had been veiled.[96] But as Edith maintained in a spirited statement to Archbishop Anselm, although she might have worn a veil for her own protection, she had never taken religious vows. Her father had been furious when he found her wearing a veil, and had torn it from her head swearing 'he had destined me as a wife . . . rather than for a community of nuns'.[97] It is evident that both Edith and her father expected she would be free to leave Wilton, and this ultimately she was able to do in order to marry William Rufus' brother after he had succeeded as Henry I. Rumours about her former religious status continued to dog her, especially as in her youth Edith-Matilda (the latter being the name she took after her marriage to Henry) had been seen veiled on more than one occasion and it was rumoured she had been oblated by her parents to the church.[98] Eadmer in his *Vita Dunstani* described an earlier occasion at Wilton whereby a laygirl being educated there (perhaps an allusion to Wulfthryth or Wulfhild) had snatched a veil from one of the nuns to try to protect herself from the attentions of King Edgar.[99] In the light of the sexual advances to which women in religious communities might be subject, it would be understandable for the nuns to do everything they could to protect their younger charges, and if laygirls were present they would not want to draw attention to the fact when there were secular male visitors. It is possible that all the young inmates of nunneries on occasion wore a veil, and differences in their status might be left deliberately ambiguous when secular visitors were present.

Education would have been provided for girls oblated in infancy, but it is only in the later Anglo-Saxon period that we have definite proof that daughters of royal and aristocratic families, apparently not intended for the church, were sent to nunneries to be educated. Wulfthryth would appear to fall into this category, and, less ambiguously, Edith, the daughter of Earl Godwin who married Edward the Confessor after spending part of her girlhood at Wilton.[100] The practice may have been more common in the later Anglo-Saxon period than earlier. Asser particularly stresses that Alfred's daughter Ælfthryth was brought up only at the royal court (unlike her elder sister Æthelgifu who at an early age entered the nunnery of Shaftesbury).[101] The presence of the nun Hundrada at the court of King Offa of Mercia may have been to provide education for his daughters,[102] and Alfred's wife Ealhswith who was of Mercian royal descent may have introduced the practice into Wessex.[103] However, in the late tenth and eleventh centuries, nunneries were apparently educating laygirls alongside girls who had been vowed to the church and their later career prospects were not necessarily that different. The question of whether children who had had vows made on their behalf were free to choose whether to leave or to renew those vows when they came of age was a vexed question in the medieval church. Theodore would no doubt have followed the ruling of St Basil that the oblate should be free to choose at the age of 16 or 17, but a much harsher line was taken with male oblates during the Carolingian Renaissance in which the vows taken on behalf of infants were regarded as binding.[104] It is not clear if such rulings were ever applied to Carolingian nuns, nor is there any evidence that they were followed in Anglo-Saxon nunneries, where, as we have seen, it appears women might leave nunneries in order to be married. It is possible that status was fluid and dependent on circumstances. A young girl might leave a nunnery if a suitable marriage offer was made (though her right to refuse it, as Wulfhild did, was recognized),[105] but if none was forthcoming presumably she might remain where she was. Some people are said to have considered Edith-

Matilda to be an example of a girl oblated by her parents who was subsequently brought out by her father in order to be married, an option with which she seems to have concurred.[106] The right to leave to be married might be expected by both former oblates and, it would appear, those who had entered at a later age and taken vows, for among those who were placed for safety in Wilton after the Norman Conquest was Gunnhild, daughter of King Harold II. Gunnhild was regarded as a religious by Anselm and had apparently hoped to become Abbess of Wilton, though she subsequently maintained that she had never made formal vows before a bishop.[107] It was only after she had failed to get the position of abbess that Gunnhild left to get married (eloping with Count Alan of Brittany who had come to Wilton as part of a plan that he should marry Edith-Matilda), and earned the very considerable wrath of Archbishop Anselm.

The expectations of Gunnhild and Edith-Matilda that they would be free to leave Wilton to marry no doubt reflects Anglo-Saxon custom, and would also have been regarded as acceptable in the continental houses of canonesses which the later Anglo-Saxon nunneries most obviously resemble.[108] However, the distinction between houses of canonesses and nuns does not seem to have been formally recognized in Anglo-Saxon England. The inhabitants of houses like Wilton were *sanctimoniales/mynecena*, the female equivalent of *monachi/munecas*,[109] and theoretically followed the reformed monasticism laid down in the *Regularis Concordia*, though a more relaxed attitude to vows was just one of several areas where there was variation between theory and practice. After the Norman Conquest the late Anglo-Saxon nunneries were regarded as Benedictine foundations, and Lanfranc and Anselm judged the behaviour of their inmates accordingly (as have many later commentators). The problems over the freedom of action of Edith-Matilda and Gunnhild, and the disquiet in eleventh-century authors about the exact status of Wulfthryth, reflect this conflict between Benedictine expectations and the more relaxed Anglo-Saxon practices which had traditionally recognized that concessions should be made for the dynastic needs of royal and aristocratic families when it came to formulating attitudes to marriage and the cloister.

Nunneries and politics

The story of Edith-Matilda demonstrates how easily royal nunneries were likely to find themselves embroiled in contemporary politics when they contained members of royal descent who had the potential to pass on their royal blood through marriage. Edith-Matilda's fortunes fluctuated as the political situation shifted, and the senior nuns of Wilton were in the difficult position of having to make allowances for the different aims and perceptions of Edith herself and her father Malcolm Canmore, the English kings, William Rufus and Henry I, and the archbishops of Canterbury, Lanfranc and Anselm. Edith-Matilda is unlikely to have been the first denizen of a royal nunnery for whom the question of whether or not she should be allowed to leave to marry was a political issue, but such examples are not particularly well represented in the sources, which are often rather limited in detail on events surrounding political crises. One of the best attested is Edward the Confessor's attempt to repudiate Edith as part of his move against the house of Godwin in 1051. After Edith's father and several of her brothers had fled overseas, Edith was deprived of her wealth and position and sent into the protective custody of the Abbess of Wherwell, who is unnamed but identified as a sister of the king.[110] Edith, in what may be regarded as her version of events in the *Vita Edwardi* which she commissioned, assigned the main enmity against her to the Archbishop of Canterbury, Robert of Jumièges, and the *Vita* records that the king suspended divorce proceedings and allowed her to withdraw to Wilton, *cum regio honore et imperiali comitatu*, where she had been brought up.[111] When the king was obliged to accept a reconciliation with her father and brothers Edith was allowed to return from Wilton to the royal court.[112] At least part of her widowhood seems also to have been spent at Wilton,[113] though she does not seem to have taken any religious vows, but perhaps her withdrawal there was a signal to the Norman regime that she was not a threat and had withdrawn from active involvement in politics.

From the ninth century onwards rulers in Francia and its successor states, following increasingly uncompromising rulings on the circumstances in which marriages could be dissolved from the Carolingian church, had on several occasions resorted to sending unwanted wives to nunneries before initiating proceedings against them.[114] The Anglo-Saxon tradition, stretching back to the rulings of Theodore,[115] that withdrawal of one party to a religious community was grounds for dissolution of a marriage, seems to have been used successfully by later Anglo-Saxon kings on at least one occasion, though the Anglo-Saxon practice of allowing remarriage in such circumstances would not have been approved by many medieval experts in canon law. Wulfthryth's agreement to abandon her marriage in order to become Abbess of Wilton left King Edgar free to marry Queen Ælfthryth with whom, rumour had it, he had been infatuated for some years.[116] Wulfthryth's political dimension as Abbess of Wilton is considered in greater detail below. It has been suspected that other royal wives of the tenth century had been similarly persuaded to withdraw from a nunnery, but the evidence stops short of certainty. The fact that Edward the Elder's second wife Ælfflaed was buried at Wilton may be an indication that she had withdrawn there, leaving Edward free to marry his third wife Eadgifu, but there is no definite proof of this and a later medieval identification of her with a *religiosa femina* of the same name is not necessarily correct.[117] The fate of the one, or possibly two wives that Æthelred II had before Emma is even more shadowy.[118] There are, of course, numerous examples of ex-queens withdrawing to nunneries after their marriages ended in the earlier Anglo-Saxon period, though the context was different then. These women returned from the kingdoms into which they had married to their home provinces, and their entry into nunneries was part of their renewed relationship with their own families. Dissolution of marriage seems to have been relatively easily achieved under traditional Anglo-Saxon secular practice, and a pattern of relatively short diplomatic marriages seems to have been already in place before conversion was achieved[119] – shifting political alliances and patterns of overlordship probably provide the main explanations. Theodore's ruling provided a way in which the church could sanction such separation, and the creation of nunneries gave a role for ex-queens that they may have lacked before and was evidently enthusiastically embraced.

Carolingian Francia provides examples of the daughters of rival dynasties being confined in nunneries, presumably to remove them from the marriage market, a fate meted out, for instance, by Charlemagne to the daughters of Duke Tassilo of Bavaria.[120] The many rival kingdoms and cadet lines in early Anglo-Saxon England might suggest the utility of similar practices here, but such instances are remarkably hard to find. One possible example is Ælfwyn, the daughter of Æthelred and Æthelflaed of Mercia, who succeeded briefly to the control of Mercia on the death of her mother in 918 until she was removed by her uncle King Edward the Elder so that he could take control of the province himself.[121] It has been suggested that she was sent into the church and can be identified with the *religiosa femina* called Ælfwyn to whom King Eadred granted an estate at Wichhambreux in Kent in 948.[122] However, there is no proof that they are the same person, and Eadred does not refer to any ties of kinship in his grant. Comparable scenarios may have occurred in earlier Anglo-Saxon England and gone unrecorded, though the emphasis we do have seems to have been rather on kings anxious to take control of nunneries that had been in the hands of women from rival families. In the eighth and early ninth centuries there are examples of princesses, like Æthelthryth, the daughter of Æthelwald Moll and Eadburh, the daughter of Offa and widow of Beorhtric of Wessex, retreating to foreign nunneries when their families were replaced by rival lines.[123] But it was not only women who might be confined in religious houses under female control. When Eadbert Praen of Kent was captured by King Coenwulf of Mercia he was taken in chains (and according to some accounts with his hands cut off and his eyes put out) to the king's family monastery at Winchcombe that was under the control of Coenwulf's daughter Cwoenthryth.[124] As Eadbert had apparently been in holy orders, confinement in a religious community may have been deemed particularly suitable; one wonders if there are other comparable examples that have gone unrecorded.[125]

Although the record of the political involvement of nunneries is incomplete, on the whole they appear not so much as passive places where individuals were detained against their will as playing a pro-active role in promoting the interests of royal kinsmen. Some of their activities have been mentioned already, for there was not always a clear separation between what could be classed as 'religious' and what 'political'. Promotion of murdered kinsmen as saints, for instance, was often an overtly political act which raised the status of the murdered king's family and cast aspersions on the murderer and his relatives. Unfortunately detailed accounts of political crises are all too rare, and those that do exist are often brief and enigmatic about the roles of different individuals or communities especially when recorded in annals. What, for instance, was Wimborne nunnery's role, or reaction, to the revolt of Æthelwold, and what was the identity and attitude of the nun whom he abducted? The active political roles of nuns and their communities can be explored through a small number of case studies. Saints' *Lives,* particularly those written soon after the event or able to draw on contemporary sources, have proved some of the more informative sources for the involvement of female monastics in political events. The value of such hagiographies, when carefully decoded, for elucidating political intrigue has been demonstrated for later Merovingian Francia[126] and Ottonian Germany,[127] and it may be possible to suggest some parallels from Anglo-Saxon England.

Whitby: Hild and Ælfflaed

The first Abbess of Whitby, Hild, was persuaded to return to Northumbria in 647 by Bishop Aidan of Lindisfarne when she had been on the point of setting out from East Anglia to join her sister at Chelles and was given charge of a community at Hartlepool.[128] At this time her second cousin Oswine was ruler of Deira. He seems to have made no attempt to revive the See of York, founded by his cousin King Edwin, but worked in close co-operation with Bishop Aidan, in spite of the fact that the latter had his see in the kingdom of his rival King Oswiu of Bernicia.[129] Nicholas Higham has provided a convincing case for Aidan's preference for Oswine over Oswiu (that was inherited by Bede who is markedly less enthusiastic about Oswiu than he is about other Bernician kings) representing a deliberate decision by the bishop to ally himself with the Deiran ruler who proved much more willing to follow his advice on appropriate behaviour for a Christian king.[130] The recall of Hild to Deira and the support Aidan provided for her in her ambition to follow the religious life can be interpreted in this context of *rapprochement* between the bishop and Oswine, which involved the deliberate cultivation by the Deiran royal house of a Christian identity. Whether Aidan had hopes that Oswine might also become king of Bernicia is not known, but Oswiu may have feared his ambitions, for he arranged the murder of his rival on 20 August 651; Aidan died – whether or not coincidentally is unknown – a few days later, on 31 August.[131]

Hild was now in a potentially vulnerable position with her two main protectors dead, but seems to have continued as Abbess of Hartlepool. A clear sign that she had Oswiu's favour is that he entrusted his infant daughter Ælfflaed to her charge after the Battle of Winwaed in 655, and two years later Hild received the estate at *Streanæshalch*/Whitby from him.[132] Oswiu's support for Hild is made understandable by the fact that his queen, and the mother of Ælfflaed, was Hild's own cousin Eanflaed, daughter of Edwin of Deira. However, his patronage of Hild may be seen as more than a polite interest in his wife's kinswoman. Rather it was part of a deliberate policy of allying himself with the surviving female contingent of the Deiran royal house in order to consolidate his control of Northumbria as a whole that he had initiated with the murder of their kinsman Oswine. Ecgfrith, the son of Oswiu and Eanflaed, would inherit both Deiran and Bernician royal blood, and his sister

Ælfflaed as abbess would be able to cultivate a dual shrine to both families from which the royal line of Oswiu could claim descent – a process begun by Hild.[133]

Hild's religious career may be said to have had political connotations from the start in which her Deiran royal descent was all-important. Not surprisingly, Bede stresses her role as a monastic leader, but he also refers briefly to a wider political influence when he describes how *reges et principes* turned to her for advice[134] – presumably Oswine, Oswiu and his sons are indicated here. What Bede also does not stress is that Hild was a woman with considerable influence in the general running of the Northumbrian church. The tally of five bishops appointed to a range of English sees from among her clergy at Whitby can have been matched by few other foundations.[135] She may well have been the dominant figure in the Deiran church for the first part of Oswiu's reign, for until 664 the Northumbrian bishopric continued to be based at Lindisfarne. Although James the Deacon may have been still active in York itself,[136] the church which Paulinus had built in York was apparently in a poor state when Wilfrid took over the see in the 670s,[137] and until then Hild's may have been the more significant foundation. If, as some would argue, her centre was at Strensall rather than Whitby, she was in a significant location, based close to the city that had been the Deiran ecclesiastical centre.[138] Her hosting of the famous synod (of Whitby) is another indication of her important role in the Northumbrian church, but for Hild there was more at stake in the outcome of the synod than the calculation of Easter. A realignment with Canterbury meant the revival of York as a bishopric, presumably with implications for Hild's own powerbase. So it may not have been only loyalty to Aidan that made her a supporter of the Irish side and hostile to Wilfrid, the rising star of the Northumbrian church, who was appointed Bishop of York in the aftermath of the synod. Wilfrid's biographer Stephen speaks of opponents of Wilfrid favouring the Irish side who intrigued to have Chad appointed to the See of York while Wilfrid was being consecrated in Francia,[139] and Hild may well have been one of these. She is said to have sent her own representatives to Rome when Wilfrid appealed following his expulsion from Northumbria in 678,[140] and there is an implication that she was working with Archbishop Theodore, who also despatched spokesmen. Hild may well have been pleased with the results of the division of the Northumbrian see that Theodore was able to achieve after Wilfrid's departure, for the new Bishop of York was her own priest Bosa.[141] Hild may therefore have been as significant in the tumultuous church politics of the latter part of the seventh century as some of the male players whose role is more often stressed.

Church affairs could also be closely interwoven with secular politics. Wilfrid's failure to succeed immediately to the See of York in 664 was linked with the fall from power of Oswiu's son Alhfrith who had been ruling as subking of Deira, and the whole issue may have been bound up with a bid for political independence by the prince.[142] The expulsion of Wilfrid in 678 seems to have been the result of the conjunction of Theodore's desire to divide the Northumbrian bishopric with the king and queen's dislike of Wilfrid's ostentatious lifestyle and large entourage;

Stephen particularly singles out the role of Queen Iurminburh in the bishop's downfall.[143] Hild, who proffered advice to kings and princes, was no doubt drawn into the broader political dimensions of the religious issues of her day even if this is not overtly stated in the surviving sources.

When Hild died in 680, she was succeeded by Ælfflaed who to begin with shared control with her mother Eanflaed, though we know little about the latter's career within the nunnery.[144] If the nunnery had been based originally at Strensall, it is likely that by Ælfflaed's abbacy the focus had shifted to the Whitby headland, possibly as a reaction to the re-establishment of the See of York. Ælfflaed was also a major figure in the Northumbrian church praised by Bede as *devota deo doctrix*,[145] and the person whom Archbishop Theodore contacted when he wished to make peace with Wilfrid.[146] Whitby even had its own resident bishop after 685 when Trumwine retired there after he had been forced to flee his see at Abercorn.[147] But Ælfflaed's most significant ally in the church was Cuthbert, with whom she communed not only on spiritual matters but also on the continuation of the political status quo. For Ælfflaed was not only a *doctrix*, she also became a king-maker. When Ælfflaed was concerned about what might happen should her brother Ecgfrith die (for he apparently had no children), Cuthbert was able to reveal the existence of a half-brother Aldfrith in an Irish monastery,[148] and when Ecgfrith fell fighting the Picts in 685, no doubt the combined influence and con-nections of Cuthbert and Ælfflaed were instrumental in securing Aldfrith's succession. Cuthbert died in 687, but Ælfflaed moved on to what must have been her most powerful phase, for, with her own bishop installed in Whitby and a half-brother who had spent all his life outside Northumbria on the throne, she was poised to become *totius provinciae consolatrix optimaque consiliatrix*,[149] both a religious and a political counsellor. She was present when Aldfrith died in 705, and her account of his last wishes at the Synod of Nidd the following year was instru-mental in ensuring the succession of Aldfrith's under-age son Osred through promising a settlement to Bishop Wilfrid if he withdrew his support from a rival candidate.[150]

Hild and Ælfflaed appear to have had much in common as abbesses of the same foundation whose royal connections enabled them to be both influential in church and state. But although Bede is full of praise for Hild as the follower of Aidan and the founder of Whitby, her memory does not seem to have been actively promoted there and, as Catherine Karkov has argued, appears to have been eclipsed by that of Ælfflaed, who seems to have been commemorated on a cross at the nunnery of late eighth or ninth century date.[151] Hild is not mentioned in the *Vita Gregorii* commissioned when Ælfflaed was abbess, nor does she appear in the Northum-brian *liber vitae* that seems to have been begun in the reign of Ecgfrith. There is little sign that Hild was actively promoted as a saint at Whitby, and not even the full version of her name is known.[152] Ælfflaed does not appear to have seen herself as continuing a tradition begun by Hild, and the focus of their family interests was different.[153] Hild may have been responsible for memorializing the lost Deiran royal family, but Ælfflaed, the daughter of one Bernician/Northumbrian king, sister, half-sister and aunt of three more, had other priorities in which the only one of her Deiran forebears to have a significant role was her grandfather Edwin, whose links with the papal conversion of England were so skilfully and influentially developed in the *Vita Gregorii* that she commissioned.[154] There were many shifts and turns in the early political history of Northumbria that are reflected in the histories of the first abbesses of Whitby and may help to explain why Hild came to be so little honoured in the house she had founded, but where her successor became the more significant political figure. There may be parallels in the eclipse of Hild by Ælfflaed at Minster-in-Thanet where Mildrith ultimately became a more significant saint than her mother Æbbe who had founded the community. Eadburh, Mildrith's successor, may have decided to promote her cult at a time of increased Mercian influence in Kent because of her father's links with the Mercian ruling house.[155]

Repton, Guthlac and Æthelbald

The few known facts of the early history of Repton include the burial there of King Æthelbald of Mercia following his murder in 757,[156] and the entry into the community of his kinsman Guthlac in *c.* 697.[157] These two events are linked because even in his fenland retreat Guthlac provided advice and encouragement to the exiled ætheling Æthelbald, and prophecied that he would one day be king of Mercia. Are we also justified in linking the nunnery of Repton with the opposition to the descendants of Penda that would lead to Æthelbald's accession? Unfortunately any references at all to the history of Repton in the seventh and eighth centuries – let alone to a political role – are limited. It is only through the Guthlac's *Vita* that we know Repton was a double community, and that the abbess at the time of his entry was called Ælfthryth.[158] Her ancestry is not known, but as Guthlac was a member of a cadet royal line, and the community was deemed appropriate for a king's burial, it can probably be regarded as a Mercian royal foundation. As we hear relatively little about the male members of double houses, Guthlac's association with Repton is of particular interest, and an indication that men from cadet lines of royal houses might join such communities (perhaps under a female relative of higher rank), and also that their political involvements could cause problems. According to his biographer Felix, Guthlac had lived the normal life of an aristocrat of royal birth (i.e. plundering with his warband), until suddenly experiencing a call to the religious life.[159] However, George Henderson has suggested a rather different reason for Guthlac's sudden change in career by drawing attention to another event that occurred at about the same time Guthlac entered the community – the murder of Osthryth, the Northumbrian wife of the reigning Mercian king Æthelred.[160] The entry of Guthlac and the murder of Osthryth are recorded together for the year 697 in the *Chronicle* of John of Worcester.[161] Was Guthlac involved in the murder, and was his entry into Repton, and retreat two years later into the fenlands where Æthelbald was already in exile, a consequence of that involvement? The evidence is tantalizing and not conclusive, but does at least suggest ways in which the associations of male members of double houses might involve their communities in political controversy. Even after Guthlac left Repton he remained in contact with the foundation, and revisited it on at least one occasion.[162] That Repton did experience difficulties with the Mercian ruling line at the turn of the seventh century could be substantiated if Guthlac's Abbess Ælfthryth was the same person as the Ælfthryth, referred to in a letter written by Bishop Wealdhere of London in 705 or 706, who needed to be reconciled with King Cenred of Mercia (nephew of Æthelred), his bishops and other leaders.[163]

It is possible that Repton found itself in a difficult position in relation to the Mercian royal house because of the kinship links and political affiliations of at least one of its members. If we knew more of Abbess Ælfthryth's background all might be much clearer, for, like Abbess Eangyth who wrote to Boniface from one of the Kentish minsters,[164] her own kinship with a rival line of the royal house could have caused her to be viewed with dislike and suspicion at court. Such kinship might also have influenced her own loyalties, of course, and the burial of Æthelbald at Repton, where he may also have been commemorated with a splendid sculpture portraying him as a kind of Germanized Roman emperor,[165] is perhaps the best evidence for a close association between Æthelbald and the community. Guthlac is one link between Repton and Æthelbald, and possibly his sister Pega was another. Pega is described as 'a holy virgin of Christ',[166] but is not directly associated with a particular religious community. However, as her brother had been one of the *clerici* at Repton, there must be a good possibility that Pega either was, or had been, a member of the community as well. The little we know of her is of particular interest for showing how a female religious might play her part in promoting the interests of a royal claimant, for Pega's promotion of Guthlac as a saint and her management of his cult can be seen not just as the duty of a sister to a brother, but as something which actively supported the bid of Æthelbald for the Mercian kingship. After Guthlac died in 714, it was Pega who translated his remains, and thus initiated his cult as a saint only a year later, which is remarkably soon by Anglo-Saxon standards, since a longer period was usually allowed to elapse in part so that one of the main signs of sanctity, the undecayed state of the body, could be unambiguously asserted.[167] The reason for Pega's speed may have been Æthelbald's political ambitions that reached fruition in 716 when he became king of Mercia. Guthlac had prophesied on a number of occasions that Æthelbald would become king; the last of these had apparently been when Æthelbald visited his tomb soon after his death when Guthlac had appeared to him in a dream and predicted that he would be king before another year had passed.[168] Thus Guthlac's sanctity and Æthelbald's succession occurred within a close time-frame, and it seems likely that the two events were linked in order to stress that Æthelbald's political success had been foretold by a saint and was therefore pre-ordained by God. After his accession Guthlac's shrine was richly endowed by the king,[169] and perhaps Repton was similarly rewarded.

In the ninth century Repton was associated with another branch of the royal house when King Wiglaf (d. 840) was buried there. In 849 his murdered grandson Wigstan was buried in the same mausoleum, probably the structure that was eventually incorporated as the crypt of the church, and in which Æthelbald may originally have been buried.[170] This parvenu royal dynasty seems to have wanted to increase its legitimacy through association with an earlier ruler. A charter reveals that Repton was still under control of the abbess at this time,[171] but unfortunately the presumably not insignificant role of the community in the affairs of the family of Wiglaf is lost to us. We are fortunate that even a little survives to flesh out Repton's probable involvement with the political agenda of Guthlac and Æthelbald.

Wilton and Barking: Wulfthryth and Wulfhild

Where the marriages of kings were concerned the personal could easily become political, and how that might affect nunneries is demonstrated very well by the lives of the abbesses Wulfthryth and her cousin Wulfhild who, through their links with King Edgar, were drawn into the fraught politics of the latter part of the tenth century. In the later Anglo-Saxon period succession became restricted to æthelings who were the sons of kings, and royal marriages and the status of individual royal wives became issues that could help sway matters in favour of one candidate or another.[172] Noble factions tended to amass around rival princes, particularly when they had different mothers, and by the time of Edgar's reign severe tensions were becoming apparent between the leading noble families.[173] Even major churchmen like Æthelwold and Dunstan were drawn into the disputes, perhaps influenced by long-standing family ties.[174] Like a number of his predecessors King Edgar had a series of marriages. He had a son Edward (the Martyr) by his first wife; little is known about Edward's mother and she may have died soon after his birth. For his second marriage, Edgar, as recounted earlier, seems to have desired a union with the family of Wulfthryth and Wulfhild, and married the former after her cousin had made clear her preference for a religious life. Wulfthryth and Edgar had a daughter Edith, but soon after her birth in 963 or 964 the marriage was dissolved, leaving Edgar free to marry his third wife Ælfthryth.[175] According to later gossip Edgar had been enamoured with Ælfthryth for some time, but she was married to one of the sons of the powerful ealdorman Athelstan Half-King. Her husband seems to have died suddenly around the time that Edgar married Wulfthryth.[176]

Edgar's dilemma would appear to have been how to separate from Wulfthryth in a way that enabled him to marry Ælfthryth without unduly incurring the censure of the church or the wrath of Wulfthryth's family. That the family was a significant one which might need to be placated is implied by his provision for her cousin Wulfhild to whom he made amends for his attempted assault by installing her as Abbess of Barking. Entry, or rather return to a nunnery also provided the means by which Edgar could separate from Wulfthryth and be free to marry Ælfthryth, for Anglo-Saxon custom, stretching back to the seventh century, allowed an individual to remarry if a partner withdrew to a monastery,[177] though even the Greek custom which Theodore cited to justify Anglo-Saxon practice balked at allowing this to occur if it was a second marriage.[178] The withdrawal of Wulfthryth to Wilton after a marriage of two years or less, with the wedding of Edgar and Ælfthryth soon after, provides one of the best attested examples of retreat to a nunnery being used to enable a new marriage to take place. Wulfthryth seems to have received a generous settlement. She was not only installed as Abbess of Wilton (what happened to the previous incumbent is not known), but seems to have received generous grants of land, some or all of which she donated to the nunnery.[179] Goscelin provides many instances of the great wealth available to Wulfthryth and her daughter Edith, much of which they lavished on Wilton, and no doubt Wulfthryth's tenure is one of the reasons Wilton became the wealthiest of the later Anglo-Saxon royal nunneries.[180]

Although Ælfthryth's marriage to Edgar may have had Anglo-Saxon precedents it was uncanonical, and in other areas of the Western church it would have been regarded as highly irregular that Edgar should have remarried while Wulfthryth was alive. Such issues would have been of considerable interest to the supporters of Edgar's eldest son Edward, particularly since after the birth of two sons to Edgar and Ælfthryth a campaign was begun by her supporters to disinherit Edward. For instance, Gaimar knew a tradition that Archbishop Dunstan, who can be presumed to be familiar with canon law and who later supported the accession of Edward, refused to recognize the legitimacy of the marriage of Edgar and Ælfthryth and upbraided them for adultery.[181] One of the ways in which Ælfthryth could have supported her position was to attack the legitimacy of Edgar's marriage to Wulfthryth, and it may have been in this context that the stories known to some Anglo-Norman historians were circulated in which Wulfthryth was said to have been a vowed nun and the concubine, rather than wife, of the king.[182] If Wulfthryth had been illegally married to Edgar, or only his mistress, he would of course have been free to marry Ælfthryth and there would have been no question of the legitimacy of her sons, but Wulfthryth evidently maintained the legitimacy of her marriage which is acknowledged by a number of Anglo-Norman historians.[183] The question of the union's legitimacy, and therefore of Edith's status, may well have been an issue, for the material that Goscelin was able to use for the latter's *Vita* appears to go out of its way to stress that Edith was Edgar's legitimate daughter and acknowledged as such by him.[184] That this was material inherited by Goscelin, rather than invented by him, is suggested by the extreme difficulty he had in wrestling it into conformity with hagiographical norms,[185] and by the disapproval he shows of some of the manifestations of Edith's high secular status, such as her menagerie of animals provided by foreign visitors.[186] The question of the status of his two later marriages seems to have been a major issue in the last years of Edgar's reign and the immediate aftermath of his death, and, because one of his wives was an abbess, her nunnery, and apparently others, was affected by the fall-out.

Another way in which the claims of Ælfthryth's sons could be boosted was by building up Ælfthryth's position as queen.[187] The argument was apparently advanced that Ælfthryth's sons were the more throneworthy as they were born to a consecrated king and queen, while Edward had been born before Edgar had been anointed as king and his mother had never been a consecrated queen.[188] One of Ælfthryth's supporters would seem to have been Bishop Æthelwold of Winchester, because documents produced at Winchester at his time stress the primacy of her sons over Edward.[189] There were various other ways in which Æthelwold could enhance Ælfthryth's position as queen, including the apparently new provision in the *Regularis Concordia*, composed by Æthelwold, whereby she was entrusted with care of the nunneries in a way that paralleled Edgar's overall lordship of monasteries.[190] Edgar's earlier behaviour with Wulfhild might seem to provide justification for removing nunneries from the king's protection, and Æthelwold may well be alluding to the long-established problem of kingly lust when he says that the arrangement was to avoid scandal. However, when the rival whom Ælfthryth had replaced as queen was abbess of one of the most prestigious royal nunneries, the granting of supervisory rights could be seen as having an extra edge to it. The relative status of Wulfthryth and Ælfthryth was being asserted in the latter's favour, and Ælfthryth was given a potentially valuable weapon in any dispute between them. Such suspicions are fuelled further by one of the few things Ælfthryth is known to have done in her new capacity, which was to remove her rival's cousin from her position as Abbess of Barking and to exile her to Horton in Dorset.[191] It is even possible that Ælfthryth's supervisory role over the nunneries replaced a position that had been granted originally to Wulfhild herself. Goscelin says that in addition to Barking, Wulfhild was granted five *domos familiarum*, each with a church, at Wilton, Shaftesbury, Wareham, Southampton and Horton.[192] Four of these places were (or had been) nunneries, but, as Sarah Foot has discussed, interpretation of this passage is very difficult.[193] Goscelin's phrase translates as 'houses of households'. If he meant to say that Wulfhild was being given some kind of authority over nunneries he should have written *domos famularum*. Perhaps this is what he intended; the words are very similar and a simple mistake could have been made in copying. If that was the case, the question of supervision of nunneries may be seen to have played its part in a complex political situation in which Ælfthryth and Wulfthryth were major players.

If Ælfthryth had hoped also to oust Wulfthryth from Wilton she was to be disappointed, for Wulfthryth was probably in a stronger position than her cousin had been at Barking. Wulfhild had apparently had no previous connection with Barking, which may not have returned to being a nunnery at the time she went there.[194] Its *officiarii* – presumably male clerics attached to the foundation – apparently connived with Ælfthryth to have Wulfhild expelled. Wulfthryth, on the other hand, had spent her early years at Wilton, and it is possible that her family had long-standing links with the nunnery. If Goscelin's *Vita* of Edith is to be believed, she also remained on good terms with Edgar, who visited his daughter at the nunnery. Wilton hosted various court events, and foreign visitors were received there.[195] Although Wulfthryth may have had powerful enemies, she would also have had friends at court, especially among those who were not supporters of Ælfthryth.

When Edgar died dissension broke out between the factions centred on his rival sons. Edward was crowned, and ruled between 975 and 978. During this period Edith would have reached her majority and it is probably at this time that her seal, which later became the conventual seal, was produced.[196] On it she is unusually described as *regalis adelpha*, 'royal sister', emphasizing her relationship and alliance with the new King Edward. However, in 978 Edward was murdered at Corfe where he was visiting his stepmother and half-brother whose supporters probably carried out the attack.[197] Æthelred was not crowned king immediately, and there appears to be a period of negotiation between different noble groups before his accession was accepted.[198] It is in the immediate aftermath of Edward's death that Goscelin places a visit to Wilton by leading nobles in which Edith was offered the crown.[199] The veracity of Goscelin's account has been doubted, and it has been seen as included merely to provide an opportunity for him to stress Edith's humility and commitment to the religious life in declining the offer.[200] However, in addition to the fact that Goscelin's technique was to gloss the material he was given rather than to invent scenes (a practice he condemned),[201] is the episode really so unbelievable given the lack of other male heirs besides Æthelred and the antipathy of members of the rival factions? There were no precedents for rule from a virgin queen, but in the early medieval world several instances could generally be found where a royal heiress married a leading member of the nobility and so sanctioned the foundation of a new dynasty. Ealdorman Ælfhere, one of the leading noblemen said by Goscelin to have visited Edith at this time, had the stature to carry off such a marriage, especially as he appears to have claimed royal blood himself, probably through descent from King Alfred's elder brother King Æthelred I.[202] Nor would the fact that Edith had been vowed in infancy to Wilton have necessarily been a bar, because, as we have seen, Anglo-Saxon practice seems to have tolerated women leaving monastic communities in order to be married. So although much of this is hypothetical, it is not necessarily implausible, and we should not rule out the fact that Wulfthryth and Edith may have been major players in the political manoeuvring in the aftermath of Edward's murder. The delay between Edward's death and Æthelred's coronation suggests that the latter's accession was not easily accepted. Before Æthelred became king complex negotiations and bargaining had to take place, and Wulfthryth and Edith would no doubt have been able to secure their positions at Wilton as the price of their co-operation. Another concession was that Edward should be reburied with the ceremony appropriate for a murdered king, and Wulfthryth and Edith seem to have been involved in these negotiations, and may have been influential in ensuring the transfer of his body to the nunnery of Shaftesbury.[203] We can now shift attention to that foundation in order to pursue further the involvement of nunneries with the politics of the tenth century.

Shaftesbury and the cult of Edward the Martyr

We do not know the exact thinking that led to Shaftesbury being chosen as the ultimate place for Edward's reburial, and there are several different ways in which the choice of location may be read. Burial in a nunnery was a break with a tenth-century tradition that the kings of England were buried in male minsters.[204] It meant that Edward was reburied with female kin rather than male relatives, for his grandmother Ælfgifu, the wife of King Edmund, was interred at Shaftesbury and her cult seems to have been well established by the 970s.[205] Two of his great-grandmothers, Wynflaed and Eadgifu, also seem to have been closely associated with the nunnery.[206] The choice of burial in a nunnery could be seen as something of a slight to Edward's claims to the throne, and a reflection of the arguments of Æthelred's faction that Edward was not a true ætheling. Queen Ælfthryth may have hoped that her position as protectoress of the nunneries would have enabled her to influence how Shaftesbury handled affairs connected with the dead Edward. However, on the other hand, those not well disposed towards Ælfthryth and Æthelred could have taken some comfort from the fact that Shaftesbury was not one of the nunneries with which she had a close association. There are no signs that Ælfthryth was ever a patron or remembered there with any affection; rather it was one of the places that promoted her as an *impissima regina* responsible for the murder of Edward.[207] So it may be that the choice of Shaftesbury was a compromise between the faction that wished to have the dead king appropriately honoured, and their opponents who maintained that he should never have succeeded to the throne in the first place. Very unusually, the deaths of the two abbesses whose houses were involved in the translation of Edward's remains, Wulfwyn of Wareham[208] and Herelufu of Shaftesbury, are recorded in the *Anglo-Saxon Chronicle* (MS C) in 982, during Æthelred's minority. As Simon Keynes has commented, 'one does wonder whether anything might lie behind the record . . . but perhaps it was simply the coincidence of their deaths in the same year, coupled with the role they may be presumed to have played in the events of February 979, which earned them their place in the record'.[209] The deaths may or may not have been sinister, but the entry at least demonstrates how two abbesses had been brought into the public arena by their involvement in the politically sensitive issue of what to do with Edward's remains.

In discussing the choice of Shaftesbury, we should not overlook the role the abbess and nuns of Shaftesbury may have played in lobbying for a royal burial that had the potential to be a valuable asset. Shaftesbury had already successfully promoted Ælfgifu as a saint, and Shaftesbury's experience in handling a royal cult may well have been deemed significant, because the question of Edward's potential sanctity in the tradition of other murdered royal saints seems to have been a major issue after his death. Modern historians have differed over whether Edward's cult was used to try to undermine Æthelred's position or to support it.[210] The truth may be that it was something that had the potential to do the former, but that Æthelred, with the aid of Shaftesbury, handled it in such a way that it developed in a way favourable to his interests. Byrhtferth and the poem included in the D manuscript of the *Anglo-Saxon Chronicle* for 979 express the view that the residual problem with Edward's murder was that no one had ever been punished for it, and, in the absence of anyone else doing anything about it, that God had become his avenger through the renewal of Scandinavian attacks.[211] Byrhtferth appears to have regarded the removal of Edward's undecayed body from its initial hiding-place as a translation that marked recognition of Edward as *martyr Dei*, for miracles had been reported at the place of his original burial. Once his murder was known, a popular reaction promoting the dead king as a martyred saint like others before him can be expected, and it would have been fuelled by current interest in the cults of several other murdered young princes.[212] However, it was not necessarily a simple matter for the king to act towards his dead half-brother as Byrhtferth would have liked. If, as Byrhtferth also asserted, it was some of Æthelred's thegns who had carried out the murder at the behest of major nobles, the king was faced with a serious dilemma, for these men were his own supporters and some of them may have been his kinsmen as well. In later, post-Conquest accounts of Edward's murder, Æthelred's mother Ælfthryth becomes the prime instigator, and in some traditions the actual murderer.[213] The details of her involvement are hard to verify at this remove, but the fact that Edward was murdered on a visit to her as part of what appears to have been a premeditated plot would make it unlikely that she was completely innocent, and, of course, she was one of the main beneficiaries of the murder in that her son became king. On the other hand, it was in Æthelred's interests to have his kingdom reminded that God watched over kings and that a crime against a king was a crime against God, partly to discourage any would-be assassins, but also to encourage compliance with increasing royal and other financial demands due to the Scandinavian attacks.[214]

In all this Shaftesbury had a pivotal role, for as guardians of the body the nuns were in the best position to provide evidence on whether miracles did or did not occur at his tomb. Æthelred may be seen as courting the support of Shaftesbury in 984 when he restored lands to them at Tisbury, and reconfirmed ownership of one of their key estates that some of his predecessors had wished to reclaim.[215] There is no reference to Shaftesbury's possession of Edward's body, yet it is possible that some significant stage in the potential development of a cult had been reached at the time the charter was granted, as Byrhtferth reports that after Edward's body came to Shaftesbury it rested for five years in paradise and then (that is, in *c.* 984), came into God's sight.[216] It was also in 984 that Bishop Æthelwold, who had been a major power during Æthelred's minority, died, and Æthelred may have been able to fully exercise total authority for the first time. Charters suggest some major shifts in policy as a result,[217] and the question of what to do about the dead Edward and the nature of the king's relations with Shaftesbury nunnery may have been among them.

According to Byrhtferth's chronology, miracles began at Edward's tomb at Shaftesbury *c.* 990, and in the following decade, as Scandinavian attacks increased in severity, Æthelred seems to have come under further pressure to deal with the problem of Edward's death. In *c.* 994 he founded Cholsey abbey to provide for the soul of Edward,[218] but initiated the official recognition of his cult only at the beginning of the new millennium. The *Passio Edwardi*, which seems to represent Shaftesbury tradition, gives the king a central role in the development of the cult, but mediated through Shaftesbury where miracles had been taking place at the tomb.[219] The final stage towards the full initiation of the cult occurred when Edward appeared to a male religious and instructed him to approach the abbess, who was to inform the king that the saint was ready to be translated which duly took place on 20 June 1001. Shortly after the event the nunnery received a major grant of land at Bradford-on-Avon to help nurture Edward's cult and provide an alternative place for his relics because of the recent viking attacks.[220]

Before Edward's cult had been launched, Æthelred had acquired another saintly sibling. Some time between 997 and 1000 Æthelred had been involved in the translation at Wilton of his half-sister Edith who is said to have appeared both to the king himself and – rather more surprisingly – to his uncle Ordulf, the brother of Ælfthryth to encourage their involvement.[221] Once again the way had been carefully prepared by the recording of miracles and other appearances of Edith,[222] and similarities between the initiation of the two cults so close together in time encourages the belief that they were part of a co-ordinated campaign.[223] The initiation of the cult of Edith demonstrated that Æthelred and his uncle accepted her as the king's legitimate sister. It may also be seen as marking a reconciliation with Wulfthryth and probably other members of her family, for it was probably also within this timespan that Wulfhild was allowed to return to Barking after an exile of twenty years.[224] Increasing Scandinavian attacks and other political problems may have persuaded Æthelred of the desirability of saintly siblings to underscore his position as an anointed ruler under God's special protection, but their promotion may also be seen as part of a wider movement of family reconciliation and reconstruction as Æthelred moved towards his second marriage to Emma of Normandy.[225] What may have made all these things possible, or at least easier was the decline of the great matriarch Ælfthryth who died on 17 November in 1000 or 1001.

The successful promotion of the cults of Edith and Edward was not a foregone conclusion, but depended on the right combination of kingdom and family politics. The cults were promoted by kings and nunneries in conjunction, with other ecclesiastics playing a subsidiary role in the actual creation of the cults. Once established they ensured the future prosperity of the two nunneries, as succeeding kings and queens also patronized the cults,[226] and their successful promotion may help to explain how Shaftesbury and Wilton came to be the two richest Anglo-Saxon nunneries at the time of Domesday Book.[227] Queen Emma is said to have loved Edith as a kinswoman,[228] while Cnut had a golden shrine made for her remains when she saved him from drowning and 'was bound to her by so much love and affection that he might have been her own brother Æthelred or nephew

Edmund',[229] a telling indication of his desire to be seen as the legitimate successor of the West Saxon royal house. He also upheld the celebration of the feast day of Edward in his laws, possibly continuing legislation initiated by Æthelred.[230]

Conclusion

Royal nunneries may have owed their initial popularity to the desire of rulers to have their families intimately connected with the propagation of the new Christian religion, possibly in imitation of pre-Christian cultic practices. The intimate connection of the royal nunneries with the families that founded them was a feature throughout their existence, and one result was that it would have been difficult for nunneries, even if they had wished to do so, to have completely distanced themselves from the secular affairs of their families. As royal nunneries contained women who were close relatives of kings, and were often commanded by abbesses who had once been queens, it was inevitable that they would have an interest in the wider political concerns of their kinsfolk. The entry, or departure, of a woman from a nunnery could be in itself an event which carried major political ramifications. The secular links of the royal nunneries were not fatal to their purity as religious communities, not least because one of their major functions was to ensure God's support for the families that patronized them. Their patrons therefore had a vested interest in the houses being pleasing to God. But nunneries did have a role to play in broader family strategies, and as a result developed some characteristics, such as a liberal policy in allowing women who had taken vows to leave in order to be married, that could appear aberrant if measured against the standards of strict Benedictine monasticism. Values and customs of the secular world might also impinge on life in the royal nunneries. Some of these, such as a continuing attachment to secular symbols of status such as dress, drew the concern of reforming churchmen, but were not in themselves fatal to the religious lives of the communities. Much more intrusive were predatory royal males who expected free access to the nunneries, and who not only violated the chastity that was a basic tenet of monasticism, but also showed how permeable these institutions could be to intrusions from the secular world. Many religious women must have had cause to resent interference from relatives in the secular world, but as many again probably found satisfaction and fulfilment in being able to advance the interests of their families through their positions in the church and were able to exploit such connections for the lasting benefit of their communities.

What we have as a result are examples of strong, active women who were implicated in some of the key political crises of the Anglo-Saxon period. When considering the course and outcome of these events, due allowance should be made for the role of religious women who need not be seen as passive players manipulated by the principal male participants, but as people whose intervention was crucial to the outcome of events. Such powerful religious women may be found at all points during the Anglo-Saxon period and are not just a feature of the 'golden age' of seventh-century female monasticism that produced Hild and Ælfflaed. Throughout the Anglo-Saxon period politics was to a large extent 'family politics', and involved issues of descent and marriageable status as well as the ability and power of claimants and their standing with lay and secular nobility – the latter might also be dictated by family alignments and intermarriage including with the royal house itself. In other words, key issues concerning succession and deposition of kings of necessity involved women of the royal house as well as men. They also involved ecclesiastical as well as customary law. Ecclesiastical concepts of legitimate and illegitimate marriage affecting succession became increasingly important as the period progressed. It was therefore inevitable that royal nunneries would be drawn into politics, for they often contained women whose past or future marriages might be the deciding factor in such disputes, something that could bring danger to nunneries and their inmates, but also opened up possibilities and meant that many abbesses could not afford to be passive at such times.

The political significance of women who lived in nunneries is not something that declined as the period progressed. Indeed, one could claim the opposite, namely that as the descent group narrowed in the tenth century so that only those who were the sons of kings became eligible for the throne, so the status of marriages and legitimacy of sons became major issues.[231] Often, the women who could decide such issues either were living or had lived in one of the major royal nunneries of the later Anglo-Saxon period, and included women such as Ælfgifu of Shaftesbury (mother of Eadwig and Edgar) and Wulfthryth of Wilton and her daughter Edith. Although reformers might have (as they saw it) good ecclesiastical reasons for wanting to enforce stricter claustration and separation from the world on religious women, one should consider whether attempts to do so in the later tenth century were directly influenced by the political crises of the time. Bishop Æthelwold's support for Queen Ælfthryth and her son Æthelred in the dispute over who should succeed King Edgar seems to be well documented.[232] By giving her authority over the nunneries in the *Regularis Concordia* he not only boosted the sacerdotal implications of queenship, but also helped her to the means to coerce her rival Wulfthryth whose testimony concerning the status of her marriage to King Edgar and the circumstances of their separation had the potential to bring the legitimacy of her own son into dispute and unseat his claim to the throne.

Looked at through ecclesiastical legislation, the history of early medieval nunneries may be represented as one of decline and oppression by the male hierarchy of the church. But legislation should always be seen as a sign of what is wanted to be achieved, of the theoretical ideals of legislators, rather than what happened in practice. It was often the case in the early middle ages that political necessities won out over religious theory, and so it proves to be the case with royal nunneries. Their vitality throughout the Anglo-Saxon period can at least in part be explained by their usefulness in family politics and the prestige their female leaders could claim because of their membership of a royal house. Throughout the period canon law made relatively little headway over such matters as the ease with which marriages could be dissolved or women could leave nunneries in order to marry in Anglo-Saxon England. Secular, political needs had precedent in such areas, and no doubt in many others which affected nunneries and the relationship of women within them with their families and their role in family strategies. The royal nunneries in particular cannot be understood solely as religious institutions. Leave out their political role and one is in danger of ignoring a key factor that governed their lives and helps to explain the fluctuating fortunes of individual communities as well as enabling us to identify some extremely influential Anglo-Saxon women.

Notes

1. See Chapter 1.
2. J. Jochens, *Old Norse Images of Women* (Philadelphia, 1996), 45–9; T. A. DuBois, *Nordic Religions in the Viking Age* (Philadelphia, 1999), 50–3. Seeresses had a significant role in Old Norse religious practices, but there is insufficient evidence to indicate whether they were also a feature of Anglo-Saxon pre-Christian beliefs. Seeresses may be an example of Saami influence within Scandinavia.
3. G. Speake, *A Saxon Bed Burial at Swallowcliffe Down*, English Heritage Archaeological Report, 10 (1989), 58–80.
4. See Chapter 4.
5. M. J. Enright, 'Lady with a mead-cup. Ritual, group-cohesion and hierarchy in the Germanic warband', *Frühmittelalterliche Studien*, 22 (1988), 170–203.
6. S. Brink, 'Political and social structures in early Scandinavia. A settlement-historical pre-study of the central place', *Tor*, 28 (1996), 235–81.
7. C. Clover, 'Regardless of sex: men, women and power in early northern Europe', *Speculum*, 69 (1993), 363–87; see Introduction.
8. Dowager queens were most likely to be influential if their sons became kings, especially if they were minors when their mothers might act as regents. With a few exceptions, rule by minors was not the norm in early Anglo-Saxon England, but was a feature of the more restricted succession patterns of the later period. See P. Stafford, *Queens, Concubines and Dowagers: The King's Wife in the Early Middle Ages* (London, 1983).
9. BL Cotton Domitian, A.VIII. J. Gerchow, *Gedenküberlieferung der Angelsachsen, mit einem Katalog der libri vitae und Necrologien*, Arbeiten zur Frühmittelalterforschung, 20 (Berlin, 1988), 109–54, 304–20.
10. Raegnmaeld and Eanflaed were wives of Oswiu; Iurminburh was the second wife of Ecgfrith. Eanflaed joined her daughter at Whitby; Iurminburh her sister at Carlisle (see Appendix 1).
11. J. Lang, *Corpus of Anglo-Saxon Stone Sculpture, Vol. III: York and Eastern Yorkshire* (London, 1991), 135–41. The inscriptions imply that Œðilburg was venerated as a saint. It is quite possible that, like the first four names in the *liber vitae* list of queens and abbesses, she was related to Ecgfrith, a likelihood that is increased if she can be identified with the Abbess Æthelburh who was present with Abbess Ælfflaed at the death of King Aldfrith. See *V. Wilfredi*, ch. 49; R. Sermon, 'The Hackness cross cryptic inscriptions', *Yorkshire Archaeological Journal*, 68 (1996), 101–11.
12. *HE*, IV, 26 says that Ælfflaed presided over Whitby with her mother Eanflaed, and so it is usually assumed that she retired there on the death of Oswiu in 670 and

became abbess. However, in 670 Hild was still alive. Did Eanflaed share control with her, or only with Ælfflaed, after her death? It is possible that Eanflaed's retirement could have been the occasion for dividing the nunnery of *Streanæshalch* between two centres at Strensall, near York and Whitby itself – see further below.

13. *V. Wilfredi*, ch. 2.
14. *Ibid.*, ch. 3.
15. *HE*, IV, 23. In this chapter Bede refers only to the travels of Oftfor who became bishop of the Hwicce, but in V, 3, John of Beverley, who had also received his early training at Whitby, refers to Theodore's medical teachings in terms which suggest that he had studied with him. For Hild's influence within early Northumbria, see further below.
16. S. Hollis, *Anglo-Saxon Women and the Church* (Woodbridge, 1992), 151–78.
17. P. Wormald, 'Bede, Beowulf and the conversion of the Anglo-Saxon aristocracy', in R. T. Farrell (ed.), *Bede and Anglo-Saxon England*, BAR, 46 (Oxford, 1978), 32–95; C. Cubitt, *Anglo-Saxon Church Councils c. 650–c. 850* (Leicester, 1995), 100–5.
18. *HE*, IV, 25 (Coldingham); R. Ehwald (ed.), *Aldhelm, De Virginitate*, in *Aldhelmi Opera Omnia*, MGH Auctores Antiquissimi, XV (Berlin, 1919), 317–18, and M. Lapidge and M. Herren, *Aldhelm: The Prose Works* (Woodbridge, 1979), 127–8.
19. L. Webster and J. Backhouse (eds), *The Making of England: Anglo-Saxon Art and Culture AD 600–900* (London, 1991).
20. J.-P. Laporte and R. Boyer, *Trésors de Chelles: sépultures et reliques de la Reine Bathilde et de l'Abbesse Bertille* (Chelles, 1991).
21. B. Krusch and W. Levison (eds), *Gregory of Tours, Decem Libri Historiarum*, MGH Scriptores Rerum Merovingicarum (Hanover, 1902), I, 1; IX, 39–43; X, 15.
22. *Ibid.*, X, 16; in her defence the abbess said she had used a silk mantle that a nun had given her as a present to make both an altar cloth and edging for her niece's tunic – the niece was not a member of the community but the arrangements for her marriage had been made by the abbess and the engagement party was held in the nunnery.
23. *V. Edithae*, ch. 12.
24. *V. Edithae*, ch. 13; a clothes chest containing some of her glorious robes was preserved at Wilton and had miraculously survived a fire.
25. The classic example is the court dress of Empress Theodora and her ladies as depicted in mosaic at San Vitale, Ravenna. For its adoption in the West, see further below.
26. *HE*, IV, 23. Hild is described by Bede as an infant at the time of her mother's dream, but as Christine Fell points out, the story would make more sense if Breguswith had been pregnant with Hild at that point: C. Fell, 'Hild, abbess of *Streonaeshalch*', in H. Bekker-Nielsen (ed.), *Hagiography and Medieval Literature* (Odense, 1981), 76–99, at 79.
27. *HE*, III, 8.
28. Webster and Backhouse, *The Making of England*; M. Gaimster, 'Scandinavian gold bracteates in Britain. Money and media in the Dark Ages', *Medieval Archaeology*, 36 (1992), 1–28.
29. *V. Wilfredi*, ch. 34.
30. *HE*, IV, 19.
31. J.-P. Laporte, *Le Trésor des Saints de Chelles* (Chelles, 1998), 89–90.
32. S. Ridyard, *The Royal Saints of Anglo-Saxon England* (Cambridge, 1988), 98–9, text, 267–9.

33. See n. 21; as Gregory was one of those bishops and the matter concerned episcopal authority, his account cannot be seen as straightforward or unbiased.
34. Ridyard, *Royal Saints*, ch. 5, 269 and ch. 7, 271–4.
35. Cubitt, *Church Councils*, 100–1; *HS*, III, chs 20 and 29.
36. *V. Wilfredi*, ch. 39.
37. *HE*, IV, 19.
38. Bede, *VC*, ch. 27; Anon., *VC*, IV, 8.
39. S 1782; P. Sims-Williams, *Religion and Literature in Western England, 600–800* (Cambridge, 1990), 123.
40. J. Blair, 'Minster churches in the landscape', in D. Hooke (ed.), *Anglo-Saxon Settlements* (London, 1988), 35–58; *idem*, 'Anglo-Saxon minsters: a topographical review', in J. Blair and R. Sharpe (eds), *Pastoral Care before the Parish* (Leicester, 1992), 226–66; *idem*, *The Church in Anglo-Saxon Society* (Oxford, forthcoming).
41. For charter evidence for the Kentish nunneries' involvement in trade, see S. Kelly, 'Trading privileges from eighth-century England', *Early Medieval Europe*, 1 (1992), 3–27.
42. L. Alcock, E. A. Alcock and S. Foster, 'Reconnaissance excavations of early historic fortifications and other royal sites in Scotland, 1974–84: 1, Excavations near St Abb's Head, Berwickshire, 1980', *Proceedings of the Society of Antiquaries of Scotland*, 116 (1986), 255–79.
43. B. Colgrave (ed.), *Two Lives of St Cuthbert* (Cambridge, 1940), 318.
44. See Chapter 3.
45. Anon., *VC*, IV, 8.
46. There is some uncertainty about the location of the defences and whether the nunnery lay inside or outside them, though the former seems more likely. L. Keen, 'The towns of Dorset', in J. Haslam (ed.), *Anglo-Saxon Towns in Southern England* (Chichester, 1984), 203–47, at 232–3; S. Keynes, 'King Alfred the Great and Shaftesbury Abbey', in L. Keen (ed.), *Studies in the Early History of Shaftesbury Abbey* (Dorchester, 1999), 17–72, at 37–9.
47. J. W. Bernhardt, *Itinerant Kingship and Royal Monasteries in Early Medieval Germany, c. 936–1075* (Cambridge, 1993).
48. See Chapter 3.
49. S 1438 (AD 838); S 300 (AD 850); S 302–5, 307–11, 1862 (AD 854); 379 (AD 921). I am grateful to Ryan Lavelle for supplying these references.
50. *Gesta Regum*, ii, 126.
51. *V. Edithae*, ch. 10.
52. B. A. E. Yorke, 'The legitimacy of St Edith', *Haskins Society Journal* (forthcoming).
53. J. Haslam, 'The towns of Wiltshire', in *Anglo-Saxon Towns in Southern England* (Chichester, 1984), 87–147, at 125–8.
54. Bernhardt, *Itinerant Kingship*, 138–49.
55. M. Biddle, 'Seasonal festivals and residence; Winchester, Westminster and Gloucester in the tenth to eleventh centuries', *Anglo-Norman Studies*, 8 (1986), 51–72; M. Hare, 'Kings, crowns and festivals: the origins of Gloucester as a royal ceremonial centre', *Transactions of the Bristol and Gloucestershire Archaeological Society*, 115 (1997), 41–78. However, Hare (47–8) also points to charters indicating that Easter 854 was spent at Wilton (see n. 49 above).
56. On which see further below.
57. Ridyard, *Royal Saints*, 99–101, 270–4.

58. Tangl, no. 63; *EHD*, I, no. 175.

59. K. Cooper, *The Virgin and the Bride: Idealized Womanhood in Late Antiquity* (Cambridge, MA, 1996), 45–67; J. T. Schulenberg, *Forgetful of Their Sex: Female Sanctity and Society ca. 500–1100* (Chicago, IL, 1998), 127–75.

60. *HE*, IV, 19; C. Fell, 'Saint Æthelthryth: a historical-hagiographical dichotomy revisited', *Nottingham Medieval Studies*, 38 (1994), 18–34.

61. *HE*, IV, 19; Bede does say that she achieved her separation from Ecgfrith 'with difficulty', but does not elaborate on what that entailed. Ecgfrith must have separated from her soon after his accession in 670, as Æthelthryth had returned to Ely by 672 (Bede says she was abbess for seven years before her death in 679).

62. On the modern historian's dilemma on how to interpret Æthelthryth's apparent virginity after twelve years of married life, see P. A. Thompson, 'St Æthelthryth: the making of history from hagiography', in M. J. Toswell and E. M. Tyler (eds), *Studies in English Language and Literature: 'Doubt Wisely': Papers in Honour of E. G. Stanley* (London, 1996), 475–92. One should remember that there may have been a disparity in their ages and Ecgfrith may have been only about 15 when they married.

63. Fell ('Hild', 79–80) suggests that Hild, one of Bede's favoured female religious, is likely to have been married before she entered the religious life, but that Bede conceals the fact, though he also does not describe her as a virgin.

64. Theodore, *Penitential*, II, 12.8 and II, 3.7. See Hollis, *Anglo-Saxon Women and the Church*, 46–74.

65. *Aldhelm, De virginitate*, ch. 13: Ehwald, *Aldhelmi Opera Omnia*, 242–3; Lapidge and Herren, *Aldhelm: The Prose Works*, 69–70; S. O'Sullivan, 'Aldhelm's *De Virginitate* – patristic pastiche or innovative exposition?', *Peritia*, 12 (1998), 271–95.

66. But elsewhere marriage is 'the foul excrement of the latrine'; the prejudices of Aldhelm's patristic sources keep asserting themselves so that his final message is contradictory (O'Sullivan, 'Aldhelm's *De Virginitate*').

67. Theodore, *Penitential*, I, 14.5 and I, 8.6.

68. *Ibid.*, I, 9.3.

69. Tangl, no. 73; *EHD*, I, no. 177.

70. *V. Leobae*, ch. 12.

71. *HS*, III, 455–6; ch. 16.

72. P. Wormald, *The Making of English Law: King Alfred to the Twelfth Century, Vol. I, Legislation and Its Limits* (Oxford, 1999), 280–1.

73. Alfred, *Laws*, ch. 8: 1–3; F. L. Attenborough, *The Laws of the Earliest English Kings* (Cambridge, 1922), 68–9.

74. Alfred, *Laws*, chs 8 and 18; Attenborough, *Laws*, 68–9, 72–3.

75. *Councils and Synods*, I, no. 20, ch. 7.

76. *HE*, IV, 25.

77. See, for instance, the deference with which Lull and his brothers address their superior, the royally born Abbess Cyneburh, in Tangl, no. 49. I am indebted to John Blair for discussion on this point.

78. Tangl, no. 73; *EHD*, I, no. 177.

79. Alfred, *Laws*, ch. 8, 68–9.

80. *A-SC, s.a.* 900; there seems to be an allusion to Alfred's legislation about the removal of nuns from nunneries cited above.

81. M. Clunies Ross, 'Concubinage in Anglo-Saxon England', *Past and Present*, 108 (1985), 3–34, 31–2.

82. *A-SC*, C, 1046.

83. *Worcester, s.a.* 1049, 548–9; T. Hearne (ed.), *Hemingi Chartularium Ecclesiae Wigornensis*, 2 vols (Oxford, 1723), I, 275–6.

84. S. Millinger, 'Humility and power: Anglo-Saxon nuns in Anglo-Norman hagiography', in J. Nichols and L. T. Shank (eds), *Medieval Religious Women. I: Distant Echoes* (Kalamazoo, 1984), 115–30.

85. Goscelin deplored this tendency in other writers (*V. Edithae*, ch. 1, 37).

86. *V. Wulfhildae*, chs 2–3; Yorke, 'Legitimacy of St Edith'.

87. Probably what was meant is one of the small detached privies that have been excavated at some high-status tenth-century sites such as the royal palace of Cheddar or the thegnly residence at Faccombe Netherton (Hants); see Yorke, 'Legitimacy of Edith'.

88. *V. Wulfhildae*, ch. 4.

89. I am grateful to Shashi Jayakumar of Balliol College, Oxford, for the suggestion that 'Wihtburd' who appears as an ancestor of Wulfhild (*V. Wulfhildae*, ch. 1) may be the West Saxon nobleman Wihtbrord who appears prominently in charters of King Edward the Elder. See also ch. 3.

90. Yorke, 'Legitimacy of St Edith'.

91. *V. Wulfhildae*, ch. 4.

92. Eadmer, *V. Dunstani*, in W. Stubbs (ed.), *Memorials of St Dunstan Archbishop of Canterbury*, Rolls Series, 63 (London, 1874), 209–10; Yorke, 'Legitimacy of St Edith'.

93. M. Rule (ed.), *Eadmer, Historia Novorum in Anglia*, Rolls Series, 81 (London, 1884), 124–5; J. Burton, *Monastic and Religious Orders in Britain 1000–1300* (London, 1994), 87–8.

94. *A-SC*, E, 1086; D. K. Coldicott, *Hampshire Nunneries before and after the Norman Conquest* (Chichester, 1989), 26.

95. There is confusion in the secondary literature about whether Edith was based at Romsey or Wilton. The suggestion that she was first at Romsey and then moved to Wilton reconciles information in Eadmer placing Edith under Christina's command as a young girl, but locating her at Wilton at the time of her projected marriage (Rule, *Historia Novorum*, 121–6).

96. R. W. Southern, *Saint Anselm and His Biographer* (Cambridge, 1966), 182–93; E. Searle, 'Women and the succession at the Norman Conquest', *Anglo-Norman Studies*, 3 (1980), 159–70.

97. Rule, *Historia Novorum*, 122–3.

98. *Ibid.*, 121.

99. Stubbs (ed.), *Memorials of St Dunstan*, 209–10; the interest in Edgar's advances to Wulfthryth and Wulfhild in the twelfth century obviously has to be related to the contemporary issue of the religious status of Edith-Matilda.

100. F. Barlow (ed.), *The Life of King Edward Who Rests at Westminster*, 2nd edn (Oxford, 1992), 22–5; P. Stafford, *Queen Emma and Queen Edith: Queenship and Women's Power in Eleventh-Century England* (Oxford, 1997), 257–9.

101. Asser, ch. 75; the motive may have been to stress her suitability for the type of diplomatic royal marriage that she eventually achieved; see B. A. E. Yorke, 'Edward as Ætheling', in N. J. Higham and D. H. Hill (eds), *Edward the Elder 899–924* (London, 2001), 25–39, at 27–9.

102. Dümmler, no. 62.

103. Asser (ch. 75) speaks of the instruction of *nutritorum et nutricum* (male and female 'tutors') at the Alfredian court.

104. M. de Jong, 'Growing up in a Carolingian monastery; magister Hildemer and his oblates', *Journal of Medieval History*, 9 (1983), 99–128; J. Doran, 'Oblation or obligation? A canonical ambiguity', in D. Wood (ed.), *The Church and Childhood*, Studies in Church History, 31 (Oxford, 1994), 127–41.

105. Theodore, *Penitential*, II, 12.34 and 37; it was also possible, in the early Anglo-Saxon period at least, for one family member to be substituted for another (*ibid.*, II, 14.5).

106. Rule, *Historia Novorum*, 121–2.

107. Southern, *Saint Anselm*, 185–90; Searle, 'Women and succession', 166–70.

108. M. Parisse, 'Les chanoinesses dans l'empire Germanique (ix–xi siècles)', *Francia*, 6 (1978), 107–28.

109. S. Foot, 'Language and method: the Dictionary of Old English and the historian', in M. J. Toswell (ed.), *The Dictionary of Old English: Retrospects and Prospects*, Old English Newsletter Subsidia, 26 (1998), 73–87; S. Foot, *Veiled Women*, 2 vols (Aldershot, 2000), 26–30.

110. *A-SC*, D and E, 1051; *Worcester* (1051, 562–3) adds the details that she was sent without honour and with only one waiting woman.

111. Barlow (ed.), *The Life of King Edward*, l, 36–9; Stafford, *Queen Emma and Queen Edith*, 262–6. The apparent discrepancy in the accounts about whether Edith was sent to Wherwell or Wilton has occasioned some concern (see Barlow, *The Life of King Edward*, l), but they can be reconciled if Edith was sent first to Wherwell and then allowed to withdraw to Wilton.

112. Barlow, *The Life of King Edward*, 44–5.

113. *Ibid.*, 137–9; Stafford, *Queen Emma and Queen Edith*, 274–9.

114. Stafford, *Queens, Concubines and Dowagers*, 175–90.

115. Theodore, *Penitential*, II, 12.13.

116. *Gesta Regum*, II, 157–9. It has been questioned whether Wulfthryth was a legitimate wife of King Edgar, but Goscelin, John of Worcester (*Worcester*, 416–17) and William of Malmesbury (*Gesta Regum*, I, 180) all refer to her as such (Yorke, 'Legitimacy of St Edith').

117. *Gesta Regum*, II, 126. The identification of her with a *religiosa femina* called Ælfflaed who received an estate from King Edmund seems extremely suspect and is discussed in detail in Foot, *Veiled Women* (I, 180–1; II, 94–5).

118. Stafford, *Queen Emma and Queen Edith*, 66, n. 3.

119. For instance, the repudiation by Cenwalh of Wessex of the sister of Penda of Mercia soon after the former's accession *c.* 642 (*HE*, III, 7). None of the individuals involved seems to have been Christian, and Penda interpreted Cenwalh's action as a political slight to himself.

120. S. Wemple, *Women in Frankish Society: Marriage and the Cloister 500–900* (Philadelphia, 1981), 171; S. Airlie, 'Narratives of triumph and rituals of submission: Charlemagne's mastering of Bavaria', *TRHS*, 6th Series, 9 (1999), 93–119, at 116–18.

121. *ASC Mercian Register, s.a.* 918 or 919.

122. S 535; M. Bailey, 'Ælfwyn, second lady of the Mercians', in N. Higham and D. H. Hill (eds), *King Edward the Elder 899–924* (London, 2001), 112–27.

123. Both established themselves in Carolingian Italy; see B. A. E. Yorke, 'Æthelbald, Offa and the patronage of nunneries', in D. Hill (ed.), *Æthelbald and Offa* (Oxford, forthcoming).

124. *A-SC*, 798 (F, *s.a.* 796); *Gesta Regum*, I, 95; N. Brooks, *The Early History of the Church of Canterbury* (Leicester, 1984), 120–5. According to William of Malmesbury's source, Eadbert was released when Coenwulf dedicated a new church at Winchcombe (possibly in 811).

125. *A-SC* (A, 962) records that King Sigeferth (a tributary king presumably from the Scottish Isles) killed himself and was buried at Wimborne. But it is not clear if he was being held in Wimborne at this time, or whether Wimborne still had a female element in that period.

126. P. Fouracre, 'Merovingian history and Merovingian hagiography', *Past and Present*, 127 (1990), 3–38; P. Fouracre and R. Gerberding, *Late Merovingian France: History and Hagiography 640–720* (Manchester, 1996).

127. P. Corbet, *Les Saints ottoniens: sainteté dynastique, sainteté royale et sainteté féminine autour de l'an Mil*, Beihefte von Francia, bd, 15 (Sigmaringen, 1986).

128. *HE*, IV, 23.

129. *HE*, III, 14. It would be interesting to know when Edwin's head was retrieved and placed in the church at York (possibly after it had been ritually displayed like that of Oswald). Oswiu performed this service for his brother and predecessor Oswald, and possibly Oswine did the same at much the same time for his cousin Edwin.

130. N. Higham, 'Dynasty and cult: the utility of Christian mission to Northumbrian kings between 642 and 654', in J. Hawkes and S. Mills (eds), *Northumbria's Golden Age* (Stroud, 1999), 95–104.

131. *HE*, III, 14 and 17; Bede says Aidan died after an illness.

132. *HE*, III, 24 and IV, 23. For discussion of whether *Streanæshalch* was Whitby or should be identified as Strensall near York see Chapter 1 and n. 138 below.

133. M. Miller, 'The dates of Deira', *A-SE*, 8 (1979), 35–61.

134. *HE*, IV, 23; one should recognize though the possibility that this passage is no more than a hagiographical topos.

135. *HE*, IV, 23.

136. *HE*, II, 20.

137. *V. Wilfredi*, ch. 16.

138. Barnwell, pers. comm. However, even if her original foundation was at Strensall, by the time Bede wrote, the centre of the foundation he associated with Hild and Ælfflaed would appear to have been at what would later be known as Whitby. His description of Hild's death with its reference to Hackness as being thirteen miles away fits Whitby but not Strensall, and his rather unsuccessful attempts to explain the place-name *Streanæshalch* are based on the assumption that it was a headland site (*HE*, III, 25). For some of the circumstances that may have lain behind the shift of site, see below.

139. *V. Wilfredi*, ch. 14. For the complicated events surrounding Wilfrid and the Northumbrian see (though without consideration of Hild's possible role) see C. Cubitt, 'Wilfrid's "usurping bishops": episcopal elections in Anglo-Saxon England, *c.* 600–*c.* 800', *Northern History*, 25 (1989), 18–38.

140. *V. Wilfredi*, ch. 54.

141. *HE*, IV, 12 and 23.

142. D. Kirby, 'Northumbria in the time of Wilfrid', in D. Kirby (ed.), *Saint Wilfrid at Hexham* (Newcastle, 1974), 1–32.

143. *V. Wilfredi*, ch. 24.

144. *HE* (IV, 26) says that both were presiding over the nunnery in 685; it is possible that

Eanflaed had retired there as early as 670 when her husband Oswiu died. A split site at Strensall and Whitby would have allowed both women to have had their own sphere of influence.

145. *HE*, IV, 26; see Hollis (*Anglo-Saxon Women and the Church*, 179–207) for what seems to be a rather more critical portrayal of Ælfflaed in his *V. Cuthberti*, and Chapter 4 for discussion of this.

146. *V. Wilfredi*, ch. 43.

147. *HE*, IV, 26.

148. Anon., *VC*, ch. 6; Bede, *VC*, ch. 24 – Bede links discussion of this matter with Cuthbert's appointment as bishop soon after. Did Ælfflaed have a hand in the latter once Cuthbert had revealed his potential usefulness concerning Aldfrith? For Aldfrith's Irish background see C. Ireland, 'Aldfrith of Northumbria and the Irish genealogies', *Celtica*, 22 (1991), 64–78.

149. *V. Wilfredi*, ch. 60. The phrase is recalled on a surviving inscription on a cross from Whitby; see n. 151.

150. *V. Wilfredi*, chs 59 and 60.

151. C. Karkov, 'Whitby, Jarrow and the commemoration of death in Northumbria', in J. Hawkes and S. Mills (eds), *Northumbria's Golden Age* (Stroud, 1999), 126–35; J. Higgitt, 'Monasteries and inscriptions in early Northumbria, the evidence of Whitby', in C. Bourke (ed.), *From the Isles of the North: Early Medieval Art in Ireland and Britain* (Belfast, 1995), 229–36.

152. Fell, 'Hild'.

153. Karkov, 'Whitby, Jarrow', 132–4.

154. A. T. Thacker, 'Memorialising Gregory the Great: the origin and transmission of a papal cult in the seventh and early eighth centuries', *Early Medieval Europe*, 7 (1998), 59–84; N. Brooks, *Bede and the English* (Jarrow, 1999), 14–15, 19–22.

155. S. Hollis, 'The Minster-in-Thanet foundation story', *A-SE*, 27 (1998), 41–74, and see Chapter 2.

156. *A-SC*, 757; certain princes of the royal house had been buried at Repton in the late seventh century: see Chapter 1, and Yorke, 'Æthelbald, Offa and the patronage of nunneries'.

157. *V. Guthlaci*, chs 19–23.

158. The case for Repton's link with Guthlac and Æthelbald would be stronger if one followed Alan Thacker's suggestion that Felix's *Life of Guthlac* was written there: A. T. Thacker, 'The Social and Political Background to Early Anglo-Saxon Hagiography', unpublished D.Phil. thesis (University of Oxford, 1977), 327ff.

159. *V. Guthlaci*, chs 17–19.

160. G. Henderson, *Vision and Image in Early Christian England* (Cambridge, 1999), 215–16.

161. *HE* (V, 24) records that Osthryth was murdered by Mercian primates. The dates of various events in Guthlac's life can be worked out from information provided by Felix.

162. *V. Guthlaci*, ch. 27.

163. P. Chaplais, 'The letter from Bishop Wealdhere of London to Archbishop Brihtwold of Canterbury: the earliest original "letter close" in the west', in M. B. Parkes and A. G. Watson (eds), *Medieval Scribes, Manuscripts and Libraries: Essays Presented to N. R. Ker* (London, 1978), 3–23.

164. Tangl, no. 14.

165. M. Biddle and B. Kjølbye-Biddle, 'The Repton stone', *A-SE*, 14 (1985), 233–92.

166. *V. Guthlaci*, ch. 50 (158–9).

167. D. Rollason, *Saints and Relics in Anglo-Saxon England* (Oxford, 1989), 34–41. The translation of Æthelthryth of Ely occurred sixteen years after her death, that of Cuthbert after eleven years.

168. *V. Guthlaci*, ch. 52.

169. *Ibid.*, ch. 51.

170. D. Rollason, *The Search for St Wigstan*, Vaughan Paper, 27 (Leicester, 1981); H. M. Taylor, 'St Wystan's church, Repton, Derbyshire: a reconstruction essay', *Archaeological Journal*, 144 (1987), 205–45.

171. S 1624, 835; Abbess Cynewara.

172. A. Williams, 'Some notes and considerations on problems connected with the English royal succession, 800–1066', *Anglo-Norman Studies*, 1 (1978), 144–67; P. Stafford, 'The king's wife in Wessex 800–1066', *Past and Present*, 91 (1981), 3–27.

173. D. Fisher, 'The anti-monastic reaction in the reign of Edward the Martyr', *Cambridge Historical Journal*, 10 (1950–52), 254–70; C. R. Hart, 'Æthelstan "Half King" and his family', *A-SE*, 2 (1973), 115–44; A. Williams, '*Princeps Merciorum gentis*: the family, career and connections of Ælfhere, ealdorman of Mercia, 956–983' *A-SE*, 10 (1982), 143–72.

174. B. A. E. Yorke, 'Æthelwold and the politics of the tenth century', in *idem* (ed.), *Bishop Æthelwold: His Career and Influence* (Woodbridge, 1988), 65–88.

175. For the dating of Edgar's marriages see Yorke, 'Legitimacy of St Edith'.

176. The rumours included claims that Edgar and Ælfthryth had plotted her husband's death (*Gesta Regum*, I, 178–9).

177. Ecgfrith of Northumbria, for instance, married Iurminburh after his first wife Æthelthryth retired to a nunnery.

178. Theodore, *Penitential*, II, xii, 8.

179. In S 766 King Edgar confirmed to Wilton Abbey a number of estates previously granted *temporaliter* to Wulfthryth and then granted by her to the nunnery. The grant shows some signs of having been reworked, but may preserve a record of Wulfthryth's settlement made at the time of her separation. See also *V. Edithae*, ch. 5.

180. J. Crick, 'The wealth, patronage and connections of women's houses in late Anglo-Saxon England', *Revue Bénédictine*, 109 (1999), 161–4.

181. A. Bell (ed.), *Geffrei Gaimar, l'estoire des Engleis*, Anglo-Norman Text Society, vols 14–16 (Oxford, 1960), ll, 3939 ff.

182. Discussed above, pp. 156–8.

183. *Gesta Regum*, I, 80; *Worcester*, 416–17.

184. Yorke, 'Legitimacy of St Edith'.

185. Millinger, 'Humility and power', 115–30.

186. *V. Edithae*, ch. 9; the animals were housed by the south wall of the nunnery and were apparently remembered by some of his informants in the community.

187. Stafford, 'King's wife in Wessex', 24–5; Yorke, 'Æthelwold and politics', 82–7.

188. J. Nelson, 'Inauguration rituals', in P. Sawyer and I. Wood (eds), *Early Medieval Kingship* (Leeds, 1977), 50–71, at 63–7.

189. See in particular S 745, the grant of privileges from King Edgar to New Minster where Edmund (the elder of the two sons of Edgar and Ælfthryth who died in infancy) *clito legitimus prefati regis filius* is given precedence over Edward *eodem rege clito procreatus*; Yorke, 'Æthelwold and politics', 82–3.

190. T. Symons (ed.), *Regularis Concordia Anglicae nationis monachorum sanctimonia-liumque* (London, 1953), 2.

191. *V. Wulfhildae*, ch. 8; the expulsion may have occurred after Edgar's death, as in Goscelin's account Ælfthryth is described as the mother of King Æthelred (Yorke, 'Legitimacy of St Edith').

192. *V. Wulfhildae*, ch. 4. In *V. Edithae* (I, 16), Goscelin says Edgar intended to make Edith head of three nunneries, including Barking and Nunnaminster (the third perhaps being Wilton).

193. Foot, 'Veiled Women', II, 6, 179–80; there is no other evidence for a female religious community at Southampton.

194. See Chapter 3.

195. *V. Edithae* I, ch. 7 and 10; Yorke, 'Legitimacy of St Edith'.

196. F. Douce, 'Some remarks on the original seal belonging to the abbey of Wilton', *Archaeologia*, 18 (1817), 40–54; T. A. Heslop, 'English seals from the mid ninth century to 1100', *Journal of the British Archaeological Association*, 133 (1980), 1–16, at 4.

197. Byrhtferth of Ramsey who provides one of the earliest accounts of the murder blames 'zealous thegns' of Prince Æthelred for the attack: J. Raine (ed.), *The Historians of the Church of York and Its Archbishops*, Rolls Series, 71 (London, 1879), I, 449. *EHD*, I, no. 236.

198. S. Keynes, *The Diplomas of Æthelred 'the Unready', 978–1016: A Study in Their Use as Historical Evidence* (Cambridge, 1978), 173–6.

199. *V. Edithae*, I, ch. 19.

200. Millinger, 'Humility and power'; Ridyard, *Royal Saints*, 87–8.

201. *V. Edithae*, I, ch. 1; Barlow, *The Life of King Edward*, 105–8.

202. Yorke, 'Æthelwold and politics', 76–7.

203. *Passio Edwardi*, 8–9; see also *V. Edithae*, I, ch. 18. Ealdorman Ælfhere played a prominent role in the translation as well.

204. See Chapter 3.

205. Keynes, 'Alfred and Shaftesbury Abbey', 45–6.

206. See Chapter 3.

207. A role she already plays in the eleventh-century *Passio* that may have been written by Goscelin; P. Stafford ('Queens, nunneries and reforming churchmen: gender, religious status and reform in tenth- and eleventh-century England', *Past and Present*, 163 (1999), 3–35, at 28–30) points out that estates of Ælfthryth bordered those of Shaftesbury and that they may have been rival claimants to some lands that had been the dower of other tenth-century queens.

208. Wulfwyn may have been related to one of the most important noble families of Æthelred's reign if she was the Wulfwyn who is described as a kinswoman of Æthelmaer the Fat in the foundation charter of Eynsham Abbey (see L. Whitbread, 'Æthelweard and the Anglo-Saxon Chronicle', *EHR*, 74 (1959), 577–89, at 583, and Chapter 3).

209. Keynes, 'Alfred and Shaftesbury Abbey', 49–50.

210. Significant discussion includes Keynes, *Diplomas of Æthelred*, 163–74; D. Rollason, 'Cults of murdered royal saints in Anglo-Saxon England', *A-SE*, 11 (1983), 1–22, at 17–19; Rollason, *Saints and Relics*, 142–4; Ridyard, *Royal Saints*, 154–71; Keynes, 'Alfred and Shaftesbury Abbey', 48–55.

211. *V. Oswaldi*, IV, 20–1. Byrhtferth and the author of the *A-SC* poem may have

expressed one school of thought, but it is unlikely that such views prevailed through-out the whole country or throughout the whole of Æthelred's reign: S. Keynes, 'The declining reputation of King Æthelred the Unready', in D. Hill (ed.), *Ethelred the Unready: Papers from the Millenary Conference*, BAR, 59 (Oxford, 1978), 227–53.

212. C. Cubitt, 'Sites and sanctity: revisiting the cult of murdered and martyred Anglo-Saxon royal saints', *Early Medieval Europe*, 9 (2000), 53–84.

213. C. Fell, 'Edward King and Martyr and the Anglo-Saxon hagiographic tradition', in D. Hill (ed.), *Ethelred the Unready: Papers from the Millenary Conference*, BAR, 59 (Oxford, 1978), 1–13; Keynes, 'Declining reputation'.

214. Ridyard, *Royal Saints*, 165–7.

215. S 850; S. Kelly (ed.), *Charters of Shaftesbury Abbey*, British Academy, Anglo-Saxon Charters, V (Oxford, 1996), 107–14. The charter also refers to woodland annexed by one of the king's reeves.

216. *V. Oswaldi*, IV, 21; Keynes, 'Alfred and Shaftesbury Abbey', 50–1.

217. Keynes, *Diplomas of Æthelred*, 174–86.

218. *Ibid.*, 186–9.

219. *Passio Edwardi*, 11–15.

220. S 899; Kelly, *Charters of Shaftesbury*, 114–22. Æthelred states in the charter that he is acting for the salvation of his soul and that of his lineage. Why Bradford should have been deemed safer than Shaftesbury with its burghal defences remains a mystery.

221. *V. Edithae*, II, 1.

222. *Ibid.*, and I, 25–7.

223. Ridyard, *Royal Saints*, 154–71.

224. *V. Wulfhildae*, ch. 8; Yorke, 'Legitimacy of St Edith'.

225. Stafford, *Queen Emma and Queen Edith*, 218–20.

226. Ridyard, *Royal Saints*, 168–9.

227. Crick, 'Wealth, patronage and connections', 161–4.

228. *V. Edithae*, II, 13.

229. *Ibid.*, 12; translated Ridyard, *Royal Saints*, 168; this is in contrast to Cnut's alleged scepticism that a daughter of Edgar could have been a saint reported by William of Malmesbury (*Gesta Pontificum*, ch. 87).

230. Wormald, *Making of English Law*, 343–4.

231. P. Stafford, 'Sons and mothers: family politics in the early middle ages', in D. Baker (ed.), *Medieval Women*, Studies in Church History Subsidia, 1 (1978), 79–100; Stafford, *Queens, Concubines and Dowagers*.

232. Yorke, 'Æthelwold and politics'.

Conclusion: Nunneries, Royal Families and Power

The survey of the history of royal nunneries has demonstrated a close interconnection with the affairs of the families which founded and supported them, and from which many of their leading members were recruited. Once kings had accepted that religious communities commanded by female relatives were the closest they would get to holding office in the church, nunneries became an accepted part of what defined a royal house for the Anglo-Saxons. Successive new regimes within the Anglo-Saxon period, as they sought to consolidate their positions, founded or annexed religious houses which kinswomen could control as abbesses. There was kudos to be obtained from this patronage, for Anglo-Saxon rulers could not fail to observe that many successive dominant regimes in Europe – Merovingian, Lombardic, Carolingian and Ottonian – also supported nunneries commanded by their female kinswomen. Such houses had important practical roles to play particularly through intercession by prayer for both living and dead family members. The holy lives of the royal nuns could also be seen as a manifestation of the royal house's distinctive qualities as a *beata stirps*. Such considerations had a particular resonance in the conversion period when kings may have been anxious about how their authority which had been in part supported by Woden and other gods could be manifested in a similar way under the new religion. An initial stage in which kings of different dynasties sought to have recently murdered kinsmen recognized as saints or tried to earn that title for themselves by retreating to monasteries they had founded was swiftly followed by one where the onus of being religious specialists was passed to the women of the house. They were acceptable to the church as royal religious who were not involved in the spilling of blood, and it was possible by such means as allowing separated married women to enter to become nuns and permitting the unmarried to leave to take husbands for the nunneries to be able to satisfy both spiritual demands and dynastic needs.

But, however great the appeal of the nunneries may have been to kings and royal families as a whole, one can assume that they would not have achieved the popularity they enjoyed if they had not been an attractive proposition to the royal women who entered them. Nunneries, of course, offered the opportunity of a life devoted to the new religion and ensuring personal and family salvation. It has often been noted that women may be among the most fervent supporters of Christianity when it is newly introduced, and this has been attributed in part to the inclusiveness of Christianity as a religion that offered opportunities for participation and salvation to individuals like women and slaves who did not always have the chance to participate so fully in non-Christian cults.[1] The idea of Christianity providing new opportunities, including improvements in status and self-worth, may well be relevant to understanding the reception of Christianity by Anglo-Saxon royal women, though one would not want to rule out the possibility of some continuation of earlier cult practices involving elite women, particularly perhaps those concerned with the welfare of family and household.

Nunneries provided an alternative life-pattern to marriage (or remarriage), and the position of abbess had more to offer still, since it was the only position besides that of queen which could give a royal woman the authority of a public role, albeit one that was also grounded in the private life of the royal household. Perhaps for these reasons abbesses and queens were entered together in the Northumbrian *liber vitae*. As abbess a woman was able to command a large *familia* of nuns, *clerici* and servants, and controlled substantial lands with their dependent inhabitants. For those who had been queens the position of abbess provided an opportunity to continue to exercise many of the attributes of their former position, but for an abbess who had remained a virgin it offered opportunities that it is unlikely an unmarried woman would have enjoyed otherwise in the early Anglo-Saxon world. One factor that would have been particularly significant for giving status was the fact that an abbess had a position which paralleled that of a male equivalent in the church. It was a rare opportunity for a woman to cross the line and become a 'social man', a person of status.[2] Headship of a royal monastery was furthermore a gendered role that generally was not considered open to princes of the royal house. It was one that only royal women could perform from the royal kin-group and must have raised their status within the family circle. It is one of the things that distinguished royal nunneries from the family monasteries of the aristocracy whose headship might be held by either a man or a woman.

Although Anglo-Saxon conciliar legislation of the pre-viking period for the most part drew no distinction between the position of abbot and abbess, the opportunities for an Anglo-Saxon woman in the church could never be wholly equal to those available to a man because she could never be a priest and so hold its highest positions. The men who did reach the highest positions, especially those who were celibate, often manifested a distrust of women. Although in theory all men and women were equal in the sight of God, there was also, as many studies have stressed, an inherent misogyny in much early Christian writing that devalued the position of women, abhorred their sexuality, and led to calls throughout the period for strict claustration of nuns. The rhetoric of Christian misogyny can be found throughout the period, and has been detected in the historical works of Bede,[3] and in the writings of Aldhelm.[4] However, it is most obviously manifest in writings of the tenth-century monastic reform period when the impression is sometimes given that the only true servant of Christ was a male Benedictine.[5] Prejudices against women in Christian writings had their counterparts in the secular Germanic world where male superiority was also assumed. Pressures from both directions mitigated against even the most powerful women having a fully public role and moving too far outside the private sphere. Abbesses are generally found less frequently than abbots attending synods of the church, just as queens are found only occasionally in the witness-lists of charters. On the other hand, the secular world had its own hierarchies, and respect for high birth might temper the disadvantages of having been born a member of the weaker sex. Royal women may not have been always regarded as the equals of the men of the royal house, but they were still of higher birth than men who were not of royal descent. As the expectations of the Anglo-Saxon secular world permeated that of the church, one might expect that prejudices inherited from early Christian writings would have been offset by the respect due to an abbess who was of royal birth. The history of royal nunneries has to be read in the light of the fact that they contained the highest ranking seculars to pursue ecclesiastical careers.

The general pattern given to monastic history in Anglo-Saxon England is to see conversion leading to the foundation of a large number of monasteries or minsters that were very diverse in their practices and eclectic in their culture. Early enthusiasm is seen as giving way to decline by the ninth century. Traditionally the viking attacks were believed to be a major catalyst towards the disappearance of religious houses founded in the Bedan Golden Age, but currently there is a greater emphasis on the desire of kings, nobles and bishops (as well as Scandinavian incomers) to take over the lands and other assets of minsters which had turned out to be extremely effective exploiters of their resources.[6] A variant reading for female communities blames influence from Carolingian church legislation with its emphasis on strict claustration for religious women for restricting the richer lives that had been enjoyed by women in the early double houses.[7] Asser's observation that by the later ninth century there were few Anglo-Saxons following the monastic way of life is generally felt to have been accurate.[8] A gradual revival of interest in monasticism for both men and women is traced as a result of Alfred's initiatives, culminating in the movement towards reform of religious communities as Benedictine foundations led by the monastic bishops Æthelwold, Dunstan and Oswald as part of a broader tenth-century reform of the church.

How well does the history of the royal nunneries fit this template? It is certainly true that some abbesses of the late seventh and early eighth centuries like Hild and Ælfflaed of *Streanæshalch*/Whitby had a greater involvement in the general running of their province's ecclesiastical affairs than would later abbesses. Both are recorded as attending Northumbrian church councils, and Hild, of course, hosted the famous Synod of Whitby in her own foundation, while after the mid-eighth century abbesses did not usually attend major ecclesiastical councils unless directly involved in business which was to be transacted.[9] The late seventh century was a period in which episcopal authority was not fully developed and where there were often not enough bishops or episcopal centres for it to function fully. *Streanæshalch*/Whitby in the time of Hild performed a valuable necessary service that might in a later period be expected to be a male preserve and under episcopal supervision, that is, the training of men who would become leaders of the church in the next generation. Under Æfflaed the foundation provided a base for the exiled bishop of Abercorn whom one suspects did not try to pull rank on his powerful patroness.

The late seventh and early eighth centuries were a time of transition and experimentation for minsters generally, and in which as a result there were unusual opportunities available for religious women. Kings no doubt hoped in this stage to be able to have a vicarious involvement in the activities of the church in their kingdoms through their female kin. As bishops gathered their collective strength they naturally wanted to assert episcopal authority, but conciliar legislation in the eighth and ninth centuries should not be seen as directed specifically against female communities; the whole range of anomalous minsters was in its sights. Two issues which particularly exercised the bishops were, on the one hand, the relative authority of bishops and the heads of minster communities, particularly those which were secular *eigenklöster*, and, on the other, the limits of royal control over the church. There is no overt prejudice against female communities as such visible in the surviving documentation, but the royal nunneries were in effect subject to episcopal disapproval on both these counts. The hostility shown by archbishops of Canterbury to the Mercian royal abbesses Cynethryth and Cwoenthryth stemmed not from the fact that they were women, but because they controlled monastic empires which included church lands that might otherwise have come under episcopal control, and which Offa and Coenwulf had attempted to remove from all episcopal supervision with the support of papal privileges.

There can be no doubt that by the end of the ninth century most of the royal nunneries founded in the late seventh and early eighth centuries had ceased to function as such, though many of the locations still contained religious communities of some sort, generally represented by a small group of male clerics. However, the chronology and explanations for decline need careful unpacking for each kingdom. For the late eighth and ninth centuries were not only a time of viking attacks and secular appropriation of former monastic estates, but also of the decline and disappearance of Anglo-Saxon kingdoms, until only that of Wessex survived. As royal dynasties waned, so the fortunes of their nunneries fell as well. This is particularly well recorded for the kingdom of the Hwicce where at the end of the eighth century the female survivors of the dynasty found some protection from the bishopric of Worcester, though at the price of eventually enabling the bishopric to absorb many of their estates. Archbishops of Canterbury and kings of Mercia battled it out for control of the wealthy nunneries of the destroyed Kentish royal house, though ultimately it was the kings of Wessex who took over the richest spoils. But royal nunneries might be threatened not only by the complete annihilation of their royal house, but also by dynastic changes within it. Cwoenthryth ultimately lost parts of her monastic empire after the deaths of her father and uncle, because the throne of Mercia passed to a ruler from another branch of the royal house who was not inclined to support her case. That the early nunneries did not fare any better in Wessex than in the kingdoms that vanished was due largely, one suspects, to the family of Alfred having little interest in supporting expensive foundations that were associated with rivals within the royal house. One early nunnery which did survive was Wimborne that had been founded by their own ancestors, but after Wimborne was implicated in the rebellion of Alfred's nephew Æthelwold, whose father had been buried there, it is not heard of again as a nunnery. At the end of the Anglo-Saxon period Wimborne appears as a secular minster supporting a small body of priests.[10] No doubt the broader estates which it must once have possessed were absorbed into the royal demesne. Therefore although many of the royal nunneries disappeared within the same broad timespan as other early minsters and formed part of a trend in which minster lands passed under secular or episcopal control, the precise circumstances surrounding their suppression were peculiar to their status as foundations of a particular royal family. Royal nunneries flourished only for as long as there was a royal kin-group that wished to support them.

But although individual royal nunneries founded in the Bedan period disappeared, the desire to have such foundations never waned and in this sense they can be said to have bucked the trend outlined above for what can be broadly termed monastic foundations.[11] There was never a period in the Anglo-Saxon centuries in which there were no royal nunneries. At the very point at which so many early minsters were disappearing, new nunneries were being founded. Both the competing Mercian dynasties of the late eighth and ninth centuries and the house of Ecgbert of Wessex in the ninth and early tenth centuries founded nunneries that were controlled by their kinswomen. As far as we can see, they performed much the same services for their families as the earlier foundations, that is, intercession for living and dead family members, the nurturing of family saints and a general contribution to the culture of a civilized Christian court. Their continuing functions as royal foundations meant that there was no major contrast between them and the earlier double houses. The nunneries of the ninth and tenth centuries also had some attached clerics, even if the numbers may not have been as considerable as in some of the earlier foundations, and like all minsters they had responsibilities for pastoral care. There were, of course, not as many royal nunneries as there had been previously because there were fewer – and ultimately only one – dynasty to support them.

The institution of the royal nunnery never had to be reintroduced into Anglo-Saxon England because it never died out; individual nunneries waned with the fortunes of the families that had supported them, but then there were new royal lines with their own foundations to take their place. Although there was only one royal line by the tenth century there was still competition for the succession fuelled by the serial marriages of many of the later kings. Individual nunneries became associated not so much with rival kin-groups as with rival queens and their aristocratic families. A major question is whether the tenth-century reformation marked as significant a watershed for the royal nunneries as it seems to have done for male monasticism. There were new nunneries founded at the height of the reform period – Romsey, Amesbury and Wherwell, all of which were connected in one way or another with Queen Ælfthryth. But the more significant royal nunneries in terms of wealth and landed endowments – Barking, Shaftesbury and Wilton – had all been founded many years before. Neither Æthelwold, Dunstan nor Oswald attempted to found a nunnery, and one of the most famous of the early double houses at Ely was refounded by Æthelwold as a strictly male community. Chatteris, founded by Bishop Eadnoth of Dorchester for his sister, is the only known example of a nunnery founded by a bishop of the reform period.

That is not to say that the royal nunneries were unaffected by the reform movement. They presumably adopted the liturgy advocated in the *Regularis Concordia,* though extensive prayers on behalf of the king and royal house seem already to have been a feature of their religious life. There is evidence of other facets of the reform period being adopted as well that were in keeping with aspects of the Benedictine Rule such as elections of abbesses by the community or the reorganization of the bounds of Nunnaminster to provide greater separation of the nuns from the urban life of Winchester. At Wilton, Wulfthryth, like her male counterparts, was a major patron of new building and decorative arts with the aid of foreign craftsman. But it would be wrong to see the royal nunneries suddenly transformed into strict Benedictine foundations. Certain aspects of life in them continued which were contrary to the Benedictine Rule, but were relevant to their roles as dynastic foundations including retention of private wealth and the ability of members to leave in order to be married. In fact, throughout the tenth century the royal nunneries most closely resemble the continental houses of canonesses that may well have been their model, even though this is not apparent from the terminology applied to religious women in England.[12]

There were ways in which the tenth-century reform movement adversely affected the royal nunneries not least in attracting patronage away from them; no new royal nunneries were founded after the reign of Edgar and those founded during his reign seem to have been less well endowed than their predecessors. By the latter part of the tenth century fewer royal women were going into the church, though this seems in part to be the result of greater acceptance that widowed or separated queens could live independently on their estates without having to take a religious vow, and was also due to the practice of princesses who married abroad not returning home. But it is also possible that the development of the office of queen, which seems to have been one of the services Æthelwold performed for Ælfthryth, may have led to changes in attitude.[13] If queenship came to be seen as something more like kingship it became a divinely ordained position in its own right which could not be resigned at will. As an anointed queen, Ælfthryth retained her status after King Edgar's death and it would have been unnecessary, if not inappropriate, for her to have become an abbess in her widowhood as had so many of her predecessors. Her successors Emma and Edith may have thought the same way. Although in the earlier Anglo-Saxon period the positions of queen and abbess may have been regarded as comparable and of similar status, Ælfthryth and Æthelwold wanted to assert the superiority of queenship.

However, one should not press a decline of interest in royal nunneries or any apparent decline in the status of the position of abbess too far. In Wulfthryth we have a former queen who as a royal abbess was a major patron and an influential political figure who can be placed alongside earlier influential figures such as Ælfflaed or Cwoenthryth. Indeed, one may suspect that the antagonism of Wulfthryth and Ælfthryth, both of them wives of Edgar, may have much to do with any attempts to redefine the relative status of royal abbess and anointed queen. In the tense political situation surrounding rival æthelings at the end of Edgar's reign Ælfthryth's status as an anointed queen was one of the means of enhancing the claims of her son Æthelred, and the idea of queenship as a position for life would have enhanced her ability to act as his regent. However, when Ælfthryth retired to end her days at or near the nunnery of Wherwell which she had founded she was following the practice of other former queens of the house, and whether or not a vow was taken may not have made much difference to the style in which they lived or their relationship to their host nunneries. When reviewing later royal patronage of the nunneries one must remember that the pattern was broken by the Danish conquest and accession of Cnut. When Edward the Confessor came to the throne former practices seem to have been resumed. One of his sisters became Abbess of Wherwell which their grandmother had founded, and after the Norman Conquest royal nunneries became the natural place to lodge surviving royal princesses. In the dispute over the status of Gunnhild and Edith-Matilda and whether they were entitled to withdraw from Wilton in order to be married we can see a clash between the traditions of the Anglo-Saxon nunneries as dynastic foundations and the expectations of Benedictine monasticism to which they may have been expected to conform for the first time.

If the history of royal nunneries does not completely conform to that of male minsters, how does it compare with that of other foundations for female religious in the Anglo-Saxon period? The same instincts that led to the foundation of royal nunneries may be presumed to have worked on the secular nobility as well, and there are examples of women of noble houses heading minsters on land which had been given to their kinsmen for this purpose.[14] These early noble foundations need a study in their own right, but an initial impression is that they were less likely to survive as long as the royal nunneries as religious houses that were always commanded by a woman. It is difficult to point to a noble nunnery that has a continual history under female leadership from the foundation period into the late eighth or early ninth centuries, while, on the other hand, there appear to be examples of minsters passing from male to female headship and vice versa. In the royal house only women went into the church; kings or princes only did so in adverse circumstances. In noble families, on the other hand, there was a greater possibility of a male member entering the church. It is probably more appropriate to speak of family monasteries of the nobility rather than of nunneries that were exclusively under female control. Opportunity and inclination of individual family members might decide whether such houses were commanded by men or women and what proportion of either sex they might contain at any one time.

There was not necessarily a major contrast between the provisions made by families for noble women who wanted to follow a religious life in the periods before and after the viking attacks. In the later period we seem to see noble houses making temporary arrangements for female members who wanted to live as religious in which they might be linked with local minsters with which presumably the families are likely to have had a close association. Such arrangements may account for the appearance of anomalous abbesses linked to foundations which appear to have no continuous history as female houses in the later period and may appear only once as having possessed an 'abbess' during that time.[15] Widowed noble women, on the other hand, might take religious vows which enabled them to remain chaste and to enjoy their dower with a bishop or other powerful male religious as their protector against kinsmen who might try to pressurize them to remarry or renounce claims on estates.[16] No doubt this also happened in the earlier Anglo-Saxon period, and the 'wary widow' is well attested in Merovingian and Carolingian sources.[17] The powerful rights of entail on family land restricted the property rights of women and their ability to alienate land where they wished, thus making the permanent endowment of noble nunneries extremely difficult. This was another aspect affecting religious provision where there would eventually be substantial change after the Norman Conquest.[18]

A subsection of the provision for religious women by noble houses was that made by ecclesiastical nobility for female relatives, though relatively few seem to have followed the example of Bishop Eorcenwald of London who arranged generous provision for his sister's foundation at Barking. Among the most notable religious women to have benefited from a kinsman's ecclesiastical career are Leoba and her kinswomen who joined their relative Boniface in Germany. Leoba and her relatives shared in their kinsman's work of Christianization and the establishment of correct religious practices, and Leoba in particular exercised considerable responsibility as the main Christian leader in the district in which she worked. Her freedom of action is envied by her modern counterparts,[19] but can be seen as a delegation of the activities and power of Boniface himself. The kin-group of Boniface and Leoba worked as a family promoting common aims and sharing in the results. They are a reminder that houses commanded by women should be seen as family minsters, and that although they share common features they will also vary in detail depending upon the nature and history of their host family. The royal nunneries were the family minsters of the royal houses, and although they need to be studied alongside other minsters, they also form a distinct group in their own right. The private life of royal families often had broader political ramifications and because of this their nunneries had political as well as religious roles to play in a way that most other minsters did not.

The Anglo-Saxon royal nunneries seem to exemplify the observation that medieval women received their main opportunities to exercise power through their families.[20] Support for their kin through prayer and other services they could perform by virtue of being religious communities were probably the main *raison d'être* for the royal nunneries in the eyes of their families, and these activities could often be directed towards achieving broader familial and political aims. Not that all royal female religious would always have been in harmony with other members of their families. Entry to nunneries might not always have been voluntary, and was on occasion used as a means to end a marriage (as was the experience of Wulfthryth) or to remove a woman from circulation whose position or potential to be married was perceived as a threat to the family's interests (as may have occurred with Ælfwyn, the niece of Edward the Elder), though there are relatively few such examples in recorded Anglo-Saxon history. Nor did kinsmen necessarily behave well towards nunneries. Sexual predatoriness and violence towards nuns seem to have been problems, with vows of chastity not being sufficient to deter powerful laymen from following their own inclinations.

Such negative examples can make the royal nunneries appear victims of the whims of more powerful kinsmen or to have little say in their own affairs. Undoubtedly such things did happen, but in studying the history of these communities what makes an even greater impression is the succession of strong and powerful abbesses who attempted to direct affairs in ways that they wanted them to go. We see them using their kinship with different rulers to obtain benefits such as the toll concessions acquired by abbesses of Thanet who may also have adapted versions of their house's history to accommodate changes in the overlordship of Kent.[21] Saints' cults were not just a pious duty, but could be manipulated to win support and financial gains.[22] One can even glimpse occasionally an abbess like Ælfflaed of *Streanæshalch*/Whitby who was a power behind the throne and used her connections in church and secular society to broker arrangements for the succession. The royal nunneries have often been seen as rather marginal to the concerns of Anglo-Saxon history, treated as an addendum to ecclesiastical history in which the main players are naturally the bishops and a handful of other influential men. Their histories are often subsumed in general accounts of developments in monasticism. But nunneries spanned two worlds, the monastic and the royal; they had a foot in both camps and their full histories cannot be written without considering both aspects. Nor were these foundations on the periphery of their family's interests, for much was invested in them, and promotion of nunneries was a recurring feature of how new dynasties coming to power sought to legitimize their rule. Above all they are an example of how, given the opportunity, women were able to exercise power in the male-dominated world of the middle ages, and showed that they were able to do so just as effectively as their male counterparts.

Notes

1. R. MacMullen, *Christianising the Roman Empire (AD 100–400)* (London, 1984); A.-S. Gräslund, 'Pagan and Christian in the age of conversion', in J. E. Knirk (ed.), *Proceedings of the Tenth Viking Congress; Larkollen, Norway 1985* (Oslo, 1987), 81–94.

2. C. Clover, 'Regardless of sex: men, women and power in early northern Europe', *Speculum*, 69 (1993), 363–87.
3. S. Hollis, *Anglo-Saxon Women and the Church* (Woodbridge, 1992).
4. S. O'Sullivan, 'Aldhelm's *De Virginitate* – patristic pastiche or innovative exposition?', *Peritia*, 12 (1998), 271–95.
5. P. Stafford, 'Queens, nunneries and reforming churchmen: gender, religious status and reform in tenth- and eleventh-century England', *Past and Present*, 163 (1999), 3–35.
6. J. Blair, *The Church in Anglo-Saxon Society* (Oxford, forthcoming).
7. See e.g., J. T. Schulenberg, 'Strict active enclosure and its effects on the female monastic experience (500–1100)', in J. A. Nichols and L. T. Shank (eds), *Medieval Religious Women. I: Distant Echoes* (Kalamazoo, 1984), 51–86. For a corrective view see J. Smith, 'Gender and ideology in the early middle ages', in R. N. Swanson (ed.), *Studies in Church History*, 34 (1998), 51–73.
8. Asser, ch. 93.
9. C. Cubitt, *Anglo-Saxon Church Councils c. 650–c. 850* (Leicester, 1995), 43–4.
10. P. Coulstock, *The Collegiate Church of Wimborne Minster* (Woodbridge, 1993).
11. This is not to say that there were no significant male minsters at the end of the ninth century in Wessex – Glastonbury and Malmesbury were major centres and places of learning where possibly some monastic element remained; Alfred founded a monastery at Athelney and his son Edward New Minster, Winchester, a house of secular priests.
12. M. Parisse, 'Les chanoinesses dans l'empire Germanique (ix–xi siècles)', *Francia*, 6 (1978), 107–28.
13. P. Stafford, *Queen Emma and Queen Edith: Queenship and Women's Power in Eleventh-Century England* (Oxford, 1997), esp. 162–92.
14. See, e.g., S. Kelly (ed.), *Charters of Selsey*, British Academy, Anglo-Saxon Charters, VI (Oxford, 1998) no. 7, and *idem* (ed.), *Charters of Abingdon Abbey, Part I*, British Academy, Anglo-Saxon Charters, VII (Oxford, 2000) nos 3 and 4. Further exemplification for this section will be found in Chapter 2.
15. For instance, Abbess Wulfwyn of Wareham whose death is recorded in the *Anglo-Saxon Chronicle* for 982 – there were nuns at Wareham in the ninth century, but there is no evidence that it had a continuous history as a nunnery in the tenth century. For other examples and discussion, see S. Foot, *Veiled Women*, 2 vols (Aldershot, 2000) *passim*, but esp. I, 145–98.
16. J. Crick, 'Men, women and widows; widowhood in pre-Conquest England', in S. Cavallo and L. Warner (eds), *Widowhood in Medieval and Early Modern Europe* (Harlow, 1999), 24–36.
17. J. Nelson, 'The wary widow', in W. Davies and P. Fouracre (eds), *Property and Power in the Early Middle Ages* (Cambridge, 1995), 54–82.
18. For the great upsurge in the foundation of noble nunneries in the twelfth century see S. K. Elkins, *Holy Women of the Twelfth Century* (Chapel Hill, NC, 1988).
19. C. Wybourne, 'Leoba: a study in humanity and holiness', in M. Schmitt and L. Kulzer (eds), *Medieval Women Monastics* (Collegeville, MN, 1996), 81–96.
20. J. A. McNamara and S. Wemple, 'The power of women through the family in medieval Europe, 500–1100', in M. Erler and M. Kowaleski (eds), *Women and Power in the Middle Ages* (Athens, GA, 1988), 83–101.
21. S. Hollis, 'The Minster-in-Thanet foundation story', *A-SE*, 27 (1998), 41–74; and see further in Chapters 2 and 5.
22. S. Ridyard, *The Royal Saints of Anglo-Saxon England: A Study of West Saxon and East Anglian Cults* (Cambridge, 1988).

Appendix

(a) Royal nunneries founded by *c.* 735

Where possible, location, date of foundation and the name of the first abbess have been given; an asterisk indicates problem cases on which further discussion will be found in Chapter 1, where references will also be found. Where a foundress has been associated with more than one location, separate entries are provided only if there is good evidence for each being the site of a nunnery.

East Angles
1. Dereham. Wihtburh.
2. Ely. 673. Æthelthryth.

East Saxons
1. Barking. By 675. Æthelburh.
2. Chich. 653(?). Osyth.
3. Nazeing. Late seventh century. Ffymme.

Hwicce
1. Bath. 675–676. Bertha.
2. Fladbury. Late seventh century. 'Flaede'.
3. Gloucester. 674–679. Cyneburh.
4. Inkberrow. 693–699. Cuthswith.
*5. Twyning.
6. Withington. 674–704. Dunne and Bugga.

Kent
1. Folkestone. Second half seventh century. Eanswith.
*2. Hoo.
3. Lyminge. Late seventh century. Eormenburh(?).
4. Minster-in-Thanet. 664–673. Æbbe.
5. Sheppey. 664–679/80. Seaxburh and Eormenhild.

Magonsaetan
1. Much Wenlock. Late seventh century. Mildburh.

Mercia
*1. Abingdon. Late seventh century. Æbbe.
*2. Adderbury/Bicester. Late seventh century. Eadburh.
*3. Aylesbury. Late seventh century. Edith and Osyth.
4. Castor. Late seventh century. Cyneswith and Cyneburh.
5. Hanbury. Late seventh century. Werburh.
*6. Oxford, Bampton, Binsley. Late seventh century. Frideswide.
7. Repton. Second half seventh century. Unknown.

Northumbria
1. Carlisle. Second half seventh century. Iurminburh and her sister.
2. Coldingham. Second half seventh century. Æbbe.
3. Hackness. 680. Hild.
4. Hartlepool. *c.* 648. Heiu/Hild.
5. Whitby. 657. Hild.

South Saxons
1. 692. Nothgyth.

West Saxons
1. Late seventh century. Bugga.
2. Wimborne. Late seventh century. Cuthburh and Cwenburh.
*3. North Wessex. Early eighth century(?). Cyneburh.

(b) Nunneries founded by *c.* 735, but with no firm evidence of royal associations

Lindsey
1. Partney. Second half seventh century. Æthelhild [*HE*, III, 11].

Northumbria
1. South Shields. Second half seventh century. Verca(?) [Bede, *VC*, chs 35–7].
2. Watton. Late seventh century. Hereburh [*HE*, V, 3].
3. Near Melrose. Late seventh century [Bede, *VC*, ch. 30].

Bibliography

L. Abrams, *Anglo-Saxon Glastonbury* (Woodbridge, 1996).

L. Abrams, 'Edward the Elder's Danelaw', in N. Higham and D. Hill (eds), *Edward the Elder 899–924* (Manchester, 2001), 128–43.

W. Aird, 'Frustrated masculinity: the relationship between William the Conqueror and his eldest son', in D. Hadley (ed.), *Masculinity in Medieval Europe* (Harlow, 1999), 39–55.

S. Airlie, 'Narratives of triumph and rituals of submission: Charlemagne's mastering of Bavaria', *TRHS*, 6th Series, 9 (1999), 93–119.

L. Alcock, E. A. Alcock and S. Foster, 'Reconnaissance excavations of early historic fortifications and other royal sites in Scotland, 1974–84: 1, Excavations near St Abb's Head, Berwickshire, 1980', *Proceedings of the Society of Antiquaries of Scotland*, 116 (1986), 255–79.

S. Allott, *Alcuin of York* (York, 1974).

A. Angenendt, 'Theologie und Liturgie der mittelalterlichen Toten-Memoria', in K. Schmidt and J. Wollasch (eds), *Memoria: Der geschichtliche Zeugniswert des liturgischen Gedenkens im Mittelalter* (Munich, 1984), 79–199.

T. Arnold, '*Historia Regum*', in *idem* (ed.), *Symeonis Monachi Opera Omnia*, Vol. II (London, 1885).

F. L. Attenborough, *The Laws of the Earliest English Kings* (Cambridge, 1922).

M. Bailey, 'Ælfwyn, second lady of the Mercians', in N. Higham and D. H. Hill (eds), *King Edward the Elder 899–924* (London, 2001), 112–27.

R. N. Bailey, *England's Earliest Sculptors* (Toronto, 1996).

R. N. Bailey and R. Cramp (eds), *Corpus of Saxon Stone Sculpture, Vol. II: Cumberland, Westmorland and Lancashire North-of-the-Sands* (London, 1988).

D. B. Baltrusch-Schneider, 'Die Angelsächsen Doppelklöster', in K. Elm and M. Parisse (eds), *Doppelklöster und andere Formen der Symbiose männlicher und weiblicher Religiosen im Mittelalter*, Berliner Historische Studien, 18.8 (Berlin, 1992), 57–79.

F. Barlow, *The English Church 1000–1066*, 2nd edn (London, 1979).

F. Barlow (ed.), *The Life of King Edward Who Rests at Westminster*, 2nd edn (Oxford, 1992).

J. Barrow, 'Cathedrals, provosts and prebends: a comparison of twelfth-century German and English practice', *Journal of Ecclesiastical History*, 37 (1986), 536–63.

R. Bartlett, 'Symbolic meanings of hair in the middle ages', *TRHS*, 6th Series, 4 (1994), 43–60.

K. Bascombe, 'Two charters of King Suebred of Essex', in K. Neale (ed.), *An Essex Tribute: Essays Presented to F. G. Emmison* (Cambridge, 1987), 85–96.

S. Bassett, 'A probable Mercian royal mausoleum at Winchcombe, Gloucestershire', *Antiquaries Journal*, 65 (1985), 82–100.

S. Bassett, 'In search of the origins of Anglo-Saxon kingdoms', in *idem* (ed.), *The Origins of Anglo-Saxon Kingdoms* (London, 1989), 3–27.

M. Bateson, 'Origin and early history of double monasteries', *TRHS*, 1st Series, 13 (1899), 137–98.

H. Becher, 'Das königliche Frauenkloster San Salvatore/Santa Giulia in Brescia im Spiegel seiner Memorialüberlieferung', *Frühmittelalterliche Studien*, 17 (1983), 299–392.

A. Bell (ed.), *Geffrei Gaimar, l'estoire des Engleis*, Anglo-Norman Text Society, vols 14–16 (Oxford, 1960).

J. W. Bernhardt, *Itinerant Kingship and Royal Monasteries in Early Medieval Germany, c. 936–1075* (Cambridge, 1993).

D. Bethell, 'The Lives of St. Osyth of Essex and St. Osyth of Aylesbury', *Analecta Bollandiana*, 88 (1980), 75–127.

M. Biddle (ed.), *Winchester in the Early Middle Ages*, Winchester Studies, I (Oxford, 1976).

M. Biddle, 'Archaeology, architecture and the cult of saints in Anglo-Saxon England', in L. Butler and R. Morris (eds), *The Anglo-Saxon Church: Papers on History, Architecture and Archaeology in Honour of Dr H. M. Taylor* (London, 1986), 1–31.

M. Biddle, 'Seasonal festivals and residence; Winchester, Westminster and Gloucester in the tenth to eleventh centuries', *Anglo-Norman Studies*, 8 (1986), 51–72.

M. Biddle and D. Keene, 'Winchester in the eleventh and twelfth centuries', in M. Biddle (ed.), *Winchester in the Early Middle Ages*, Winchester Studies, I (Oxford, 1976).

M. Biddle and B. Kjølbye-Biddle, 'The Repton stone', *A-SE*, 14 (1985), 233–92.

M. Biddle and B. Kjølbye-Biddle, 'Repton and the Vikings', *Antiquity*, 66 (1992), 36–51.

W. de Gray Birch (ed.), *Cartularium Saxonicum*, 3 vols (London, 1885–99).

W. de Gray Birch (ed.), *An Ancient Manuscript of the Eighth or Ninth Century* (London, 1889).

W. de Gray Birch (ed.), *Liber Vitae: Register and Martyrology of New Minster and Hyde Abbey, Winchester* (London, 1892).

J. Blair, 'Saint Frideswide reconsidered', *Oxoniensia*, 52 (1987), 71–127.

J. Blair, 'Minster churches in the landscape', in D. Hooke (ed.), *Anglo-Saxon Settlements* (Oxford, 1988), 35–58.

J. Blair (ed.), *Minsters and Parish Churches* (Oxford, 1988).

J. Blair, 'St Frideswide's monastery: problems and possibilities', *Oxoniensia*, 53 (1988), 221–58.

J. Blair, 'Frithuwold's kingdom and the origins of Surrey', in S. Bassett (ed.), *The Origins of Anglo-Saxon Kingdoms* (Leicester, 1989), 97–107.

J. Blair, 'Anglo-Saxon minsters: a topographical review', in J. Blair and R. Sharpe (eds), *Pastoral Care before the Parish* (Leicester, 1992), 226–66.

J. Blair, *Anglo-Saxon Oxfordshire* (Stroud, 1994).

J. Blair, 'Debate: ecclesiastical organization and pastoral care in Anglo-Saxon England', *Early Medieval Europe*, 4 (1995), 193–212.

J. Blair, 'The minsters of the Thames', in J. Blair and B. Golding (eds), *The Cloister and the World* (Oxford, 1996), 5–28.

J. Blair, 'Palaces or minsters? Northampton and Cheddar reconsidered', *A-SE*, 25 (1996), 97–122.

J. Blair, 'A handlist of Anglo-Saxon saints', in A. Thacker and R. Sharpe (eds), *Local Saints and Local Churches in the Early Medieval West* (Oxford, 2002), 495–565.

J. Blair, 'A saint for every minster?', in A. Thacker and R. Sharpe (eds), *Local Saints and Local Churches in the Early Medieval West* (Oxford, 2002), 455–94.

J. Blair, *The Church in Anglo-Saxon Society* (Oxford, forthcoming).

J. Blair and R. Sharpe (eds), *Pastoral Care before the Parish* (Leicester, 1992).

P. Hunter Blair, 'Whitby as a centre of learning in the seventh century', in M. Lapidge and H. Gneuss (eds), *Learning and Literature in Anglo-Saxon England* (Cambridge, 1985), 3–32.

E. O. Blake (ed.), *Liber Eliensis*, Royal Historical Society, Camden Third Series, 92 (London, 1962).

L. Braswell, 'St Edburga of Winchester; a study of her cult a.d. 950–1500, with an edition of the fourteenth-century Middle English and Latin Lives', *Medieval Studies*, 33 (1971), 292–333.

S. Brink, 'Political and social structures in early Scandinavia. A settlement-historical pre-study of the central place', *Tor*, 28 (1996), 235–81.

B. Brooks, 'Archbishop Wulfred (825–32) and the lordship of Minster-in-Thanet in the early ninth century', *Downside Review*, 111 (1994), 211–27.

N. Brooks, 'The development of military obligations in eighth- and ninth-century England', in P. Clemoes and K. Hughes (eds), *England before the Conquest: Studies in Primary Sources Presented to Dorothy Whitelock* (Cambridge, 1971), 69–84.

N. Brooks, *The Early History of the Church of Canterbury* (Leicester, 1984).

N. Brooks, 'The creation and early structure of the kingdom of Kent', in S. Bassett (ed.), *The Origins of Anglo-Saxon Kingdoms* (Leicester, 1989), 55–74.

N. Brooks, 'The career of St Dunstan', in N. Ramsay and M. Sparkes (eds), *St Dunstan: His Life, Times and Cult* (Woodbridge, 1992), 1–23.

N. Brooks, *Bede and the English* (Jarrow, 1999).

J. Burton, *Monastic and Religious Orders in Britain 1000–1300* (London, 1994).

E. Cambridge and D. Rollason, 'Debate: the pastoral organization of the Anglo-Saxon church: a review of the "minster hypothesis"', *Early Medieval Europe*, 4 (1995), 87–104.

A. Campbell (ed.), *The Chronicle of Æthelweard* (London, 1962).

W. A. Chaney, *The Cult of Kingship in Anglo-Saxon England: The Transition from Paganism to Christianity* (Manchester, 1970).

P. Chaplais, 'The letter from Bishop Wealdhere of London to Archbishop Brihtwold of Canterbury: the earliest original "letter close" in the west', in M. B. Parkes and A. G. Watson (eds), *Medieval Scribes, Manuscripts and Libraries: Essays Presented to N. R. Ker* (London, 1978), 3–23.

C. Clover, 'Regardless of sex: men, women and power in early northern Europe', *Speculum*, 69 (1993), 363–87.

S. Coates, 'Regendering Radegund? Fortunatus, Baudonivia and the problem of female sanctity in Merovingian Gaul', in R. N. Swanson (ed.), *Studies in Church History*, 35 (Woodbridge, 1998), 37–50.

E. Coatsworth, 'Late pre-conquest sculptures with the crucifixion south of the Humber', in B. A. E. Yorke (ed.), *Bishop Æthelwold: His Career and Influence* (Woodbridge, 1988), 161–93.

D. K. Coldicott, *Hampshire Nunneries before and after the Norman Conquest* (Chichester, 1989).

B. Colgrave (ed.), *The Life of Bishop Wilfrid by Eddius Stephanus* (Cambridge, 1927).

B. Colgrave (ed.), *Two Lives of Saint Cuthbert* (Cambridge 1940).

B. Colgrave (ed.), *Felix's Life of Saint Guthlac* (Cambridge, 1956).

B. Colgrave (ed.), *The Earliest Life of Gregory the Great* (Cambridge, 1968).

B. Colgrave and R. A. B. Mynors (eds), *Bede's Ecclesiastical History of the English People* (Oxford, 1969).

K. Cooke, 'Donors and daughters: Shaftesbury Abbey's benefactors, endowments and nuns c. 1086–1130', *Anglo-Norman Studies*, 12 (1989), 29–45.

L. Coon, *Sacred Fictions: Holy Women and Hagiography in Late Antiquity* (Philadelphia, 1997).

K. Cooper, *The Virgin and the Bride: Idealized Womanhood in Late Antiquity* (Cambridge, MA, 1996).

P. Corbet, *Les Saints ottoniens: sainteté dynastique, sainteté royale et sainteté féminine autour de l'an Mil*, Beihefte von *Francia*, bd 15 (Sigmaringen, 1986).

P. Coulstock, *The Collegiate Church of Wimborne Minster* (Woodbridge, 1993).

S. Coupland, 'The rod of God's wrath? The Carolingian theology of the Viking invasions', *Journal of Ecclesiastical History*, 42 (1991), 535–54.

J. Cox, 'Religious houses', in *VCH Warwickshire*, Vol. 2 (London, 1908), 62–5.

H. O. Coxe (ed.), *Roger of Wendover, Flores Historiarum* (London, 1841–44).

R. Cramp, 'Monastic sites', in D. Wilson (ed.), *The Archaeology of Anglo-Saxon England* (London, 1976), 201–52.

R. Cramp, *Corpus of Anglo-Saxon Stone Sculpture, Vol. I: County Durham and North-umberland* (London, 1984).

R. Cramp, 'A reconsideration of the monastic site of Whitby', in R. M. Spearman and J. Higgitt (eds), *The Age of Migrating Ideas* (Edinburgh, 1993), 64–73.

S. Crawford, *Childhood in Anglo-Saxon England* (Stroud, 1999).

J. Crick, 'Church, land and nobility in early ninth-century Kent', *Bulletin of the Institute of Historical Research*, 61 (1988), 251–69.

J. Crick, 'Men, women and widows; widowhood in pre-Conquest England', in S. Cavallo and L. Warner (eds), *Widowhood in Medieval and Early Modern Europe* (Harlow, 1999), 24–36.

J. Crick, 'The wealth, patronage and connections of women's houses in late Anglo-Saxon England', *Revue Bénédictine*, 109 (1999), 154–85.

J. Crick, 'Women, posthumous benefaction and family strategy in pre-conquest England', *Journal of British Studies*, 38 (1999), 399–422.

C. Cubitt, 'Wilfred's "usurping bishops": episcopal elections in Anglo-Saxon England, *c.* 600–*c.* 800', *Northern History*, 25 (1989), 18–38.

C. Cubitt, 'Pastoral care and conciliar canons: the provisions of the 747 council of *Clofesho*', in J. Blair and R. Sharpe (eds), *Pastoral Care before the Parish* (Leicester, 1992), 193–211.

C. Cubitt, *Anglo-Saxon Church Councils c. 650–c. 850* (Leicester, 1995).

C. Cubitt, 'Sites and sanctity: revisiting the cult of murdered and martyred Anglo-Saxon royal saints', *Early Medieval Europe*, 9 (2000), 53–84.

R. Daniels, 'The Anglo-Saxon monastery at Church Close, Hartlepool, Cleveland', *Archaeological Journal*, 145 (1988), 158–210.

R. Daniels, 'The Anglo-Saxon monastery at Hartlepool, England', in J. Hawkes and S. Mills (eds), *Northumbria's Golden Age* (Stroud, 1999), 105–12.

R. R. Darlington and P. McGurk (eds), *The Chronicle of John of Worcester, Volume II, The Annals from 450 to 1066* (Oxford, 1995).

M. Deanesly, 'English and Gallic minsters', *TRHS*, 4th Series, 23 (1941), 25–69.

D. Mauskopf Deliyannis, 'Church burial in Anglo-Saxon England: the pre-rogative of kings', *Frühmittelalterliche Studien*, 29 (1995), 96–119.

R. Deshman, '"Christus rex and magi reges": kingship and Christology in Anglo-Saxon and Ottonian art', *Frühmittelalterliche Studien*, 10 (1986), 367–405.

R. Deshman, *The Benedictional of Æthelwold*, Studies in Manuscript Illumination, 9 (Princeton, NJ, 1995).

A. Dierkens, 'Prolégomènes à une historie des relationes culturelles entre les Îles Britanniques et le continent pendant le haut moyen âge', in H. Atsma (ed.), *La Neustrie: les pays au nord de la Loire de 650 à 850*, 2 vols (Sigmaringen, 1989), II, 371–94.

S. C. Dietrich, 'An introduction to women in Anglo-Saxon society (c. 600–1066)', in B. Kanner (ed.), *The Women of England from Anglo-Saxon Times to the Present* (Hamden, CT, 1979), 32–56.

J. Doran, 'Oblation or obligation? A canonical ambiguity', in D. Wood (ed.), *The Church and Childhood*, Studies in Church History, 31 (Oxford, 1994), 127–41.

A. Dornier, 'The Anglo-Saxon monastery at Breedon-on-the-Hill, Leicestershire', in A. Dornier (ed.), *Mercian Studies* (Leicester, 1997), 155–68.

F. Douce, 'Some remarks on the original seal belonging to the abbey of Wilton', *Archaeologia*, 18 (1817), 40–54.

K. F. Drew, 'The Italian monasteries of Nonantola, San Salvatore and Santa Maria Teodata in the eighth and ninth centuries', *Manuscripta*, 9 (1965), 131–54.

T. A. DuBois, *Nordic Religions in the Viking Age* (Philadelphia, 1999).

E. Dümmler (ed.), 'Alcuini Epistolae', *MGH Epistolae*, IV, Vol. 2 (Berlin, 1895).

D. N. Dumville, 'The Anglian collection of royal genealogies and regnal lists', *A-SE*, 5 (1976), 23–50.

D. N. Dumville, 'Kingship, genealogies and regnal lists', in P. Sawyer and I. N. Wood (eds), *Early Medieval Kingship* (Leeds, 1977), 72–104.

D. N. Dumville, *Wessex and England from Alfred to Edgar* (Woodbridge, 1992).

D. N. Dumville, *The Churches of North Britain in the First Viking Age* (Whithorn, 1997).

L. Eckenstein, *Woman under Monasticism: Chapters on Saint-Lore and Convent Life between A.D. 500 and A.D. 1500* (Cambridge, 1896).

E. Edwards (ed.), *Liber Monasterii de Hyde*, Rolls Series (London, 1866).

R. Ehwald (ed.), *Aldhelmi Opera Omnia, MGH Auctores Antiquissimi*, XV (Berlin, 1919).

S. K. Elkins, *Holy Women of the Twelfth Century* (Chapel Hill, NC, 1988).

K. Elm and M. Parisse, *Doppelklöster und andere Formen der Symbiose männlicher und weiblicher Religiosen im Mittelalter*, Berliner Historische Studien, 18.8 (Berlin, 1992).

M. J. Enright, 'Lady with a mead-cup. Ritual, group-cohesion and hierarchy in the Germanic warband', *Frühmittelalterliche Studien*, 22 (1988), 170–203.

M. Erler and M. Kowaleski (eds), *Women and Power in the Middle Ages* (Athens, GA, 1988).

M. Esposito, 'La vie de Saint Wulfhilda par Goscelin de Cantorbery', *Analecta Bollandiana*, 32 (1913), 10–26.

E. Ewig, 'Beobachtungen zu den Klosterprivilegien des 7. und frühen 8. Jahrhunderts', in J. Fleckenstein and K. Schmid (eds), *Adel und Kirche: Gerd Tellenbach zum 65ten Geburtstag* (Freiburg, 1968), 52–65.

E. Ewig, *Die Merowinger und das Frankenreich* (Stuttgart, 1988).

C. Fell, *Edward King and Martyr*, Leeds Texts and Monographs, New Series, 3 (Leeds, 1971).

C. Fell, 'Edward King and Martyr and the Anglo-Saxon hagiographic tradition', in D. Hill (ed.), *Ethelred the Unready: Papers from the Millenary Conference*, BAR, 59 (Oxford, 1978), 1–13.

C. Fell, 'Hild, abbess of *Streonaeshalch*', in H. Bekker-Nielsen (ed.), *Hagiography and Medieval Literature* (Odense, 1981), 76–99.

C. Fell, *Women in Anglo-Saxon England* (London, 1984).

C. Fell, 'Saint Æthelthryth: a historical-hagiographical dichotomy revisited', *Nottingham Medieval Studies*, 38 (1994), 18–34.

C. Fell, C. Clark and E. Williams, *Women in Anglo-Saxon England and the Impact of 1066* (London, 1984).

H. P. R. Finberg, 'The house of Ordgar and the foundation of Tavistock Abbey', *EHR*, 58 (1943), 190–201.

H. P. R. Finberg, *Early Charters of Wessex* (Leicester, 1964).

H. P. R. Finberg, *Early Charters of the West Midlands*, 2nd edn (Leicester, 1972).

P. W. Finsterwalder (ed.), *Die Canones Theodoris Cantuariensis und ihre Überlieferungsformen* (Weimar, 1929), 285–334.

D. Fisher, 'The anti-monastic reaction in the reign of Edward the Martyr', *Cambridge Historical Journal*, 10 (1950–52), 254–70.

J. M. J. Fletcher, 'The marriage of St Cuthburga, who was afterwards foundress of the monastery at Wimborne', *Dorset Natural History and Antiquarian Field Club*, 34 (1931), 167–85.

R. Fleming, 'Monastic lands and England's defence in the viking age', *EHR*, 100 (1985), 247–65.

H. Foerster (ed.), *Liber Diurnus Romanorum Pontificum* (Bern, 1958).

S. Foot, 'Violence against Christians? The vikings and the church in ninth-century England', *Medieval History*, 1.3 (1991), 3–16.

S. Foot, 'Anglo-Saxon minsters: a review of terminology', in J. Blair and R. Sharpe (eds), *Pastoral Care before the Parish* (Leicester, 1992), 212–25.

S. Foot, 'The making of *Angelcynn*: English identity before the Norman Conquest', *TRHS*, 6th Series, 6 (1996), 25–49.

S. Foot, 'Language and method: the Dictionary of Old English and the historian', in M. J. Toswell (ed.), *The Dictionary of Old English: Retrospects and Prospects*, Old English Newsletter Subsidia, 26 (1998), 73–87.

S. Foot, 'Remembering, forgetting and inventing; attitudes to the past in England at the end of the first viking age', *TRHS*, 6th Series, 9 (1999), 185–200.

S. Foot, *Veiled Women*, 2 vols (Aldershot, 2000).

P. Fouracre, 'Merovingian history and Merovingian hagiography', *Past and Present*, 127 (1990), 3–38.

P. Fouracre and R. Gerberding, *Late Merovingian France: History and Hagiography 640–720* (Manchester, 1996).

A. Frantzen, 'When women aren't enough', *Speculum*, 68 (1993), 445–77.

M. Gaimster, 'Scandinavian gold bracteates in Britain. Money and media in the Dark Ages', *Medieval Archaeology*, 36 (1992), 1–28.

H. Geake, *The Use of Grave-Goods in Conversion Period England, c. 600–c. 850*, BAR, 261 (1997).

P. J. Geary, *Before France and Germany: The Creation and Transformation of the Merovingian World* (Oxford, 1988).

P. J. Geary, *Phantoms of Remembrance: Memory and Oblivion at the End of the First Millennium* (Princeton, NJ, 1994).

J. Gerchow, *Gedenküberlieferung der Angelsachsen, mit einem Katalog der libri vitae und Necrologien*, Arbeiten zur Frühmittelalterforschung, 20 (Berlin, 1988).

R. Gilchrist, *Gender and Material Culture: The Archaeology of Religious Women* (London, 1994).

J. Godfrey, 'The place of the double monastery in the Anglo-Saxon minster system', in G. Bonner (ed.), *Famulus Christi: Essays in Commemoration of the Thirteenth Centenary of the Birth of the Venerable Bede* (London, 1976), 344–50.

W. Goffart, *The Narrators of Barbarian History* (Princeton, NJ, 1988).

B. J. Golding, *Gilbert of Sempringham and the Gilbertine Order c. 1130–c. 1300* (Oxford, 1995).

P. Goodman (ed.), *Alcuin: The Bishops, Kings and Saints of York* (Oxford, 1982).

A. Gransden, 'Traditionalism and continuity during the last century of Anglo-Saxon monasticism', *Journal of Ecclesiastical History*, 40 (1989), 159–207.

A.-S. Gräslund, 'Pagan and Christian in the age of conversion', in J. E. Knirk (ed.), *Proceedings of the Tenth Viking Congress; Larkollen, Norway 1985* (Oslo, 1987), 81–94.

M. Gretsch, *Die Regula Sancti Benedicti in England und ihre altenglische Übersetzung* (Munich, 1973).

M. Gretsch, 'The Benedictine Rule in Old English: a document of Bishop Æthelwold's reform politics', in M. Korhammer (ed.), *Words, Texts and Manuscripts: Studies in Anglo-Saxon Culture Presented to Helmut Gneuss* (Cambridge, 1992), 131–58.

R. Gryson, *The Ministry of Women in the Early Church*, trans. J. Laporte and M. L. Hall (Collegeville, MN, 1976).

V. A. Gunn, 'Bede and the martyrdom of St Oswald', *Studies in Church History*, 30 (1993), 57–66.

A. W. Haddan and W. Stubbs (eds), *Councils and Ecclesiastical Documents Relating to Great Britain and Ireland. III, The English Church 595–1066*, 3 vols (Oxford, 1869–79, repr. 1964).

D. M. Hadley, 'Conquest, colonisation and the church. Ecclesiastical organisation in the Danelaw', *Historical Research*, 69 (1996), 109–28.

D. M. Hadley, '"And they proceeded to plough and support themselves"; the Scandinavian settlement of England', *Anglo-Norman England*, 19 (1997), 69–96.

D. M. Hadley, *The Northern Danelaw: Its Social Structure c. 800–1100* (London, 2000).

D. M. Hadley and J. M. Moore, '"Death makes the man"? Burial rite and the construction of masculinities in the early middle ages', in D. M. Hadley (ed.), *Masculinity in Medieval Europe* (Harlow, 1999), 21–38.

T. A. Hall, 'Minster Churches in the Dorset Landscape', unpublished M.Phil. thesis (University of Leicester, 1997).

P. Halpin, 'Women religious in late Anglo-Saxon England', *Haskins Society Journal*, 6 (1994), 97–110.

N. Hamilton (ed.), *Willelmi Malmesbiriensis Monachi de Gestis Pontificum Anglorum Libri Quinque*, Rolls Series (London, 1870).

M. Hare, 'Kings, crowns and festivals: the origins of Gloucester as a royal ceremonial centre', *Transactions of the Bristol and Gloucestershire Archaeological Society*, 115 (1997), 41–78.

H. Härke, '"Warrior graves?" The background of the Anglo-Saxon burial rite', *Past and Present*, 126 (1990), 22–43.

C. Harrington, 'Women of the Church in Early Medieval Ireland *c.* A.D. 450–1150', unpublished Ph.D. thesis (University College, London, 1997).

C. R. Hart, 'Eadnoth, first abbot of Ramsey and the foundation of Chatteris and St Ives', *Proceedings of the Cambridge Antiquarian Society*, 56–7 (1964), 61–7.

C. R. Hart, *The Early Charters of Eastern England* (Leicester, 1966).

C. R. Hart, 'Æthelstan "Half King" and his family', *A-SE*, 2 (1973), 115–44.

C. R. Hart, 'The ealdordom of Essex', in K. Neale (ed.), *An Essex Tribute: Essays Presented to F. G. Emmison* (Cambridge, 1987), 57–81.

C. R. Hart, 'Eadnoth I of Ramsey and Dorchester', in *The Danelaw* (London, 1992), 613–23.

W. H. Hart, *Historia et Cartularium Monasterii Sancti Petri Gloucestriae*, 3 vols, Rolls Series (London, 1863–67).

P. Hase, 'The mother churches of Hampshire', in J. Blair (ed.), *Minster and Parish Churches: The Local Church in Transition 950–1200* (Oxford, 1988), 45–66.

P. Hase, 'The church in the Wessex heartlands', in M. Aston and C. Lewis (eds), *The Medieval Landscape of Wessex* (Oxford, 1994), 47–81.

J. Haslam, 'The towns of Wiltshire', in *idem* (ed.), *Anglo-Saxon Towns in Southern England* (Chichester, 1984), 87–148.

P. Hayward, 'The idea of innocent martyrdom in late tenth- and eleventh-century English hagiography', *Studies in Church History*, 30 (1993), 81–92.

T. Hearne (ed.), *Hemingi Chartularium Ecclesiae Wigornensis*, 2 vols (Oxford, 1723), I, 275–6.

C. Heighway and R. Bryant, *The Golden Minster: The Anglo-Saxon Minster and Later Medieval Priory of St Oswald at Gloucester*, CBA Report, 117 (York, 1999).

Y. Hen, '*Milites Christi Utriusque Sexus*, gender and the politics of conversion in the circle of Boniface', *Revue Bénédictine*, 109 (1999), 17–31.

G. Henderson, *Vision and Image in Early Christian England* (Cambridge, 1999).

T. A. Heslop, 'English seals from the mid ninth century to 1100', *Journal of the British Archaeological Association*, 133 (1980), 1–16.

J. Higgitt, 'Monasteries and inscriptions in early Northumbria, the evidence of Whitby', in C. Bourke (ed.), *From the Isles of the North: Early Medieval Art in Ireland and Britain* (Belfast, 1995), 229–36.

N. Higham, 'Dynasty and cult: the utility of Christian mission to Northumbrian kings between 642 and 654', in J. Hawkes and S. Mills (eds), *Northumbria's Golden Age* (Stroud, 1999), 95–104.

J. Hillaby, 'Early Christian and pre-Conquest Leominster: an exploration of the sources', *Transactions of the Woolhope Naturalists Field Club*, 45 (1986–87), 557–685.

S. Hilpisch, *Die Doppelklöster: Entstehung und Organisation* (Munster, 1928).

D. Hinton, 'Amesbury and the early history of its abbey', in J. Chandler (ed.), *The Amesbury Millennium Lectures* (Amesbury, 1979), 20–31.

R. C. Hoare (ed.), *Registrum Wiltunense* (London, 1827).

C. Hohler, 'St Osyth and Aylesbury', *Records of Buckinghamshire*, 18 (1966), 61–72.

S. Hollis, *Anglo-Saxon Women and the Church* (Woodbridge, 1992).

S. Hollis, 'The Minster-in-Thanet foundation story', *A-SE*, 27 (1998), 41–74.

R. Holtzmann (ed.), *Thietmari Merseburgensis Episcopi Chronicon*, MGH SRG, NS 9, 2nd edn (Berlin, 1955).

H. Homeyer (ed.), *Hrotsvithae Opera* (Munich, 1970).

E. van Houts, 'Women and the writing of history in the early middle ages: the case of Abbess Matilda of Essen and Æthelweard', *Early Medieval Europe*, 1 (1992), 53–68.

E. van Houts, *Memory and Gender in Medieval Europe 900–1200* (Basingstoke, 1999).

C. Horstmann (ed.), *S. Edithe sive Chronicon Vilodunense* (Heilbronn, 1883).

C. Horstmann (ed.), *Nova Legenda Angliae*, 2 vols (Oxford, 1901).

P. J. Huggins, 'Excavations of a Belgic and Romano-British farm with Middle Saxon cemetery and churches at Nazeingbury, Essex, 1975–6', *Essex Archaeology and History*, 10 (1978), 3rd Series, 29–117.

C. Ireland, 'Aldfrith of Northumbria and the Irish genealogies', *Celtica*, 22 (1991), 64–78.

R. H. Jackson, 'The Tisbury landholdings granted to Shaftesbury monastery by the Saxon kings', *Wiltshire Archaeological Magazine*, 79 (1985), 164–77.

J. Jochens, *Old Norse Images of Women* (Philadelphia, 1996).

M. de Jong, 'Growing up in a Carolingian monastery; magister Hildemer and his oblates', *Journal of Medieval History*, 9 (1983), 99–128.

M. de Jong, 'Carolingian monasticism: the power of prayer', in R. McKitterick (ed.), *The New Cambridge Medieval History, Vol. II. c. 700–c. 900* (Cambridge, 1995), 622–53.

C. Karkov, 'The Bewcastle cross. Some iconographic problems', in C. Karkov, R. T. Farrell and M. Ryan (eds), *The Insular Tradition* (Albany, NY, 1997), 9–26.

C. Karkov, 'Whitby, Jarrow and the commemoration of death in Northumbria', in J. Hawkes and S. Mills (eds), *Northumbria's Golden Age* (Stroud, 1999), 126–35.

L. Keen, 'The towns of Dorset', in J. Haslam (ed.), *Anglo-Saxon Towns in Southern England* (Chichester, 1984), 203–47.

S. Kelly, 'Trading privileges from eighth-century England', *Early Medieval Europe*, 1 (1992), 3–27.

S. Kelly (ed.), *Charters of St Augustine's Abbey, Canterbury and Minster-in-Thanet*, British Academy, Anglo-Saxon Charters, IV (Oxford, 1995).

S. Kelly (ed.), *Charters of Shaftesbury Abbey*, British Academy, Anglo-Saxon Charters, V (Oxford, 1996).

S. Kelly (ed.), *Charters of Selsey*, British Academy, Anglo-Saxon Charters, VI (Oxford, 1998).

S. Kelly (ed.), *Charters of Abingdon Abbey, Part I*, British Academy, Anglo-Saxon Charters, VII (Oxford, 2000).

J. M. Kemble, *Codex Diplomaticus Aevi Saxonici*, 6 vols (1839–48).

T. Kempf, 'Benna Treverensis Canonicus de Sancti Paulini Patrocino', in *Mainz und der Mittelrhein in der europäischen Kunstgeschichte* (Mainz, 1966), 179–84.

S. Keynes, 'The declining reputation of King Æthelred the Unready', in D. Hill (ed.), *Ethelred the Unready: Papers from the Millenary Conference*, BAR, 59 (Oxford, 1978), 227–53.

S. Keynes, *The Diplomas of Æthelred 'the Unready', 978–1016: A Study in Their Use as Historical Evidence* (Cambridge, 1978).

S. Keynes, 'The control of Kent in the ninth century', *Early Medieval Europe*, 2 (1993), 111–31.

S. Keynes, 'The "Dunstan B" charters', *A-SE*, 23 (1994), 165–93.

S. Keynes (ed.), *The Liber Vitae of the New Minster and Hyde Abbey, Winchester* (Copenhagen, 1995).

S. Keynes, 'Anglo-Saxon entries in the "Liber Vitae" of Brescia', in J. Roberts and J. L. Nelson (eds), *Alfred the Wise: Studies in Honour of Janet Bately* (Woodbridge, 1997), 99–119.

S. Keynes, 'King Alfred and the Mercians', in M. Blackburn and D. N. Dumville (eds), *Kings, Currency and Alliances* (Woodbridge, 1998), 1–45.

S. Keynes, 'King Alfred the Great and Shaftesbury Abbey', in L. Keen (ed.), *Studies in the Early History of Shaftesbury Abbey* (Dorchester, 1999), 17–72.

S. Keynes, *Anglo-Saxon Charters: Archives and Single Sheets*, British Academy (Oxford, forthcoming)

S. Keynes and M. Lapidge (eds), *Alfred the Great: Asser's Life of King Alfred and Other Contemporary Sources* (Harmondsworth, 1983).

D. Kirby, 'Northumbria in the time of Wilfrid', in *idem* (ed.), *Saint Wilfrid at Hexham* (Newcastle, 1974), 1–32.

D. Kirby, *The Earliest English Kings* (London, 1991).

A. Klinck, 'Anglo-Saxon women and the law', *Journal of Medieval History*, 8 (1982), 107–21.

D. Knowles, *The Monastic Order in England 940–1216*, 2nd edn (Cambridge, 1963).

D. Knowles and R. N. Hadcock, *Medieval Religious Houses: England and Wales*, 2nd edn (London, 1971).

D. Knowles, C. N. L. Brooke and V. C. M. London, *The Heads of Religious Houses: England and Wales, 940–1216* (Cambridge, 1972).

B. Krusch (ed.), *Additamentum Nivialense de Fuliano*, MGH Scriptores Rerum Merovingicarum, IV (Hanover, 1902), 449–51.

B. Krusch (ed.), *Ionas, Vitae Columbani Discipulorumque eius*, MGH Scriptores Rerum Merovingicarum, IV (Hanover, 1902), 130–43.

B. Krusch (ed.), *Virtutes Fursei Abbatis Latiniacensis*, MGH Scriptores Rerum Merovingicarum, IV (Hanover, 1902), 440–9.

B. Krusch and W. Levison (eds), *Gregory of Tours, Decem Libri Historiarum, MGH Scriptores Rerum Merovingicarum*, I (Hanover, 1951), 1.

L. Lancaster, 'Kinship in Anglo-Saxon society; parts I and II', *British Journal of Sociology*, 9 (1958), 230–50, 359–77.

J. Lang, *Corpus of Anglo-Saxon Stone Sculpture, Vol. III: York and Eastern Yorkshire* (London, 1991).

M. Lapidge, 'Some remnants of Bede's lost *Liber Epigrammatum*', *EHR*, 90 (1975), 798–820.

M. Lapidge, *Anglo-Saxon Litanies of the Saints*, Henry Bradshaw Society, 106 (London, 1991).

M. Lapidge and M. Herren, *Aldhelm: The Prose Works* (Woodbridge, 1979).

M. Lapidge and J. Rosier, *Aldhelm: The Poetic Works* (Woodbridge, 1985).

M. Lapidge and M. Winterbottom (eds), *Wulfstan of Winchester, Life of St Æthelwold* (Oxford, 1991).

J.-P. Laporte, *Le Trésor des Saints de Chelles* (Chelles, 1998).

J.-P. Laporte and R. Boyer, *Trésors de Chelles: Sépultures et Reliques de la Reine Bathilde et de l'Abbesse Bertille* (Chelles, 1991).

R. Lavelle, 'Royal Estates in Wessex', unpublished Ph.D. thesis (University of Southampton, 2002).

M. K. Lawson, 'The collection of danegeld and heregeld in the reigns of Æthelred II and Cnut', *EHR*, 99 (1984), 721–38.

W. Levison, *England and the Continent in the Eighth Century* (Oxford, 1946).

E. Levy, *West-Roman Vulgar Law: The Law of Property* (Philadelphia, 1954).

K. Leyser, *Rule and Conflict in an Early Medieval Society: Ottonian Saxony* (London, 1979).

K. Leyser, 'The Ottonians and Wessex', repr. and trans. in T. Reuter (ed.), *Communications and Power in Medieval Europe: The Carolingian and Ottonian Centuries* (London, 1994), 73–104.

F. Liebermann, *Gesetze der Angelsachsen*, 3 vols (Halle, 1898–1916).

H. G. Liveing, *Records of Romsey Abbey 907–1558* (Winchester, 1906).

H. E. Lohmann and P. Hirsch (eds), *Widukind of Corvey, Rerum Gestarum Saxonicarum libri tres, MGH SRG*, 5th edn (Hanover, 1935).

R. Love, *Three Eleventh-Century Anglo-Latin Saints' Lives* (Oxford, 1996).

H. Loyn, 'Kinship in Anglo-Saxon England', *A-SE*, 3 (1974), 197–209.

H. R. Luard (ed.), *Matthew Paris, Chronica Majora*, Rolls Series (London, 1872–83).

S. Lucy, 'Housewives, warriors and slaves? Sex and gender in Anglo-Saxon burials', in J. Moore and E. Scott (eds), *Invisible People and Processes: Writing Gender and Childhood into European Archaeology* (London, 1997), 150–68.

J. Mabillon (ed.), *Acta Sanctorum Ordinis Sancti Benedicti*, 6 vols (Paris, 1668–71).

M. McLaughlin, *Consorting with Saints: Prayer for the Dead in Early Medieval France* (Ithaca, NY, 1994).

R. MacMullen, *Christianising the Roman Empire (AD 100–400)* (London, 1984).

J. A. McNamara, 'The need to give: suffering and female sanctity in the Middle Ages', in R. Blumenfeld-Kosinski and T. Szell (eds), *Images of Sainthood in Medieval Europe* (Ithaca, NY, 1991), 199–221.

J. A. McNamara and S. Wemple, 'The power of women through the family in medieval Europe, 500–1100', in M. Erler and M. Kowaleski (eds), *Women and Power in the Middle Ages* (Athens, GA, 1988), 83–101.

J. A. McNamara, J. E. Halborg and E. G. Whatley (eds and trans.), *Sainted Women of the Dark Ages* (Durham, NC, 1992).

J. T. McNeill and H. A. Gamer (eds), *Medieval Handbooks of Penance* (New York, 1979).

W. D. Macray (ed.), *Chronicon Abbatiae de Evesham*, Rolls Series, 29 (London, 1983).

J. Maddicott, 'Plague in seventh-century England', *Past and Present*, 156 (1997), 7–54.

M. de Maillé, *Les Cryptes de Jouarre* (Paris, 1971).

W. T. Mellows (ed.), *The Peterborough Chronicle of Hugh Candidus* (Peterborough, 1941).

M. A. Meyer, 'Women and the tenth-century English monastic reform', *Revue Bénédictine*, 87 (1977), 34–61.

M. A. Meyer, 'Patronage of the West Saxon nunneries in late Anglo-Saxon England', *Revue Bénédictine*, 91 (1981), 332–58.

M. A. Meyer, 'Queens, converts and conversion in early Anglo-Saxon England', *Revue Bénédictine*, 109 (1999), 90–116.

E. Miller, *The Abbey and Bishopric of Ely: The Social History of an Ecclesiastical Estate from the Tenth Century to the Early Fourteenth Century* (Cambridge, 1951).

M. Miller, 'The dates of Deira', *A-SE*, 8 (1979), 35–61.

S. Millinger, 'Humility and power: Anglo-Saxon nuns in Anglo-Norman hagiography', in J. Nichols and L. T. Shank (eds), *Medieval Religious Women. I: Distant Echoes* (Kalamazoo, 1984), 115–30.

J. Milner, *The History and Survey of the Antiquities of Winchester*, 2 vols, 3rd edn (London, 1839).

A. Morton, *Excavations in Hamwic: Volume I*, CBA Research Report, 84 (London, 1992).

B. J. Muir (ed.), *A Pre-Conquest English Prayer-Book (BL MSS Cotton Galba Axiv and Nero Aii (ff. 3–13)*, Henry Bradshaw Society, 103 (Woodbridge, 1988).

E. Murphy, 'Anglo-Saxon Shaftesbury – Bectun's base or Alfred's foundation?', *Proceedings of the Dorset Natural History and Archaeology Society*, 113 (1992), 23–32.

R. A. B. Mynors, R. M. Thomson and M. Winterbottom (eds), *William of Malmesbury, Gesta Regum Anglorum*, Vol. I (Oxford, 1998).

J. Nelson, 'Royal saints and early medieval kingship', in D. Baker (ed.), *Sanctity and Secularity*, Studies in Church History, 10 (Oxford, 1974), 39–44.

J. Nelson, 'Inauguration rituals', in P. Sawyer and I. Wood (eds), *Early Medieval Kingship* (Leeds, 1977), 50–71.

J. Nelson, 'The earliest surviving royal *ordo*: some liturgical and historical aspects', in *Politics and Ritual in Early Medieval Europe* (London, 1986), 341–60.

J. Nelson, '"A king across the sea": Alfred in continental perspective', *TRHS*, 5th Series, 36 (1986), 45–68.

J. Nelson, 'Women and the word in the earlier middle ages', in W. J. Shiels and D. Wood (eds), *Women in the Church*, Studies in Church History, 27 (Oxford, 1990), 53–78.

J. Nelson, 'Reconstructing a royal family: reflections on Alfred from Asser, chapter 2', in I. Wood and N. Lund (eds), *People and Places in Northern Europe, 500–1000* (Woodbridge, 1991), 47–66.

J. Nelson, 'The wary widow', in W. Davies and P. Fouracre (eds), *Property and Power in the Early Middle Ages* (Cambridge, 1995), 54–82.

J. Nelson, 'Early medieval rites of queen-making and the shaping of medieval queenship', in A. J. Duggan (ed.), *Queens and Queenship in Medieval Europe* (Woodbridge, 1997), 301–15.

J. Nelson, 'Family, gender and sexuality in the middle ages', in M. Bentley (ed.), *Companion to Historiography* (London, 1997), 153–76.

J. Nelson, 'Making a difference in eighth-century politics; the daughters of Desiderius', in A. C. Murray (ed.), *After Rome's Fall: Narrators and Sources of Early Medieval History. Essays Presented to Walter Goffart* (Toronto, 1998), 171–90.

J. Nelson, 'Monks, secular men and masculinity c. 900', in D. M. Hadley (ed.), *Masculinity in Medieval Europe* (Harlow, 1999), 121–42.

C. Neuman de Vegvar, 'Saints and companions to saints: Anglo-Saxon royal women monastics in context', in P. Szarmach (ed.), *Holy Men and Holy Women: Old English Prose Saints' Lives and Their Contexts* (Albany, NY, 1996), 51–94.

R. North, *Heathen Gods and Old English Literature* (Cambridge, 1997).

E. O'Carragain, 'A liturgical interpretation of the Bewcastle cross', in M. Stokes and T. Burton (eds), *Medieval Literature and Antiquities: Studies in Honour of Basil Cottle* (Woodbridge, 1987), 15–42.

D. Ó Cróinín, 'The Salaberga Psalter', in C. Bourke (ed.), *From the Isles of the North: Early Medieval Art in Ireland and Britain* (Belfast, 1995), 127–35.

M. A. O'Donovan (ed.), *Charters of Sherborne*, British Academy, Anglo-Saxon Charters, III (Oxford, 1988).

O. G. Oexle, 'Memoria und Memorialüberlieferung im frühen Mittelalter', *Frühmittelalterliche Studien*, 10 (1976), 70–95.

V. Ortenberg, *The English Church and the Continent in the Tenth and Eleventh Centuries: Cultural, Spiritual and Artistic Changes* (Oxford, 1992).

S. O'Sullivan, 'Aldhelm's *De Virginitate* – patristic pastiche or innovative exposition?', *Peritia*, 12 (1998), 271–95.

G. Owen, 'Wynflaed's wardrobe', *A-SE*, 8 (1979), 195–22.

R. Page, *'A Most Vile People': Early English Historians on the Vikings*, Viking Society for Northern Research (London, 1987).

M. Parisse, 'Les chanoinesses dans l'empire Germanique (ix–xi siècles)', *Francia*, 6 (1978), 107–28.

M. Parker, 'An Anglo-Saxon monastery in the Lower Don valley', *Northern History*, 21 (1985), 19–32.

P. Périn and L.-C. Feffer (eds), *La Neustrie: les pays au nord de la Loire de Dagobert à Charles le Chauve (vii–ix siècles)* (Seine-Maritime, 1985).

J.-M. Picard, 'Church and politics in the seventh century: the Irish exile of King Dagobert II', in *idem* (ed.), *Ireland and Northern France* (Dublin, 1991), 27–52.

J. Pitt, 'Wiltshire Minster Parochiae and Ecclesiastical Organisation in Wessex', unpublished Ph.D. thesis (University of Southampton, 2000).

C. Plummer (ed.), *Venerabilis Baedae Opera Historica*, 2 vols (Oxford, 1896).

R. U. Potts, 'The tombs of the kings and archbishops in St Austin's Abbey, Canterbury', *Archaeologia Cantiana*, 38 (1926), 97–112.

F. Prinz, *Frühes Monchtum in Frankenreich*, 2nd edn (Munich, 1988).

P. Rahtz, 'Anglo-Saxon and later Whitby', in L. Hoey (ed.), *Yorkshire Monasticism: Archaeology, Art and Architecture, from the Seventh to the Sixteenth Century*, British Archaeological Association Transactions, 16 (London, 1995), 1–11.

J. Raine (ed.), *The Historians of the Church of York and Its Archbishops*, 3 vols, Rolls Series, 71 (London, 1879–94).

S. Ridyard, *The Royal Saints of Anglo-Saxon England: A Study of West Saxon and East Anglian Cults* (Cambridge, 1988).

S. Ridyard, 'Monk-kings and the Anglo-Saxon hagiographic tradition', *Haskins Society Journal*, 6 (1994), 13–27.

T. J. Rivers, 'Widows' rights in Anglo-Saxon law', *American Journal of Legal History*, 19 (1975), 208–15.

A. J. Robertson, *Anglo-Saxon Charters*, 2nd edn (Cambridge, 1956).

S. Robertson, 'St Eanswith's reliquary in Folkestone church', *Archaeologia Cantiana*, 16 (1886), 322–6.

D. Roffe, 'The seventh-century monastery of Stow Green, Lincolnshire', *Lincolnshire History and Archaeology*, 21 (1986), 31–2.

D. Rollason, 'Lists of saints' resting-places in Anglo-Saxon England', *A-SE*, 7 (1978), 61–94.

D. Rollason, *The Search for St Wigstan*, Vaughan Paper, 27 (Leicester, 1981).

D. Rollason, *The Mildrith Legend: A Study in Early Medieval Hagiography in England* (Leicester, 1982).

D. Rollason, 'Cults of murdered royal saints in Anglo-Saxon England', *A-SE*, 11 (1983), 1–22.

D. Rollason, 'Relic-cults as instruments of royal policy c. 900–c. 1050', *A-SE*, 15 (1986), 91–103.

D. Rollason, 'The shrines of saints in later Anglo-Saxon England: distribution and significance', in L. Butler and R. Morris (eds), *The Anglo-Saxon Church* (London, 1986), 32–43.

D. Rollason, *Saints and Relics in Anglo-Saxon England* (Oxford, 1989).

D. Rollason, 'Hagiography and politics in early Northumbria', in P. Szarmach (ed.), *Holy Men and Holy Women: Old English Prose Saints' Lives and Their Contexts* (Albany, NY, 1996), 95–114.

B. Rosenwein, *To Be the Neighbor of Saint Peter: The Social Meaning of Cluny's Property, 909–1049* (Ithaca, NY, 1989).

M. Clunies Ross, 'Concubinage in Anglo-Saxon England', *Past and Present*, 108 (1985), 3–34.

Royal Commission on Historical Monuments (RCHM), *Churches of South-East Wiltshire* (London, 1987).

M. Rule (ed.), *Eadmer, Historia Novorum in Anglia*, Rolls Series, 81 (London, 1884).

A. R. Rumble, '*Ad Lapidem* in Bede and a Mercian martyrdom', in A. R. Rumble and A. D. Mills (eds), *Names, Places and People* (Stamford, 1997), 307–19.

J. Salisbury, *Church Fathers and Independent Virgins* (London, 1991).

P. Sawyer, *Anglo-Saxon Charters: An Annotated List and Bibliography* (London, 1968).

P. Sawyer, *Anglo-Saxon Lincolnshire* (Lincoln, 1998).

D. B. Schneider, 'Anglo-Saxon Women in the Religious Life: A Study of the Status and Position of Women in an Early Medieval Society', unpublished Ph.D. thesis (University of Cambridge, 1985).

J. T. Schulenberg, 'Strict active enclosure and its effects on the female monastic experience (*ca.* 500–1100)', in J. A. Nichols and L. T. Shank (eds), *Medieval Religious Women. I: Distant Echoes* (Kalamazoo, 1984), 51–86.

J. T. Schulenberg, *Forgetful of Their Sex: Female Sanctity and Society ca. 500–1100* (Chicago, 1998).

G. Scobie and K. Qualmann, *Nunnaminster: A Saxon and Medieval Community of Nuns* (Winchester, 1993).

I. R. Scott, *Romsey Abbey: Report on the Excavations 1973–1991*, Hampshire Field Club Monograph, 8 (Stroud, 1996).

E. Searle, 'Women and the succession at the Norman Conquest', *Anglo-Norman Studies*, 3 (1980), 159–70.

R. Sermon, 'The Hackness cross cryptic inscriptions', *Yorkshire Archaeological Journal*, 68 (1996), 101–11.

J. Shephard, 'The social identity of the individual in isolated barrows and barrow cemeteries in Anglo-Saxon England', in B. C. Burnham and J. Kingsbury (eds), *Space, Hierarchy and Society: Interdisciplinary Studies in Social Area Analysis*, BAR International Series, 59 (1979), 47–79.

T. A. Shippey, *Poems of Wisdom and Learning in Old English* (Cambridge, 1976).

P. Sims-Williams, 'Continental influence at Bath monastery in the seventh century', *A-SE*, 4 (1975), 1–10.

P. Sims-Williams, 'Cuthswith, seventh-century abbess of Inkberrow, near Worcester, and the Wurzburg manuscript of Jerome on Ecclesiastes', *A-SE*, 5 (1976), 1–21.

P. Sims-Williams, *Religion and Literature in Western England, 600–800* (Cambridge, 1990).

J. A. Smith, 'The earliest queen-making rites', *Church History*, 66 (1997), 18–35.

J. Smith, 'The problem of female sanctity in Carolingian Europe c. 780–920', *Past and Present*, 146 (1995), 3–37.

J. Smith, 'Gender and ideology in the early middle ages', in R. N. Swanson (ed.), *Studies in Church History*, 34 (1998), 51–73.

A. Smyth, *Scandinavian Kings in the British Isles, 850–880* (Oxford, 1977).

A. Smyth, *King Alfred the Great* (Oxford, 1995).

R. W. Southern, *Saint Anselm and His Biographer* (Cambridge, 1966).

R. W. Southern, *Western Society and the Church in the Middle Ages* (Harmondsworth, 1970).

G. Speake, *A Saxon Bed Burial at Swallowcliffe Down*, English Heritage Archaeological Report, 10 (1989).

P. Stafford, 'Sons and mothers: family politics in the early middle ages', in D. Baker (ed.), *Medieval Women*, Studies in Church History Subsidia, 1 (1978), 79–100.

P. Stafford, 'The king's wife in Wessex 800–1066', *Past and Present*, 91 (1981), 3–27.

P. Stafford, *Queens, Concubines and Dowagers: The King's Wife in the Early Middle Ages* (London, 1983).

P. Stafford, 'Emma: the powers of the queen in the eleventh century', in A. J. Duggan (ed.), *Queens and Queenship in Medieval Europe* (Woodbridge, 1997), 3–26.

P. Stafford, *Queen Emma and Queen Edith: Queenship and Women's Power in Eleventh-Century England* (Oxford, 1997).

P. Stafford, 'Queens, nunneries and reforming churchmen: gender, religious status and reform in tenth- and eleventh-century England', *Past and Present*, 163 (1999), 3–35.

P. Stafford, '"Cherchez la femme": queens, queens' lands and nunneries: missing links in the foundation of Reading abbey', *History*, 85 (2000), 4–27.

C. Stancliffe, 'Kings who opted out', in P. Wormald (ed.), *Ideal and Reality in Frankish and Anglo-Saxon Society* (Oxford, 1983), 154–76.

C. Stancliffe, 'Where was Oswald killed?', in C. Stancliffe and E. Cambridge (eds), *Oswald: Northumbrian King to European Saint* (Stamford, 1995), 84–96.

D. M. Stenton, *The English Woman in History* (London, 1957).

F. M. Stenton, 'The East Anglian kings of the seventh century', in D. M. Stenton (ed.), *Preparatory to Anglo-Saxon England* (Oxford, 1970), 394–402.

F. M. Stenton, '*Medehamstede* and its colonies', in D. Stenton (ed.), *Preparatory to Anglo-Saxon England* (Oxford, 1970), 179–92.

W. H. Stevenson (ed.), *Asser's Life of King Alfred* (Oxford, 1904, repr. 1959).

N. Stoodley, *The Spindle and the Spear: A Critical Enquiry into the Construction and Meaning of Gender in the Early Anglo-Saxon Inhumation Burial Rite*, BAR, 288 (Oxford, 1999).

K. Streckler (ed.), 'Gesta Ottonis', *Hrotsvithae Opera* (Leipzig, 1906).

W. Stubbs (ed.), *Memorials of St Dunstan Archbishop of Canterbury*, Rolls Series, 63 (London, 1874).

M. Swanton, 'A fragmentary life of St Mildred and other Kentish royal saints', *Archaeologia Cantiana*, 91 (1975), 15–27.

T. Symons (ed.), *Regularis Concordia Anglicae nationis monachorum sanctimonialiumque* (London, 1953).

C. H. Talbot, 'Amesbury Church. Reasons for thinking that it was not the church of the priory,' *Wiltshire Archaeological Magazine*, 31 (1900–1), 8–20.

C. H. Talbot, *The Anglo-Saxon Missionaries in Germany* (London, 1954).

M. Tangl (ed.), *S. Bonifatii et Lulli Epistolae, MGH Epistolae Selecta I* (Berlin, 1916).

C. S. Taylor, 'Berkeley minster', *Transactions of the Bristol and Gloucestershire Archaeological Society*, 19 (1894–95), 70–84.

H. M. Taylor, 'The Anglo-Saxon church at Bradford-on-Avon', *Archaeological Journal*, 130 (1973), 141–71.

H. M. Taylor, 'St Wystan's church, Repton, Derbyshire: a reconstruction essay', *Archaeological Journal*, 144 (1987), 205–45.

H. M. and J. Taylor, *Anglo-Saxon Church Architecture*, 2 vols (Cambridge, 1965).

A. T. Thacker, 'The Social and Political Background to Early Anglo-Saxon Hagiography', unpublished D.Phil. thesis (University of Oxford, 1977).

A. T. Thacker, 'Kings, saints and monasteries in pre-viking Mercia', *Midland History*, 10 (1985), 1–25.

A. T. Thacker, 'Æthelwold and Abingdon', in B. A. E. Yorke (ed.), *Bishop Æthelwold: His Career and Influence* (Woodbridge, 1988), 43–64.

A. T. Thacker, 'Monks, preaching and pastoral care in early Anglo-Saxon England', in J. Blair and R. Sharpe (eds), *Pastoral Care before the Parish* (Leicester, 1992), 137–70.

A. T. Thacker, '*Membra disjecta*: the division of the body and the diffusion of the cult', in C. Stancliffe and E. Cambridge (eds), *Oswald: Northumbrian King to European Saint* (Stamford, 1995), 97–127.

A. T. Thacker, 'Memorialising Gregory the Great: the origin and transmission of a papal cult in the seventh and early eighth centuries', *Early Medieval Europe*, 7 (1998), 59–84.

A. T. Thacker, 'Dynastic monasteries and family cults: Edward the Elder's sainted kindred', in N. Higham and D. Hill (eds), *Edward the Elder 899–924* (London, 2001), 248–63.

A. T. Thacker, 'The making of a local saint', in A. Thacker and R. Sharpe (eds), *Local Saints and Local Churches in the Early Medieval West* (Oxford, 2002).

A. Hamilton Thompson, 'Double monasteries and the male element in nunneries', in *The Ministry of Women: A Report by a Committee Appointed by His Grace the Lord Archbishop of Canterbury* (London, 1919), Appendix 7, 145–64.

P. A. Thompson, 'St Æthelthryth: the making of history from hagiography', in M. J. Toswell and E. M. Tyler (eds), *Studies in English Language and Literature: 'Doubt Wisely': Papers in Honour of E. G. Stanley* (London, 1996), 475–92.

S. Thompson, 'Why English nunneries had no history; a study of the problems of the English nunneries founded after the Conquest,' in J. A. Nichols and L. T. Shank (eds), *Medieval Religious Women. I: Distant Echoes* (Kalamazoo, 1984), 131–49.

R. M. Thomson, *William of Malmesbury* (Woodbridge, 1987).

R. M. Thomson and M. Winterbottom, *William of Malmesbury, Gesta Regum Anglorum: General Introduction and Commentary* (Oxford, 1999).

L. Thorpe (trans.), *Gregory of Tours: The History of the Franks* (Harmondsworth, 1974).

D. Tweddle, M. Biddle and B. Kjølbye-Biddle, *Corpus of Anglo-Saxon Stone Sculpture, Vol. IV. South-East England* (Oxford, 1995).

M. Varin, *Mémoire sur les causes de la dissidence entre l'Eglise bretonne et l'Eglise romaine* (Paris, 1858).

B. L. Venarde, *Women's Monasticism and Medieval Society: Nunneries in France and England, 890–1215* (Ithaca, NY, 1997).

Vita SS. Kyneburgae et Kineswidae, ed. *AA SS*. 1 March (1668), 441–7.

Vita S. Werburgae, ed. *AA SS*. 1 February (1658), 386–90.

G. Waitz (ed.), *Vitae Leobae Abbatissae Biscofesheimensis auctore Rudolfo Fuldensi, MGH Scriptores*, XV (Hanover, 1887), 118–31.

J. M. Wallace-Hadrill, *Bede's Ecclesiastical History of the English People: A Historical Commentary* (Oxford, 1988).

B. Ward, "'To my dearest sister": Bede and the educated woman', in L. Smith and J. Taylor (eds), *Women, the Book and the Godly* (Woodbridge, 1995), 105–11.

A. Wareham, 'St Oswald's family and kin', in N. Brooks and C. Cubbitt (eds), *St Oswald of Worcester: Life and Influence* (London, 1996), 117–28.

W. Watts (ed.), *Matthei Paris Monachi Albanensis Angli, Historia Maior* (Paris, 1644).

L. Webster and J. Backhouse (eds), *The Making of England: Anglo-Saxon Art and Culture AD 600–900* (London, 1991).

S. Wemple, *Women in Frankish Society: Marriage and the Cloister 500–900* (Philadelphia, 1981).

S. Wemple, 'S.Salvatore/S.Guilia; a case study in the endowment and patronage of a major female monastery in northern Italy', in J. Kirschner and S. F. Wemple (eds), *Women of the Medieval World* (Oxford, 1985), 85–102.

S. Wemple, 'Female spirituality and mysticism in Frankish monasticism: Radegund, Balthild and Aldegund', in J. A. Nichols and L. T. Shank (eds), *Medieval Religious Women. II: Peace Weavers* (Kalamazoo, 1987), 39–54.

G. Whalen, 'Patronage engendered; how Goscelin allayed the concerns of nuns' discriminatory publics', in L. Smith and J. H. M. Taylor (eds), *Women, the Book and the Godly* (Woodbridge, 1995), 123–35.

L. Whitbread, 'Æthelweard and the Anglo-Saxon Chronicle', *EHR*, 74 (1959), 577–89.

D. Whitelock, *Anglo-Saxon Wills* (Cambridge, 1930).

D. Whitelock, 'The pre-Viking age church in East Anglia', *A-SE*, 1 (1972), 1–22.

D. Whitelock (ed.), *English Historical Documents, I, c. 500–1042*, 2nd edn (London, 1979).

D. Whitelock, with D. C. Douglas and S. I. Tucker (eds), *The Anglo-Saxon Chronicle* (London, 1961).

D. Whitelock, M. Brett and C. N. L. Brooke, *Councils and Synods with Other Documents Relating to the English Church*, 2 vols (Oxford, 1981).

A. Williams, 'Some notes and considerations on problems connected with the English royal succession, 800–1066', *Anglo-Norman Studies*, 1 (1978), 144–67.

A. Williams, '*Princeps Merciorum gentis*: the family, career and connections of Ælfhere, ealdorman of Mercia, 956–983', *A-SE*, 10 (1982), 143–72.

A. Williams, *The English and the Norman Conquest* (Woodbridge, 1995).

A. Wilmart, 'La légende de Ste Edith en prose et vers par le moine Goscelin', *Analecta Bollandiana*, 56 (1938), 5–101, 265–307.

M. Winterbottom (ed.), *Gildas: The Ruin of Britain and Other Documents* (Chichester, 1978).

I. N. Wood, 'The Franks and Sutton Hoo', in I. N. Wood and N. Lund (eds), *People and Places in Northern Europe 500–1600: Essays in Honour of Peter Sawyer* (Woodbridge, 1991), 1–14.

I. N. Wood, 'Pagan religions and superstitions east of the Rhine from the fifth to the ninth century', in G. Ausenda (ed.), *After Empire: Towards an Ethnology of Europe's Barbarians* (Woodbridge, 1995), 253–79.

M. Wood, 'The making of King Athelstan's empire: an English Charlemagne?', in P. Wormald (ed.), *Ideal and Reality in Frankish and Anglo-Saxon Society* (Oxford, 1983), 250–72.

F. Wormald (ed.), *English Kalendars before A.D. 1100*, Henry Bradshaw Society, 72 (London, 1934).

P. Wormald, 'Bede, Beowulf and the conversion of the Anglo-Saxon aristocracy', in R. T. Farrell (ed.), *Bede and Anglo-Saxon England*, BAR, 46 (Oxford, 1978), 32–95.

P. Wormald, *Bede and the Conversion of England: The Charter Evidence*, Jarrow Lecture, 1984 (Newcastle, 1985).

P. Wormald, '*Engla Lond*; the making of an allegiance', *Journal of Historical Sociology*, 7 (1994), 1–24.

P. Wormald, *The Making of English Law: King Alfred to the Twelfth Century, Vol. I, Legislation and Its Limits* (Oxford, 1999).

C. Wybourne, 'Leoba: a study in humanity and holiness', in M. Schmitt and L. Kulzer (eds), *Medieval Women Monastics* (Collegeville, MN, 1996), 81–96.

B. A. E. Yorke, 'The bishops of Winchester, the kings of Wessex and the development of Winchester in the ninth and early tenth centuries', *Proceedings of Hampshire Field Club and Archaeological Society*, 40 (1984), 61–70.

B. A. E. Yorke, 'The kingdom of the East Saxons', *A-SE*, 14 (1985), 1–36.

B. A. E. Yorke, 'Æthelwold and the politics of the tenth century', in *idem* (ed.), *Bishop Æthelwold: His Career and Influence* (Woodbridge, 1988), 65–88.

B. A. E. Yorke, '"Sisters under the skin"? Anglo-Saxon nuns and nunneries in southern England', *Medieval Women in Southern England*, Reading Medieval Studies, 15 (1989), 95–117.

B. A. E. Yorke, *Kings and Kingdoms of Early Anglo-Saxon England* (London, 1990).

B. A. E. Yorke, 'Lindsey: the lost kingdom found?', in A. Vince (ed.), *Pre-Viking Lindsey* (Lincoln, 1993), 141–50.

B. A. E. Yorke, 'The Bonifacian mission and female religious in Wessex', *Early Medieval Europe*, 7 (1998), 145–72.

B. A. E. Yorke, 'Edward King and Martyr; a Saxon murder mystery', in L. Keen (ed.), *Studies in the Early History of Shaftesbury Abbey* (Dorchester, 1999), 99–116.

B. A. E. Yorke, 'The reception of Christianity at the Anglo-Saxon royal courts', in R. Gameson (ed.), *St Augustine and the Conversion of England* (Stroud, 1999), 152–73.

B. A. E. Yorke, 'Edward as Ætheling', in N. J. Higham and D. H. Hill (eds), *Edward the Elder 899–924* (London, 2001), 25–39.

B. A. E. Yorke, 'The acceptance of Christianity at the Anglo-Saxon royal courts', in M. Carver (ed.), *The Cross Goes North* (Woodbridge, forthcoming).

B. A. E. Yorke, 'Æthelbald, Offa and the patronage of nunneries', in D. Hill (ed.), *Æthelbald and Offa* (Oxford, forthcoming).

B. A. E. Yorke, 'The legitimacy of St Edith', *Haskins Society Journal* (forthcoming).

Index

Lightning Source UK Ltd.
Milton Keynes UK
UKHW020709250122
397662UK00002B/60

9 780826 460400